THE ESSENTIAL
vegetarian
COOKBOOK

MURDOCH BOOKS®

Sydney • London • Vancouver • New York

Published by Murdoch Books® a division of Murdoch Magazines Pty Ltd,
213 Miller Street, North Sydney NSW 2060

Editorial Director: Susan Tomnay
Creative Director: Marylouise Brammer
Editors: Wendy Stephen, Deirdre Blayney, Jane Price
Photographer (cover and special features): Luis Martin
Stylist (cover and special features): Rosemary De Santis
Stylist's Assistant (cover and special features): Tracey Port
Background painter (special features): Sandra Anderson from Painted Vision, Mudgee NSW
Food Editors: Kerrie Ray, Tracy Rutherford
Additional recipes: Jody Vassallo
Additional text: Maggie Pickering, Karen Hammial
Editorial assistants: Justine Upex, Rebecca Myors, Alison Turner
Picture Librarian: Dianne Bedford

CEO & Publisher: Anne Wilson
Publishing Director: Catie Ziller
General Manager: Mark Smith
International Sales Director: Mark Newman

National Library of Australia
Cataloguing-in-Publication Data
The essential vegetarian cookbook. Includes index.
Cased edition ISBN 086411 510 5
Limp edition ISBN 0 86411 584 9
1. Vegetarian cookery 641.5636

Printed by Toppan Printing (S) Pte Ltd

Cased edition first printed 1996. Reprinted 1996, 1997.
Limp edition first printed 1996. Reprinted 1997.

FOREWORD

Vegetarian fare is no longer a poor relation on the restaurant menu, no more regarded as the province of the brown-rice-and-lentils brigade. Our eating habits have evolved to such a point that, in fact, very many of us live on a virtually meat-free diet without considering ourselves strict vegetarians—and not because of a particular philosophy, nor for reasons of health or economy. Today's widespread interest in food and cooking, our discovery of the infinite range of non-meat dishes from other lands, and the seemingly daily increase in the variety of vegetables, grains, nuts and pulses now available, have combined to make vegetarian cooking exciting and innovative and, simultaneously, extended our appreciation of good food.

CONTENTS

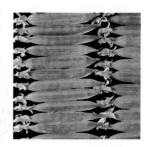

THE VEGETARIAN ADVENTURE

A good vegetarian diet meets all today's requirements: it's nutritionally sound, both quick to prepare and easy to follow, and gastronomically sensational. With the days of overcooked vegetables and a-hundred-ways-with-soya-beans long gone, a vegetarian menu is now first choice for a growing number of people of all ages and lifestyles.

THE VEGETARIAN CHOICE

People can be drawn to a vegetarian diet for a variety of reasons. Some have ethical or health concerns, for others it is a matter of religious belief. But the decision to eat this way could just as easily be an aesthetic or gastronomic one. The variety of ingredients, abundance of possible dishes and scope that vegetarian cuisine offers for creative cooking and eating are often dismissed or not recognised by confirmed meat-eaters.

For many in the developed world, meat—and less often chicken or fish—has always been the easy option. Certainly flesh foods have formed the centrepiece of most meals. This tradition has led to a diet often lacking in variety and, consequently, in a beneficial balance of nutrients, as well as to the health consequences of eating too many saturated fats. A diet which overemphasises meat is a product of affluence, and not necessarily a good one.

Many people have recognised an imbalance in their way of eating and are modifying the amount of flesh foods included in their diets. The discovery of vegetarian food often begins in this way. As people gain confidence, experiment more and discover the pleasures of cooking vegetarian foods—the wealth of colours, flavours, textures and aromas—they often welcome increased vitality and say goodbye to weight problems. Other benefits people report include clearer skin and less constipation. Many choose to abandon eating meat and fish altogether.

The term 'vegetarian' is used quite loosely. Some people call themselves vegetarian (or semi-vegetarian) while still eating a little fish or chicken and no red meat. Many just exclude all meat and fish from their diets. Vegans, on the other hand, exclude all other animal products such as milk, cheese and eggs as well. Most vegetarians, however, are lacto-ovo vegetarians who still eat eggs and dairy products.

Meatless meals need never be bland or boring. They offer enormous variety, stimulating the imagination and sometimes offering the opportunity to learn new cooking skills. Vegetarian food, it could be argued, offers the cook more scope to be inventive.

ABOUT THIS BOOK

This book features recipes using no flesh foods, but occasionally an option like fish sauce is included for flavouring. It is not specifically a vegan cookbook, in that eggs, butter, milk and cream are used liberally. However, there are plenty of recipes suitable for vegans, particularly using grains. Nor is it a book of vegetarian substitutes for a meat-centred diet, offering recipes for pale imitations of meatloaf or burgers. The recipes are for anyone who loves preparing, serving and eating good food.

All the delights of richer foods are available for vegetarians—there are plenty of luscious desserts to be sampled here. This is neither a diet book nor a health food book, but is designed to expand the menu of possibilities, to show that one can be a connoisseur of good food, a fine cook *and* a vegetarian.

RIGHT: These Crispy Fried Mushroom Crepes (page 94) and Pepper and Black Olive Pikelets (page 95) show just how tempting and innovative vegetarian food can be.

SOME PRINCIPLES

Many people who have discovered the joys of vegetarian eating are unaware of a few dietary pitfalls which they could easily avoid with a little knowledge. With the increasing popularity of vegetarian food, and despite a high level of awareness of the facts about nutrition, there are still gaps in many people's knowledge about how to get the most out of their diet. Filling in these gaps can enhance the vegetarian experience and make it beneficial as well as enjoyable.

If you were raised as a vegetarian, you are probably already in the habit of making sure all your nutritional needs are met, but for those making the transition from eating flesh foods, or even to eating substantially less of them, there are a few important things to bear in mind.

● It is perfectly possible, and not at all difficult, to live a healthy life eating only vegetarian foods. The key is to ensure variety in the diet: eat as many different kinds of food as possible and all the essential nutrients that the body requires will be available.

● It is a common mistake to think in terms of 'substituting' the nutrients provided by meat, fish or poultry. A little knowledge, awareness and enthusiasm for trying new things, plus a willingness to broaden your culinary repertoire to include delicious vegetarian dishes from all over the world, is more important than any specialised scientific knowledge about nutrition.

● Make sure you include grains, pulses, vegetables, fruit, and, if not a vegan, eggs and dairy food in your diet, and you can't go wrong.

● Many studies have shown that populations that have a diet high in unrefined foods and fibre and low in salt and sugar have a lower incidence of blood pressure problems, heart disease, bowel disease (including cancer), diabetes and gallstones. Unrefined whole foods are best. (The term 'unprocessed' is misleading since many valuable foods must undergo change of some sort before we eat them: think of pasta and rice, many other grains, and bread.)

● It is important that any produce you buy be as fresh as possible so that the nutrients have not had time to deteriorate. For this reason, as well as for economy, it is a good idea to get into the habit of shopping and eating seasonally, when fruit and vegetables are at their best and cheapest.

● Similarly, it is wise to freeze some fruits and vegetables when they are in season. Make sauces from tomatoes and red peppers (capsicums), purées from berries and stone fruits, and enjoy the taste of summer throughout the year.

IS IT SAFE FOR CHILDREN?

Children thrive on a vegetarian diet and, in fact, many make the choice for themselves at quite an early age. When planning meals for vegetarian children, the principle of maximising the number of different kinds of food in the diet is even more vital. Most of the nutritional needs of children will be met this way, but there are a few important things to remember.

Pulses, eaten at the same meal with grains, nuts or seeds, provide complete protein, an absolute necessity for children. This is not as daunting as it may sound: baked beans on toast; lentils and rice; felafel sandwich; kidney bean chilli with tortillas or tacos.

Growing children need concentrated foods rich in the many nutrients their bodies require, and they need more fat in their diets than adults. There are lots of healthy ways for children to obtain fats: peanut butter, avocado, cheese, yoghurt, nuts. Most children enjoy all these foods anyway, which means there is no excuse for resorting to nutritionally bankrupt sources such as cakes, biscuits, chocolate, or fried take-away foods.

Make sure your children eat a good breakfast. Avoid sugary, processed cereals. If you start them off eating home-made muesli and wholemeal toast, you'll set up a pattern that will benefit them all their life.

ABOVE: A vegetarian diet does not have to be strict and puritan. Strawberry and Passionfruit Muffins (page 278) make a delicious afternoon tea or a special breakfast treat.

THE HEALTHY FOOD PYRAMID

It is as possible to have a poor diet eating exclusively vegetarian foods as it is eating excessive amounts of animal products. The Vegetarian Food Pyramid is a good starting point if you want to check whether your diet is adequate. Its principles are simple:

● EAT MOST

GRAINS: *wheat, rice, barley, corn, oats, rye, millet, buckwheat*

FOODS MADE FROM GRAINS: *pasta, bread, wholegrain breakfast cereals*

FRUIT AND VEGETABLES

● EAT MODERATELY

DAIRY: *milk, yoghurt, cheese*

PULSES: *peas, beans of all kinds, lentils*

NUTS

EGGS

● EAT LEAST

SUGAR, HONEY

BUTTER, CREAM

MARGARINE, OILS

ALCOHOL, TEA, COFFEE

Meal planning becomes easier if you make a habit of using the food pyramid as a guide. There should be in each day a preponderance of foods from the 'Eat Most' group: fruit, cereals and toast for breakfast, bread or bread rolls, salads or cooked vegetable dishes and fruit for lunch; pasta or rice-based main course for dinner with fresh bread or rolls, and more fruit for dessert or snacks.

Small amounts of dairy foods from the 'Eat Moderately' group can be part of the day's meals (unless you are a vegan): yoghurt with breakfast or lunch, a little cheese with lunch or dinner. Dinner can include filling dishes and hearty soups made from dried beans or lentils, as well as tasty egg dishes. Nuts are great for snacking.

The 'Eat Least' category means exactly that—a small amount of butter or margarine on your breakfast toast, a little virgin olive oil with the salad or to stir-fry the onions for the evening meal, the occasional glass of wine with dinner. A sugary treat is fine if it isn't a regular occurrence and tea and coffee can be enjoyed in moderation.

You can balance the nutritional content of the day's meals so that the overall pattern easily satisfies the food pyramid guidelines. Compensate for an unavoidably fatty lunch, for example, with an evening meal made up of vegetables, grains and fruit.

Eating out can be a trap, but it is easy to keep the food pyramid in mind when ordering food (salads, first courses, soups and bread, plus fruit and cheese instead of dessert), and to compensate for any imbalances when preparing food for yourself at home.

Changing the habits of a lifetime is not something we can do overnight. If your usual diet doesn't bear much resemblance to the food pyramid, you can move gradually towards a healthier way of eating. Don't worry if every meal is not perfectly balanced. You can correct the proportions over the course of each week as you adjust to buying and cooking healthier foods, and experiment with new dishes. Replace refined foods with whole foods, high-fat dairy products with reduced-fat versions. Check labels for salt, sugar and fat content, and for food additives. Have fun making your own versions of soups, sauces and even breakfast cereals—rather than buying the ready-made product. This way you control what goes into your body.

Children generally enjoy healthy eating. Pastas, fruit, yoghurt, peanut butter, cheese, milk and nuts are usually popular. The difficulties only arise if you are trying to change bad habits: doing it gradually is best.

MENU PLANNING

Aim to shop and eat for health, using the food pyramid as a guide. Buy several different kinds of rice, couscous, a variety of pastas, lots of breads (freeze loaves and flatbreads if you have room), breakfast cereals and interesting flours.

Get into the habit of replenishing your store of fresh produce regularly, but do it systematically. Shop with some idea of your meal plans from week to week to avoid wastage. Taking advantage of enticing seasonal produce by buying up big is pointless if fruit and vegetables languish at the bottom of your refrigerator while you think of a way to use them. Vary your choices as much as possible to keep your diet interesting and to maximise the nutritional benefits.

Buy cheeses, milk, yoghurt and eggs regularly but plan how much you are likely to need to avoid introducing too much fat.

Canned foods are an essential pantry item: canned beans of every variety are great time-savers if you don't want to soak and cook your own. Tomato pastes and canned tomatoes will be invaluable. Olive oils—extra virgin for flavour, lighter grades for cooking—and other vegetable oils should be kept on hand. Bottled sauces such as pesto, basic pasta sauces and chilli sauce are invaluable flavour enhancers.

VEGETARIAN PYRAMID

The Vegetarian Food Pyramid shows graphically the amazing choice available to you.

By following the simple principles, you will not only enjoy your food, but good health.

EAT LEAST

EAT MODERATELY

EAT MOST

CARBOHYDRATES

The critical importance of complex carbohydrates in a good diet cannot be overstated. Carbohydrates are vital for energy. They occur in the form of starches and sugars from grains and their products—flour, bread and pasta; in potatoes, pulses and to a lesser degree nuts; and in fruits and sugars.

There are probably still people who think potatoes are fattening, but fortunately we now have a far greater awareness of the benefits of loading our diet with pasta, rice, breads, cereals and, yes—potatoes. It is difficult to eat too much carbohydrate—usually excess flab comes from eating too much fat, not too much carbohydrate.

There is a whole world of delicious grain foods that has only recently come into its own in the Western diet: couscous, buckwheat and hybrid grains like triticale (bred from wheat and rye and with a deliciously nutty flavour—try it instead of or as well as rolled oats in home-made muesli). Take advantage of these to add variety to your menus.

Many different rices are also readily available now: fragrant basmati and jasmine rice; pearly arborio, essential for the perfect risotto; and wild rice (an aquatic grass), which, although expensive, is available in more economical mixtures and makes a delicious change.

The fibre component of carbohydrate foods is a bonus, and the less processing the food has undergone the more of it there will be. The presence of fibre in complex carbohydrates allows the energy from sugars to be used by the body at an even rate, whereas refined sugars hit the bloodstream rapidly and are quickly used,

leaving energy levels depleted. This is why you may feel elated and then lethargic in quick succession after eating sugary foods. Complex carbohydrates, with their sustained release of energy, provide more stamina.

FOODS RICH IN COMPLEX CARBOHYDRATES

- BREADS
- POTATOES
- RICES
- WHEAT
- BARLEY
- CORN
- BUCKWHEAT
- RYE
- DRIED BEANS
- LENTILS
- BANANAS
- PASTA

TEA AND COFFEE SUBSTITUTES

If you wish to reduce your intake of caffeine, there are a number of tasty alternatives to coffee and tea available from supermarkets as well as health food stores. Decaffeinated coffees which have been processed using water extraction rather than chemicals are best. Cereal-based coffee substitutes, made from roasted grains, can be an acquired taste but many are quite palatable. Various brands of low-tannin teas are also available, and it's worth remembering that Chinese tea is low in caffeine and very refreshing. There is a huge range of fragrant herbal teas that are delicious by themselves or with a little honey or lemon juice added. Carob powder makes a warming drink to replace caffeine-rich cocoa. Make it with skim milk and add a cinnamon stick.
Instead of cola drinks, try unsweetened fruit juice mixed with mineral water, or plain mineral water with a squeeze of fresh lime juice—heaven on a hot day. Many refreshing fruit juice and yoghurt drinks can be whipped up in the blender with some crushed ice. Make a deliciously filling and healthy smoothie with skim milk, yoghurt, a couple of very ripe bananas and a sprinkling of nutmeg. Or try a frappé—crushed ice and fresh fruit whipped together in a blender. A mango frappé is one of life's little joys.

BELOW: Pasta is one of the best sources of carbohydrates. Combined with fresh and frozen green vegetables as here in Spaghetti with Primavera Sauce (page 116), it is a quick and delicious source of energy.

FIBRE

Fibre includes the cellulose and gums in fruit and vegetables. Animal products do not contain any fibre at all—there is none in dairy foods, fish, poultry or meat, despite their sometimes chewy texture. A well-balanced vegetarian diet, on the other hand, is rich in fibre.

Among other things, fibre acts as a broom in the bowel by moving food along at a such a rate that the potential for problems is minimised. It prevents constipation and lowers the risk of bowel cancer and other intestinal malfunctions.

Because different types of dietary fibre have different functions, again it is important to vary the diet as much as possible. Some types of fibre (mainly from fruit and vegetables) help lower blood cholesterol. It is not enough—as was the fad at one time—to simply heap spoonfuls of unprocessed bran onto your breakfast cereal. Apart from some uncomfortable consequences while the body adjusts to the unfamiliar onslaught of fibre, unprocessed bran contains large amounts of phytic acid, which inhibits the uptake of iron. Since non-meat eaters need to maximise their intake of iron from sources other than meat, this is to be avoided. It's a good rule to include some fibre-rich foods in every meal.

FOODS RICH IN FIBRE

- DRIED BEANS AND PEAS
- FRESH GREEN BEANS AND PEAS
- CABBAGES
- CARROTS
- POTATOES (*especially in their jackets*)
- SPINACH
- CORN
- CEREALS SUCH AS OATS AND WHEAT (*if wholegrain—germ and husk included*)
- PRODUCTS MADE FROM WHOLE GRAINS (*eg, wholewheat bread*)
- DRIED FRUITS (*apricots are good*)
- FRESH FRUIT (*especially apples, bananas and oranges. It is important to eat the whole fruit and not just drink the juice.*)

A WORD ABOUT SUGAR

Excessive amounts of sugar in the diet interfere with the body's ability to metabolise fat. If you eat lots of sugar, the fat you eat will be stored more readily as body fat instead of burned off with physical activity.

Few people, however, are going to eliminate sugar entirely from their diets as they simply enjoy the taste too much. Like all good things, sugar is fine in moderation. A delicious pudding or sweet treat enjoyed on a special occasion does no harm. It is when these foods displace others

of more nutritional value that problems arise.

Cane sugar, however, is valueless in terms of vitamins and minerals. A sweet tooth can always indulge itself in the many delicious fruits available in season: their sugar content comes accompanied by fibre and other nutrients. Fruits are also more filling than other forms of sweet foods so there is less danger of overeating.

SMART SHOPPING

- **NEVER** shop for food when you are hungry. Foods high in sugar and fat never look so inviting as when you're desperate for a quick snack.
- **RESIST** sweet and fat-laden food at the supermarket and you won't have to resist it again, while you're watching TV and feel the urge for a chocolate biscuit.
- **KEEPING** unhealthy food out of your kitchen means that your children will naturally grow up healthier. If there are no chips in the house, they'll eat fruit.
- **READ** labels. When you are at the supermarket, take the time to read the labels of any canned, bottled or frozen food. You'll be surprised at how much salt, sugar, oil and additives some foods contain. For example, you might think that all brands of tomato pasta sauce are the same, but some contain sugar and some do not.

ABOVE: Although there is more fibre in wholewheat bread than white, even white bread contains some (and you can buy white flour boosted with added fibre). Lemon Pepper Bread (page 228) is an example of a quick-to-make yeast-free bread. It has a chewy crust, a delicious cheesy taste and plenty of fibre.

CARBOHYDRATES

Complex carbohydrates fill you up while adding valuable vitamins and minerals to your diet, with little fat. They are economical, tasty, and should make up about 50 per cent of your daily energy intake.

KIDNEY BEANS, COOKED
Carbohydrate per 100 g: 9 g
Fat per 100 g: 0.5 g

PEARL BARLEY, COOKED
Carbohydrate per 100 g: 21 g
Fat per 100 g: 0.9 g

POLENTA, COOKED
Carbohydrate per 100 g: 40 g
Fat per 100 g: 1 g

LIMA BEANS, COOKED
Carbohydrate per 100 g: 10.2 g
Fat per 100 g: 0.3 g

BULGHUR, SOAKED
Carbohydrate per 100 g: 30 g
Fat per 100 g: 0.9 g

OATS, RAW
Carbohydrate per 100 g: 61 g
Fat per 100 g: 8.5 g

CHICKPEAS, COOKED
Carbohydrate per 100 g: 13 g
Fat per 100 g: 2 g

PUFFED MILLET
Carbohydrate per 100 g: 77 g
Fat per 100 g: 2.9 g

LENTILS, COOKED
Carbohydrate per 100 g: 9.5 g
Fat per 100 g: 0.4 g

POTATO, COOKED
Carbohydrate per 100 g: 10 g
Fat per 100 g: 0.1 g

SWEET POTATO, COOKED
Carbohydrate per 100 g 16.7 g
Fat per 100 g: 0.1 g

PASTA, COOKED
Carbohydrate per 100 g: 24.6 g
Fat per 100 g: 0.3 g

RICE, COOKED
Carbohydrate per 100 g: 28 g
Fat per 100 g: 0.2 g

BAKED BEANS
Carbohydrate per 100 g: 11.2 g
Fat per 100 g: 0.5 g

CORN, COOKED
Carbohydrate per 100 g: 20 g
Fat per 100 g: 1 g

QUINOA, DRY
Carbohydrate per 100 g: 70 g
Fat per 100 g: 3 g

BREAD
Carbohydrate per 100 g: 47.3 g
Fat per 100 g: 2.5 g

FINDING FIBRE
The value of fibre in our diet has been widely recognised in recent years as an aid to digestion and even a protection against disease. The recommended daily intake is 25–30 grams.

ROLLED OATS, COOKED
Fibre per 100 g: 1.0 g
Fat per 100 g: 2.2 g

BRAN CEREAL
Fibre per 100 g: 28 g
Fat per 100 g: 4 g

HAZELNUTS
Fibre per 100 g: 10 g
Fat per 100 g: 61 g

PEANUTS
Fibre per 100 g: 8 g
Fat per 100 g: 52 g

SPLIT PEAS, COOKED
Fibre per 100 g: 4 g
Fat per 100 g: 0.3 g

LENTILS, COOKED
Fibre per 100 g: 3.5 g
Fat per 100 g: 0.7 g

WALNUTS
Fibre per 100 g: 6 g
Fat per 100 g: 70 g

PISTACHIOS
Fibre per 100 g: 10 g
Fat per 100 g: 50 g

SOYA BEANS, COOKED
Fibre per 100 g: 7 g
Fat per 100 g: 7 g

HARICOT BEANS, COOKED
Fibre per 100 g: 8.0 g
Fat per 100 g: 2.2 g

PINE NUTS
Fibre per 100 g: 15 g
Fat per 100 g: 70 g

PUMPKIN SEEDS (PEPITAS)
Fibre per 100 g: 25 g
Fat per 100 g: 15 g

KIDNEY BEANS, COOKED
Fibre per 100 g: 11 g
Fat per 100 g: 0.3 g

RICE, BROWN/WILD, COOKED
Fibre per 100 g: 2 g
Fat per 100 g: 0.9 g

SUNFLOWER SEEDS
Fibre per 100 g: 3.3 g
Fat per 100 g: 47 g

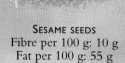

SESAME SEEDS
Fibre per 100 g: 10 g
Fat per 100 g: 55 g

APRICOTS, DRIED
Fibre per 100 g: 10 g
Fat per 100 g: 0 g

DATES, DRIED
Fibre per 100 g: 10 g
Fat per 100 g: 0 g

PEAS, FRESH
Fibre per 100 g: 7 g
Fat per 100 g: 0.6 g

CORN, CANNED
Fibre per 100 g: 3.2 g
Fat per 100 g: 1.2 g

FIGS, DRIED
Fibre per 100 g: 14 g
Fat per 100 g: 1.0 g

PRUNES, CANNED
Fibre per 100 g: 8.0 g
Fat per 100 g: 0 g

BROAD BEANS
Fibre per 100 g: 4.2 g
Fat per 100 g: 0 g

BRUSSELS SPROUTS, COOKED
Fibre per 100 g: 3.5 g
Fat per 100 g: 0 g

RAISINS
Fibre per 100 g: 5 g
Fat per 100 g: 1.0 g

TAMARILLO
Fibre per 100 g: 4.6 g
Fat per 100 g: 0 g

SILVERBEET, COOKED
Fibre per 100 g: 3.3 g
Fat per 100 g: 0 g

TOMATOES
Fibre per 100 g: 1 g
Fat per 100 g: 0 g

SULTANAS
Fibre per 100 g: 5 g
Fat per 100 g: 0 g

STRAWBERRIES
Fibre per 100 g: 2.4 g
Fat per 100 g: 0 g

PUMPKIN, COOKED
Fibre per 100 g: 1.8 g
Fat per 100 g: 0.5 g

PARSLEY
Fibre per 100 g: 5 g
Fat per 100 g: 0 g

COCONUT, FRESH
Fibre per 100 g: 8 g
Fat per 100 g: 29 g

PROTEIN

Nobody needs huge amounts of protein from any source, but everybody needs some. Growing children and pregnant women need a little more than other people.

Protein is essential for cell growth, for tissue repair and reproduction, and to manufacture the substances that protect against infection. Our daily requirements, however, are quite small.

It is easy to get too concerned about protein—this is probably a legacy of the meat-rich diets of the past. The truth is that most people in Western societies eat far more protein than they need, and if there is too much protein in the diet it is converted to body fat. Affluent communities very rarely produce a case of protein deficiency, even when the members are otherwise careless of their nutritional needs and live on too much takeaway food, for example. The real problem is too much fat, sugar and salt.

Deriving protein from vegetable sources has a distinct advantage: the high fibre content of food like legumes and grains puts the brake on overeating.

FOOD COMBINING AND 'COMPLETE' PROTEIN

Protein is made up of 23 different amino acids, substances that combine to make what is termed a 'complete' protein. Digestion breaks down complex proteins from food into these simpler units so that they can be used by the body to build up proteins of its own. Complete protein is what is needed by the human body.

BELOW: Dairy foods are a good source of complete protein and, when combined with grains and vegetables as here in Brown Rice Tart with Fresh Tomato Filling (page 148), you'll get vitamins and carbohydrates as well in one tasty dish.

Amino acids occur in different combinations and proportions in various foods. The body can make most of them itself if the diet is adequate. However, eight essential amino acids can't be made by the body and can only be obtained directly from food. Some foods have these in almost the right proportions for the body to use them immediately.

Protein from animal sources—meat, eggs, cheese, fish, poultry, milk, cheese and yoghurt—provides all the essential amino acids and is therefore termed 'complete'.

Although cheese and eggs are complete proteins, overloading on these sources of protein will introduce too much fat into the diet, and vegans do not have the option. Vegetarians need to look beyond cheese. Hence food combining.

Pulses and cereals have some but not all of the essential amino acids, but if they are eaten with other foods with the missing amino acids—for example, a grain with a pulse (say rice and beans) the body marries them to form a complete protein. These foods don't even have to be eaten at the same time—within a few hours of each other will do.

Most vegetarians are aware of the importance of getting their protein from a range of sources. Food combining needn't be a complicated business. By following a few simple principles you can invent a delicious way of eating. The proteins in dairy products, nuts and seeds, pulses and grains are complementary, so eating foods from two or more of these groups together makes plenty of protein available to the body.

In most societies, ways of combining complementary proteins have evolved in the indigenous diet. Think of dhal and rice, beans and corn, hummus and pitta bread—all are combinations of a pulse and a grain. Other common combinations include:

- PEANUT BUTTER SANDWICHES ON WHOLEMEAL BREAD
- BAKED BEANS ON WHOLEMEAL TOAST
- SPLIT PEA SOUP AND A BREAD ROLL
- BROWN RICE AND CHICKPEAS
- RICE AND TOFU
- CORN TACOS WITH KIDNEY BEANS
- LENTIL PATTY ON A BUN
- PASTA AND CHEESE
- MUESLI WITH MILK
- BEANS AND VEGETABLES
- TABOULI
- VEGETABLE PIES: POTATO, SPINACH
- MUESLI WITH NUTS AND SEEDS
- CHICKPEAS AND COUSCOUS

Tofu and other soya bean products as well as wheatgerm and oatmeal come pretty close to being complete proteins, the only non-animal products to do so. This is why they are so highly valued by vegetarians. Vegans can obtain all the protein they need by eating a wide range of foods of purely vegetable origin.

SOURCES OF PROTEIN
- DAIRY: *cheese, milk, yoghurt*
- NUTS AND SEEDS: *sunflower, sesame, pumpkin, pecans, brazil nuts, hazelnuts, almonds, walnuts, cashews, pine nuts*
- PULSES: *peanuts, peas, beans, lentils, soya beans and soya bean products like tempeh and tofu*
- GRAINS: *rice, oats, corn, wheat/flour products and pasta couscous, rye, barley*

Eating foods from at least two of the above groups together will make more protein available to the body. There is no need for mathematical calculations—making sure you eat a varied diet will ensure you get enough protein.

VEGANS
Vegans—those who eat only foods of plant origin and no animal products (dairy, eggs)—can obtain all their nutritional needs with just a little planning. Some extra care is needed with vegan children, as their needs are slightly different. Again, variety is the key. Vegans need to be especially vigilant about eating a variety of foods from the four plant food groups every day:
- GRAINS *in the form of bread, cereals, pasta and rice*
- PULSES, NUTS AND SEEDS *including peanut butter and tahini, beans of all kinds (including baked beans), chickpeas, soy products (tofu, tempeh, soy milk—fortified with calcium and vitamin B12), especially for children*
- VEGETABLES
- FRESH FRUIT *and juices*

Vegans need to make sure they do not miss out on Vitamin B12 as the usual sources in a lacto-ovo vegetarian diet are eggs and dairy products. Supplements may be necessary, although fortified soy milk is a good source. Mushrooms have plenty of vitamin B12, as does tofu.

Soy milk also supplies calcium, as do some green vegetables, sesame seeds and tahini, almonds, and breads and cereals fortified with calcium.

The iron which is found in meat and which lacto-ovo vegetarians can obtain from eggs can come also from pulses, soy products, green vegetables, breakfast cereals, dried fruits, nuts and seeds—provided you eat a wide variety. The amount of iron available from these foods is maximised if you eat them in conjunction with foods that are rich in vitamin C, such as oranges or blackcurrants.

It is important to remember that children need more fat in their diets than adults to provide them with energy for growth. Vegan children can thrive if they get this from healthy foods such as peanut butter and nuts, vegetable oils, tahini and avocados.

Snack foods can include dried fruit, nuts, seeds and fresh fruit juice.

SAMPLE DAY'S MENU FOR VEGANS
- **BREAKFAST:** Porridge or muesli with fruit and soy milk
  Wholemeal toast with jam or peanut butter
- **LUNCH:** Wholemeal salad sandwich. Or chickpea or rice salad
- **DINNER:** Pulse and grain dish with vegetables. Or vegetable dish with wholemeal bread, or rice or pasta dish with salad
- **DESSERT:** Fruit
- **SNACKS:** Fresh or dried fruit, crispbreads, nuts, vegetable sticks

ABOVE: Chickpea Curry (page 134) is a great example of vegan food. When served with chapattis or naan, it is perfectly balanced—the combination of a pulse and grain making it a complete protein meal.

COMBINING FOR PROTEIN

Combining pulses with grains or with nuts or seeds will provide all the amino acids necessary to make complete protein.

RED BEANS AND RICE

HUMMUS AND LAVASH BREAD

CHICKPEAS AND COUSCOUS

SPLIT PEA SOUP AND BREAD

BEAN SALAD AND TABOULI

DHAL AND PITTA BREAD

LENTIL BURGER ON A BREAD ROLL

PEANUT BUTTER ON TOAST

FELAFEL AND PITTA BREAD

BEANS AND CORN CHIPS

BAKED BEANS ON TOAST

ABOVE: Vegetable and bean mixtures such as Minestrone (page 40) are packed with vitamins and minerals and with a little shaved Parmesan on top, you get extra protein too.

VITAMINS AND MINERALS

Vegetarians who combine food to get enough protein can still miss out on some essential nutrients that meat-eaters obtain easily. The most important of these are the minerals iron, zinc and calcium, and vitamin B12.

Including dairy foods and eggs in the diet will generally ensure enough protein, riboflavin, calcium, iron, vitamins and minerals. Vegans, however, need to take particular care.

Freshness is important when buying fruit and vegetables. Although most nutrients are retained quite well in snap-frozen products, the flavour may not be as good.

Taking vitamin and mineral supplements is a waste of time if your diet is inadequate as they are unable to be used effectively by the body in the absence of the right kinds of foods.

VITAMINS

The body needs vitamins from the B group to metabolise food and to allow proper functioning of the nervous system. These vitamins come from wholegrain cereals, bread and pasta, nuts and seeds, peas, beans, leafy green vegetables, potatoes, fruits, avocados and yeast extract.

Vitamin B12, found in dairy foods, eggs, yeast extract, alfalfa, seaweeds and fortified soy milk, is essential for red blood cells and nerve cells. If there is one vitamin vegetarians are going to be deficient in, it will be this one.

Vitamin B1 (thiamine) is found in soya beans, wheatgerm, sunflower seeds, brazil nuts, peas and beans.

Vitamin B2 (riboflavin) is obtained from milk products, mushrooms, soya beans, leafy green vegetables, almonds, prunes and dates.

Vitamin B3 (nicotinic acid) is contained in mushrooms, sesame and sunflower seeds.

Vitamin B6 (pyridoxine) is found in currants, sultanas, raisins, bananas, sunflower seeds and soya beans.

Folic acid is found in lettuce, endive, oranges, walnuts, almonds and avocados.

Vitamin C is essential for protection from infection, for healing, and to help the body absorb iron from foods. It is found in leafy green vegetables, tomatoes, peppers (capsicums), blackcurrants, oranges, strawberries, kiwifruit and pawpaw.

Vitamins A, D, E and K are fat-soluble vitamins found in foods such as milk, butter, cheese, margarine, vegetable oils, nuts and seeds. Deficiencies in these vitamins are rare.

When exposed to sunlight, the body makes vitamin D, which is needed to allow the absorption of calcium into the bones. Vitamin A is needed for good eyesight, healthy skin, hair, nails and mucous membranes, and for resisting infection. It is found in dairy foods, green and yellow vegetables, especially carrots, and in apricots, red peppers, parsley and spinach. You

PREPARING AND COOKING VEGETABLES FOR NUTRITION

TO RETAIN the vitamins and minerals in fresh vegetables, wash them quickly (don't soak), dry and store in the crisper compartment of the refrigerator. As far as possible, use them unpeeled—brush root vegetables rather than scrape them. Sprinkle cut surfaces with lemon juice to prevent browning. Save peelings and things like carrot tops to make stock. Cook vegetables in stainless steel pans.

Many vitamins are destroyed by cooking. To minimise this loss, steam rather than boil or, even better, use the microwave, which cooks vegetables quickly and with very little water, retaining their colour and nutritional value. Vegetables taste better if undercooked rather than overcooked. Save any of the cooking water for soups and sauces.

ALTERNATIVES TO SALT

MOST people eat far more salt than the body needs. Too much salt has been implicated in high blood pressure and in an increasing susceptibility to strokes. Salt should be used sparingly and dependency on it can be reduced. Herb salts can add flavour while helping you get used to using less salt. Sprinkle chopped fresh herbs, spices, or lemon or lime juice over cooked or salad vegetables, instead of salt. Another way to cut down on salt is to replace it with *Gomasio*, a mixture of one part toasted, crushed sesame seeds to one part salt.

can see it would be difficult to develop a deficiency on a normal vegetarian diet. Vitamin E is an important antioxidant guarding against cell damage, and Vitamin K helps the blood to clot.

Vegetarians should not need to take vitamin supplements, except on medical advice. The key is variety. A well-balanced vegetarian diet will supply all the vitamins you need.

MINERALS

Iron is needed for the formation of red blood cells. One of the biggest problems for non-meat eaters can be the spectre of iron-deficiency anaemia. For women this is even more of a possibility. A varied vegetarian diet provides enough iron if it includes pulses, most especially lentils and soya beans; whole grains and products made from them, and nuts and seeds (pistachios, pumpkin seeds, sesame seeds). Dark, leafy green vegetables, brewer's yeast, wheatgerm and egg yolks, dried fruits (especially apricots and prunes) and seaweeds are also good sources of iron.

Signs that you may not be getting enough iron include tiredness and lethargy, paleness and shortness of breath.

Calcium is needed for good teeth and bones and for the healthy functioning of the muscles (including the heart) and nerves. Cheese is rich in calcium, as are milk, yoghurt and cream. It's worth remembering, if you are concerned about the amount of fat in your diet, that low-fat and skim versions of dairy products have the same amount of calcium as the full-fat variety. Eggs contain calcium as well.

For vegans, there are many non-animal sources of calcium. One of the richest is sesame seeds, which can be sprinkled on cereal or salads, or used in the form of the ground paste tahini, an essential ingredient of hummus. Soya beans

contain calcium, as do flour, figs and other dried fruits; almonds, sunflower seeds, dark green vegetables, broccoli, brewer's yeast, carob, molasses and seaweeds. Vegans need to eat these foods if they are not to be deficient in calcium.

Women have a greater need for calcium and should be aware of this from early adulthood. Getting regular supplies of calcium fortifes their store of dense bone for after the menopause. At this time of life, osteoporosis, a painful and sometimes crippling deterioration of the bones, is a very real possibility if dietary calcium has been inadequate in earlier years. Osteoporosis can be prevented but not cured.

Zinc is needed by the body for growth, healing, and the metabolising of protein and carbohydrates. Signs of a zinc deficiency include white flecks on the nails and skin problems.

Sources of zinc include wheatgerm, oatmeal, cheese, skim milk, brewer's yeast, dried figs, peanuts, nuts, sesame and pumpkin seeds, and corn and peas. Zinc also occurs in mangoes, spinach and asparagus.

Magnesium is also necessary for metabolising carbohydrates. It is not damaged by heat but is soluble so can still be used if the cooking water is saved for stock or sauces. Magnesium deficiencies are rare. Fresh fruit and vegetables. nuts and seeds, brewer's yeast, whole grains, dried fruits, pulses and soya beans, all contain some magnesium.

Iodine, needed for the functioning of the thyroid gland, is only required in tiny amounts and is present in iodised salt and seaweeds.

SEA VEGETABLES

There are many species of edible seaweeds that are worth investigating—they are an excellent source of protein, vitamins (including Vitamin B12) and the minerals calcium, sodium, potassium, iron and iodine. Nori, used to make sushi, can be cooked and used in salads. Wakame can be served as a green vegetable. Kombu sweetens the flavour of stocks and soups. They are sold in health food shops in dried form.

BELOW: Eating a balanced diet from a wide variety of food will almost certainly provide you with enough vitamins and minerals every day. Mediterranean Lentil Salad (page 146) is an unusual and delicious way to serve lentils.

THE FAT TRAP

Meat-lovers who give meat a central place in their diet face one pitfall a vegetarian largely avoids: eating a lot of animal products, including cheese and eggs, means eating a lot of fat, and of the kind that has been implicated in some serious health problems if eaten in excess.

Vegetarians tend not to suffer weight problems and the perils of a diet high in saturated fats are more easily avoided by eating this way. But it is important to realise that there are plenty of non-meat sources of saturated fat, and these are best eaten in moderation. One example is coconut oil, which is used in a lot of commercial baked goods. Coconut cream or canned coconut milk used in many curries is another.

Children need more fat than adults to help them grow but they can obtain it from a range of nutritious vegetarian foods: milk, avocados, peanut butter, yoghurt and cheese.

Everyone needs some fat as fatty acids are essential to the formation of cells in the body, especially those of the nervous system. It would be harmful to try to eliminate all fat from the diet, but eating a variety of foods will supply plenty without any special effort.

BELOW: To reduce the amount of fat in your diet, don't simply give up fat, but eat more pulses, grains and vegetables which provide bulk and therefore sustain you. Borlotti Bean Moussaka (page 152) contains yoghurt, eggs and cheese, but each serving is so full of nutrients that you'd be unlikely to eat any more fat at that meal.

HEALTHY FATS

Dietary fat comes from two sources: animals and plants. Sources of animal fats that vegetarians (excluding vegans) can use include butter, cheese, cream, yoghurt and egg yolks. Plants provide oils and margarine and the hard vegetable fats made from them. Fats containing essential fatty acids and occurring in foods that have other nutrients (olive and other vegetable oils, nuts, seeds, avocados, grains) are a better source of fat in the diet than fried takeaway food, cakes, biscuits, chocolates or ice cream.

KINDS OF FAT

● Saturated fats solidify at room temperature. Most animal fats are saturated. Some examples are lard, butter and dripping. Saturated fats are thought to raise the level of the harmful type of cholesterol in the blood and lower the amount of the beneficial type. They are also thought to be implicated in some cancers.

● Polyunsaturated fats include vegetable oils like safflower, sunflower, corn and soya bean oil. These lower the overall amount of cholesterol in the blood. They are liquid at room temperature but can be chemically processed into margarines.

The effects on the body of eating a lot of polyunsaturated fats are still being investigated. It used to be thought that they had a beneficial effect on the amount of cholesterol in the blood but it is now known that this effect is indiscriminate and reduces 'good cholesterol' as well as 'bad cholesterol'.

Margarine in the diet in large amounts is thought to contribute a kind of fatty acid implicated in heart disease. Large quantities of polyunsaturated fats can also oxidise to form free radicals in the blood. These are responsible for tissue damage and contribute to the formation of plaque on the artery walls. Eating lots of fruit and vegetables reduces this effect as these foods contain antioxidants.

● Monounsaturated fats have recently come into favour, for a number of reasons. When it began to be noticed that the people of countries like Spain and Italy had a lower incidence of heart disease than that occurring in other cultures, it was realised that the so-called Mediterranean diet was high in olive oil and low in dairy fats.

Large amounts of monounsaturated fats occur in olive and canola oils. These kinds of fats reduce the levels of 'bad' cholesterol and increase 'good' cholesterol, protecting against heart disease. In addition, populations using olive oil as the main fat in their diets have been shown to have lower rates of breast and bowel cancer, although the exact reason why this should be so is still disputed.

DIETING

The different kinds of fat usually occur in combination in foods. More important than worrying about which kind of fat you are eating is being aware of the overall amount of fat in your diet. This means being conscious of hidden fats in things like pies, crisps, chocolate (and carob) bars, cakes, biscuits and other commercially produced, ready-to-eat foods. Many people worry about the sugar in these foods and forget about the fats.

Eating out a lot and eating takeaway foods and commercially produced snacks can easily lead to an excess of fat in the diet. A good guide is to aim at getting only about a quarter of your total daily kilojoules from fat, or to eat about 30–40 g of fat per day if you are a woman or a child, and 40–60 g if you are a man. Very active adults and teenagers need about 70 g a day, and athletes and those engaged in heavy physical work, about 70–80 g.

There also hidden fats in many innocuous-looking so-called 'health foods', for example toasted muesli, which contains a lot of vegetable oil. Avocados and nuts are also high in fat and should be eaten in moderation. Remember, also, that foods labelled 'low cholesterol' are not necessarily low in fat.

The body only needs small amounts of fat, and nobody eating a western diet is ever in danger of suffering a fat deficiency. It is very important, as much for someone on a non-meat diet as for meat eaters, to be aware of how much fat they are eating. The pitfalls for vegetarians are just different.

Vegetarians can sometimes be under the illusion they are eating a healthy diet simply because they have eliminated meat with its hidden and not-so-hidden fats. But unthinkingly loading up on cheeses, cream, sour cream or even vegetable oils is just as hazardous for health.

Excessive amounts of fried food will lead to weight gain whether they're fried in animal or vegetable fats. The only difference is a that a vegetarian eating lots of food fried in, say, olive oil—and not burning up kilojoules with increased physical activity—will gain weight without increasing blood cholesterol levels the way a meat-eater on a high fat diet will.

If you are concerned about your weight, it is more important to be aware of the amount of fat in foods you eat on a daily basis than to try counting kilojoules from all sources, as was done in the past. Excess kilojoules from fat are readily stored as body fat, whereas those from carbohydrates, for example, are made available to the body as energy.

HERO FOODS

Some foods have been called the 'heroes' of a vegetarian diet because they are rich sources of certain essential nutrients which meat-eaters obtain in abundance. Including these in your diet will help to ensure there are not any deficiency problems.

● LENTILS contain protein, fibre and complex carbohydrate and the B vitamins, as well as potassium, magnesium and zinc.

● SOYA BEANS have the best quality protein of all pulses, some B vitamins, polyunsaturated fat, and fibre.

● ROLLED OATS are good for protein, thiamin, niacin and iron, fibre and carbohydrate.

● WHEAT BRAN is an excellent source of soluble fibre, iron, thiamine and niacin.

● EGGS supply iron, phosphorus, Vitamin B12, Vitamins A and D, and protein.

● DRIED APRICOTS contain beta carotene (the plant form of Vitamin A), fibre and vitamin C. Almonds are a good source of monounsaturated oil, dietary fibre and Vitamin E.

● MILK, YOGHURT AND CHEESE provide calcium, phosphorus, protein and Vitamin A. Milk and yoghurt retain the B vitamins which are removed in the processing of cheese.

● SPINACH contains fibre and most of the vitamins and minerals normally found in meats.

● UNHULLED SESAME SEEDS are rich in calcium and contain Vitamin E, magnesium, phosphate and zinc.

● TOFU AND TEMPEH provide magnesium, calcium, phosphorus and iron as well as protein.

● YEAST EXTRACT is a concentrated source of B vitamins.

ABOVE: One of the best ways a vegetarian can ensure good nutrition is to eat a proper breakfast. Crunchy Nut Muesli (page 151) provides a perfect start to the day. It is a genuine hero food.

FAT IN FOOD

We all need some fat in our diet but many of us have far too much. It is recommended that men limit their fat intake to about 70 g per day, and women to about 50 g per day.

CROISSANT
Fat per 100 g: 23.6 g

EGG
Fat per 100 g: 10 g

ALMONDS
Fat per 100 g: 54.7 g

BREAD
Fat per 100 g: 2.5 g

PECANS
Fat per 100 g: 72 g

MACADAMIAS
Fat per 100 g: 7.6 g

POTATO CHIPS, THICK CUT
Fat per 100 g: 10 g

PRETZELS
Fat per 100 g: 7.2 g

AVOCADO
Fat per 100 g: 22.6 g

MUESLI
Fat per 100 g: 9 g

BAKED JACKET POTATO
Fat per 100 g: 0.1 g

CORN CHIPS
Fat per 100 g: 26.7 g

TOASTED MUESLI
Fat per 100 g: 16.6 g

POTATO CHIPS, THIN CUT
Fat per 100 g: 20 g

WHOLE MILK
Fat per 100 g: 3.8 g

CHEDDAR CHEESE
Fat per 100 g: 33.8 g

BUTTER
Fat per 100 g: 80 g

SKIM MILK
Fat per 100 g: 0.1 g

BRIE
Fat per 100 g: 29 g

MARGARINE
Fat per 100 g: 80 g

OIL, ANY KIND
Fat per 100 g: 100 g

RICOTTA, LOW FAT
Fat per 100 g: 4 g

YOGHURT, NATURAL
Fat per 100 g: 4.4 g

SOUR CREAM
Fat per 100 g: 37.7 g

RICOTTA
Fat per 100 g: 11.3 g

YOGHURT, NATURAL, LOW FAT
Fat per 100 g: 0.2 g

COCONUT CREAM
Fat per 100 g: 20 g

HERO FOODS

The foods shown here contain significant amounts of the nutrients which, without care, may be lacking in a vegetarian diet. The recommended daily intakes are given below.

ROLLED OATS, RAW
Protein per 100 g: 10.7 g
Iron per 100 g: 3.7 mg
Zinc per 100 g: 1.9 mg

SOYA BEANS, COOKED
Protein per 100 g: 13.5 g
Calcium per 100 g: 76 mg
Iron per 100 g: 2.2 mg
Zinc per 100 g: 1.6 mg

ALMONDS
Protein per 100 g: 20 g
Calcium per 100 g: 250 mg
Iron per 100 g: 3.9 mg
Zinc per 100 g: 3.8 mg
Folate per 100 g: 96 ug

SUNFLOWER SEEDS
Protein per 100 g: 22.7 g
Calcium per 100 g: 100 mg
Iron per 100 g: 4.6 mg
Zinc per 100 g: 6.4 mg

SESAME SEEDS
Protein per 100 g: 22.2 g
Calcium per 100 g: 62 mg
Iron per 100 g: 5.2 mg
Zinc per 100 g: 5.5 mg

PARSLEY
Calcium per 100 g: 200 mg
Iron per 100 g: 9.4 mg

ENDIVE
Folate per 100 g: 330 ug

BRAN, WHEAT
Iron per 100 g: 12 mg
Zinc per 100 g: 4.7 mg
Folate per 100 g: 260 ug

LENTILS, COOKED
Protein per 100 g: 6.8 g
Calcium per 100 g: 17 mg
Iron per 100 g: 2 mg

YEAST EXTRACT
Protein per 100 g: 24.4 g
Zinc per 100 g: 5.1 mg
B12 per 100 g: 5 ug

YOGHURT
Protein per 100 g: 5.8 g
Calcium per 100 g: 195 mg

EGG
Protein per 100 g: 13.2 g
Calcium per 100 g: 43 mg
Iron per 100 g: 1.8 mg
B12 per 100 g: 1.7 ug

TEMPEH
Protein per 100 g: 19 g

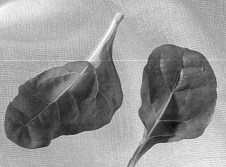

SPINACH
Calcium per 100 g: 53 mg
Iron per 100 g: 3.2 mg
Zinc per 100 g: 0.6 mg
Folate per 100 g: 120 ug

CHEDDAR CHEESE
Protein per 100 g: 26 g
B12 per 100 g: 1.5 ug
Folate per 100 g: 60 ug

TOFU
Protein per 100 g: 10 g

DRIED APRICOTS
Calcium per 100 g: 67 mg
Iron per 100 g: 3.1 mg
Zinc per 100 g: 0.8 mg

MILK
Protein per 100 g: 3.3 g
Calcium per 100 g: 120 mg

Recommended daily intakes: Iron 7 mg (men), 12–16 mg (women), Vitamin B12 2 ug, Folate 200 ug,
Protein 55 g (men) 45 g (women), Calcium 800 mg, Zinc 12–16 mg.
(Women who are pregnant, breast-feeding, or over 54 require different amounts.)

A WORLD OF FLAVOURS

One of the great joys of vegetarian eating lies in its versatility. There are many exotic detours available through the world's cuisines which can broaden your options and expand your cooking skills. The limitations of the Western diet of the past will soon become very obvious.

Many cultures feature a strong vegetarian component and some are exclusively vegetarian, having evolved this way of eating for economic as well as religious reasons. These cuisines are the source of delicious, nutritious dishes that any cook can easily master.

Some dishes are classic examples of efficient and tasty food combining. From Mexico we get tortillas and beans; from the Orient, silken tofu, tempeh and rice; from the Middle East, hummus with lavash or pitta bread; from North Africa and the Mediterranean, couscous and chickpeas. And there are many more possibilities.

Asian food is one of the best and most interesting sources of vegetarian food. If you've never tried Asian cooking before, becoming a vegetarian offers an ideal opportunity to start.

Many exotic vegetarian dishes can be served as either a side-dish, main course, light meal or snack. All you need is a little knowledge, a few interesting ingredients, and some thought about complementary flavours and textures. You will then discover perhaps the biggest advantage of vegetarian eating: the opportunity to cook and eat a whole glorious palette of flavours, colours and textures. It is impossible to be bored by vegetarian food.

ABOVE: Trying new foods and different combinations of food is one of the joys of vegetarian eating. It's hard to get into a rut when there's so much fresh produce to be sampled. If you've only ever tasted pumpkin baked or mashed, try this lovely Asian-inspired dish Pumpkin with Chilli and Avocado (page 199).

WAKE UP YOUR TASTEBUDS

The incomparable flavours of fresh whole foods can be enhanced with spices and condiments: harissa, chermoula, chilli pastes and curry spice mixtures. Herbs are indispensable, and pickles, chutneys, sauces, mustards and relishes can be used to dress up a number of dishes.

Certain herbs and spices go particularly well with certain foods:

- BASIL *with tomatoes and cheeses*
- CINNAMON, CARDAMOM, CLOVES *with yoghurt, cream and milk dishes*
- CLOVES *with oranges*
- CHIVES *in soups, dips, salads, sandwiches and sauces; with eggs, potatoes and cheese*
- DILL *in salads, with potatoes, in egg dishes*
- CHOPPED HERBS *with pasta and rice*
- GINGER *with carrots*
- LEMON GRASS *in rice dishes, Asian-style sauces*
- LEMON THYME *in salads, with cooked vegetables*
- OREGANO AND MARJORAM *with eggs, in salads and marinades, with cauliflower and tomatoes*
- MINT *with potatoes, in tabouli, with rice*
- PAPRIKA *with eggs, cheeses and in casseroles*
- PARSLEY *in salads, with tomatoes*
- ROSEMARY *with eggplant (aubergine), tomatoes, zucchinis (courgettes)*
- SAGE *in bean, cheese or egg dishes, salads*
- GARLIC *with just about anything savoury*

Stock up the pantry before you begin to roam through the varied world of vegetarian cookery. This will ensure you have the necessary ingredients for a successful dish always to hand and don't have to compromise on flavour.

Most supermarkets these days stock a huge variety of the things you will need, but don't forget to explore delicatessens, and Asian and other ethnic food stores and markets, especially for condiments and unusual flavourings.

SERVING A VEGETARIAN MEAL

Old habits die hard and the old tradition of meat and two vegetables is very hard to break. But vegetarian eating can make things a whole lot easier. When you don't have to make the meat (or chicken or fish) the centrepiece, it becomes much easier to serve food buffet-style. Many ethnic cuisines demand this way of serving and eating, with platters of complementary dishes from which people help themselves, adding accompaniments of their choice.

Vegetarian food makes mealtime much more interesting. You can break all the rules. Serve first courses as main courses, change what you would normally serve as a main course into a starter. Make a soup the star of your meal. Except for soups and starters, which are grouped together because many people want a quick idea for a light meal, this book does not divide recipes traditionally into particular courses. It is designed so that the cook can browse and plunder recipes at will.

Consider colour and texture as well as taste and nutritive value. Serve Layered Potato and Apple Bake (page 164) or Cauliflower and Pasta Bake (page 166) with a green salad or crisp-textured green vegetables, such as asparagus or snow peas (mange tout) to provide additional colour and a crunchy texture. Make simple vegetable dishes and salads more interesting (and nutritious) by sprinkling with chopped nuts or seeds. Try a mixture of pumpkin and sesame seeds tossed in soy sauce and roasted in the oven. It's delicious with cucumber salad and even a simple green salad and will keep for months in the refrigerator in an airtight jar. Include lots of interesting breads when serving vegetarian foods, including flatbreads like lavash, chapattis, rotis, poppadums, tortillas and pitta.

HOW TO USE THIS BOOK

RECIPE FORMAT
The recipes are written in step form to break them up into their separate parts and make them easier to follow.

FAST RECIPES
All the fast recipes can be made from beginning to end within 30 minutes. They're all listed in the index under Fast Recipes for easy reference.

MARGIN NOTES
The margin notes might contain a quick recipe or describe how to deal with a particular ingredient, or just give you a little history of food. They are meant to inform and divert.

STEP-BY-STEP PICTURES
Scattered throughout the book are step-by-step instructions and photographs on some special techniques for preparing and cooking vegetarian food.

SPECIAL FEATURES
There are twelve special feature pages in the book to draw your attention to the fresh innovative food available to the vegetarian.

TABLESPOONS
We have used 20 ml tablespoon measures. If you are using a 15 ml tablespoon, for most recipes the difference will not be noticeable. However, for recipes using baking powder, bicarbonate of soda, small amounts of flour and cornflour, add an extra teaspoon for each tablespoon specified.

CUPS
Many of the ingredients are measured in cups—always with a metric and imperial equivalent. We use 250 ml (8 fl oz) measuring cups.

OVEN TEMPERATURES
Cooking times may vary slightly depending on the type of oven you are using. Check the manufacturer's instructions to ensure proper temperature control. For fan-forced ovens check your appliance manual, but as a general rule, set oven temperature to 20°C (68°F) lower than the temperature indicated in the recipe.

OUR STAR RATING
When we test our recipes, we rate them for ease of preparation. The following cookery ratings are on the recipes in this book, making them easy to use and understand.

★ A single star indicates a recipe that is simple and generally quick to make—perfect for beginners.

★★ Two stars indicate the need for just a little more care, or perhaps a little more time.

★★★ Three stars indicate special dishes that need more investment in time, care and patience—but the results are worth it. Even beginners can make these dishes as long as the recipe is carefully followed.

SOUPS AND STARTERS

Confess—who among us has never felt like ordering two (or even three) first courses rather than just the usual one, along with a main? First courses sound more appealing and there is often a wider choice for vegetarians at the top of a menu. Here, you're given free rein to realise that impulse: try a restorative soup with a gutsy antipasto. No matter how you pair these recipes, you'll love the meal.

SOUPE AU PISTOU
(VEGETABLE SOUP WITH BASIL SAUCE)

Preparation time: 45 minutes
Total cooking time: 35–40 minutes
Serves 6–8

★

2 medium onions

I leek

3 sprigs fresh parsley

I large sprig fresh rosemary

I large sprig fresh thyme

I large sprig fresh marjoram

1/4 cup (60 ml/2 fl oz) olive oil

I bay leaf

375 g (12 oz) pumpkin, cut into small pieces

250 g (8 oz) potato, cut into small pieces

I medium carrot, cut in half lengthways
   and thinly sliced

2 small zucchinis (courgettes), sliced

I teaspoon salt

8 cups (2 litres) water or vegetable stock

1/2 cup (90 g/2²/3 oz) fresh or frozen broad beans

1/2 cup (80 g/3 oz) fresh or frozen peas

2 tomatoes, peeled and roughly chopped

1/2 cup (45 g/1 1/2 oz) shell pasta

Pistou

1/2 cup (15 g/1/2 oz) fresh basil leaves

2 large cloves garlic, crushed

1/2 teaspoon black pepper

3 tablespoons freshly grated Parmesan cheese

1/3 cup (80 ml/2³/4 fl oz) olive oil

I Thinly slice the onions and leek. Tie the parsley, rosemary, thyme and marjoram together with string. Heat the oil in a heavy-based pan; add onions and leek. Cook over low heat for 10 minutes or until soft.

2 Add herb bunch, bay leaf, pumpkin, potato, carrot, zucchinis, salt, and water or stock. Cover and simmer for 10 minutes, or until vegetables are almost tender.

3 Add broad beans, peas, tomatoes and pasta. Cover; cook for 15 minutes or until vegetables are tender and pasta is cooked (add more water if necessary). Remove herbs, including bay leaf.

4 To make Pistou: Process basil, garlic, pepper and cheese in food processor for 20 seconds or until finely chopped. Pour in oil gradually, processing until smooth. Refrigerate. Reheat soup and serve with Pistou spooned on top.

ABOVE: Soupe au Pistou

WATERCRESS SOUP

Preparation time: 15 minutes
Total cooking time: 15–20 minutes
Serves 4-6

1 onion
4 spring onions
450 g (14¹/₃ oz) watercress
100 g (3¹/₃ oz) butter
¹/₃ cup (40 g/1¹/₃ oz) plain flour
3 cups (750 ml/24 fl oz) vegetable stock
1¹/₄ cups (315 ml/10 fl oz) water
salt and pepper
sour cream or cream, for serving

1 Roughly chop the onion, spring onions and watercress. Heat the butter in a large pan and add the onion, spring onions and watercress. Stir over low heat for 3 minutes or until the vegetables have softened.
2 Add flour and stir until combined. Gradually add the stock and water to the pan, stirring until smooth. Stir until mixture boils and thickens. Simmer, covered, over low heat for 10 minutes, or until the watercress is tender. Cool slightly.
3 Transfer the mixture to a food processor or blender and process in batches until smooth. Before serving, gently heat through and season with salt and pepper. Serve with a dollop of sour cream or cream and garnish with fresh watercress, if desired.

VEGETABLE STOCK

PREHEAT THE OVEN to hot 210°C (415°F/Gas 6–7). Heat 2 tablespoons of oil in a large baking dish; add the following vegetables, all unpeeled and chopped: 4 large brown onions, 5 large carrots and 2 large parsnips; toss to coat in the oil. Bake for 30 minutes. Transfer the baked vegetables to a large heavy-based pan. Add 5 chopped celery sticks (including leaves), 2 bay leaves, a fresh bouquet garni, 1 teaspoon whole black peppercorns and 3 litres water to the pan. Bring to the boil slowly, reduce heat and simmer, uncovered, for 1 hour or until liquid is reduced by half. Strain stock through a fine sieve, discarding the vegetables. Allow to cool before refrigerating. Remove any fat which sets on the top. Makes 1.5 litres.

CORN CHOWDER

Preparation time: 15 minutes
Total cooking time: 30 minutes
Serves 8

90 g (3 oz) butter
2 large onions, finely chopped
1 clove garlic, crushed
2 teaspoons cumin seeds
4 cups (1 litre) vegetable stock
2 medium potatoes, peeled and chopped
1 cup (250 g/8 oz) canned creamed-style corn
2 cups (400 g/12²/₃ oz) fresh corn kernels
3 tablespoons chopped fresh parsley
1 cup (125 g/4 oz) grated Cheddar cheese
salt and freshly ground black pepper
3 tablespoons cream (optional)
2 tablespoons chopped fresh chives, to garnish

1 Heat the butter in large heavy-based pan. Add the onions and cook over medium-high heat for 5 minutes or until golden. Add garlic and cumin seeds, cook 1 minute, stirring constantly. Add vegetable stock, bring to boil. Add potatoes and reduce heat. Simmer, uncovered, 10 minutes.
2 Add the creamed corn, corn kernels and parsley. Bring to the boil, reduce heat, simmer for 10 minutes. Stir through the cheese, salt and pepper, to taste, and cream. Heat gently until the cheese melts. Serve immediately, sprinkled with chopped chives.

CHOWDERS
A chowder is a thick soup, usually milk-based, made with vegetables, fish or chicken. The name comes from the French *chaudière*, the copper pot in which fishermen's wives cooked a communal soup from a share of each man's catch to celebrate the safe return of the fishing fleet.

ABOVE: Corn Chowder

GAZPACHO (SPANISH COLD TOMATO AND CUCUMBER SOUP)

Preparation time: 20 minutes
Total cooking time: 10–15 minutes
Serves 6–8

1 red (Spanish) onion
3 tomatoes
1/2 medium cucumber
1/2 green pepper (capsicum), seeded
1/2 red pepper (capsicum), seeded
1 clove garlic, crushed
3 1/2 cups (875 ml/28 fl oz) tomato juice
1/2 teaspoon sugar
salt and pepper
1/4 cup (60 ml/2 fl oz) olive oil
1/4 cup (60 ml/2 fl oz) white wine vinegar

Garlic Croutons

6 slices white bread
1/4 cup (60 ml/2 fl oz) olive oil
1 clove garlic, crushed

1 Finely chop the onion, tomatoes, cucumber and peppers. Place in a large bowl with garlic.
2 Stir in the juice, sugar, salt and pepper, and combined oil and vinegar and mix well. Refrigerate. Serve soup cold, with a bowl of Garlic Croutons.
3 **To make Garlic Croutons:** Preheat the oven to moderate 180°C (350°F/Gas 4). Trim the crusts from the bread and cut the bread into 1 cm (1/2 inch) cubes. Drizzle with combined oil and garlic and mix well. Spread on baking tray. Bake for 10–15 minutes, turning twice, or until golden brown.

FAST ZUCCHINI (COURGETTE) SOUP

FRY A FINELY chopped onion in about 30 g (1 oz) of butter in a medium pan. Add 4 grated zucchinis (courgettes) and 2 crushed cloves of garlic and stir-fry for 2–3 minutes, until the vegetables are soft. Add 4 cups (1 litre) of vegetable stock, bring to the boil, reduce the heat slightly and simmer, uncovered, for 10 minutes. Stir in 1/4 cup (60 ml/2 fl oz) of fresh cream and season, to taste, with salt and pepper. Serve immediately. Serves 4.

FAST SPICY BEAN SOUP

FRY A CHOPPED onion in a little oil in a medium pan until soft. Add 2 crushed cloves of garlic and 1/2 teaspoon of chilli powder, stir-fry for 1 minute, then add two 425 g (13 1/2 oz) cans mixed beans, rinsed and drained. Stir in 2 cups (500 ml/16 fl oz) of vegetable stock and 400 g (12 2/3 oz) canned tomato purée; cook until heated through. Season with salt and pepper, to taste. Garnish with a combination of finely chopped boiled egg and finely chopped parsley, and serve. Serves 4.
Note: Combinations of beans such as red kidney, cannellini and haricot, are available in cans. If you prefer, you can use just one kind of bean.

SPINACH AND LENTIL SOUP

Preparation time: 10 minutes
Total cooking time: 1 hour 25 minutes
Serves 4–6

2 cups (370 g/11 3/4 oz) brown lentils
5 cups (1.25 litres) water
2 teaspoons olive oil
1 medium onion, finely chopped
2 cloves garlic, crushed
20 English spinach leaves, stalks removed and leaves finely shredded
1 teaspoon ground cumin
1 teaspoon finely grated lemon rind
2 cups (500 ml/16 fl oz) vegetable stock
2 cups (500 ml/16 fl oz) water
2 tablespoons finely chopped fresh coriander

1 Place the lentils in a large pan with water. Bring to the boil and then simmer, uncovered, for 1 hour. Rinse and drain, then set aside. In a separate pan heat the oil; add the onion and garlic. Cook over medium heat until golden. Add spinach and cook for another 2 minutes.
2 Add the lentils, cumin, lemon rind, stock and water to the pan. Simmer, uncovered, for 15 minutes. Add the coriander and stir through. Serve immediately.

PREPARING DRIED BEANS OR SPLIT PEAS

1 Place the beans in a large bowl and cover with plenty of water (they will expand). Soak for 4 hours or time stated on the packet; drain.

2 Place beans in a pan, cover with fresh water, bring to boil, simmer over low heat. Skim any froth that gathers on the surface during cooking.

3 If the water reduces too much, top up with boiling water. When the beans are tender, drain in a colander, use as needed. Use for Fast Spicy Bean Soup, if you like.

OPPOSITE PAGE:
Gazpacho

MINESTRONE

Preparation time: 30 minutes + overnight
soaking
Total cooking time: 2 hours 45 minutes
Serves 6-8

1 1/4 cups (250 g/8 oz) haricot beans
2 tablespoons oil
2 onions, chopped
2 cloves garlic, crushed
4 tomatoes, peeled and chopped
3 tablespoons chopped parsley
9 cups (2.25 litres) vegetable stock
1/4 cup (60 ml/2 fl oz) red wine
1 carrot, chopped
1 turnip, chopped
2 potatoes, chopped
1 celery stick, chopped
3 tablespoons tomato paste
1 zucchini (courgette), sliced
1/2 cup (60 g/2 oz) sliced green beans
1/2 cup (80 g/2 2/3 oz) macaroni elbows
salt and pepper
shaved Parmesan cheese, for serving

1 Soak haricot beans overnight in water; drain.
Add to a pan of boiling water and simmer for
15 minutes; drain. Heat oil in a pan, add onions
and garlic. Cook, stirring, until onion is soft.

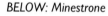

BELOW: Minestrone

2 Add the tomatoes, parsley, haricot beans, stock
and wine. Simmer, covered, over low heat for
2 hours.
3 Add the carrot, turnip, potatoes, celery and
tomato paste; simmer, covered, 15–20 minutes.
4 Add the zucchini, green beans and macaroni.
Simmer, covered, for 10–15 minutes, or until
vegetables and pasta are tender. Season with salt
and pepper. Serve topped with shavings of
Parmesan cheese.

PUMPKIN SOUP
WITH HARISSA

Preparation time: 10–40 minutes
Total cooking time: 20 minutes
Serves 6

2.5 kg (5 lb) pumpkin
3 cups (750 ml/24 fl oz) vegetable stock
3 cups (750 ml/24 fl oz) milk
sugar and black pepper, to taste

Harissa

250 g (8 oz) fresh or dried birds-eye chillies
   (or any small red chillies)
1 tablespoon caraway seeds
1 tablespoon coriander seeds
2 teaspoons cumin seeds
4–6 cloves garlic, peeled
1 tablespoon dried mint
1 teaspoon salt
1/2 cup (125 ml/4 fl oz) extra-virgin olive oil

1 Remove skin, seeds and fibre from pumpkin
and cut into pieces. Simmer, uncovered, in a
large pan with stock and milk for 15–20 minutes
or until tender. Allow to cool slightly.
2 Process mixture, in batches, until smooth.
Season with a little sugar and black pepper.
3 **To make Harissa:** Wearing rubber gloves,
remove stems of chillies, split in half, remove
seeds and soften flesh in hot water for 5 minutes
(or 30 minutes if using dried). Drain and place in
a food processor. While chillies are soaking, dry-
fry the caraway, coriander and cumin in a pan
until they become aromatic, about 1 or 2
minutes. Add the 3 spices, garlic, mint and salt to
food processor and, slowly adding the olive oil,
process until a smooth, thick paste forms. Stir
Harissa into individual bowls of soup to suit tastes.

CREAMY CORN AND TOMATO SOUP

Preparation time: 20 minutes
Total cooking time: 15 minutes
Serves 4-6

1 teaspoon olive oil
1 teaspoon vegetable stock powder
1 medium onion, finely chopped
3 medium tomatoes
425 g (13½ oz) canned tomato purée
310 g (9¾ oz) canned creamed-style corn
125 g (4 oz) canned corn kernels, drained
chilli powder
sour cream and tortillas, for serving

1 Heat the oil in a large pan. Add stock powder and onion and cook until onion is soft.
2 Peel tomatoes, remove seeds with a spoon and chop flesh. Add to the pan with the tomato purée, creamed corn and corn kernels. Season with chilli. Stir until heated through. Serve with a dollop of sour cream and some warm tortillas.

GREEN PEA SOUP

Preparation time: 20 minutes + 2 hours soaking
Total cooking time: 1 hour 40 minutes
Serves 4-6

1½ cups (330 g/10½ oz) green split peas
2 tablespoons oil
1 medium onion, finely chopped
1 celery stick, finely sliced
1 medium carrot, finely sliced
1 tablespoon ground cumin
1 tablespoon ground coriander
2 teaspoons grated fresh ginger
5 cups (1.25 litres) vegetable stock
2 cups (310 g/9¾ oz) frozen green peas
salt and freshly ground black pepper
1 tablespoon chopped fresh mint
4 tablespoons plain yoghurt or sour cream

1 Soak the split peas in cold water for 2 hours. Drain peas well. Heat oil in a large heavy-based pan and add onion, celery and carrot. Cook over medium heat for 3 minutes, stirring occasionally, until soft but not browned. Stir in cumin, coriander and ginger, then cook for 1 minute.
2 Add split peas and stock to pan. Bring to the boil; reduce heat to low. Simmer, covered, for 1½ hours, stirring occasionally.
3 Add frozen peas to pan and stir to combine; set aside to cool. When cool, purée soup in batches in a blender or food processor until smooth. Return to pan, gently reheat. Season with salt and pepper and then stir in mint. Serve in bowls with a swirl of yoghurt or sour cream.

FREEZING SOUP
Some soups take a long time to cook so it makes sense to cook a big batch and freeze it for later use. Freeze in quantities that you're most likely to use— one serving, two servings, five servings—because once the soup has thawed it is unsafe to freeze it again. Cool the soup and pour it into airtight containers, cover tightly, label and date. To thaw, place the container in the fridge up to 24 hours ahead, then reheat gently in a pan on top of the stove. If you're in a hurry, you can put the frozen soup in a pan and heat gently, or heat it in the microwave.

*ABOVE: Creamy Corn and Tomato Soup
BELOW: Green Pea Soup*

ANTIPASTO
Enticing to the eye, emanating a mouthwatering scent and captivating the palate, these seductive appetizers assault the senses, whether eaten on their own or as a tempting introduction to a meal.

MARINATED ROASTED PEPPERS (CAPSICUMS)
Grill 1 large red pepper, 1 large yellow pepper, 1 large green pepper and, if available, 1 large purple pepper, until the skin blisters and blackens. Cover the peppers with a tea towel to cool slightly before peeling. Cut the peppers into thick strips and place into a bowl, add 2 crushed cloves of garlic, 2 tablespoons of balsamic vinegar, 2 tablespoons of shredded fresh basil and ¼ cup (60 ml/ 2 fl oz) of olive oil. Cover and refrigerate for 3 hours. Return to room temperature before serving. Serve on toasted bruschetta or focaccia. Serves 4–6.

SWEET AND SOUR ONIONS
Carefully peel 3 medium (500 g/1 lb) red (Spanish) onions, keeping the ends intact so that the layers stay together. Cut the onions into eighths and place the pieces in a non-stick baking dish. Combine 2 tablespoons of wholegrain mustard, 2 tablespoons of honey,

2 tablespoons of red wine vinegar and 2 tablespoons of oil. Brush this mixture over the onions, cover the dish and bake in a preheated hot 220°C (425°F/Gas 7) oven for 20 minutes. Uncover and continue baking for another 15–20 minutes, or until the onions are soft and caramelised. Serves 4–6.

GOLDEN FRIED GOATS CHEESE
Cut 250 g (8 oz) of goats cheese into 5 mm (¼ inch) thick slices. Dust lightly with seasoned flour. Dip the slices into 2 lightly beaten eggs and gently toss to coat in a mixture of 1 cup (80 g/2⅔ oz) of fresh breadcrumbs, ½ cup (45 g/ 1½ oz) of grated pecorino cheese and 1 teaspoon of sweet paprika. Refrigerate for 1 hour. Deep-fry the crumbed goats

cheese in batches in hot oil for 2 minutes, or until the crust is crisp and golden. Serve with your favourite relish or a sweet dipping sauce. It is best to use the small logs of goats cheese for this recipe. Serves 4.

CHAR-GRILLED SPRING ONIONS AND ASPARAGUS
Cut 110 g (9¾ oz) of asparagus and 12 spring onions into 12 cm (5 inch) lengths. Brush the spring onions and asparagus lightly with macadamia nut oil and cook on a preheated char-grill or barbecue for 3 minutes, or until the vegetables are tender. Pour some balsamic vinegar over the top, sprinkle with pepper and then top with shavings of Parmesan cheese. Serves 4–6.

MUSHROOMS IN LIME AND CHILLI
Brush 250 g (8 oz) of button mushrooms with oil; cook under a preheated grill, or on a barbecue grill, until tender. Combine 1 teaspoon chilli flakes, 1 tablespoon shredded lime rind, 1 crushed clove garlic, 1 tablespoon chopped fresh coriander, 1 teaspoon soft brown sugar, 2 tablespoons of lime juice and ¼ cup (60 ml/2 fl oz) of olive oil in a bowl. Toss the mushrooms in lime and chilli mixture and refrigerate for 1 hour before serving. Serves 2–4.

CLOCKWISE, FROM TOP LEFT: Golden Fried Goats Cheese; Marinated Roasted Peppers; Sweet and Sour Onions; Char-grilled Spring Onions and Asparagus; Mushrooms in Lime and Chilli

PUREEING SOUP

Be careful when puréeing hot soup in a blender or food processor as it can shoot out of the top and scald you. If possible, cool the soup before puréeing. If you must purée while the soup is hot, do it in small batches. Thin soups may also leak from a food processor—the best way to deal with this is to remove the vegetables from the soup with a slotted spoon and process with a spoonful or two of the liquid. Mix the puréed vegetables back into the liquid in the pan.

RED PEPPER (CAPSICUM) SOUP

Preparation time: 20 minutes
Total cooking time: 30 minutes
Serves 6

★ ★

4 medium red peppers (capsicums)
4 medium tomatoes
¼ cup (60 ml/2 fl oz) oil
½ teaspoon dried marjoram
½ teaspoon dried mixed herbs
2 cloves garlic, crushed
I teaspoon mild curry paste
I medium red (Spanish) onion, sliced
I medium leek, sliced (white part only)
250 g (8 oz) green cabbage, chopped
4 cups (I litre) water
I teaspoon sweet chilli sauce
salt and freshly ground black pepper

I Cut the red peppers into quarters. Remove the seeds and membrane. Grill until the skin blackens and blisters. Place on a cutting board, cover with a tea towel and allow to cool before peeling. Mark a small cross on the top of each tomato. Place in a bowl and cover with boiling water for about 2 minutes. Drain and cool. Peel skin off downwards from the cross and discard.

Cut the tomatoes in half and gently scoop out the seeds using a small spoon.

2 Heat the oil in a large pan; add the herbs, garlic and curry paste. Stir over low heat for 1 minute, or until aromatic. Add the onion and leek and cook for 3 minutes or until golden. Add the cabbage, tomatoes, red peppers and water. Bring to the boil, reduce heat and simmer for 20 minutes. Remove from the heat; allow to cool slightly.

3 Place the soup in small batches in a food processor bowl. Process for 30 seconds or until smooth. Return the soup to a clean pan, stir through chilli sauce and season with salt and pepper. Reheat gently and serve hot.

FAST MUSHROOM SOUP

FRY 2 CHOPPED onions in 60 g (2 oz) butter until they are lightly golden. Add 500 g (1 lb) of chopped button mushrooms and cook for another 5 minutes, stirring. Add ¼ cup (30 g/1 oz) of plain flour and stir for 1 more minute. Stir in 2 cups (500 ml/16 fl oz) of milk and 1½ cups (375 ml/12 fl oz) of vegetable stock. Reduce heat and simmer, uncovered, for 10–15 minutes, until the soup has thickened and the mushrooms are tender. Serve topped with a dollop of sour cream and some chopped parsley. Serves 4.

ABOVE: Red Pepper Soup

TOMATO SOUP WITH PASTA AND BASIL

Preparation time: 25 minutes
Total cooking time: 35 minutes
Serves 4

3 large ripe tomatoes (750 g/1 1/2 lb)
2 tablespoons olive oil
1 medium onion, finely chopped
1 clove garlic, crushed
1 small red pepper (capsicum), finely chopped
4 cups (1 litre) vegetable stock
3 tablespoons tomato paste
salt and pepper
1 teaspoon sugar
1/4 cup (7 g/1/4 oz) basil leaves, or 1 1/2 teaspoons dried basil
1 cup (155 g/5 oz) small shell pasta or macaroni
fresh basil leaves, extra

1 Cut a small cross in the top of each tomato. Place in a bowl and cover with boiling water for about 2 minutes; drain and cool. Peel skin downward from the cross and discard. Roughly chop flesh. Heat oil in a large heavy-based pan. Add onion, garlic and red pepper; cook, stirring, for 10 minutes or until all ingredients are soft. Add tomatoes and cook another 10 minutes.
2 Add the stock, tomato paste, salt, pepper and sugar. Cover and simmer for 15 minutes. Remove from the heat, add the basil. Allow to cool. Process in batches, in a food processor or blender, until smooth. Return the mixture to the pan and reheat gently.

3 Cook the pasta separately in boiling salted water until tender; drain. Add to soup and heat through. Serve sprinkled with fresh basil leaves.

COUNTRY PUMPKIN AND PASTA SOUP

Preparation time: 25 minutes
Total cooking time: 20 minutes
Serves 4-6

1 large onion
750 g (1 1/2 lb) pumpkin
2 medium potatoes
1 tablespoon olive oil
30 g (1 oz) butter
2 cloves garlic, crushed
12 cups (3 litres) vegetable stock
125 g (4 oz) miniature pasta or risoni
1 tablespoon chopped fresh parsley, for serving (optional)

1 Peel the onion and chop finely. Peel pumpkin and potatoes and chop into small cubes. Heat oil and butter in a large pan. Add onion and garlic and cook, stirring, for 5 minutes over low heat.
2 Add the pumpkin, potatoes and stock. Increase heat, cover pan and cook for 10 minutes or until vegetables are tender.
3 Add pasta and cook, stirring occasionally, for 5 minutes or until just tender. Serve immediately. Sprinkle with chopped parsley, if desired.

SOUP TOPPERS
To add a boost of flavour and interest to soups, try one of the following—a dollop of garlicky pesto marries well with a hearty, tomato-based soup, while spicy Harissa adds spark to plain old pumpkin soup. Make some crunchy croutons by brushing day-old bread with olive oil, cutting into cubes and baking in a moderate oven for 10–15 minutes, or fry bread cubes in olive oil infused with garlic to make tasty sippets.

LEFT: Tomato Soup with Pasta and Basil
ABOVE: Country Pumpkin and Pasta Soup

45

MELBA TOAST

Toast thin slices of white or brown bread (with crusts) until golden on both sides. Using a serrated knife, cut off the crusts and then carefully slice the toast in half horizontally to make 2 pieces, each one with a toasted and an untoasted side. Scrape away the soft untoasted side and place the slices, untoasted side up, on a baking tray. Bake in a slow oven until they begin to curl and turn golden. Serve Melba toast with soups, salads or, with a topping, as finger food.

ABOVE: Carrot and Orange Soup

CARROT AND ORANGE SOUP

Preparation time: 20 minutes
Total cooking time: 35 minutes
Serves 4

500 g (1 lb) carrots
30 g (1 oz) butter
1/2 cup (125 ml/4 fl oz) orange juice
4–5 cups (1–1.25 litres) vegetable stock
1 small onion, roughly chopped
3–4 teaspoons chopped fresh thyme, or
   1 teaspoon dried
salt and pepper
sour cream and nutmeg, for serving

1 Peel and slice the carrots. Place carrots and butter in a large heavy-based pan and cook over medium heat for 10 minutes, stirring occasionally.
2 Add the orange juice, stock and onion. Bring to the boil, add thyme, salt and pepper. Reduce heat; cover and cook for 20 minutes, or until the carrots are tender. Allow to cool.
3 Process the mixture in batches, in a food processor or blender, until smooth. Return mixture to the pan and reheat. Serve in individual bowls. Top each with a dollop of sour cream sprinkled with nutmeg. Garnish with a small sprig of thyme, if desired.

FRENCH ONION SOUP

Preparation time: 20 minutes
Total cooking time: 1 hour 45 minutes
Serves 4-6

6 onions (about 1 kg/2 lb)
60 g (2 oz) butter
1 teaspoon sugar
3 tablespoons plain flour
9 cups (2.25 litres) vegetable stock
salt and pepper
1 stick French bread
1/2 cup (65 g/2 1/4 oz) grated Gruyère or
   Cheddar cheese, plus extra, for serving

1 Peel the onions and slice into fine rings. Heat the butter in a large pan, add onion and cook slowly over low heat for about 20 minutes, or until very tender. Add the sugar and flour and cook, stirring, for another 1–2 minutes until mixture is just starting to turn golden.
2 Stir in stock and simmer, covered, over low heat for 1 hour. Season with salt and pepper.
3 Preheat oven to moderate 180°C (350°F/Gas 4). Cut bread stick into 1 cm (1/2 inch) slices. Bake 20 minutes, turning once, until slices are dry and golden. Top each slice with some of the grated cheese and place under hot grill until cheese has melted. Serve soup topped with toasted cheese croutons. Sprinkle with extra grated cheese.

GRILLED VEGETABLES WITH GARLIC MAYONNAISE

Preparation time: 30 minutes
Total cooking time: 15 minutes
Serves 8

2 medium eggplants (aubergines), cut into
 thin slices
salt
4 small leeks, halved lengthways
2 medium red peppers (capsicums), cut
 into eighths
4 small zucchinis (courgettes), halved
 lengthways
8 large flat mushrooms

Dressing

1 tablespoon balsamic vinegar
2 tablespoons Dijon mustard
2 teaspoons dried oregano leaves
1 cup (250 ml/8 fl oz) olive oil

Garlic Mayonnaise

2 egg yolks
1 tablespoon lemon juice
2 cloves garlic, crushed
1 cup (250 ml/8 fl oz) olive oil
1 tablespoon chopped fresh chives
1 tablespoon chopped fresh parsley
1 tablespoon water

1 Sprinkle eggplant slices with salt and allow to stand for 30 minutes. Rinse under cold water, then pat dry with paper towels.
2 Place eggplants, leeks, red peppers and zucchinis in a single layer on a flat grill tray; brush with dressing. Cook under preheated grill on high for 5 minutes, turning once; brush occasionally with dressing. Add mushrooms, cap-side up, to grill tray and brush with dressing. Continue cooking vegetables for 10 minutes or until tender, turning mushrooms once. Brush vegetables with dressing during cooking. Serve with Garlic Mayonnaise.
3 To make Dressing: Combine vinegar, mustard and oregano in bowl; gradually whisk in oil.
4 To make Garlic Mayonnaise: Place egg yolks, lemon juice and garlic in a food processor or blender, blend for 5 seconds until combined. With motor running, add oil slowly in a thin, steady stream until it is all added and mayonnaise

is thick and creamy. Add chives, parsley and water and blend for 3 seconds until combined.
NOTE: Garlic mayonnaise can be made several days ahead and refrigerated. Do not worry if the dressing separates—simply brush on as required.

FAST PASTA SOUP

STIR-FRY 2 chopped spring onions, 150 g (4¾oz) of snow peas (mange tout), cut into pieces, and 200 g (6½ oz) of sliced mushrooms in a little oil for a few minutes, until all ingredients are just tender. Add 2 crushed cloves of garlic and 1 teaspoon of grated fresh ginger and stir for another minute. Pour in 4 cups (1 litre) of vegetable stock and bring to the boil. Add 150 g (4¾ oz) of angel hair pasta and cook for 3 minutes, or until the pasta is just tender. Serve immediately. Serves 4.
Note: Angel hair pasta is long like spaghetti, but very fine. It is known as *capelli d'angelo* in Italian and is used in soups, rather than served with a sauce.

ABOVE: Grilled Vegetables with Garlic Mayonnaise

FLAVOURED BUTTERS
Softened butter can be flavoured with chopped fresh herbs, garlic, blue cheese or mustard and used to liven up steamed or baked vegetables. Put the flavoured butter on a sheet of plastic wrap, roll into a log shape, wrap up tightly and refrigerate until firm. Slice and serve on top of hot vegetables.

MUSHROOMS WITH HERB NUT BUTTER

Preparation time: 20 minutes
Total cooking time: 20 minutes
Serves 4-6

12 large mushrooms
1 tablespoon olive oil
1 small onion, finely chopped
1/4 cup (40 g/1 1/3 oz) blanched almonds
1 clove garlic, peeled and chopped
1 tablespoon lemon juice
3 tablespoons parsley sprigs
3 teaspoons chopped fresh thyme or
   1 teaspoon dried thyme
3 teaspoons chopped fresh rosemary or
   1 teaspoon dried rosemary
1 tablespoon chopped fresh chives
1/2 teaspoon salt
1/4 teaspoon black pepper
75 g (2 1/2 oz) butter, chopped

1 Preheat oven to moderate 180°C (350°F/Gas 4). Brush a shallow baking dish with oil or melted butter. Remove stalks from mushrooms, chop stalks finely. Heat oil in a small pan, add onion. Cook over medium heat 2–3 minutes or until soft and golden. Add chopped stalks. Cook 2 minutes or until softened. Remove from heat.

2 Place the almonds, garlic, lemon juice, parsley, thyme, rosemary, chives, salt, pepper and butter in a food processor. Process for 20–30 seconds or until the mixture is smooth.

3 Place the mushroom caps in the baking dish. Spoon equal amounts of the onion and mushroom mixture into each cap and smooth the surface. Top each mushroom with the almond and herb mixture. Bake 10–15 minutes, or until mushrooms are cooked through and butter has melted.

NOTE: Mushrooms are best cooked just before serving. Assemble the caps up to two hours before serving and store, covered, on a flat tray, in the refrigerator.

FAST MUSHROOM PASTRIES

CUT A SHEET of thawed frozen puff pastry into 4 squares. Brush with melted butter, sprinkle with sesame seeds and bake in a moderately hot 200°C (400°F/Gas 6) oven for 15 minutes until puffed and golden. While pastry is cooking, melt 40 g (1 1/3 oz) butter in a frying pan; add 400 g (12 2/3 oz) sliced baby mushrooms and cook for 10 minutes, until tender. Stir in 170 ml (5 1/2 fl oz) cream and season with salt and black pepper. Split pastry squares in half, spoon the mushroom mixture over bottom halves. Sprinkle with Parmesan, replace the tops and serve immediately. Serves 4.

ABOVE: Mushrooms with Herb Nut Butter

EGGPLANT AND ZUCCHINI POTS WITH PEPPER RELISH
(AUBERGINE AND COURGETTE POTS WITH CAPSICUM RELISH)

Preparation time: 30 minutes
  + 20 minutes standing
Total cooking time: 1 hour 15 minutes
Makes 6

1 large eggplant (aubergine), cut into
  1 cm (1/2 inch) cubes
1 tablespoon salt
200 g (6 1/2 oz) fresh ricotta cheese
1 1/4 cups (310 g/9 3/4 oz) sour cream
3 eggs
1 tablespoon cornflour
1 cup (135 g/4 1/2 oz) grated zucchini (courgette)
1/2 teaspoon cracked black pepper

Pepper (Capsicum) Relish

3/4 cup (185 ml/6 fl oz) brown vinegar
1/3 cup (90 g/3 oz) sugar
1 teaspoon yellow mustard seeds
1 green apple, peeled and chopped
1 pear, peeled and chopped
1 red pepper (capsicum), chopped
1 green pepper (capsicum), chopped

1 Preheat the oven to hot 210°C (415°F/ Gas 6–7). Brush six 1/2–3/4 cup capacity ramekins with oil. Place the eggplant in a colander, sprinkle with salt and set aside for 20 minutes. Rinse under cold water; drain well.
2 Using electric beaters, beat ricotta and sour cream in a small bowl until light and creamy. Add eggs and cornflour and beat until smooth. Transfer to large bowl and gently fold in the eggplant, zucchini and black pepper.
3 Spoon the mixture evenly into prepared ramekins. Arrange in a deep baking dish. Fill dish two-thirds up the side of ramekins with warm water; cover baking dish loosely with foil. Bake for 40 minutes or until a skewer comes out clean when inserted into the centre of ramekins. When ready to serve, top or accompany with Pepper Relish.
4 **To make Pepper Relish:** Heat vinegar, sugar and mustard seeds in a pan for 5 minutes or until sugar dissolves and mixture boils. Add remaining ingredients. Bring to boil, reduce heat and simmer, uncovered, for 30 minutes.

POTATO PANCAKES

Preparation time: 20 minutes
Total cooking time: 15 minutes
Serves 4-6

4 large potatoes, peeled and dried
3 eggs, lightly beaten
4 spring onions, finely sliced
3 tablespoons cornflour
2 tablespoons oat bran
oil, for frying
1/2 cup (60 g/2 oz) shredded spring onion,
  grated fresh beetroot and sour cream,
  for serving (optional)

1 Coarsely grate potatoes. Squeeze out excess moisture from potatoes with your hands and dry well in tea towels. Place potatoes in a large bowl. Add the eggs, spring onions, cornflour and oat bran. Mix well to combine.
2 Drop heaped tablespoons of the mixture into a well-oiled pan, flatten slightly. Cook over medium heat until cooked through and golden brown on both sides. Drain on paper towels.
3 Serve hot, garnished with spring onion, or fresh beetroot shreds and a dollop of sour cream.

GRATING POTATOES
Grated potatoes can be made into pancakes (see recipe, left), or used for Swiss Potato Rösti. Put the grated potatoes into a pan of hot butter and oil, pressing down well to make a flat cake. Brown on one side, flip and brown the other side. It is essential that the potatoes are dry so that they fry rather than stew in the moisture. First, dry the whole peeled potato, then grate it, put it in a colander and squeeze several times until you've squeezed out all the moisture. Dry grated potatoes in a tea towel or on paper towels. This will take many sheets of paper towels or several tea towels but it is essential for a crisp finish.

ABOVE: Eggplant and Zucchini Pots with Pepper Relish

49

PEELING ASPARAGUS

Not all asparagus needs to be peeled—thin asparagus hardly ever does and there would not be much left to eat if you did. Thick asparagus is fine unpeeled if it's really fresh, but if you have any doubts, peel the stalks. Do this with a vegetable peeler, working from just under the tip towards the base. Laying the asparagus on a board will make it easier. Cut or snap off the base of the stalk as well, as the end tends to be woody.

ABOVE: Asparagus with Citrus Hollandaise

ASPARAGUS WITH CITRUS HOLLANDAISE

Preparation time: 15 minutes
Total cooking time: 8 minutes
Makes 6

 ☆

315–440 g (10–14 oz) asparagus spears
180 g (5³⁄₄ oz) butter
2 tablespoons water
4 egg yolks
1–2 tablespoons lemon, lime or orange juice
salt and white pepper
shavings of Parmesan or pecorino
    cheese (optional)

1 Trim any woody ends from asparagus. Place in a pan of boiling water; simmer 1–2 minutes until just tender; drain.
2 Melt the butter in a small pan. Skim any froth from the top and discard. Allow the butter to cool. Combine the water and egg yolks in a small pan and whisk for 30 seconds or until pale and creamy. Place the pan over very low heat and continue whisking for 3 minutes or until mixture thickens.
3 Remove from heat; add the cooled butter gradually, whisking constantly (leave whey in the bottom of the pan). Stir in the juice; season to taste. Drizzle sauce over the asparagus. Garnish with cheese shavings, if desired.

CHILLI PUFFS WITH CURRIED VEGETABLES

Preparation time: 35 minutes
Total cooking time: 1 hour 5 minutes
Makes 12

☆☆

Choux Pastry

90 g (3 oz) butter
1¼ cups (315 ml/10 fl oz) water
1¼ cups (155 g/5 oz) plain flour, sifted
¼ teaspoon chilli powder
4 eggs, lightly beaten

Curried Vegetables

4 yellow squash
100 g (3¹⁄₃ oz) snow peas (mange tout)
1 carrot
50 g (1²⁄₃ oz) butter, extra
2 medium onions, sliced
2 tablespoons mild curry paste
300 g (9²⁄₃ oz) small oyster mushrooms
1 tablespoon lemon juice

1 Preheat the oven to very hot 240°C (475°F/ Gas 9). Sprinkle two 32 x 28 cm (13 x 11 inch) oven trays with water.
2 To make Choux Pastry: Combine the butter and water in a medium pan. Stir over low heat for 5 minutes, or until the butter melts and the

mixture comes to the boil. Remove from heat; add the flour and chilli powder all at once and stir with a wooden spoon until just combined.

3 Return pan to heat and beat constantly over low heat for 3 minutes or until the mixture thickens and comes away from the sides and base of pan. Transfer mixture to large bowl. Using electric beaters, beat the mixture on high speed for 1 minute. Add eggs gradually, beating until mixture is stiff and glossy. (This stage could take up to 5 minutes.)

4 Place Choux Pastry mixture, in mounds measuring about 2 tablespoons each, onto the prepared trays, spacing them about 10 cm (4 inches) apart. Sprinkle with a little water. Bake for 20 minutes. Reduce the heat to hot 210°C (415°/Gas 6–7) and bake for 30 minutes more, or until the puffs are crisp and well browned. (Cut a small slit into each puff halfway through cooking to allow excess steam to escape and puff to dry out.) Transfer the puffs to a wire rack to cool.

5 To make Curried Vegetables: Slice the squash thinly. Cut the snow peas in half diagonally. Cut the carrot into thin strips. Heat the extra butter in a medium pan and add onions. Cook over low heat for 5 minutes or until golden; stir in curry paste. Add the mushrooms and prepared vegetables and stir over high heat for 1 minute. Add the lemon juice, remove from heat and stir. Cut the puffs in half, remove any uncooked mixture from the centre with a spoon. Fill with vegetables. Serve immediately.

GRILLED TOMATOES WITH BRUSCHETTA

Preparation time: 15 minutes
Total cooking time: 35 minutes
Serves 4

1 loaf Italian bread
4 large ripe tomatoes
1/2 teaspoon dried marjoram leaves
salt and freshly ground black pepper
1/3 cup (80 ml/2³/4 fl oz) olive oil
2 tablespoons red wine vinegar
1 teaspoon soft brown sugar
1 clove garlic, cut in half
1/2 cup (110 g/3²/3 oz) chopped, marinated artichokes
1 tablespoon finely chopped flat-leaf parsley

1 Cut bread into thick slices. Preheat grill. Cut the tomatoes in half; gently squeeze out seeds. Place tomatoes, cut side down, in a shallow, ovenproof dish. Place marjoram, salt and pepper, oil, vinegar and sugar in a small screw-top jar; shake well. Pour half over the tomatoes.

2 Cook the tomatoes under a hot grill for 30 minutes; turn halfway during cooking. Pour remaining oil mixture over the tomatoes. Remove from heat and keep warm.

3 Brush the bread slices liberally with some oil, on both sides, and toast until golden. Rub cut surface of garlic over bread. Place cooked tomatoes onto bread, top with artichokes and sprinkle with parsley.

QUICK AND EASY STARTERS
Baby leeks cooked in butter and then baked in a filo casing; steamed snow peas (mange tout) tossed in herb-flavoured cream; asparagus with melted butter and Parmesan; steamed beans tossed in garlic butter; roasted garlic cloves slipped out of their skins and spread on bread; rocket salad with shavings of Parmesan and a lemony vinaigrette; cooked shell pasta combined with peas and garlic-flavoured cream.

LEFT: Chilli Puffs with Curried Vegetables
ABOVE: Grilled Tomatoes with Bruschetta

GOATS CHEESE SALAD

Preparation time: 20 minutes
Total cooking time: 15 minutes
Serves 4

★

12 slices white bread
4 x 100 g (3¹/₃ oz) rounds goats cheese
60 g (2oz) mixed salad leaves (mesclun)
60 g (2oz) rocket
250 g (8 oz) cherry tomatoes, halved
1 tablespoon white wine vinegar
¼ cup (60 ml/2 fl oz) olive oil
½ teaspoon wholegrain mustard

1 Preheat the oven to moderate 180°C (350°F/Gas 4). Using a biscuit cutter, cut a round out of each slice of bread. (The bread must not be larger than the cheese or the edges will burn under the grill.) Place the bread on a baking tray and bake for 10 minutes. Slice each cheese into three.
2 Place a slice of cheese on each piece of bread. Arrange a bed of salad leaves and rocket on small individual serving plates; top with several tomato halves. Cook cheese and bread rounds under a preheated hot grill for 5 minutes or until the cheese turns golden and bubbles. Drizzle salad leaves with dressing and place 3 cheese rounds on top of each salad. Sprinkle with chopped chives to serve, if desired.
3 To make Dressing: Combine vinegar, oil and mustard in a small screw-top jar; shake vigorously for a minute or so until well combined.

AVOCADO WITH LIME AND CHILLIES

Preparation time: 20 minutes
Total cooking time: Nil
Serves 6

★

1 teaspoon finely grated lime rind
2 tablespoons lime juice
1 teaspoon soft brown sugar
1 tablespoon olive oil
1 tablespoon chopped fresh parsley
2–3 jalapeño chillies, seeded and diced
2 ripe avocados, peeled and sliced

1 Thoroughly combine lime rind and juice, sugar, oil, parsley and chillies in a small bowl. Pour over sliced avocado and serve.
NOTE: The lime juice prevents the avocados browning. Lemon juice may be substituted.

GOATS CHEESE
Although most cheeses are made from cows milk, other animal milks are used to make some famous cheeses. Goats cheese or *chèvre* has a very distinctive, tart flavour that may take some getting used to. Depending on its age, it ranges from fresh and soft to crumbly and dry. When very young, it is soft enough to spread and it matures to a chalky consistency.

RIGHT: Goats Cheese Salad

EGGPLANT (AUBERGINE) FRITTERS

Preparation time: 40 minutes + 20 minutes
    standing
Total cooking time: 15–20 minutes
Serves 4-6

Yoghurt Dip

200 g (6¹/2 oz) natural yoghurt
2 tablespoons finely grated onion
¹/2 teaspoon dried mint leaves
¹/2 teaspoon salt
¹/4 teaspoon ground coriander
pinch ground cumin

1 large, long eggplant (aubergine)
1 tablespoon salt
2 tablespoons besan flour (chickpea flour)
¹/4 teaspoon black pepper
¹/4 cup (30 g/1 oz) self-raising flour
¹/2 cup (55 g/1³/4 oz) besan flour, extra
2 eggs, lightly beaten
¹/2 cup (60 ml/4 fl oz) cold beer
2 teaspoons lemon juice
²/3 cup (170 ml/5¹/2 fl oz) olive oil, for
    shallow-frying

1 To make Yoghurt Dip: Beat all ingredients in
a small bowl until well combined. Cover bowl
with plastic wrap and refrigerate.
2 Cut eggplant into 20 slices, each about 5 mm
(¹/4 inch) thick. Sprinkle both sides of each slice
with salt. Leave in a colander for about
20 minutes. Rinse the eggplant, drain well and
pat dry with paper towels.
3 Combine the 2 tablespoons besan flour and
pepper on a sheet of greaseproof paper. Dust the
eggplant slices lightly in seasoned flour and shake
off excess.
4 Sift remaining flours into a medium bowl;
make a well in the centre. Add eggs, beer and
lemon juice all at once. Beat until all liquid is
incorporated and batter is free of lumps.
5 Heat oil in a large heavy-based frying pan.
Using two forks, dip floured eggplant into batter
a few pieces at a time; drain off excess. Cook in
oil over medium–high heat for 2 minutes or
until underside is golden and crisp. Turn fritter
over, cook other side. Transfer to a large plate;
keep warm. Repeat with remaining batter and
eggplant. Serve with chilled Yoghurt Dip.

EGGPLANT (AUBERGINE) MARINATED IN CHERMOULA

Preparation time: 40 minutes
    + 1 hour refrigeration
Total cooking time: 10 minutes
Serves 4

2 medium eggplants (aubergines)
salt
olive oil

Chermoula

2 cloves garlic, crushed
1 tablespoon ground cumin
1 teaspoon ground cinnamon
¹/4 teaspoon cayenne pepper
1 teaspoon allspice
¹/4 cup (60 ml/2 fl oz) lemon juice
3 tablespoons chopped fresh coriander
2 tablespoons chopped fresh mint
¹/2 cup (125 ml/4 fl oz) olive oil

1 Cut eggplants into 1 cm (¹/2 inch) thick slices
and sprinkle with salt. Set aside for 30 minutes,
then rinse and pat dry.
2 Brush the eggplant slices liberally with olive
oil and cook under a preheated grill until golden
brown on both sides. Drain on paper towels.
3 To make Chermoula: Combine all ingredients.
Add eggplant and toss. Cover and refrigerate for
1 hour. Serve at room temperature.

CHERMOULA
Chermoula is a pungent
Moroccan condiment used
to flavour vegetable dishes.
It can be used as a
marinade—either before or
after the vegetables are
cooked—or as a sauce to
serve with the vegetables.

*ABOVE: Eggplant
Fritters*

EATING ARTICHOKES
Whole fresh artichokes are always eaten with the fingers, so be sure to provide finger bowls for guests. To eat artichokes, take off a leaf at a time, dip the bottom of the leaf in mayonnaise and scrape off the fleshy base with your teeth. Towards the centre of the artichoke, the leaves are more tender and more of the leaf is edible. Provide a bowl for the discarded leaves.

ABOVE: Marinated Baby Mushrooms

MARINATED BABY MUSHROOMS

Preparation time: 30 minutes
Total cooking time: Nil
Serves 6–8

500 g (1 lb) button mushrooms, halved
1/2 cup (125 ml/4 fl oz) olive oil
1/2 cup (125 ml/4 fl oz) white wine vinegar
3 cloves garlic, chopped
2 tablespoons chopped fresh parsley
2 teaspoons chopped chilli
1 teaspoon caster sugar
salt and pepper

1 Wipe the mushrooms with a damp cloth and trim the stalks to the level of the cap. Place the mushroom caps in a large bowl. Combine the olive oil, vinegar, garlic, parsley, chilli, sugar, salt and pepper in a screw-top jar; shake well.
2 Pour the marinade over the mushrooms and toss to combine. Cover with plastic wrap and refrigerate for at least 1 hour. Mushrooms can be marinated for up to 2 days, depending on how intense you want the flavour. Turn mushrooms occasionally as they marinate.
3 Serve mushrooms at room temperature with other marinated vegetables as part of an antipasto platter, if desired.

ARTICHOKES WITH TARRAGON MAYONNAISE

Preparation time: 30 minutes
Total cooking time: 30 minutes
Serves 4

4 medium globe artichokes
1/4 cup (60 ml/2 fl oz) lemon juice

Tarragon Mayonnaise

1 egg yolk
1 tablespoon tarragon vinegar
1/2 teaspoon French mustard
2/3 cup (170 ml/5 1/2 fl oz) olive oil
salt and white pepper

1 Trim stalks from base of artichokes. Using scissors, trim points from outer leaves. Using a sharp knife, cut tops from artichokes. Brush all cut areas of artichokes with lemon juice to prevent discolouration.
2 Steam artichokes for 30 minutes, until tender; top up pan with boiling water if necessary. Remove from heat and set aside to cool.
3 To make Tarragon Mayonnaise: Place the egg yolk, vinegar and mustard in a medium mixing bowl. Using a wire whisk, beat for 1 minute. At first, add the oil a teaspoon at a time, whisking constantly until the mixture is thick and creamy. As the mayonnaise thickens, pour oil in a thin, steady stream. Continue whisking until all the

oil is added. Season to taste. To serve, place a cooled artichoke on each plate with a little Tarragon Mayonnaise.

NOTE: Artichokes may be cooked up to 4 hours in advance. Mayonnaise may be made up to 2 hours in advance; cover and refrigerate.

CRUDITES WITH GARLIC SAUCE

Preparation time: 30 minutes
Total cooking time: 20 minutes
Serves 4–6

a selection of fresh vegetable sticks, for serving

Garlic Sauce

2 large old potatoes, peeled and cubed
4–5 cloves garlic, crushed
1 tablespoon white wine vinegar
freshly ground white pepper
lemon juice
salt
1/3 cup (80 ml/2 3/4 fl oz) olive oil

1 Cover and refrigerate the prepared vegetables.
2 **To make Garlic Sauce:** Cook the potatoes in a pan of boiling water until tender. Test with a sharp knife or a fork. If the knife comes away easily, the potato should be ready to mash; alternatively, try to mash a cube with the fork.

Drain the potatoes well and place in a bowl. Mash the potato until smooth. Add the crushed garlic and vinegar and mix well. Season with pepper, a little lemon juice, and salt, to taste.
3 Add olive oil a few drops at a time, beating well after each addition. Continue adding the oil and beating until the mixture is quite smooth and thick—this process may take up to 5 minutes. Serve the sauce warm with vegetable sticks and crusty bread or toasted flatbread.

NOTE: This garlic sauce is often made using almonds and soaked white bread instead of potato. Substitute 4 tablespoons of ground almonds and 90 g (3 oz) of stale white bread that has been soaked in water and squeezed dry. Blend in a food processor, adding the oil in drops through the feed tube while the motor is running. The consistency should be that of a thick mayonnaise. If mixture is too thick, add a little more oil or lemon juice.

FAST SALSA TOASTS

CUT A SHORT bread stick into diagonal slices about 4 cm (1½ inches) thick—you should get about 6 slices. Toast one side under a preheated grill until golden. Scrape some of the bread out from the untoasted side. Finely chop 2 small, ripe tomatoes, half a small red (Spanish) onion and a few pitted black olives. Combine, spoon tomato mixture into the bread cavities, then top with 125 g (4 oz) crumbled feta cheese and some fresh thyme leaves. Drizzle lightly with olive oil, grill until golden on top.

ABOVE: Crudités with Garlic Sauce

1 Preheat oven to hot 210°C (415°F/Gas 6–7). Brush an oven tray with melted butter or oil. Wash the spinach leaves thoroughly and steam or microwave them until they are just softened. Squeeze out excess moisture and spread the leaves out to dry.

2 Heat the oil in a frying pan, add the onion and cook over medium heat for 3 minutes. Add the peppers, zucchinis and eggplants; cook, stirring, for another 5 minutes or until vegetables have softened. Season and then set aside to cool.

3 Brush 1 sheet of filo pastry with melted butter, top with a second sheet. Repeat with remaining pastry, brushing with butter between each layer. Place the spinach, cooled vegetable mixture, basil and cheese along one long side of pastry, about 5 cm (2 inches) in from the edge. Fold the sides over the filling, fold short end over and roll up tightly.

4 Place the strudel, seam-side down, on prepared tray. Brush with remaining melted butter and sprinkle with sesame seeds. Bake for 25 minutes, or until golden brown and crisp. NOTE: This dish is best made just before serving. Serve sliced as a first course, or with a green salad as a main meal.

SAMOSAS

Preparation time: 30 minutes
Total cooking time: 10 minutes
Makes about 24

⭐

2 potatoes, peeled
1/2 cup (80 g/2 2/3 oz) frozen peas
3 tablespoons currants
2 tablespoons chopped fresh coriander
2 tablespoons lemon juice
1 tablespoon soy sauce
1 teaspoon ground cumin
1 teaspoon ground chilli powder
1/2 teaspoon chopped fresh chilli
1/4 teaspoon ground cinnamon
4 sheets ready-rolled frozen puff pastry, thawed
oil, for shallow-frying

Mint Sauce
1/2 cup (125 g/4 oz) plain yoghurt
1/2 cup (125 ml/4 fl oz) buttermilk
3 tablespoons chopped fresh mint
1/2 teaspoon ground cumin

VEGETABLE STRUDEL

Preparation time: 30 minutes
Total cooking time: 35 minutes
Serves 4-6

⭐⭐

12 English spinach leaves
2 tablespoons olive oil
1 medium onion, finely sliced
1 medium red pepper (capsicum),
   cut into strips
1 medium green pepper (capsicum),
   cut into strips
2 medium zucchinis (courgettes), sliced
2 slender eggplants (aubergines), sliced
salt and pepper
6 sheets filo pastry
40 g (1 1/3 oz) butter, melted
1/3 cup (20 g/2/3 oz) finely sliced fresh basil leaves
1/2 cup (60 g/2 oz) grated Cheddar cheese
2 tablespoons sesame seeds

ABOVE: Vegetable Strudel

1 Cook potatoes until tender, then chop finely. Combine the potatoes, peas, currants, coriander, lemon juice, soy sauce, cumin, chilli powder, chilli and cinnamon in a bowl.

2 Cut pastry into rounds using a 10 cm (4 inch) cutter. Place heaped teaspoonsful of the mixture on one side of each round. Fold the pastry over the filling to make a semi-circle. Press the edges together firmly with a fork.

3 Heat 2 cm (³/₄ inch) oil in pan; add pastries and cook for 2–3 minutes on each side or until golden brown and puffed. Drain on paper towels. Serve with Mint Sauce or Peach Relish.

4 To make Mint Sauce: Combine the yoghurt, buttermilk, mint and cumin in a small bowl and stir until smooth.

FAST PEACH RELISH

PLACE 6 large peeled and roughly chopped fresh peaches in a large heavy-based pan. Add 1 tablespoon finely chopped preserved ginger, 2 tablespoons soft brown sugar, 2 finely chopped spring onions, ¼ teaspoon mixed spice, 2 whole cloves, 4 whole black peppercorns, 2 tablespoons brown vinegar and 2 teaspoons soy sauce. Stir over medium heat until sugar dissolves. Cover, simmer mixture gently for about 15 minutes or until it becomes soft and pulpy. Remove from heat, discard the cloves and peppercorns. Allow to cool, then serve with Pakoras or Samosas. Refrigerate any remaining relish in an airtight container. Makes about 3 cups.

VEGETABLE PAKORAS

Preparation time: 15 minutes
Total cooking time: 10 minutes
Serves 4

1 cup (110 g/3²/₃ oz) besan flour (chickpea flour)
½ teaspoon ground coriander
1 teaspoon salt
½ teaspoon ground turmeric
½ teaspoon chilli powder
½ teaspoon garam masala
1–2 cloves garlic, crushed
³/₄ cup (185 ml/6 fl oz) water
½ cauliflower, cut into florets
2 onions, sliced into rings (see note)
oil, for deep-frying

1 Sift flour into a bowl; add coriander, salt, turmeric, chilli powder, garam masala and garlic.

2 Make a well in the centre of the flour. Gradually add the water and mix to form a thick, smooth batter.

3 Coat cauliflower and onions in batter. Heat 4 cm (1½ inches) oil in a deep pan and add cauliflower and onions in batches. Cook for 4–5 minutes or until golden. Drain on paper towels, serve with Mint Sauce (see Samosas recipe), Chilli Sauce or Peach Relish (below).

NOTE: Small pickling onions are best for Pakoras. You can also use thick slices of eggplant or potato.

BESAN FLOUR
Besan flour is a heavy-textured flour which is made from dried chick-peas. It has a strong flavour and is used in Indian cooking, most famously to make pakoras.

ABOVE: Samosas
BELOW: Vegetable Pakoras

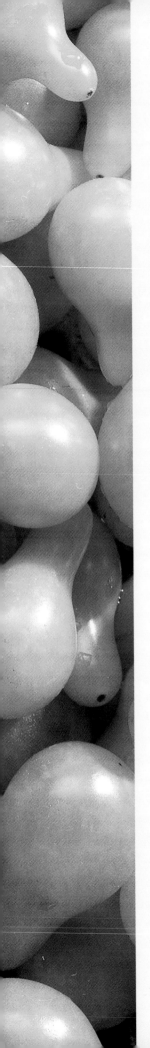

SNACKS AND PARTY FOOD

Beautifully presented party food always looks truly spectacular and the vegetarian variety is no exception to the rule. Leave the tired party pies and ribbon sandwiches on the shelf and impress your guests with this tempting array of inspired suggestions. Next day, when the party's over, sit down with the family and relive the event over a sensational snack.

VEGETABLE OMELETTE WITH PITTA BREAD

Preparation time: 50 minutes
Total cooking time: 20 minutes
Serves 4

✸

4 baby beetroot, peeled and grated

2¹/₂ teaspoons grated fresh ginger

2 cloves garlic, crushed

1 teaspoon rice vinegar

1 teaspoon sesame oil

4–5 teaspoons soy sauce

2 spring onions, finely chopped

few drops Tabasco sauce

3 tablespoons peanut oil

1 onion, thinly sliced

1 red pepper (capsicum), cut in thin strips

1 medium carrot, peeled and grated

4 baby bok choy leaves, shredded

1 tablespoon sweet chilli sauce

3 eggs, lightly beaten

1 tablespoon cornflour

8 round pitta breads

*ABOVE: Vegetable
Omelette with Pitta Bread*

1 Place the beetroot, ¹/₂ teaspoon of ginger, half the garlic, rice vinegar, sesame oil, 1 teaspoon of soy sauce, spring onions and Tabasco sauce in a medium bowl. Mix until well combined, then set aside.

2 Heat half the peanut oil in a wok or frying pan. Add the onion and remaining garlic and cook over medium heat for 1 minute. Stir in the red pepper, carrot, bok choy, remaining ginger and chilli sauce. Cook for another 1–2 minutes, or until just tender. Remove from the heat and transfer the mixture to a large bowl; allow to cool slightly. Combine the eggs, cornflour and remaining soy sauce in a bowl. Add to cooled vegetable mixture and stir well to combine.

3 Heat remaining oil in a frying pan. Spoon a quarter of the egg and vegetable mixture into pan to make a thick circle. Cook for 1–2 minutes each side. Repeat with remaining mixture.

4 Lightly toast the pitta breads on both sides. Drain the excess liquid from the beetroot mixture. Place four pitta breads on individual serving plates. On each pitta bread, place a vegetable omelette and some of the beetroot mixture. Garnish with yellow pepper, if desired, and serve with the remaining pitta bread.

SPINACH CROQUETTES WITH MINTED YOGHURT SAUCE

Preparation time: 50 minutes +
  1 hour refrigeration
Total cooking time: 25 minutes
Makes 18

1 1/2 cups (285 g/9 1/4 oz) short-grain rice
250 g (8 oz) feta cheese, crumbled
1/4 cup (25 g/3/4 oz) grated Parmesan cheese
2 eggs, lightly beaten
1 clove garlic, crushed
2 teaspoons grated lemon rind
1/3 cup (40 g/1 1/3 oz) chopped spring onions
250 g (8 oz) packet frozen spinach, thawed,
  squeezed of excess moisture
1 tablespoon chopped fresh dill
2 cups (200 g/6 1/2 oz) dry breadcrumbs
2 eggs, lightly beaten, extra
oil, for deep-frying

Minted Yoghurt Sauce

200 g (6 1/2 oz) plain yoghurt
2 tablespoons chopped fresh mint
2 tablespoons lemon juice
salt and freshly ground black pepper

1 Cook the rice in a large pan of boiling water until just tender; drain; rinse under cold water, then drain again. Combine the rice, cheeses, eggs, garlic, lemon rind, spring onions, spinach and dill in a large bowl. Using wet hands, divide the mixture into 18 portions. Roll each portion into even-sized sausage shapes. Place on a tray and refrigerate for 30 minutes.
2 Spread breadcrumbs on a sheet of greaseproof paper. Dip the croquettes into the extra beaten egg. Coat with the breadcrumbs; shake off excess. Refrigerate for another 30 minutes.
3 **To make Minted Yoghurt Sauce:** Combine the yoghurt, fresh mint, lemon juice, salt and pepper in a bowl. Mix well. Cover and refrigerate until needed.
4 Heat oil in a deep heavy-based pan. Gently lower batches of croquettes into moderately hot oil with tongs or a slotted spoon. Cook for 2–3 minutes or until golden and crisp and cooked through. Drain on paper towels. Repeat with the remaining croquettes. Serve the croquettes hot or cold with Minted Yoghurt Sauce.

CAJUN POTATO WEDGES

Preparation time: 10 minutes
Total cooking time: 25–30 minutes
Serves 4

vegetable oil
4 medium potatoes
1–2 tablespoons Cajun spice mix

1 Preheat the oven to moderately hot 190°C (375°F/Gas 5). Pour 1 cm (1/2 inch) of oil into a baking dish and place in the oven until hot (about 5 minutes).
2 Cut the potatoes into wedge shapes or chunks. Roll the wedges in the Cajun spice mix until well coated.
3 Add the potatoes to the hot oil and toss to coat. Bake for 20–25 minutes or until golden brown, turning occasionally. Drain on paper towels. Serve immediately with ready-made tomato salsa and sour cream, if desired.
NOTE: Cajun spice mix is available from supermarkets, or you can make up your own.

CAJUN SPICES
Cajun spice mix gives Cajun dishes their tasty distinctive flavour. You can make your own by mixing 1 tablespoon of garlic powder with 1 tablespoon onion powder, 2 teaspoons each of white and cracked black pepper, 2 teaspoons dried thyme, 1/2 teaspoon dried oregano and 1 1/2 teaspoons cayenne pepper.

ABOVE: Cajun Potato Wedges

CHEESE AND MUSHROOM PIES

Preparation time: 40 minutes
Total cooking time: 30 minutes
Makes 6

✷ ✷

40 g (1 1/3 oz) butter

2 cloves garlic, crushed

500 g (1 lb) button mushrooms, sliced

1 small red pepper (capsicum), finely chopped

2/3 cup (160 g/5 1/4 oz) sour cream

3 teaspoons seeded mustard

1/2 cup (65 g/2 1/4 oz) finely grated Gruyère or
     Cheddar cheese

6 sheets ready-rolled puff pastry

1/2 cup (65 g/2 1/4 oz) finely grated Gruyère or
     Cheddar cheese, extra

1 egg, lightly beaten

1 Preheat the oven to moderately hot 190°C (375°F/Gas 5). Lightly grease two oven trays with melted butter or oil. Heat the butter in a large pan. Add the garlic and mushrooms, cook over medium heat, stirring occasionally, until mushrooms are tender and liquid has evaporated. Remove from heat and cool. Stir in red pepper.
2 Combine the sour cream, mustard and cheese in a small bowl and mix well. Cut twelve circles with a 14 cm (5 1/2 inch) diameter from pastry.

Spread cream mixture over six of the circles, leaving a 1 cm (1/2 inch) border. Top each with mushroom mixture.
3 Sprinkle each with two teaspoons of extra grated cheese. Brush around the outer edges with beaten egg; place reserved pastry rounds on top of the filling, sealing the edges with a fork. Brush the tops of the pastry with egg. Sprinkle the remaining cheese over the pastry. Place the pies on oven trays and bake for 20 minutes or until lightly browned and puffed.

POLENTA (CORNMEAL) CHILLIES

Preparation time: 30 minutes
    + 2 hours refrigeration
Total cooking time: 2–3 minutes each batch
Serves 6

✷ ✷

330 g (10 1/2 oz) jar mild, whole chillies

1/2 cup (60 g/2 oz) grated Cheddar cheese

100 g (3 1/3 oz) soft cream cheese

1/3 cup (40 g/1 1/3 oz) plain flour

2 eggs, lightly beaten

3/4 cup (110 g/3 2/3 oz) polenta (cornmeal)

3/4 cup (75 g/2 1/2 oz) dry breadcrumbs

oil, for deep-frying

sour cream, for serving (optional)

SWISS CHEESE
Both Gruyère and Emmenthal cheeses are often called 'Swiss cheese'. They are, however, quite different. Gruyère has only a few holes the size of peas, while Emmenthal has eyes the size of cherries. From the chef's point of view, the important difference is in the texture of the cheeses when cooked: Gruyère is often preferred as Emmenthal becomes stringy when melted.

RIGHT: Cheese and Mushroom Pies

FRESH VEGETABLE SPRING ROLLS

Preparation time: 40 minutes
Total cooking time: Nil
Makes 12

✷ ✷

1 cup (155 g/5 oz) grated carrot

100 g (3 1/3 oz) snow peas (mange tout), sliced

1 cup (90 g/3 oz) bean sprouts, trimmed

30 g (1 oz) rice vermicelli, soaked, drained and cooled

2 tablespoons chopped fresh coriander

2 tablespoons chopped fresh mint

1/4 cup (40 g/1 1/3 oz) chopped, dry-roasted peanuts

12 rice paper rounds

Dipping Sauce

1 tablespoon caster sugar

1/4 cup (60 ml/2 fl oz) warm water

2 tablespoons fish sauce (optional)

1 clove garlic, crushed

1/4 cup (60 ml/2 fl oz) lime juice

1 small fresh chilli, finely sliced

1 tablespoon chopped fresh coriander

1 Combine the carrot, snow peas and bean sprouts in a large bowl. Chop the cooked vermicelli roughly and add to the vegetables with the coriander, mint and peanuts.
2 Dip each rice paper round into a bowl of warm water for about 1 minute, until softened. Carefully remove from the water and lay on a clean, flat surface. Place about 2 level tablespoons of vegetable mixture on the lower half of the rice paper; roll up gently but firmly into a spring roll shape. (The moist rice paper will adhere to itself on rolling.) Serve with Dipping Sauce.
3 To make Dipping Sauce: Place the sugar in a bowl; add water and stir until dissolved. Add the remaining ingredients and stir.
NOTE: Rice vermicelli should be soaked in boiling water for about 30 seconds for this recipe. Rice paper rounds are about 23 cm (9 inches) in diameter and can be purchased in packets in Asian food stores.

1 Select twelve large, similar-sized chillies from the jar. Drain well and dry with paper towels. With a sharp knife, cut a slit down the length of one side of each chilli. Remove all the seeds and membrane. Combine the grated Cheddar and cream cheeses; fill each chilli with the cheese mixture.
2 Place the flour onto a large plate and beaten eggs in a small bowl. Combine the polenta and breadcrumbs in a small plastic bag; transfer to a large plate. Roll each chilli in flour; shake off excess; dip in egg and roll in crumb mixture to coat chillies thoroughly. Refrigerate for 1 hour. Re-dip in egg and re-roll in the breadcrumbs. Return to the refrigerator for 1 hour.
3 Heat the oil in a medium pan. Test the oil by frying a small cube of bread; if it browns in 30 seconds, the oil is ready. Deep-fry the prepared chillies in small batches until golden; drain on paper towels.
NOTE: Delicious served with sour cream and your favourite salsa.

FAST FRENCH SANDWICH

CUT TWO diagonal slices of crusty French bread; spread each with butter. Top one slice with Swiss cheese and a little seeded mustard. Place the other slice on top; press firmly. Beat together an egg and a dash of milk; season with salt and pepper. Add some finely chopped fresh herbs. Dip sandwich in egg mixture, turning to soak both sides. Heat a little butter in a frying pan and when sizzling cook sandwich for 2–3 minutes each side or until golden. Serve at once, plain or with a salad. Serves 1.

RICE VERMICELLI
Rice vermicelli are white and folded into a block. Thickness and widths vary. They are commonly used in stir-fries and soups, and need to be soaked briefly in hot water or boiled, until soft, and drained before use. (Follow the instructions on the packet.) Some recipes require fried rice vermicelli—it separates and puffs up when deep-fried and a little goes a long way so always deep-fry in small quantities.

ABOVE: Polenta Chillies

ABOVE: Spinach and Olive Turnovers

PINE NUTS
These are the most protein-rich of the nut family and are obtained from the cones of certain pine trees—most commonly the European Stone and Pinon pines. The Stone pine is the romantic, umbrella-shaped tree often seen in Italian landscape paintings. Pine nuts are usually sold blanched but frying or roasting in a moderate oven improves their flavour. Take care though—they burn easily.

SPINACH AND OLIVE TURNOVERS

Preparation time: 1 hour 20 minutes
  + 1 hour refrigeration
Total cooking time: 15 minutes
Makes 30

★★★

2 cups (250 g/8 oz) plain flour
200 g (6¹/₂ oz) butter, cut into
  small cubes
³/₄ cup (185 ml/6 fl oz) water
1 egg, lightly beaten, for glazing

Filling

60 g (2 oz) English spinach leaves
100 g (3¹/₃ oz) feta cheese
2 tablespoons chopped pitted black olives
2 teaspoons chopped fresh rosemary
1 clove garlic, crushed
2 tablespoons pistachio nuts, shelled
1 egg, lightly beaten

1 Sift the flour into a large bowl and stir in the cubed butter until just combined. Make a well in the centre of the flour, add almost all the water and mix to a slightly sticky dough with a knife, adding more water if necessary. Gather the dough together.

2 Turn the dough onto a well-floured surface, and lightly press together until almost smooth, taking care not to overwork the dough. Roll out to a neat 20 x 40 cm (8 x 16 inch) rectangle, trying to keep the corners fairly square. Fold the top third of the pastry down and fold the bottom third of the pastry up over it. Make a quarter turn to the right so that the edge of the top fold is on the right. Re-roll the pastry to a rectangle 20 x 40 cm (8 x 16 inches), and repeat the folding step. Wrap in plastic wrap and refrigerate for 30 minutes.

3 Repeat the previous step, giving a roll, fold and turn twice more. Refrigerate for another 30 minutes. The folding and rolling give the pastry its flaky characteristics. Roll out the pastry on a well-floured surface to a 3 mm (¹/₈ inch) thickness, and then cut out thirty 8 cm (3 inch) rounds.

4 Preheat the oven to moderate 180°C (350°F/Gas 4). Brush a large baking tray with melted butter or oil.

5 To make Filling: Wash and dry the spinach leaves thoroughly. Shred the spinach finely and place in a medium bowl. Crumble the feta cheese over the spinach; add the olives, rosemary and garlic. Spread the pistachio nuts on a baking tray and toast under a moderately hot grill for 1–2 minutes. Cool and chop finely. Add to spinach mixture with beaten egg and stir until well combined.

6 Place two teaspoonsful of mixture in the centre of each pastry round; fold in half and pinch edges to seal. Place on the prepared tray; brush lightly with beaten egg and bake for 15 minutes or until golden and crisp. Serve hot.

FAST BRUSCHETTA WITH HERBS AND CAPERS

TOAST ONE or two slices of thick crusty Italian bread or a mini pizza base until lightly golden on both sides. Rub each slice or base with a little crushed garlic. Top with chunks of vine-ripened or egg (Roma) tomato and sprinkle with salt and freshly cracked black pepper. Sprinkle with some fresh herbs such as basil or lemon thyme. Quickly deep-fry some capers until they are crisp and opened up like flowers. Drain the capers and sprinkle on top of the tomato. Serve immediately with shaved Parmesan cheese or sour cream. Serves 1.

EGGPLANT AND PEPPER GRILL (AUBERGINE AND CAPSICUM GRILL)

Preparation time: 20 minutes
Total cooking time: 8 minutes
Serves 4

2 tablespoons oil
1 small eggplant (aubergine), cut into
  1 cm (1/2 inch) slices
1 large 30 x 30 cm (12 x 12 inch) focaccia
4 tablespoons tomato paste
1 small onion, finely sliced
1 small red pepper (capsicum), cut into thin
  strips
3 tablespoons chopped fresh coriander leaves
1/2 cup (60 g/2 oz) grated Cheddar cheese
3 tablespoons shredded Parmesan cheese

1 Heat the oil in a large frying pan. Cook the eggplant slices for 2 minutes or until soft and just golden. Drain on paper towels.
2 Cut the focaccia into four squares, then in half horizontally. Toast each side until golden and spread with tomato paste.
3 Layer the eggplant, onion, red pepper, fresh coriander and the combined cheeses on each square. Place under a moderately hot grill for 2–3 minutes or until the cheese has melted. Serve immediately.

CHEESE, BASIL AND PINE NUT TRIANGLES

Preparation time: 40 minutes
Total cooking time: 15 minutes
Makes 28

125 g (4 oz) feta cheese
1/2 cup (125 g/4 oz) ricotta cheese
2 tablespoons chopped fresh basil
3 tablespoons pine nuts, toasted
1 egg, lightly beaten
salt and pepper
14 sheets filo pastry
125 g (4 oz) butter, melted

1 Preheat the oven to moderately hot 190°C (375°F/Gas 5). Combine the cheeses, basil, pine nuts and egg in a medium bowl; season with salt and pepper.
2 Place a sheet of pastry on a work surface and brush all over with melted butter. Top with another sheet of pastry and brush with butter. Cut the pastry lengthways into four strips.
3 Place 3 level teaspoonsful of the filling mixture on the end of each pastry strip. Fold the pastry over and up to enclose filling and form a triangle. Brush the triangles with butter and place on lightly greased oven trays. Repeat the process with the remaining pastry and filling. Bake the triangles for 15 minutes or until golden brown. Serve hot.
VARIATION: Heat 1 tablespoon of oil in a medium pan. Add 1 finely chopped onion, 2 cloves of crushed garlic and 2 small finely chopped red chillies. Cook, stirring, over medium heat for about 2–3 minutes or until the onion is tender. Stir in 425 g canned, drained and mashed pinto or kidney beans, 1 cup (250 g/8 oz) ready-made tomato salsa and 2 tablespoons chopped fresh coriander; mix well. Place a teaspoon of bean mixture onto each pastry sheet (as above). Sprinkle with a little grated Cheddar cheese. Fold into triangles as specified and bake. These are delicious served with sour cream and guacamole for dipping.

FILO PASTRY
You need swift hands to work with filo—the pastry sheets must be handled quickly and carefully as they become dry and brittle when exposed to the air. Work with one sheet at a time and keep the others covered with a damp tea towel.

LEFT: Eggplant and Pepper Grill

TOMATOES
Versatile, reliable and available year-round, eaten sliced on its own or used as the base for a myriad of dishes, very few foods evoke the same common chord of pleasure as an appealing, red-ripe tomato.

TOMATO SALAD
Arrange sliced egg (Roma) tomatoes on a platter with sliced bocconcini. Scatter with shredded basil and drizzle with the best extra virgin olive oil you can afford. You can sprinkle with rock salt and freshly cracked black pepper and serve with rocket leaves and crusty fresh bread.

HOME-DRIED TOMATOES
Cut 500 g (1 lb) tomatoes, either round or egg (Roma), in half; place in one layer on a baking tray, cut-side up. Sprinkle with salt; put in a preheated very slow 120°C (250°F/Gas ½) oven for 7–8 hours for egg (Roma) tomatoes or up to 10 hours for round. The tomatoes will

wrinkle up and become darker. Allow to cool, then pack into clean, sterilised jars with a little chopped fresh parsley; cover with olive oil. Store in a cool place.
ROASTED TOMATOES are made by the same method but cooked for only 4 to 5 hours. Serve the same day with cracked black pepper and olive oil.

TOMATO PIZZETTAS

Spread small home-made or ready-made pizza bases with fresh tomato sauce. Top with sliced ripe tomatoes, halved black olives and slivers of anchovy fillets (optional). Sprinkle with a little shredded mozzarella and crumbled goats cheese; put on a baking tray. Bake 15–20 minutes at hot 220°C (425°F/Gas 7) until crisp. Scatter with oregano leaves to serve.

WARM TOMATO SAUCE

Heat ¼ cup (60 ml/2 fl oz) olive oil in a frying pan; add 6 finely chopped spring onions. Cook over low heat for 5 minutes or until soft, being careful not to allow them to brown. Cut a cross in the bottom of 3 ripe tomatoes; put into a bowl of boiling water for 2 minutes. Plunge into cold water; remove and peel. Chop them finely and add to the pan. Simmer for 5 minutes and add ¼ cup (60 ml/2 fl oz) red wine vinegar, 2 cloves chopped garlic, ⅔ cup (170 ml/5½ fl oz) dry white wine, salt and pepper. Simmer for another 15 minutes or until the sauce has reduced and is quite thick. Just before serving, add 2 tablespoons finely chopped gherkins and 1 tablespoon chopped capers. Serve with fried or grilled zucchinis (courgettes) or eggplants (aubergines), topped with caperberries. Serves 4.

BRUSCHETTA WITH TOMATO

Peel 500 g (1 lb) ripe tomatoes by cutting a cross in the bottom of each and putting them in a bowl of boiling water for 2 minutes. Plunge them into cold water; remove and peel. Cut the tomatoes in half; remove the seeds by squeezing gently; dice the flesh. Put the flesh in a bowl and pour ¼ cup (60 ml/ 2 fl oz) of olive oil over the top. Add 8 finely chopped fresh basil leaves and salt and freshly ground black pepper, to taste. Toast 8 thick slices of crusty Italian bread and rub both sides with whole cut cloves of garlic. Spoon the tomato over the warm toast and serve. Serves 4.

CLOKWISE, FROM TOP LEFT:
Bruschetta with Tomato; Warm Tomato Sauce (served with grilled eggplant); Tomato Pizzetta; Roasted Tomatoes; Tomato Salad; Home-dried Tomatoes

2 Cut each sheet into twenty squares. Cut each piece in half to make triangles. Place triangles on baking trays. Bake for 5 minutes or until crisp. Remove and cool. Serve with Blue Cheese Dip.

3 To make Blue Cheese Dip: Using electric beaters, beat the cheese and butter in a small bowl until smooth and creamy. Add the wine, mint, rosemary and oregano; mix well. Fold through the crème fraîche or sour cream. Season to taste. Spoon the mixture into serving dishes.

NOTE: Crisps may be stored in an airtight container for up to 2 weeks. For a variation, combine 2 cloves crushed garlic with melted butter before brushing over lavash bread. Sprinkle with grated Parmesan cheese and chives, cut into squares and triangles and bake.

DOLMADES

Preparation time: 40 minutes + 1 hour soaking
Total cooking time: 50 minutes
Makes about 35

250 g (8 oz) vine leaves in brine
3/4 cup (185 ml/6 fl oz) olive oil
2 large onions, finely chopped
3/4 cup (165 g/5 1/2 oz) short-grain rice
6 spring onions, chopped
4 tablespoons coarsely chopped fresh dill
1 tablespoon finely chopped fresh mint
salt and freshly ground black pepper
1 tablespoon lemon juice

LAVASH BREAD

Lavash bread is thin, rectangular slices of wheat bread and can be found in most supermarkets. It can be rolled around a filling and eaten cold as a sandwich or perhaps used for burritos. Alternatively, sprinkle slices with oil or butter and salt, crushed garlic or herbs and then heat in the oven until crisp. Break into pieces and serve with dips. Lavash bread also makes a good (if thin) pizza base.

ABOVE: Herb Pepper Crisps with Blue Cheese Dip
RIGHT: Dolmades

HERB PEPPER CRISPS WITH BLUE CHEESE DIP

Preparation time: 30 minutes
Total cooking time: 5 minutes
Serves 10

☆

4 sheets lavash bread
90 g (3 oz) butter, melted
1 small jar herb pepper seasoning
1 tablespoon finely chopped fresh chives

Blue Cheese Dip

250 g (8 oz) blue vein cheese, chopped
60 g (2 oz) butter, softened
1 tablespoon sweet white wine
2 teaspoons chopped fresh mint
1 teaspoon chopped fresh rosemary
2 teaspoons chopped fresh oregano
1/3 cup (90 g/3 oz) crème fraîche or
    sour cream
salt and pepper

1 Preheat the oven to moderate 180°C (350°F/Gas 4). Brush each sheet of lavash bread with butter. Sprinkle with herb pepper seasoning and chives.

1 Rinse the vine leaves in cold water and soak in warm water for 1 hour; drain. Heat ½ cup (125 ml/4 fl oz) of the oil in a small heavy-based pan. Add the onions; cook over low heat for 5 minutes. Remove from the heat; set aside, covered, for 5 minutes. Add the rice, spring onions, herbs, salt and pepper to the pan and mix thoroughly.

2 Lay out a vine leaf, vein-side up. Place 3 teaspoons of the rice mixture onto the centre of the leaf. Fold the sides over the mixture and then roll towards the tip of the vine leaf. Repeat the process with the remaining filling and leaves.

3 Place five vine leaves over the base of a medium heavy-based pan. Arrange the rolled dolmades in the pan in two layers and drizzle with the remaining oil. Place a heatproof plate on top of the dolmades and cover the dolmades with water. Bring to the boil, reduce the heat and simmer, covered, for 45 minutes. Remove the plate, drain the dolmades and drizzle with lemon juice. Serve warm or cold.

NOTE: Fresh vine leaves can be used in this recipe if they are available. Use small leaves, blanched briefly in boiling water.

MEDITERRANEAN SQUARES

Preparation time: 15 minutes
Total cooking time: 15 minutes
Makes about 20 pieces

1 medium red (Spanish) onion
3 tablespoons pitted black olives
1 medium red pepper (capsicum)
1 medium green pepper (capsicum)
2 tablespoons fresh basil leaves
3 teaspoons balsamic vinegar
2 cloves garlic, crushed
¼ cup (60 ml/2 fl oz) oil
3 cloves garlic, crushed, extra
1 large 30 x 40 cm (12 x 16 inch) piece of focaccia
¾ cup (90 g/3 oz) Cheddar cheese, grated

1 Preheat the oven to moderate 180°C (350°F/Gas 4) and line an oven tray with foil. Slice the onion and olives. Cut the peppers in half, remove the seeds and membrane and cut the remaining flesh into fine strips. Finely shred the basil leaves.

2 Combine the onions, olives, peppers, basil, vinegar and garlic in a medium bowl. Mix well, then cover and set aside.

3 Combine oil and extra garlic in a small bowl. Using a serrated knife, split focaccia through the centre. Brush focaccia halves with combined oil and garlic. Arrange the combined olive and pepper filling evenly over the bottom half of the focaccia. Sprinkle with the cheese and top with the remaining piece of focaccia. Place on prepared oven tray; bake for 15 minutes or until cheese melts. Cut into squares and serve hot or at room temperature.

FAST SAVOURY BITES

BRUSH 4 sheets ready-rolled puff pastry with melted butter or oil. Place on 4 greased oven trays. Spread 2 sheets thinly with tomato paste and remaining 2 with Dijon mustard. Top tomato sheets with ⅔ cup (140 g/4⅔ oz) of quartered marinated artichoke hearts, ⅓ cup (40 g/1⅓ oz) sliced black olives, finely shredded basil and a little grated mozzarella cheese. Sprinkle with crushed garlic. Top mustard sheets with thin wedges of egg (Roma) tomatoes, chopped fresh herbs and thin slices of camembert cheese. Bake in a hot 210°C (415°F/Gas 6–7) oven 10–15 minutes. Cut in triangles for serving. Serves 2–6.

BALSAMIC VINEGAR
Balsamic vinegar has an intense, sweet flavour and is almost syrupy in consistency. It is used sparingly in salad dressings or sauces. Made in the area of Modena, Italy, there are strict guidelines governing its production. The vinegar is aged in wooden casks for at least three and up to 12 years. The older it is, the more mellow the flavour (and the higher the price).

ABOVE: Mediterranean Squares

PEELING GARLIC

1 Place the clove of garlic on a board. Lay a wide-bladed knife on top and give a sharp blow with the heel of the hand.

2 The papery skin can then be easily peeled away.

ABOVE: Tangy Tomato Dip with Pitta Crisps

TANGY TOMATO DIP WITH PITTA CRISPS

Preparation time: 20 minutes
Total cooking time: 20 minutes
Makes 2 cups

2 tablespoons oil
1 onion, chopped
2 cloves garlic, crushed
2 small red chillies, chopped
425 g (13½ oz) canned tomatoes, crushed
2 pimientos, chopped
2 tablespoons lemon juice
4 tablespoons chopped fresh parsley
3 pitta bread pockets
3 tablespoons sour cream

1 Preheat the oven to moderate 180°C (350°F/Gas 4). Heat oil in a medium pan and add onion, garlic and chillies. Stir over medium heat for 2 minutes or until onion is tender.
2 Add the tomatoes, pimientos and lemon juice; bring to the boil. Reduce heat to low; simmer, uncovered, for 5 minutes or until reduced and thickened. Remove from heat; stir in parsley.
3 Split the pitta pockets in half and cut each half into eight wedges; brush with a little oil. Place in a single layer on an oven tray and bake for 10 minutes or until golden and crisp. Spoon the tomato dip into a bowl and top with sour cream. Serve warm or cold, as a dip for pitta crisps.

BABA GHANNOUJ

Preparation time: 20 minutes
  + 15 minutes resting
Total cooking time: 20 minutes
Serves 6–8

2 small eggplants (aubergines), halved lengthways
salt
2 cloves garlic, crushed
2 tablespoons lemon juice
3 tablespoons tahini
1 tablespoon olive oil
1 tablespoon finely chopped fresh mint

1 Preheat the oven to moderately hot 190°C (375°F/Gas 5). Sprinkle the eggplant flesh with salt and set aside for 15 minutes. Rinse off the salt and pat the eggplant dry with paper towels.
2 Place the eggplants, flesh-side-up, on a baking tray. Bake for 20 minutes or until the flesh is soft. Peel off the skin and discard.
3 Place the eggplant flesh, garlic, lemon juice, tahini and olive oil into a food processor. Process for 30 seconds or until smooth. Season, to taste, with salt. Garnish with mint and serve with pitta bread or lavash bread wedges.
NOTE: This dip is a favourite appetiser in the Middle East. It can be made in advance, covered and refrigerated. Tahini is a paste made from ground toasted sesame seeds and is available from supermarkets and speciality stores.

POTATO AND CASHEW SAMOSAS

Preparation time: 20 minutes + refrigeration
Total cooking time: 40 minutes
Makes 16

1 tablespoon olive oil
2 teaspoons chopped fresh ginger
3 medium potatoes, peeled and finely diced
90 g (3 oz) roasted cashew nuts, chopped
1/4 cup (15 g/1/2 oz) shredded coconut
3 tablespoons coconut cream
3 tablespoons chopped fresh coriander leaves
salt and ground black pepper
4 sheets shortcrust pastry
oil, for frying

1 Heat the oil in a large heavy-based frying pan and cook the ginger and potatoes for 8 minutes over medium heat, stirring constantly. Add the cashews, coconut, coconut cream and coriander; stir to combine. Season. Allow to cool.
2 Cut each pastry sheet into four. Place quarter cupfuls of the filling in the centre of each square; brush the edges of the pastry with water. Press the edges of the pastry together, twist to seal, then chill for 15 minutes.
3 Heat the oil in a deep heavy-based pan; deep-fry the samosas in batches for 6 minutes or until golden and crisp. Drain on paper towels and serve immediately with a dip made from plain yoghurt, finely chopped cucumber, chopped chilli and perhaps some chopped mint.

AVOCADO SALSA

Preparation time: 15 minutes
Total cooking time: 1 minute
Serves 6

1 medium red (Spanish) onion
2 large avocados
1 tablespoon lime juice
1 medium tomato
1 small red pepper (capsicum)
1 teaspoon ground coriander
1 teaspoon ground cumin
3 tablespoons chopped fresh coriander leaves
2 tablespoons olive oil
4–5 drops Tabasco sauce

1 Finely chop the onion. Cut the avocados in half; remove the seed and carefully peel. Finely chop the flesh; place in a medium bowl and toss lightly with lime juice.
2 Cut the tomato in half horizontally, squeeze gently to remove seeds; chop finely. Remove seeds and membrane from pepper, chop finely.
3 Place the ground coriander and cumin in a small pan; stir over medium heat for 1 minute to enhance fragrance and flavour; cool. Add all the ingredients to the avocado in a bowl and gently combine, so that the avocado retains its shape and is not mashed. Refrigerate until required and serve at room temperature with corn chips.

BUYING AVOCADOS

An avocado that is ready to eat should be firm, but just yield to pressure when gently squeezed. The skin should be blemish-free. There are three common varieties of avocado: Hass has a rough knobbly skin which changes from green to purple-black; Fuerte is more pear-shaped, with a thinner, smoother green skin and there is also a cocktail avocado about 5 cm (2 inches) long.

LEFT: Potato and Cashew Samosas
ABOVE: Avocado Salsa

NACHOS WITH GUACAMOLE

Preparation time: 20 minutes
Total cooking time: 3–5 minutes
Serves 4

★

440 g (14 oz) canned red kidney beans,
   rinsed and drained
4 tablespoons ready-made tomato salsa
250 g (8 oz) corn chips
2 cups (250 g/8 oz) grated Cheddar cheese
1 1/2 cups (375 g/12 oz) ready-made
   tomato salsa, extra
4 tablespoons sour cream

Guacamole

1 large avocado
1 spring onion, finely chopped
1 small tomato, finely chopped
1 tablespoon lemon juice
freshly ground black pepper

1 Preheat oven to moderate 180°C (350°F/Gas 4).
Combine kidney beans and salsa; divide mixture
between four ovenproof serving plates. Cover
with corn chips and grated cheese. Place in the
oven for 3–5 minutes, until cheese has melted.
2 To assemble, spoon the extra salsa onto melted
cheese; top with guacamole and sour cream.
3 To make Guacamole: Cut the avocado in
half, discard the skin and stone. Mash the flesh
lightly with a fork and combine with spring
onion, tomato, lemon juice and pepper.

BELOW: Nachos
with Guacamole

FAST CRISPY KEFALOTYRI CHEESE STICKS

CUT 500 g (1 lb) Kefalotyri cheese into
sticks 1 cm (1/2 inch) thick. Dip in water and
toss to coat in a mixture of 1 cup (125 g/
4 oz) of plain flour, 1 cup (100 g/3 1/3 oz) of
dried breadcrumbs, 2 tablespoons of sweet
paprika, 1 teaspoon of ground cumin and
1 tablespoon chopped fresh parsley. Repeat
dipping process; cover sticks with plastic
wrap; refrigerate until needed. Shallow-fry in
hot oil until sticks are crisp. Don't overcook
or the cheese will start to melt through the
crust. Gruyère or Romano cheese may be
used instead of Kefalotyri. Serves 6–8.

INDIVIDUAL HERB TARTS

Preparation time: 20 minutes
Total cooking time: 35 minutes
Makes 18

★

18 slices white bread, crusts removed
40 g (1 1/3 oz) butter, softened

Filling

2 eggs
2 tablespoons milk
1/2 cup (125 ml/4 fl oz) cream
2 teaspoons chopped fresh chives
1 teaspoon chopped fresh dill
1 teaspoon chopped fresh thyme
1 tablespoon chopped fresh parsley
2 tablespoons freshly grated Parmesan cheese

1 Preheat the oven to hot 210°C (415°C/
Gas 6–7). Brush two 12-cup muffin or patty pan
trays with melted butter or oil. Cut bread into
rounds using a 7 cm (2 3/4 inch) plain biscuit
cutter. Flatten out each round with a rolling pin.
2 Spread both sides of rounds with butter
and gently press into muffin pan. Bake for
10 minutes or until lightly browned and crisp.
Do not overcook.
3 To make Filling: Reduce the heat to moderate
180°C (350°F/Gas 4). Combine the eggs, milk,
cream and herbs in a medium bowl and mix
well. Pour the egg mixture into the bread cases
and sprinkle with Parmesan cheese. Bake for
25 minutes or until the filling is lightly browned
and set. Serve the tarts immediately.

MUSHROOMS EN CROUTE

Preparation time: 40 minutes
Total cooking time: 20–25 minutes
Makes 48

8 slices white bread

90 g (3 oz) butter, melted

1 tablespoon olive oil

1 clove garlic, crushed

1/2 small onion, finely chopped

375 g (12 oz) small button mushrooms,
    finely sliced

salt and pepper

1 tablespoon dry sherry

2 teaspoons cornflour

1/3 cup (90 g/3 oz) sour cream

1 tablespoon finely chopped fresh parsley

1 teaspoon finely chopped fresh thyme

3 tablespoons shredded Parmesan cheese

1 Preheat the oven to moderate 180°C (350°F/Gas 4). Cut crusts from bread. Brush both sides of bread with melted butter. Cut each slice in half vertically, then each half into three horizontally. Place croûtes onto a foil-lined tray. Bake for 5–10 minutes or until golden and crisp.

2 Heat oil in a large frying pan; add garlic and onion. Cook, stirring, over low heat, until onion is soft. Add mushrooms; cook over medium heat 5 minutes or until tender. Add salt and pepper.
3 Pour in sherry. Blend the cornflour and sour cream; add to mushroom mixture and stir until mixture boils and thickens. Remove from heat and stir in parsley and thyme. Set aside to cool.
4 Spread some mushroom mixture onto each croûte. Sprinkle with Parmesan cheese. Place on a baking tray and bake for 5 minutes or until heated through.

FAST PARMESAN LACE BISCUITS

FINELY SHRED 100 g (3¹/₃ oz) of good quality Parmesan cheese. Combine in a small bowl with 1 tablespoon each of finely chopped fresh parsley and chives, and ¹/₄ teaspoon of paprika. Heat a non-stick frying pan until moderately hot. Sprinkle a heaped tablespoon of the cheese mixture in a round (about 5 cm/2 inches in diameter) in the pan. Cook until melted and bubbling, then remove the pan from the heat. When the bubbling subsides and the cheese firms slightly, lift the crisp out of the pan with a spatula onto paper towel. Repeat with the rest of the mixture. Makes 8 crisps.

ABOVE: Mushrooms en Croûte

THE VEGETARIAN PARTY

Bright, fresh vegetarian food is perfect for parties. Make pizzas from lavash bread, spread with a tapenade of sun-dried tomatoes and olives. Serve warm, cut into wedges, as you hand out drinks chilled with herb ice cubes. Set out large platters of roasted and marinated vegetables such as peppers (capsicums), zucchinis (courgettes) and eggplants (aubergines). These taste just as good (or better) at room temperature than hot. Cut into pieces and serve with plenty of different kinds of bread.

ABOVE: Eggplant Sandwiches

EGGPLANT (AUBERGINE) SANDWICHES

Preparation time: 30 minutes +
30 minutes standing
Total cooking time: 25–30 minutes
Serves 4

3 medium eggplants (aubergines)
olive oil, for frying
salt and cracked black pepper
ground cumin (optional)
2 red peppers (capsicums)
10–12 sun-dried tomatoes
200 g (6½ oz) ricotta or goats cheese
4 tablespoons small fresh basil leaves
fresh basil leaves, extra

1 Cut the eggplants lengthways into slices about 1 cm (½ inch) thick. Choose the eight largest slices and place on a tray or board. Refrigerate the remaining eggplant (see Note). Sprinkle the eight eggplant slices with salt and allow to stand for 30 minutes. Rinse well and pat dry with paper towels.
2 Heat a large frying pan over medium heat. Add enough oil to cover the base of the pan. When the oil is hot, add the eggplant slices, a few at a time. Cook for 2–3 minutes each side or until brown. Drain on paper towels. Season each slice with salt and pepper. Sprinkle with cumin, if desired.
3 Cut the peppers in half lengthways. Remove the seeds and membrane and then cut into large, flattish pieces. Grill until the skin blackens and blisters. Place on a cutting board, cover with a tea towel and allow to cool. Peel the peppers and cut the flesh into strips.
4 Cut the sun-dried tomatoes into strips. On each of four serving plates, place a slice of eggplant. Spread the slices with ricotta or goats cheese. Top with sun-dried tomatoes and peppers, reserving some for garnish. Sprinkle with basil leaves. Cover each with a second slice of eggplant. Decorate the top with strips of peppers and sun-dried tomatoes. Garnish with extra basil leaves.
NOTE: The unused eggplant slices will last a day or two in the refrigerator. Finely chop and then brown in olive oil with crushed garlic; season well with salt and pepper. Spread on toast or on pitta bread as a snack or add to a soup or casserole.

SWEET AND SPICY NUTS

Preparation time: 20 minutes
Total cooking time: 15 minutes
Serves 6–8

250 g (8 oz) blanched almonds
250 g (8 oz) pecans
3 tablespoons sugar
1 teaspoon salt
1/2 teaspoon ground black pepper
1 teaspoon ground cinnamon
pinch ground cloves
1/2 teaspoon curry powder
1/4 teaspoon ground cumin

1 Preheat oven to moderate 180°C (350°F/Gas 4). Place almonds and pecans on a large baking tray. Bake for 5–10 minutes or until the nuts are golden and crisp. Remove from the oven and allow to cool.
2 Combine the sugar, salt, pepper and spices in a small bowl. Mix well.
3 Heat a large frying pan. Add the almonds and pecans. Sprinkle the spice mixture over the nuts. Cook the nuts, stirring over medium heat for 5 minutes or until they turn golden—the sugar will melt and coat the nuts. Shake the frying pan often to ensure even cooking. If the nuts stick together, separate them with a wooden spoon. When nuts are cooked, remove them from heat. Spread on a lightly oiled baking tray to cool.

PARMESAN AND PESTO TOASTS

Preparation time: 30 minutes
Total cooking time: 5 minutes
Makes about 40

1 bread stick
16 large sun-dried tomatoes, cut into thin strips
150 g (4 3/4 oz) fresh Parmesan cheese, shaved thinly

Pesto

1 cup (50 g/1 2/3 oz) firmly packed fresh basil leaves
2 tablespoons chopped fresh chives
4 tablespoons pine nuts
2–3 cloves garlic, peeled
1/4 cup (60 ml/2 fl oz) olive oil

1 Freeze the bread stick until firm. Cut it into very thin slices, using a sharp serrated knife. Toast the slices under a hot grill until they are golden brown on both sides.
2 **To make Pesto:** Place the basil leaves, chives, pine nuts, garlic and olive oil in a food processor. Process for 20–30 seconds or until smooth.
3 Spread the pesto mixture evenly over the toasted slices. Top with strips of tomato and shavings of Parmesan cheese.

*LEFT: Sweet and Spicy Nuts
ABOVE: Parmesan and Pesto Toasts*

PIES FLANS
AND PIZZAS

A deliciously familiar and much-loved way to combine fresh vegetables with crisp pastry, and often a creamy sauce, home-baked pies also have a healthy dollop of nostalgia buried within their crusts. These pastry-based recipes, whether a rich, classic onion tart or piquant tomato pizzettas, will travel from picnic to party, light lunch to family meal, with scarcely a single golden crumb out of place.

¹/₄ cup (60 ml/2 fl oz) good-quality red wine
¹/₄ cup (60 ml/2 fl oz) vegetable stock
2 tablespoons tomato paste
¹/₂ teaspoon dried basil
¹/₂ teaspoon dried oregano

1 Preheat the oven to hot 210°C (415°F/ Gas 6–7). Brush an oven tray with melted butter or oil. Peel and cut the potato, carrot, parsnip and pumpkin into 1 cm (¹/₂ inch) cubes. Heat the oil in a frying pan and cook the onion over medium heat for 2 minutes, or until soft. Add potato, carrot, parsnip, pumpkin and stock; bring to the boil. Reduce heat and simmer for 10 minutes, stirring occasionally, until the vegetables are soft and the liquid has evaporated. Stir in the peas and parsley and leave to cool.
2 Using a plate as a guide, cut four 12 cm (5 inch) circles from each sheet of pastry. Place 1 level tablespoon of mixture onto each round, brush the edges of pastry with water and fold the pastry over so the edges meet. Twist the edges together decoratively to seal. Brush with beaten egg, place on prepared tray and bake for 25 minutes, until puffed and golden.
3 To make Tomato Sauce: Heat the oil in a small pan and add the onion and garlic. Cook over medium heat for 2 minutes, or until soft. Add the tomatoes, wine and stock and bring to boil. Reduce heat and simmer for 15 minutes, stirring occasionally. Remove from heat; cool. Process tomato mixture in a food processor until smooth. Return to pan, add tomato paste, basil and oregano and stir until hot. Serve hot or cold.

VEGETABLE PASTIES WITH RICH TOMATO SAUCE

Preparation time: 40 minutes
Total cooking time: 50 minutes
Makes 12

★

1 potato
1 carrot
1 parsnip
100 g (3¹/₃ oz) pumpkin
2 teaspoons oil
1 onion, finely chopped
¹/₂ cup (125 ml/4 fl oz) vegetable stock
¹/₃ cup (50 g/1²/₃ oz) fresh or frozen peas
1 tablespoon finely chopped fresh parsley
3 sheets ready-rolled puff pastry
1 egg, lightly beaten

Tomato Sauce

1 tablespoon oil
1 small onion, chopped
1 clove garlic, crushed
2 tomatoes, peeled and chopped

PICNIC PIES
Most vegetable pies taste just as good at room temperature as they do hot and so are perfect as picnic food. If they've been refrigerated, you may like to warm them up in the oven before you leave the house. Wrap them in foil for transporting.

ABOVE: Vegetable Pasties with Rich Tomato Sauce

SPINACH PIE

Preparation time: 35 minutes
Total cooking time: 40 minutes
Serves 6-8

★

500 g (1 lb) English spinach
1 tablespoon oil
6 spring onions, finely chopped
125 g (4 oz) feta cheese, crumbled
³/₄ cup (90 g/3 oz) grated Cheddar cheese
5 eggs, lightly beaten
salt and freshly ground black pepper
16 sheets filo pastry
¹/₃ cup (80 ml/2³/₄ fl oz) olive oil
1 egg, extra, lightly beaten, for glazing
1 tablespoon poppy seeds

1 Preheat oven to hot 210°C (415°F/Gas 6–7). Brush a 30 x 25 cm (12 x 10 inch) baking dish with oil. Wash spinach thoroughly and shred finely. Place in a large pan with just the water that is clinging to the leaves; cook, covered, over low heat for 2 minutes or until just wilted. Cool, wring out excess water and spread out strands.

2 Heat oil in a small pan and cook spring onions for 3 minutes or until soft. Transfer to a large bowl and add spinach, cheeses, eggs, salt and pepper. Stir until cheeses are distributed evenly.

3 Place 1 sheet of pastry in dish, letting edges overhang. Cover remaining pastry with a clean, damp tea towel to prevent drying out. Brush pastry in dish with oil. Repeat with another 7 layers of pastry, brushing each lightly with oil.

4 Spread filling over pastry then fold in edges of pastry. Brush each remaining sheet of pastry lightly with oil and place on top of pie. Tuck edges down the sides, brush top with egg and sprinkle with poppy seeds. Bake 35–40 minutes or until pastry is golden. Serve immediately.

NOTE: Sesame seeds can be used instead of poppy seeds, if you prefer.

INDIVIDUAL VEGETABLE POT PIES

Preparation time: 40 minutes
Total cooking time: 45 minutes
Makes 6

1 medium potato, peeled, cut into small cubes

150 g (4³/4 oz) pumpkin, peeled, cut into 1 cm (¹/2 inch) cubes

1 large carrot, peeled, cut into 1 cm (¹/2 inch) cubes

150 g (4³/4 oz) small broccoli florets

1 tablespoon oil

1 onion, finely chopped

1 red pepper (capsicum), cut into 1 cm (¹/2 inch) squares

50 g (1²/3 oz) butter

2 tablespoons plain flour

1¹/2 cups (375 ml/12 fl oz) milk

1 cup (125 g/4 oz) grated Cheddar cheese

2 egg yolks

salt and cayenne pepper, to taste

2 sheets ready-rolled puff pastry

1 egg, lightly beaten

1 teaspoon poppy seeds

1 Preheat the oven to hot 210°C (415°F/ Gas 6–7). Brush six 1-cup capacity ramekins with oil. Steam or microwave the potato, pumpkin, carrot and broccoli until just tender. Drain well and place in a large bowl. Heat the oil in a frying pan and cook the onion and red pepper over medium heat for 2 minutes until soft. Add to the bowl.

2 Heat the butter in a pan and add the flour. Stir over low heat for 2 minutes or until lightly golden. Add the milk gradually, stirring until smooth. Stir over medium heat for 3 minutes or until the mixture boils and thickens. Boil for another minute, then remove from the heat and cool slightly. Add the cheese and yolks to the sauce and stir to combine. Season to taste.

3 Add the sauce to the vegetables and stir to combine. Divide between the ramekins. Cut 6 circles from the pastry to fit the top of the ramekins and press the edges to seal. Brush with beaten egg and sprinkle with poppy seeds. Bake for 30 minutes or until golden brown.

NOTE: These pies are best eaten on the day they are made.

ABOVE: Individual Vegetable Pot Pies

The secret of a light and crisp pastry is to make sure the dough is not overworked. Whether the mixing is done by hand or with a food processor, as long as you do it quickly, the dough will be easy to handle and roll. The amount of liquid required varies depending on the texture of the flour so it must be added gradually in small amounts until the mixture just comes together. It should then be gathered up into a ball, wrapped and refrigerated. Pastry should always be cooked in a preheated oven, never one that has not yet reached the required temperature.

ABOVE: Silverbeet Pie

SILVERBEET (SWISS CHARD) PIE

Preparation time: 40 minutes + refrigeration
Total cooking time: 45–50 minutes
Serves 6-8

Pastry

2 cups (250 g/8 oz) plain flour
1/2 cup (75 g/2 1/2 oz) wholemeal plain flour
125 g (4 oz) butter, chopped
1/3 cup (80 ml/2 3/4 fl oz) iced water

Filling

800 g (1 lb 10 oz) silverbeet (Swiss chard)
1/2 cup (65 g/2 1/4 oz) chopped pistachio nuts
3 tablespoons chopped raisins
1/3 cup (35 g/1 1/4 oz) freshly grated
   Parmesan cheese
1/2 cup (60 g/2 oz) grated Cheddar cheese
4 eggs
2/3 cup (170 ml/5 1/2 fl oz) cream
1/4 teaspoon ground nutmeg

1 To make Pastry: Sift the flours into a large bowl and add the butter. With your fingertips, rub the butter into the flour for 2 minutes, or until the mixture is fine and crumbly. Add enough water to mix to a firm dough, adding more water if necessary. Turn the dough onto a lightly floured surface and press together until smooth. Roll out two-thirds of the pastry and line a greased 23 cm (9 inch) pie dish. Wrap the remaining pastry in plastic wrap and refrigerate both for 20 minutes.

2 To make Filling: Preheat the oven to moderate 180°C (350°F/Gas 4). Remove the stems from the silverbeet and wash the leaves thoroughly. Shred finely. Steam or microwave for 3 minutes or until tender. Cool, squeeze thoroughly to remove excess moisture and spread out to dry in separate strands.

3 Sprinkle the pistachios onto the pastry base. Combine the silverbeet, raisins and cheeses and spread over the pistachios. Whisk 3 of the eggs with the cream and nutmeg and pour over silverbeet mixture.

4 Roll out the remaining pastry to cover the top of the pie and trim the edges with a sharp knife. Press the edges together to seal. Beat the remaining egg and use it to brush the pie top. Decorate with pastry trimmings. Bake for 45 minutes or until golden. Serve warm, with a tomato salad.

NOTE: This is best eaten on the day it is made.

HARVEST PIE

Preparation time: 40 minutes + refrigeration
Total cooking time: 1 hour
Serves 6

175 g (5²/₃ oz) butter
2 cups (250 g/8 oz) plain flour
¹/₄ cup (60 ml/2 fl oz) iced water
1 tablespoon oil
1 onion, finely chopped
1 small red pepper (capsicum), chopped
1 small green pepper (capsicum), chopped
150 g (4³/₄ oz) pumpkin, chopped
1 small potato, chopped
100 g (3¹/₃ oz) broccoli, cut into small florets
1 carrot, chopped
¹/₄ cup (30 g/1 oz) plain flour
1 cup (250 ml/8 fl oz) milk
2 egg yolks
¹/₂ cup (60 g/2 oz) grated Cheddar cheese
1 egg, lightly beaten, for glazing

1 Preheat the oven to moderate 180°C (350°F/Gas 4). Chop 125 g (4 oz) of the butter. Sift the flour into a large bowl and add the chopped butter. Using your fingertips, rub the butter into the flour until it is fine and crumbly. Add almost all the water and use a knife to mix to a firm dough, adding more water if necessary. Turn onto a lightly floured surface and press together until smooth.
2 Divide the dough in half, roll out one portion and line a deep 21 cm (8¹/₂ inch) fluted flan tin. Refrigerate for 20 minutes. Roll the remaining pastry out to a 25 cm (10 inch) diameter circle. Cut into strips and lay half of them on a sheet of baking paper, leaving a 1 cm (¹/₂ inch) gap between each strip. Interweave the remaining strips to form a lattice pattern. Cover with plastic wrap and refrigerate, keeping flat, until firm.
3 Cut a sheet of greaseproof paper to cover the pastry-lined tin. Spread a layer of dried beans or rice over the paper. Bake for 10 minutes, remove from oven and discard paper and beans or rice. Bake for another 10 minutes or until lightly golden; allow to cool.
4 Heat the oil in a frying pan. Add the onion and cook for 2 minutes or until soft. Add the peppers and cook, stirring, for another 3 minutes. Steam or boil remaining vegetables until just tender; drain and cool. Mix the onion, peppers and the other vegetables in a large bowl.

5 Heat the remaining butter in a small pan. Add the flour and cook, stirring, for 2 minutes. Add the milk gradually, stirring until smooth between each addition. Stir constantly over medium heat until the mixture boils and thickens. Boil for 1 minute and then remove from the heat. Add the egg yolks and cheese and stir until smooth. Pour the sauce over the vegetables and stir to combine. Pour the mixture into the pastry case and brush the edges with egg. Using baking paper to lift, invert the pastry lattice over the vegetables, trim the edges and brush with a little beaten egg, sealing to the cooked pastry. Brush the top with egg and bake for 30 minutes or until golden brown.

DECORATING PIES
Traditionally, savoury pies were decorated while sweet ones were left plain, so that diners could easily choose between them when a selection was presented on the sideboard. Individual pies for little children can be given a personal touch by using pastry scraps to put their initials or first name on top.

ABOVE: Harvest Pie

POTATOES This ultimate comfort food has a

long history of keeping famine at bay and families together and, with its many

varieties and unlimited number of ways to cook them, its staying power seems assured.

CRISPY POTATO WEDGES
Scrub and pat dry 8 medium Sebago potatoes, and cut into thick wedges. Brush the wedges lightly with olive oil, sprinkle with sea salt and sweet paprika (or chilli powder for a spicier flavour). Bake in a preheated hot 220°C (425°F/Gas 7) oven for 35–40 minutes, or until the wedges are crisp and golden. Serves 4.

CLASSIC POTATO GNOCCHI
Boil 1.2 kg (2 lb 6½ oz) unpeeled Desiree or Pontiac potatoes in salted water until tender. Rinse and allow to cool slightly before peeling and mashing. (Do not use a food processor for mashing.) Place the mashed potato onto a lightly floured surface. Make a well in the centre and add 2 egg yolks and 1 cup

(125 g/4 oz) of plain flour. Knead the mixture to form a soft dough. If dough is too sticky, add more flour—the amount needed will differ with the type of potato used. Coat your hands with flour, divide the mixture into 8 pieces and roll into logs 3 cm (1¼ inches) thick and 22 cm (8¾ inches) long. Cut the logs into 1 cm (½ inch) lengths and roll the pieces over

the prongs of a lightly floured fork. Cook the gnocchi in a large pan of salted boiling water—they are cooked when they float to the surface. Serve with your favourite pasta sauce. Serves 4.

ROSEMARY OVEN-ROASTED POTATOES

Peel and chop 500 g (1 lb) Kipfler or other variety of new potatoes into 1 cm (½ inch) cubes. Place the potatoes in a non-stick baking dish, drizzle with ¼ cup (60 ml/2 fl oz) of olive oil, sprinkle liberally with sea salt and freshly cracked black pepper and toss through 2 tablespoons of fresh rosemary sprigs. Bake in a preheated hot 220°C (425°F/Gas 7) oven for 45 minutes, turning frequently until the potatoes are crisp and golden. Serves 4.

WARM AND SPICY POTATO SALAD

Peel and cut 1 kg (2 lb) Pontiac potatoes into thick slices. Heat ½ cup (125 ml/ 4 fl oz) of olive oil in a large non-stick frying pan; add the sliced potatoes, 2 tablespoons tomato paste, ½ teaspoon turmeric and 1 teaspoon each chilli flakes, saffron threads, black mustard seeds and cumin seeds. Cook over medium heat for 5 minutes. Stir in 1½ cups (375 ml/ 12 fl oz) of vegetable stock and 2 bay leaves. Bring to boil, reduce heat, cover, simmer 30 minutes or until tender. Stir in 3 tablespoons chopped fresh mint. Can be served with natural yoghurt. Serves 4–6.

POTATOES WITH CREME FRAICHE AND AVOCADO SALSA

Place 500 g (1 lb) new potatoes in a large non-stick baking tray, drizzle with

3 tablespoons olive oil and sprinkle with sea salt. Bake in preheated moderately hot 200°C (400°F/Gas 6) oven for 40 minutes or until crisp and golden. To make Avocado Salsa, combine 1 crushed clove of garlic, 1 finely chopped small red chilli, 1 small finely chopped red (Spanish) onion, 1 chopped avocado, 1 tablespoon lime juice, 2 tablespoons chopped fresh coriander, 1 finely chopped tomato and 1 finely chopped peach in a bowl. Serve potatoes topped with a spoonful each of crème fraîche and Avocado Salsa. Serves 4.

CLOCKWISE, FROM TOP LEFT: Potatoes with Crème Fraîche and Avocado Salsa; Crispy Potato Wedges; Warm and Spicy Potato Salad; Rosemary Oven-Roasted Potatoes; Classic Potato Gnocchi

then spread a layer of dried beans or rice evenly over paper. Bake 15 minutes, then remove paper and beans or rice. Bake another 10 minutes or until pastry case is lightly golden; cool. Reduce oven to moderate 180°C (350°F/Gas 4).

3 Cut the tomatoes in half; sprinkle with salt and drizzle with oil. Place in a baking dish, cut-side up; bake for 15 minutes. Arrange the tomatoes, cut-side up, over the pastry. Place the bocconcini slices and spring onion between tomatoes; scatter with rosemary and salt and pepper. Bake for 10 minutes. Remove from oven and cool for 10 minutes before serving.

MINI PUMPKIN AND CURRY QUICHES

Preparation time: 30 minutes
 + 30 minutes refrigeration
Total cooking time: 40 minutes
Makes 8

Cream Cheese Pastry

1½ cups (185 g/6 oz) plain flour
125 g (4 oz) cream cheese, chopped
125 g (4 oz) butter, chopped

Filling

1 tablespoon oil
2 onions, finely chopped
3 cloves garlic, crushed
1 teaspoon curry powder
3 eggs
½ cup (125 ml/4 oz) thick (double) cream
1 cup mashed, cooked pumpkin
  (about 350 g/11¼ oz raw)
2 teaspoons cumin seeds

1 To make Cream Cheese Pastry: Preheat the oven to hot 210°C (415°F/Gas 6–7). To make the pastry, sift the flour into a large bowl and add the cream cheese and butter. Using your fingertips, rub the ingredients together for 2 minutes or until the mixture is smooth and comes together in a ball.

2 Turn dough onto a lightly floured surface, knead for 10 seconds or until smooth. Place, covered with plastic wrap, in the refrigerator for 30 minutes. Divide the pastry into 8 equal portions, roll out and line 8 deep, greased 10 cm (4 inch) flan tins. Bake for 15 minutes or until lightly browned. Remove from the oven. Reduce

---

BOCCONCINI
Bocconcini are small rounds of fresh mozzarella cheese. They are usually served in salads so as to retain their delicate texture. If you cook them, be careful to do so only briefly or they will become dry and leathery.

ABOVE: Tomato and Bocconcini Flan

TOMATO AND BOCCONCINI FLAN

Preparation time: 30 minutes + refrigeration
Total cooking time: 50 minutes
Serves 6

1½ cups (185 g/6 oz) plain flour
100 g (3⅓ oz) butter, chopped
1 egg
2 tablespoons cold water
5–6 egg (Roma) tomatoes
salt
1 tablespoon olive oil
8 bocconcini (220 g/7 oz), sliced
6 spring onions, chopped
2 tablespoons chopped fresh rosemary
salt and pepper, to taste

1 Combine flour and butter in a food processor; process 10 seconds or until fine and crumbly. Combine egg and water in a small bowl. With motor constantly running, gradually add to flour mixture; process until mixture just comes together. Turn out onto a lightly floured surface; knead to form a smooth dough. Refrigerate, covered with plastic wrap, for 20 minutes.

2 Preheat oven to hot 210°C (415°F/Gas 6–7). On a floured board, roll pastry to fit a 23 cm (9 inch) round, loose-bottomed flan tin. Ease pastry into tin; trim edges. Cut a sheet of baking paper to cover pastry-lined tin. Place over pastry

1 Preheat oven to hot 210°C (415°F/Gas 6–7). Wash the rocket and shake off excess water; finely slice rocket leaves.

2 Sift the flour into a bowl. Using your fingertips, rub the butter into the flour for 2 minutes, or until the mixture is fine and crumbly. Add water and mix to a soft dough. Turn onto a lightly floured surface and knead for 10 seconds or until smooth. Refrigerate, covered in plastic wrap, for 30 minutes.

3 Roll the pastry, between 2 sheets of plastic wrap, to cover the base and side of a shallow 23 cm (9 inch) flan tin. Cover the pastry-lined tin with a sheet of baking paper. Spread dried beans or rice over the paper. Bake for 10 minutes and then remove from the oven and discard the beans or rice. Return pastry to the oven for 5 minutes or until lightly golden. Reduce heat to moderate 180°C (350°F/Gas 4).

4 Heat the oil in a frying pan, add the leek and garlic and stir over low heat for 5 minutes or until the leek is soft. Add the rocket and stir over heat for 1 minute. Remove from heat and allow to cool. Spread over base of pastry shell. Combine eggs, milk and cream in a bowl; whisk until smooth. Pour into pastry shell. Bake at moderate 180°C (350°F/Gas 4) for 50 minutes, or until set and golden. Serve topped with basil leaves and shaved Parmesan cheese, if desired.

ROCKET

Rocket, also called arugula or rugola, is a leafy herb with a spicy, peppery taste. It makes a wonderful and very simple salad mixed with shavings of Parmesan and tossed in a lemony olive oil dressing. If you find the taste too strong, mix rocket with other salad greens.

ABOVE: Mini Pumpkin and Curry Quiches BELOW: Rocket, Basil and Leek Quiche

the heat to moderate 180°C (350°F/Gas 4).

3 **To make Filling:** Heat oil in a small pan, add the onions and garlic and stir over low heat for 5 minutes or until soft. Add curry powder, stir for 1 minute. Spread over bases of pastry cases.

4 Combine eggs, cream and pumpkin in a large bowl, beat until combined. Pour over onion mixture, sprinkle with cumin seeds. Bake in moderate 180°C (350°F/Gas 4) oven for 20 minutes, or until filling has set.

ROCKET, BASIL AND LEEK QUICHE

Preparation time: 30 minutes + refrigeration
Total cooking time: 1 hour 10 minutes
Makes one 23 cm (9 inch) quiche

★★

150 g (4³⁄₄ oz) rocket, stalks removed
1¹⁄₂ cups (185 g/6 oz) plain flour
125 g (4 oz) butter, chopped
1–2 tablespoons water
1 tablespoon oil
1 large leek, white part only, thinly sliced
2 cloves garlic, crushed
2 eggs
¹⁄₂ cup (125 ml/4 fl oz) milk
¹⁄₂ cup (125 ml/4 fl oz) cream

TOMATO AND OLIVE FLAN

Preparation time: 30 minutes
 +30 minutes refrigeration
Total cooking time: 30–35 minutes
Makes one 20 cm (8 inch) flan

Pastry

2 cups (250 g/8 oz) plain flour
90 g (3 oz) butter, chopped
I egg yolk
I tablespoon water

Filling

2 tablespoons olive oil
I–2 tablespoons French mustard
15 g (½ oz) butter
6 small tomatoes, peeled and chopped
3 large onions, thinly sliced
I teaspoon sugar
2 tablespoons shredded fresh basil
I cup (125 g/4 oz) pitted olives, sliced
I cup (220 g/7 oz) grated Gruyère cheese

I Preheat oven to hot 210°C (415°F/Gas 6–7). Brush a 20 cm (8 inch) deep flan tin with melted butter or oil. Coat the base and sides of tin evenly with flour and shake off any excess.
2 To make Pastry: Place flour and butter in a food processor; process for 30 seconds or until mixture reaches a fine crumbly texture. Add combined egg yolk and water and process for 30 seconds or until mixture comes together. Gather together on a lightly floured surface. Store, covered with plastic wrap, in the refrigerator for 30 minutes.
3 To make Filling: Mix together the oil and French mustard to make a smooth paste.
4 Roll the pastry out to fit the prepared flan tin. Cover pastry with a large sheet of baking paper. Spread a layer of dried beans evenly over the paper. Bake for 15 minutes, remove from oven, discard paper and beans and leave pastry to cool. Spread the mustard and oil mixture over the pastry base. Heat the butter in a medium pan and cook the tomatoes and onions until soft. Remove from heat. Drain off excess liquid. Spoon the tomato mixture over the pastry base. Mix together the sugar, basil and olives and sprinkle over the tomato mixture. Top with cheese. Bake flan for 20 minutes or until the pastry is crisp and the cheese browned.

OLIVES

The golden rule when buying olives is to get the best you can afford. Two of the most delicious varieties are the purple-black Kalamata from Greece, and the tiny dark-brown Niçoise olives from France. If a recipe specifies using a certain type it is best to try to find it.

RIGHT: Tomato and Olive Flan

TRIPLE CHEESE FLAN

Preparation time: 20 minutes
Total cooking time: 35 minutes
Serves 6

6 sheets filo pastry
60 g (2 oz) butter, melted

Filling
1/4 cup (30 g/1 oz) grated Cheddar cheese
1/2 cup (60 g/2 oz) grated smoked cheese
1/2 cup (65 g/21/4 oz) grated Gruyère cheese
3 eggs, lightly beaten
1/2 cup (125 ml/4 fl oz) milk
3/4 cup (185 ml/6 fl oz) cream
1 tablespoon chopped fresh chives
2 tablespoons chopped fresh parsley

1 Preheat the oven to moderate 180°C (350°F/Gas 4). Lay out filo pastry on kitchen bench and cover with damp tea towel to prevent drying out. Remove one sheet and brush it with melted butter. Place another sheet of filo over it and brush with butter. Repeat until all the sheets have been used.
2 Brush a 23 cm (9 inch) flan tin with melted butter or oil. Line the tin with pastry, tucking in the edges.
3 To make Filling: Combine all the ingredients in a bowl and mix well. Pour the filling into the tin and bake for 35 minutes or until the filling is lightly browned and set.

SWISS ONION TART

Preparation time: 30 minutes
Total cooking time: 1 hour 10 minutes
Serves 4

2 sheets frozen shortcrust pastry
2 tablespoons oil
3 medium onions, sliced
1/2 cup (125 g/4 oz) sour cream
2 eggs
1/2 cup (65 g/21/4 oz) finely grated Gruyère cheese
cayenne pepper

1 Preheat the oven to hot 210°C (415°F/Gas 6–7). Thaw the pastry and fit the sheets, overlapping where necessary, into a 20 cm (8 inch) fluted flan tin; trim edges. Cut a sheet of baking paper large enough to cover the pastry-lined tin. Spread a layer of dried beans or rice evenly over the paper. Bake the pastry shell for 10 minutes, then remove from oven. Discard the paper and beans or rice. Return the pastry-lined tin to the oven for another 5 minutes or until the pastry is lightly golden. Reduce the oven temperature to moderate 180°C (350°F/Gas 4).
2 Heat the oil in a pan and add the onions. Cook over low heat, stirring often, for 15 minutes or until onion is lightly browned and very tender. Spread over pastry base.
3 Whisk the sour cream and eggs in a medium bowl until smooth. Add the cheese and stir until combined. Place the flan tin on a baking tray. Pour the egg mixture over the onion and sprinkle lightly with cayenne pepper. Bake for 40 minutes or until the filling is set. Serve warm or cold.
NOTE: Pastry can be cooked a day in advance and refrigerated, covered. Onion can be cooked and filling prepared several hours ahead. Cover and refrigerate. Assemble tart and bake just before serving.

BAKING BLIND
Baking blind ensures the pastry base is crisp and cooked thoroughly. Once the pastry is in the tin, lay a sheet of baking paper over it, to cover the base and sides. Spread a layer of uncooked rice, dried beans or baking beads over the base. Bake in a preheated oven for the time stated, then remove the rice, beans or beads and paper. Return the pastry to the oven until lightly golden, then fill according to the recipe. The rice or beans (chickpeas are also good) can be kept in a separate jar and re-used whenever needed.

ABOVE: Swiss Onion Tart

YEAST DOUGH

Yeast dough may be made up to the stage where it is left to double in size (this is called 'proving') well in advance. Place the dough in a lightly oiled bowl, cover with plastic wrap and refrigerate for up to eight hours. The dough will still rise, it just happens much more slowly at the cooler temperature. Never leave dough to rise in a very hot environment, thinking it will happen more quickly. The yeast will develop a sour taste, or can even be killed if it is too hot.

ABOVE: Potato Pizza with Onions and Goats Cheese

POTATO PIZZA WITH ONIONS AND GOATS CHEESE

Preparation time: 40 minutes + standing
Total cooking time: 55 minutes
Serves 4

1/2 cup (125 ml/4 fl oz) warm milk
50 g (1²/3 oz) fresh compressed yeast or
  2 x 7 g (1/4 oz) sachets dried yeast
1/2 teaspoon sugar
salt
3/4 cup (165 g/5¹/2 oz) mashed potato
1 cup (125 g/4 oz) plain flour
2 tablespoons chopped fresh parsley
freshly ground black pepper

Topping

2 tablespoons olive oil
1 kg (2 lb) red (Spanish) onions,
  thinly sliced
200 g (6¹/2 oz) roasted red pepper (capsicum),
  cut into strips
1/2 cup (90 g/3 oz) black olives
50 g (1²/3 oz) goats cheese, cut into small pieces
cracked black pepper

1 Mix together the milk and crumbled yeast with the sugar and a pinch of salt in a small bowl. Cover the bowl with plastic wrap and leave in a warm place for 10 minutes or until frothy. Stir together the mashed potato, flour, parsley, salt, pepper and yeast mixture in a large bowl until a soft dough forms. Turn out onto a lightly floured surface and knead for 10 minutes or until the dough is smooth and springs back when pressed.

2 Return the dough to a large, clean, lightly greased bowl. Cover with plastic wrap and leave in a warm place until the dough has doubled in size (1–1¹/2 hours).

3 To make Topping: Heat the oil in a heavy-based pan over low heat. Cook the onions, covered, stirring occasionally, for 20–30 minutes or until golden and glossy. Remove from heat.

4 Preheat the oven to hot 210°C (415°F/ Gas 6–7). Turn the dough out onto a floured surface and gently knock down and knead for another 2 minutes. Generously oil a pizza tray or 2 small trays. Put the dough on the tray and press out to fit. Top the dough with the onion, red pepper, olives and goats cheese and sprinkle with cracked black pepper. Bake for 20–25 minutes and serve immediately.

NOTE: The caramelised onions can be prepared a day in advance. Be careful to cook them over low heat so that they become sweet and delicious. If they burn they will be bitter.

SPANISH PIZZA

Preparation time: 30 minutes + standing
Total cooking time: 35 minutes
Serves 4-6

Base

7 g (¼ oz) sachet dried yeast
1 teaspoon caster sugar
2¼ cups (280 g/9 oz) plain flour
1 cup (250 ml/8 fl oz) warm water

Topping

10 English spinach leaves, shredded
1 tablespoon olive oil
2 cloves garlic, crushed
2 onions, chopped
440 g (14 oz) canned tomatoes, drained
   and crushed
¼ teaspoon ground pepper
12 pitted black olives, chopped

1 Preheat the oven to hot 210°C (415°F/
Gas 6–7). Brush a 30 x 25 cm (12 x 10 inch)
Swiss roll tin with melted butter or oil.
2 To make the Base: Combine the yeast, sugar
and flour in a large bowl. Gradually add the
warm water and blend until smooth. Knead the
dough on a lightly floured surface until smooth

and elastic. Place in a lightly oiled basin, cover
with a tea towel and leave to rise in a warm
position for 15 minutes or until the dough has
almost doubled in size.
3 To make the Topping: Put the spinach in a
large pan, cover and cook on low heat for
3 minutes. Drain the spinach and cool. Squeeze
out the excess moisture with your hands and set
spinach aside.
4 Heat the oil in a pan and add the garlic and
onions. Cook over low heat for 5–6 minutes.
Add the tomatoes and pepper and simmer gently
for 5 minutes.
5 Punch the dough down, remove from the
bowl and knead on a lightly floured board for
2–3 minutes. Roll the dough out and fit it in the
tin. Spread with spinach, top with the tomato
mixture and sprinkle the olives on top.
6 Bake for 25–30 minutes. Cut into small squares
or fingers and serve hot or cold.

MINI PIZZAS

Preparation time: 20 minutes
Total cooking time: 20–25 minutes
Serves 4

1 tablespoon oil
1 small green pepper (capsicum), cut into
   short, thin strips
150 g (4¾ oz) mushrooms, thinly sliced
1 zucchini (courgette), thinly sliced
4 mini pizza bases
⅔ cup (160 g/5¼ oz) ready-made napoletana
   pasta sauce
410 g (13 oz) canned artichokes, drained
   and quartered
130 g (4¼ oz) canned corn kernels, drained
1 cup (150 g/4¾ oz) grated mozzarella cheese

1 Preheat the oven to hot 210°C (415°F/
Gas 6–7). Lightly brush 2 baking trays with
melted butter or oil. Heat the oil in a frying
pan and add the green pepper, mushrooms and
zucchini. Stir over medium heat for 3 minutes,
or until soft; allow to cool.
2 Spread bases with pasta sauce. Top with the
cooked vegetables, artichokes and corn. Sprinkle
with grated mozzarella. Place on trays.
3 Bake for 15–20 minutes, until the cheese
has melted and the pizza bases are crisp. Serve
the pizzas immediately.

PIZZA BASES
Traditionally, pizza bases are made from the local baker's leftover bread dough. They can also be made from scone dough or shortcrust pastry. Pitta, Lebanese, lavash and Turkish (pide) breads also make good pizza bases.

LEFT: Spanish Pizza

SOUR CREAM TOMATO PIZZA

Preparation time: 30 minutes
  + 1 hour 30 minutes standing
Total cooking time: 40 minutes
Serves 4

☆ ☆

1 teaspoon dried yeast
1 teaspoon caster sugar
2/3 cup (170 ml/5 1/2 fl oz) warm water
2 cups (250 g/8 oz) plain flour
pinch salt
1/2 cup (125 ml/4 fl oz) olive oil

Topping

1/2 cup (125 g/4 oz) sour cream
90 g (3 oz) ricotta cheese
2 tablespoons chopped fresh herbs
  (basil, lemon thyme, sage)
2 tablespoons oil
2 medium onions, thinly sliced
5 ripe tomatoes, sliced
2 cloves garlic, thinly sliced
45 g (1 1/2 oz) marinated Niçoise olives
10 sprigs fresh lemon thyme
freshly cracked black pepper

1 Preheat oven to moderately hot 200°C (400°F/Gas 6). To make base, place yeast, sugar and warm water into a bowl and mix to dissolve the sugar. Set aside in a warm draught-free area for 5 minutes or until the mixture is foamy.
2 Place flour and salt into a food processor, add the olive oil and the yeast mixture with the motor running and process until it forms a rough dough. Turn out onto a lightly floured surface and knead until smooth. Place into a lightly oiled bowl, cover and allow to rest in a warm area for 1 1/2 hours or until doubled in volume. Punch down dough and remove from bowl. Knead and roll out to a 30 cm (12 inch) circle, or four 14 cm (about 5 1/2 inch) circles and place on a non-stick baking tray.
3 Combine sour cream, ricotta and herbs. Spread over base, leaving a 1 cm (1/2 inch) border.
4 Heat oil in a frying pan, add onions and cook for 10 minutes or until onions are caramelised. Cool slightly, spoon over ricotta mixture, top with sliced tomatoes and garlic, olives, lemon thyme and black pepper. Bake 15–30 minutes, depending on size, until base is crisp and golden.

SANTA FE PIZZETTA

Preparation time: 15 minutes
Total cooking time: 15 minutes
Serves 6

☆

6 ready-made small pizza bases
3/4 cup (185 g/6 oz) ready-made spicy
  tomato salsa
4 spring onions, sliced
1 red pepper (capsicum), sliced
440 g (14 oz) canned red kidney beans,
  drained and washed
2 tablespoons chopped fresh basil
1/2 cup (75 g/2 1/2 oz) grated mozzarella cheese
1/4 cup (30 g/1 oz) grated Cheddar cheese
1/2 cup (125 g/4 oz) sour cream
125 g (4 oz) corn chips

Guacamole

1 clove garlic, crushed
1 small red (Spanish) onion, finely chopped
1 large avocado, mashed
1 teaspoon lemon juice
1 tablespoon ready-made tomato salsa
2 tablespoons sour cream

1 Preheat oven to moderately hot 200°C (400°F/Gas 6). Spread the pizza bases with the spicy tomato salsa.
2 Top with spring onions, red pepper, kidney beans and basil.
3 Sprinkle with grated mozzarella and Cheddar cheese. Bake for 15 minutes or until the pizza bases are crisp and the cheese is golden brown. Serve topped with corn chips, guacamole and sour cream.
4 To make Guacamole: Place the garlic, onion, avocado, lemon juice, salsa and sour cream in a bowl and stir to combine.

ITALIAN PIZZAS
Pizza originated in Naples, in southern Italy, where nineteenth-century street vendors vied with each other to attract customers. The classic Neapolitan pizza has a thin crisp crust with a tomato and mozzarella topping. In Rome, pizza is made in large rectangular pans, cut into pieces and sold by weight. Sicily is the home of the thick-crust or pan pizza, rolled thicker than the Neapolitan original and baked in a greased pan.

OPPOSITE PAGE:
Sour Cream Tomato Pizza (top);
Santa Fe Pizzetta

PANCAKES FRITTERS AND OMELETTES

Good all-rounders, these scrumptious savoury

dishes provide a perfect kickstart to a busy

Saturday or a delightful late supper for friends

after the movies. No matter when you serve

your first stack of aromatic herbed potato

pancakes or a tangy chilli frittata, rest assured

you'll get calls for an encore.

MUSHROOMS

Although there are now many types available, field and button mushrooms are still most commonly used. Button mushrooms, and the slightly larger cap mushrooms, are delicately flavoured and best used in fillings and sauces or with pasta. The much more robust flavour of large field mushrooms makes them excellent for grilling or sautéeing, but they should be complemented by other strong tastes such as basil, mustard, red wine, Parmesan cheese, lemon juice or garlic.

ABOVE: Crispy Fried Mushroom Crepes (left); Pepper and Black Olive Pikelets

CRISPY FRIED MUSHROOM CREPES

Preparation time: 25 minutes + 20 minutes standing
Total cooking time: 35 minutes
Makes 12

3/4 cup (90 g/3 oz) plain flour
pinch salt
3 eggs, lightly beaten
3/4 cup (185 ml/6 fl oz) milk
1 tablespoon light olive oil
2 tablespoons finely chopped fresh chives
2 cups (160 g/5 1/4 oz) fresh breadcrumbs
oil, for frying

Mushroom Filling

1 tablespoon olive oil
1 medium onion, finely chopped
400 g (12 2/3 oz) mushrooms, finely chopped
1 tablespoon cream
1/4 teaspoon salt and 1/2 teaspoon pepper
2 tablespoons freshly grated Parmesan cheese

1 Sift the flour and salt into a medium bowl; make a well in the centre. Add the combined eggs and milk gradually. Beat until all the liquid is incorporated and the batter is free of lumps. Add the oil and chives. Set aside, covered with plastic wrap, for 20 minutes. Place 1/3 cup batter in a jug and set aside. Pour 2–3 tablespoons of remaining batter into a lightly greased small crepe pan; swirl evenly over the base. Cook over medium heat for 1 minute, or until the underside is golden. Turn crepe over and cook the other side. Transfer to a plate, cover with a tea towel and keep warm. Repeat the process with the remaining batter, greasing the pan when necessary.

2 To make Mushroom Filling: Heat the oil in a frying pan and cook the onion over medium heat until soft. Add the mushrooms and cook for 2–3 minutes. Stir in the cream, salt, pepper and cheese; cool.

3 Place crepes, one at a time, on a plate. Place 1 tablespoonful of mushroom mixture on one half of each crepe, spreading evenly and leaving a 1 cm (1/2 inch) border. Brush the edges of the crepe lightly with some reserved batter. Fold the uncovered half of the crepe over top of mushroom mixture. Repeat the process until all the crepes are filled. Spread a little reserved batter over each crepe with a pastry brush and sprinkle with breadcrumbs. Brush the top with more batter, mixing it with the breadcrumbs.

4 Cover the base of a large frying pan with the oil and heat. Add filled crepes and cook until golden on one side, then turn and cook the other side. Transfer to paper towels to drain.

NOTE: For best results, use stale bread to make the breadcrumbs for this recipe. Serve the crepes plain or with a tomato sauce, or a ready-made Italian pasta sauce.

PEPPER (CAPSICUM) AND BLACK OLIVE PIKELETS

Preparation time: 15 minutes
    + 20 minutes standing
Total cooking time: 15 minutes
Makes 16

2 medium red peppers (capsicums)
1/2 cup (125 ml/4 fl oz) milk
1/2 cup (60 g/2 oz) self-raising flour
1/2 teaspoon salt
1/4 teaspoon black pepper
3 eggs, lightly beaten
2 tablespoons finely chopped black olives
1 tablespoon finely chopped basil
olive oil, for frying

1 Cut each red pepper in half, remove the seeds and flatten the halves. Cook under a preheated grill, skin-side up, for 10 minutes or until the skin blisters and turns black. Cover with a damp tea towel, set aside and allow to cool. Remove the skin and chop the flesh roughly.

2 Process the cooked red pepper with the milk in a food processor or blender.

3 Sift the flour with salt into a bowl. Add the black pepper and make a well in the centre. Add the eggs, and the red pepper and milk mixture. Stir until all the ingredients are combined and the mixture is free of lumps. Stir in the olives and basil. Set aside, covered with plastic wrap, for 20 minutes.

4 Brush the base of a small frying pan with oil. When the oil is hot, pour 1–2 tablespoons of batter into the pan and cook over medium-high heat until the underside is golden. Turn over and cook the other side. Repeat the process with the remaining mixture. Serve with goats cheese and a sprinkling of fresh herbs.

HERBED POTATO PANCAKES

Preparation time: 10 minutes
Total cooking time: 12 minutes
Makes 10–12 pancakes

2 tablespoons chopped fresh chives
2 tablespoons chopped fresh tarragon
    or parsley
salt and black pepper
3 medium potatoes (600 g/1 1/4 lb), peeled
60 g (2 oz) unsalted butter
2 tablespoons olive oil

1 Mix the chives, tarragon or parsley, and salt and pepper in a bowl. Coarsely grate the potatoes and squeeze out excess moisture. Add to the herb mixture and combine well.

2 Heat half the butter and oil in a large non-stick frying pan over medium heat, until it starts to foam. Cook heaped tablespoonsful of the potato and herb mixture for 2 minutes. Turn and cook for approximately 2–3 minutes, or until golden. Drain on paper towels; keep warm. Add remaining butter and oil to pan. Repeat process using all the mixture.

NOTE: Pancakes may be kept for up to 1/2 hour, loosely covered with foil, in a very slow 120°C (250°F/Gas 1–2) oven. As a variation, parsnip or carrot may be substituted for one of the potatoes. Use dill instead of the tarragon or parsley, if you prefer.

TARRAGON
French tarragon (*Artemisia dracunculus*) is the best type to buy and grow. Tarragon's subtle flavour works well in omelettes or with potatoes, but its most famous marriage is with chicken. Tarragon vinegar can also be used as a salad dressing. Do not confuse Russian tarragon (*Artemisia dracunculoides*) with the French variety—it looks very similar but is, in fact, virtually tasteless.

LEFT: Herbed Potato Pancakes

MEXICAN POLENTA (CORNMEAL) PANCAKES WITH AVOCADO

Preparation time: 30 minutes
  + 20 minutes refrigeration
Total cooking time: 20 minutes
Serves 4-6

1/3 cup (50 g/1 2/3 oz) yellow polenta (cornmeal)
1/2 cup (60 g/2 oz) plain flour
1/4 teaspoon baking powder
1/4 teaspoon salt
1 teaspoon sugar
1 cup (250 ml/8 fl oz) buttermilk
2 eggs
30 g (1 oz) butter, melted
vegetable oil
2/3 cup (160 g/5 1/4 oz) sour cream, for serving

Avocado Filling

1 large ripe avocado
8 spring onions, finely chopped
2 ripe tomatoes, seeded and finely chopped
1 teaspoon chilli sauce, or to taste
2 teaspoons lemon juice
1/4–1/2 teaspoon salt
pepper

1 Sift polenta, flour, baking powder, salt and sugar into a bowl. Make a well in the centre. Place buttermilk, eggs and butter in a jug; beat to combine. Add to dry ingredients. Beat until liquid is incorporated and batter is free of lumps. Set aside, covered with plastic wrap, 20 minutes.
2 To make Avocado Filling: Cut the avocado in half lengthways, remove the seed and place the flesh in a bowl. Mash the avocado flesh with a fork. Add half the spring onions. Stir in the tomatoes, chilli sauce, lemon juice, salt and pepper. Mix well and chill for 20 minutes.
3 Brush a small frying pan with oil. When hot, pour in enough batter to thinly cover base of pan. Cook over medium heat until the underside is golden. Turn pancake over and cook the other side. Transfer to a plate; cover with a tea towel and keep warm. Repeat the process with remaining batter, greasing the pan when necessary. Spoon some avocado filling on one half of each pancake and fold the other half over. Serve with sour cream sprinkled with remaining spring onion.

POTATO AND PUMPKIN PANCAKES

Preparation time: 25 minutes
Total cooking time: 25 minutes
Makes 10

250 g (8 oz) potato, cooked and mashed
250 g (8 oz) pumpkin, cooked and mashed
30 g (1 oz) butter
3 spring onions, finely chopped
2 eggs, lightly beaten
1/4 cup (30 g/1 oz) plain flour
2 tablespoons self-raising flour
1/4 teaspoon ground nutmeg
pinch cayenne pepper
1/4 teaspoon salt
30 g (1 oz) butter, extra

1 Place the potato and pumpkin in a food processor and add the butter. Process until smooth. Transfer to a bowl and add the spring onions and eggs.
2 Sift flours, spices and salt into a bowl. Add to the pumpkin mixture and stir well to combine.
3 Heat extra butter in a non-stick frying pan. Cook heaped tablespoons of mixture for 2 minutes. Turn and cook approximately 2–3 minutes or until golden. Drain on paper towels.
4 Repeat process with the remaining mixture. Keep warm in the oven. Serve plain, or with yoghurt or butter.

FAST THAI CORN PANCAKES

PLACE THE KERNELS of 2 fresh cobs of corn in a bowl. Add 2 finely chopped spring onions, 2 tablespoons of finely chopped coriander stems, 2 cloves of crushed garlic, 2 teaspoons of drained and crushed, canned green peppercorns, 2 tablespoons of cornflour, 2 beaten eggs, 1 tablespoon of fish sauce (optional) and 2 teaspoons of soft brown sugar. Beat with a wooden spoon until all the ingredients are well combined. Heat a little oil in a heavy-based frying pan until moderately hot. Spoon tablespoonsful of the pancake mixture into the pan. Cook in batches until the pancakes are golden on both sides and drain on paper towels. Serve immediately. Serves 4–6.

POLENTA

Polenta, also known as cornmeal, is made from ground dried corn and is bright yellow in colour. Polenta also refers to the dish made from cornmeal. This is a thick, porridge-like mixture usually left to set and then brushed with oil and fried or grilled.

*OPPOSITE PAGE:
Mexican Polenta
Pancakes with Avocado
(top); Potato and
Pumpkin Pancakes*

CORN FRITTERS

Preparation time: 20 minutes
Total cooking time: 20 minutes
Serves 4-6

1¼ cups (155 g/5 oz) plain flour
1½ teaspoons baking powder
½ teaspoon ground coriander
¼ teaspoon ground cumin
130 g (4¼ oz) canned corn kernels, well-drained
130 g (4¼ oz) canned creamed-style corn
½ cup (125 ml/4 fl oz) milk
2 eggs, lightly beaten
2 tablespoons chopped fresh chives
salt and pepper
½ cup (125 ml/4 fl oz) olive oil

Dipping Sauce

1 tablespoon brown vinegar
3 teaspoons soft brown sugar
1 teaspoon sambal oelek or chilli sauce
1 tablespoon chopped fresh chives
½ teaspoon soy sauce

1 Sift the flour, baking powder, coriander and cumin into a bowl; make a well in the centre. Add the corn kernels, creamed corn, milk, eggs, chives, salt and pepper. Stir until combined.
2 Heat the oil in a large non-stick pan. Lower heaped tablespoonsful of the mixture into the pan about 2 cm (¾ inch) apart, flatten slightly.

BELOW: Corn Fritters

Cook over medium-high heat 2 minutes or until underside is golden. Turn over, cook other side. Remove and drain on paper towels; repeat with the remaining mixture. Serve with dipping sauce.
3 To make Dipping Sauce: Heat vinegar, sugar, sambal oelek, chives and soy in small pan for 1–2 minutes until sugar is dissolved.

VEGETABLE FRITTERS WITH TOMATO SAUCE

Preparation time: 30 minutes
Total cooking time: 30 minutes
Serves 4

2 medium potatoes, peeled
1 medium carrot, peeled
2 medium zucchinis (courgettes)
125 g (4 oz) sweet potato, peeled
1 small leek
2 tablespoons plain flour
3 eggs, lightly beaten
oil, for frying

Fresh Tomato Sauce

1 tablespoon oil
1 small onion, finely chopped
1 clove garlic, crushed
½ teaspoon ground paprika
3 ripe medium tomatoes, peeled and finely chopped
3 tablespoons finely shredded fresh basil

1 Finely grate the potatoes, carrot, zucchinis and sweet potato. Finely slice the leek (white part only). Cup small handfuls of grated vegetables in both hands and squeeze out as much moisture as possible. Combine in large bowl with sliced leek.
2 Sprinkle flour over vegetables and combine. Add eggs, mix well. Heat about 5 mm (¼ inch) of oil in a frying pan and lower in ¼ cup of mixture in a neat pile. Use a fork to gently form mixture into a 10 cm (4 inch) round. Fry 2–3 at a time for 3 minutes each side over medium heat until golden and crispy. Drain on paper towels; keep warm. Repeat with remaining mixture.
3 To make Tomato Sauce: Heat oil in pan. Add onion, garlic and paprika, cook over medium heat 3 minutes or until soft. Add tomatoes, reduce heat to low and cook 10 minutes, stirring occasionally. Stir in basil. Serve warm.

FRIED GREEN TOMATOES

Preparation time: 15 minutes
Total cooking time: 12 minutes
Serves 4-6

3/4 cup (90 g/3 oz) plain flour
1 teaspoon salt
1/2 teaspoon white pepper
1/4 cup (35 g/1 1/4 oz) polenta (cornmeal)
1 egg
3/4 cup (185 ml/6 fl oz) milk
4 medium green tomatoes (about 500 g/1 lb)
oil, for frying

1 Sift the flour, salt and pepper into a medium bowl. Add the polenta and stir to combine. Make a well in the centre.
2 Combine the egg and milk and add gradually to flour mixture. Whisk the batter until just combined, but do not over-beat.
3 Cut the tomatoes into thick slices. Heat about 1 cm (1/2 inch) of oil in a frying pan.
4 Dip the tomatoes into the batter; drain excess and fry for 1 minute on each side, turning only once with tongs. Drain on paper towels and serve immediately.
NOTE: Red tomatoes can be also be used.

POTATO AND HERB FRITTERS

Preparation time: 25 minutes
Total cooking time: 8 minutes
Serves 4-6

4 cups (620 g/1 lb 4 2/3 oz) finely grated peeled potato
1 1/2 cups (185 g/6 oz) peeled, finely grated orange sweet potato (kumera)
3 tablespoons finely chopped fresh chives
1 tablespoon finely chopped fresh oregano
2 tablespoons finely chopped fresh parsley
2 eggs, lightly beaten
1/4 cup (30 g/1 oz) plain flour
1 tablespoon olive oil
1 cup (250 g/8 oz) light sour cream
fresh dill sprigs, for garnish

1 Combine potato, sweet potato, chives, oregano, parsley, eggs and sifted flour in a bowl. Stir with a wooden spoon until ingredients are just combined.
2 Heat oil in heavy-based pan. Spoon heaped tablespoonsful of mixture into pan. Cook over medium-high heat 4 minutes each side, or until golden. Serve warm, topped with sour cream and sprigs of dill.

GREEN TOMATOES
Green tomatoes are not a separate variety but are simply unripe red tomatoes. They became popular in the Depression years in the Deep South of the United States as a tasty, light summer meal. It is easy to confuse green tomatoes with Tomatillos: these are small green fruit which *do* resemble the tomato. As well as fried, green tomatoes are also excellent pickled and made into a spicy sauce.

ABOVE: Fried Green Tomatoes

VEGETABLE CHIPS

Paper-thin or saw-toothed and chunky, chips are loved by everyone—and they don't

have to be made from potatoes, as these clever and surprising suggestions prove.

BEETROOT CHIPS
Using a sharp vegetable peeler or a knife, cut 500 g (1 lb) of peeled beetroot into paper-thin slices. Heat 3 cups (750 ml/24 fl oz) of oil in a pan and cook the beetroot chips in hot oil, in batches, until they are crisp and browned. Drain on paper towels and keep warm in a preheated moderate 180°C (350°F/Gas 4)

oven while cooking the remainder. Serve beetroot chips with a blend of whole egg mayonnaise and chopped fresh herbs of your choice.

CRISPY SWEET POTATO (KUMERA) DISCS
Peel 500 g (1 lb) of orange sweet potato (kumera) and cut into thin slices using a

sharp vegetable peeler or a knife. Heat 3 cups (750 ml/24 fl oz) of oil in a pan and cook the sweet potato discs in batches until crisp and golden. Drain on paper towels and keep warm in a preheated moderate 180°C (350°F/Gas 4) oven while cooking remainder. Serve with a mixture of mayonnaise, lime juice and curry powder.

ZUCCHINI (COURGETTE) RIBBONS

Using a sharp vegetable peeler, cut 500 g (1 lb) of large zucchinis (courgettes) into ribbons by running the peeler horizontally along the zucchinis. Dip the zucchini ribbons into a bowl of 4 lightly beaten eggs, then dip into a mixture of 1 cup (100 g/3$\frac{1}{3}$ oz) of dried breadcrumbs and 1 tablespoon of chopped fresh herbs. Cook the crumbed zucchini ribbons in batches in 3 cups (750 ml/24 fl oz) of hot oil until the ribbons are golden. Drain on paper towels and keep warm in a preheated moderate 180°C (350°F/ Gas 4) oven while cooking the remaining zucchini ribbons. Zucchini ribbons are delicious served with a dipping sauce made from chopped sun-dried tomatoes and natural yoghurt.

GOLDEN POTATO CHIPS

Cut 500 g (1 lb) washed old potatoes into thick country-style chips (wedges). Heat 3 cups (750 ml/24 fl oz) of oil in a pan and cook potatoes in batches until lightly golden; drain on paper towels. Repeat with remaining potatoes. Just before serving, re-fry the potatoes in batches until crisp and golden. Sprinkle with sea salt and malt vinegar, if desired.

PUMPKIN CRISPS

Peel 500 g (1 lb) butternut pumpkin and cut into crinkle-cut slices. Heat 3 cups (750 ml/24 fl oz) of oil in a pan and cook slices in batches until they are crisp and golden. Drain on paper towels and keep warm in a preheated moderate 180°C (350°F/Gas 4) oven while cooking the remaining pumpkin chips.

CARROT AND HERB RIBBONS

Peel 500 g (1 lb) carrots into ribbons by running a sharp peeler horizontally along the length of the carrot. Rinse and dry 1 cup (50 g/1$\frac{2}{3}$ oz) of large basil leaves. Heat 3 cups (750 ml/24 fl oz) of oil in a pan and cook carrot ribbons and basil leaves in batches until crisp. Drain on paper towels and keep warm in a preheated moderate 180°C (350°F/ Gas 4) oven while cooking remaining carrot and basil. Serve with a dipping sauce of sweet chilli sauce, lime juice and chopped fresh coriander.

CLOCKWISE, FROM TOP LEFT:
Golden Potato Chips; Zucchini Ribbons;
Beetroot Chips; Pumpkin Crisps;
Carrot and Herb Ribbons; Crispy
Sweet Potato Discs

FRITTATA

Freshly made, hot Frittata makes a great brunch or lunch dish, but it is also ideal picnic food. Frittata transports easily and can be eaten with a fork or fingers. Make it a day in advance and refrigerate until required—let it come to room temperature before serving.

LEEK, ZUCCHINI (COURGETTE) AND CHEESE FRITTATA

Preparation time: 20 minutes
Total cooking time: 40 minutes
Serves 4

2 tablespoons olive oil

3 leeks, thinly sliced

2 medium zucchinis (courgettes), cut into matchstick pieces

1 clove garlic, crushed

salt and pepper

5 eggs, lightly beaten

4 tablespoons freshly grated Parmesan cheese

4 tablespoons Swiss cheese, cut into small cubes

1 Heat 1 tablespoon olive oil in small pan; add the leeks and cook, stirring, over low heat until slightly softened. Cover and cook the leeks for 10 minutes. Add the zucchinis and garlic; cook for another 10 minutes. Transfer to a bowl. Allow to cool; add salt, pepper, egg and cheeses.

2 Heat remaining oil in pan; add egg mixture and smooth surface. Cook over low heat for 15 minutes or until the frittata is almost set.

3 Cook under a preheated hot grill for 3–5 minutes or until the top is set and golden. Allow the frittata to stand for 5 minutes before cutting into wedges for serving. Serve with a fresh green salad for lunch or a light meal.

FAST POTATO FRITTERS AND LIME CHILLI SAUCE

PEEL AND GRATE 4 large potatoes into a colander. Rinse well under cold water and pat dry on paper towels, squeezing out all excess moisture. Put in a bowl with 3 finely chopped spring onions, 2 cloves crushed garlic, 3 tablespoons finely chopped coriander, 2 lightly beaten eggs and 1/3 cup (40 g/1 1/3 oz) plain flour. Mix well and season with salt and pepper, to taste. Heat about 2 tablespoons each olive oil and butter in a frying pan. Drop 3 tablespoons of mixture into pan and flatten well. Cook in batches over medium heat for 3–4 minutes each side, until golden. Drain on paper towels. Serve topped with mascarpone. Combine a little sweet chilli sauce, fresh lime juice and finely grated rind and a pinch of soft brown sugar and drizzle over fritters. Serves 4.

ABOVE: Leek, Zucchini and Cheese Frittata

MIXED GRATED VEGETABLE FRITTATA

Preparation time: 25 minutes
Total cooking time: 18 minutes
Serves 2–4

1/4 cup (60 ml/2 fl oz) olive oil
1 onion, finely chopped
1 small carrot, grated
1 small zucchini (courgette), grated
1 cup (125 g/4 oz) grated pumpkin
4 tablespoons finely diced Jarlsburg
  or Cheddar cheese
1/2 teaspoon salt
1/2 teaspoon ground black pepper
5 eggs

1 Heat 2 tablespoons of the oil in a frying pan, add the onion and cook gently for 5 minutes or until onion is soft. Add the carrot, zucchini and pumpkin; cover the pan and cook over low heat for 3 minutes.
2 Transfer to a bowl and cool. Stir in cheese, salt and pepper. Beat eggs and add to the vegetables.
3 Heat the remaining oil in a small frying pan. When the oil is hot, add the egg mixture to the pan and shake the pan to spread the mixture evenly over the base. Reduce heat to low and cook for 3 minutes or until mixture is set almost all the way through. Tilt pan and lift the edges of frittata occasionally during cooking to allow uncooked egg to flow underneath. Cut frittata into wedges and serve immediately.

CHILLI AND CORIANDER FRITTATA

Preparation time: 25 minutes
Total cooking time: 30 minutes
Serves 6

3 medium potatoes, peeled and cut into
  small cubes
2 medium banana chillies
2 tablespoons olive oil
1 medium onion, finely chopped
1 small red chilli, finely chopped
1 tablespoon coriander leaves
5 eggs, lightly beaten

1 Cook potatoes in a large pan of boiling water until just tender; drain well. Remove seeds from banana chillies and slice the flesh. Heat half the oil in a non-stick frying pan. Cook the banana chillies over medium heat for 2 minutes or until softened. Remove from pan and set aside. Heat the remaining oil in pan. Add the onion and small red chilli and cook over medium heat for 3 minutes or until soft.
2 Add the potato and toss to combine. Remove from pan and set aside. Return half the banana chillies to the pan and sprinkle with coriander leaves. Layer half the potato mixture, remaining banana chillies, and remaining potato mixture.
3 Pour the eggs into the pan, swirling to distribute evenly. Cook over medium-low heat for 8 minutes until the eggs are almost cooked through, then place under a hot grill for 5 minutes to cook the top. Invert the frittata onto a plate and cut into wedges. Serve hot or cold, garnished with fresh herbs.

ABOVE: Chilli and Coriander Frittata

EGGS

A lot of vegetarians eat eggs and dairy foods, and can obtain a signifcant amount of calcium and protein by doing so. Free-range eggs are produced in an environment where the hens are allowed to move about and feed naturally, rather than be confined in batteries. These eggs are therefore preferable for people with health and humanitarian concerns.

ABOVE: Creamy Omelette (left); Omelette Rolls

CREAMY OMELETTE

Preparation time: 5 minutes
Total cooking time: 5 minutes
Serves 2

3 eggs
1/4 cup (60 ml/2 fl oz) cream
salt and pepper
20 g (2/3 oz) butter

1 Place the eggs, cream, salt and pepper in a medium bowl. Beat with a wire whisk for 2 minutes.
2 Heat the butter in a small non-stick pan over medium heat. When the butter is foaming, add mixture to the pan all at once. Stir with a wooden spoon for 15 seconds.
3 Cook until the mixture is almost set, tilting the pan and lifting the edges of the omelette occasionally to allow the uncooked egg to flow underneath. When the mixture has almost set, fold the omelette in half using an egg slice or a flat-bladed knife. The centre of the omelette should be moist and creamy. Alternatively, instead of folding the omelette, complete the cooking process by covering the pan with a lid for about 2 minutes. Sprinkle with fresh herbs and serve with sliced avocado, if desired.

OMELETTE ROLLS

Preparation time: 15 minutes
Total cooking time: 10 minutes
Makes 5

4 eggs
2 tablespoons water
2 teaspoons soy sauce
2 teaspoons peanut oil

1 Place the eggs, water and sauce in a medium bowl. Beat with a wire whisk for 2 minutes.
2 Brush the base of a small non-stick pan with oil. Heat pan on high. Pour one-fifth of the egg mixture into the base of the pan. Shake pan to spread mixture evenly over the base. Heat for 20 seconds, or until the egg has almost set. Remove pan from heat. Using an egg slice or a large flat-bladed knife, roll the omelette from one end, forming a roll. Transfer to a warm plate and cover with a tea towel.
3 Repeat the process with the remaining egg mixture, using one-fifth of the egg mixture to make each omelette.
NOTE: For extra flavour, before rolling spread the omelettes with a pesto or olive paste, or other filling of your choice. Roll up tightly and cut into rounds for serving.

OMELETTES
Omelettes come in many shapes and forms, and each country has its own traditional variety. The French make their folded omelettes to incorporate many diffent fillings, both sweet and savoury. The Italians have frittata, a more substantial dish which is cooked on both sides and cut into wedges to serve. Spanish omelette, which is called tortilla in Spain, is similar to frittata, but is always made from potatoes set with eggs.

CHEESE SOUFFLE OMELETTE

Preparation time: 10 minutes
Total cooking time: 5 minutes
Serves 2–4

5 eggs, separated
2 teaspoons water
2 teaspoons lemon juice
salt and pepper
20 g (²/₃ oz) butter
²/₃ cup (85 g/2³/₄ oz) coarsely grated
   Cheddar cheese

1 Place the egg yolks, water, juice, salt and pepper in a small bowl. Using electric beaters, beat on high for 2 minutes or until the mixture is pale and creamy.
2 Place the egg whites in a small, dry, bowl. Using electric beaters or a wire whisk, beat the egg whites until firm peaks form. Using a metal spoon, gently fold the egg whites into the yolk mixture. Preheat the grill to high.
3 Place the butter in a deep, non-stick pan and heat over high heat. When the butter is foaming, add the omelette mixture and swirl the pan to spread evenly over the base. Cook over high heat for 1 minute without stirring. Remove from heat and sprinkle with cheese.
4 Place under a hot grill for 2–3 minutes, or until the omelette is puffed and golden. Cut the omelette into serving portions and serve immediately as it may deflate quickly. Sprinkle with chopped fresh herbs, if desired.
NOTE: This is delicious accompanied by grilled or pan-fried mushrooms, or tomatoes which have been halved, sprinkled with cheese and then grilled.

ABOVE: Cheese Soufflé Omelette

3 Heat a lightly oiled small frying pan. Pour in sufficient egg mixture to cover the base. Cook for a few seconds and then tip onto a plate. Brush the pan with more oil and repeat the process to make 3 thin omelettes.

4 Place the omelettes on top of each other and roll into a cylinder shape. Using a sharp knife, cut into fine strips.

5 Reheat the sauce. Add the egg strips and warm gently, stirring until covered with tomato. If desired, serve with extra fresh shredded basil and cracked pepper.

NOTE: Serve omelette strips accompanied by a salad or as a side dish with roast chicken. They can also be used in soups, added to stir-fries or served over salads.

CREAMY ZUCCHINI (COURGETTE) OMELETTE

Preparation time: 5–10 minutes
Total cooking time: 12 minutes
Serves 2

2 medium zucchinis (courgettes)
2 tablespoons olive oil
60 g (2 oz) butter
1 clove garlic, finely chopped
5 eggs
2 tablespoons cream
1/2 teaspoon salt
1/4 teaspoon pepper
2 tablespoons freshly grated
    Parmesan cheese

OMELETTE STRIPS IN FRESH TOMATO SAUCE

Preparation time: 25 minutes
Total cooking time: 12 minutes
Serves 2

Tomato Sauce

3 ripe tomatoes, peeled and roughly
    chopped
1/2 teaspoon salt
1/2 teaspoon pepper
1 teaspoon sugar
2 tablespoons shredded fresh basil

4 eggs
2 teaspoons soy sauce
1/4 teaspoon white pepper
1 tablespoon water
light olive oil

1 To make Tomato Sauce: Cook the tomatoes in a small pan with salt, pepper and sugar for 5 minutes or until the liquid has reduced and thickened. Add the basil.

2 Using a wire whisk, beat the eggs in a medium mixing bowl with the soy sauce, pepper and water.

ABOVE: Omelette Strips in Fresh Tomato Sauce RIGHT: Creamy Zucchini Omelette

1 Slice the ends from the zucchinis and cut horizontally into very thin slices. Place half the oil and half the butter in a frying pan and heat until the butter melts. Add the zucchini and cook, stirring, for 2–3 minutes or until the zucchini is golden. Sprinkle chopped garlic on top and mix gently. Cook for another 30 seconds. Using a slotted spoon, lift onto a plate. Wipe out the pan with a paper towel.

2 Beat the eggs with the cream, salt and pepper. Reheat the pan, add the remaining oil and butter and, when very hot, add the eggs. Stir the eggs with the back of a fork. Cook the mixture for 1 minute, tilting the pan and lifting the omelette edges occasionally to allow the uncooked egg to flow underneath.

3 When the mixture is partly set, spread the zucchini evenly over the top, covering the egg mixture. Reduce heat and cook for 5 minutes, or until set around the edges. Remove from heat and sprinkle grated Parmesan cheese over the top. Cover with a lid and leave the omelette to rest in the pan for 2 minutes. Slide onto a plate and cut into wedges. Serve with a salad.

NOTE: Buy Parmesan cheese in block form and grate it yourself for a fresher taste.

SPANISH OMELETTE

Preparation time: 20 minutes
Total cooking time: 40 minutes
Serves 4-6

1 kg (2 lb) potatoes, peeled
salt
2 large red (Spanish) onions
50 g (1²/₃ oz) butter
2 tablespoons olive oil
1 clove garlic, crushed
2 tablespoons finely chopped fresh parsley
4 eggs, lightly beaten

1 Cut the peeled potatoes into small cubes and place in a large pan with the salt; cover with water. Bring to the boil and cook, uncovered, for 3 minutes. Remove the pan from the heat and allow to stand, covered, for 8 minutes or until the potato is just tender; drain well.

2 Chop the onions coarsely. Heat the butter and oil in a deep, non-stick frying pan over medium heat. Add the onions and garlic and cook for 8 minutes, stirring occasionally. Add the potato and cook for another 5 minutes. Remove the vegetables with a slotted spoon and transfer them to a large bowl. Add the chopped parsley and beaten eggs to the potato and onion and mix until well combined.

3 Pour the mixture into the hot oiled frying pan, reduce the heat to low and cook, covered, for 10 minutes, or until the underside is golden. Brown the top of the omelette under a hot grill, if desired.

NOTE: Spanish omelette is delicious served with olives, lettuce and slices of red onion, and garnished with sprigs of fresh herbs.

FAST HERBED MUSHROOM OMELETTE

HEAT ABOUT 20 g (²/₃ oz) butter in a medium non-stick frying pan. Add 6 thinly sliced mushrooms. Stir over medium heat until softened and golden. Whisk together 1 clove crushed garlic, 2 eggs, 1 tablespoon milk and a little freshly grated Parmesan cheese. Pour over the mushrooms and sprinkle with 3–4 tablespoons finely chopped fresh basil and chives. Season with salt and pepper and cook for about 4 minutes or until omelette has almost set. Place under a preheated grill to complete the cooking. Serve immediately. Top with a dollop of sour cream if you wish. Serves 1.

RED (SPANISH) ONIONS
Red onions are generally less strongly flavoured than white or brown, which makes them ideal to use raw in salads. Cooking, unfortunately, robs them of their vibrant colour. Cut or chopped onion of any variety soon takes on an unpleasant smell—if you need to chop onion ahead of time, fry it in butter and store in the refrigerator.

ABOVE: Spanish Omelette

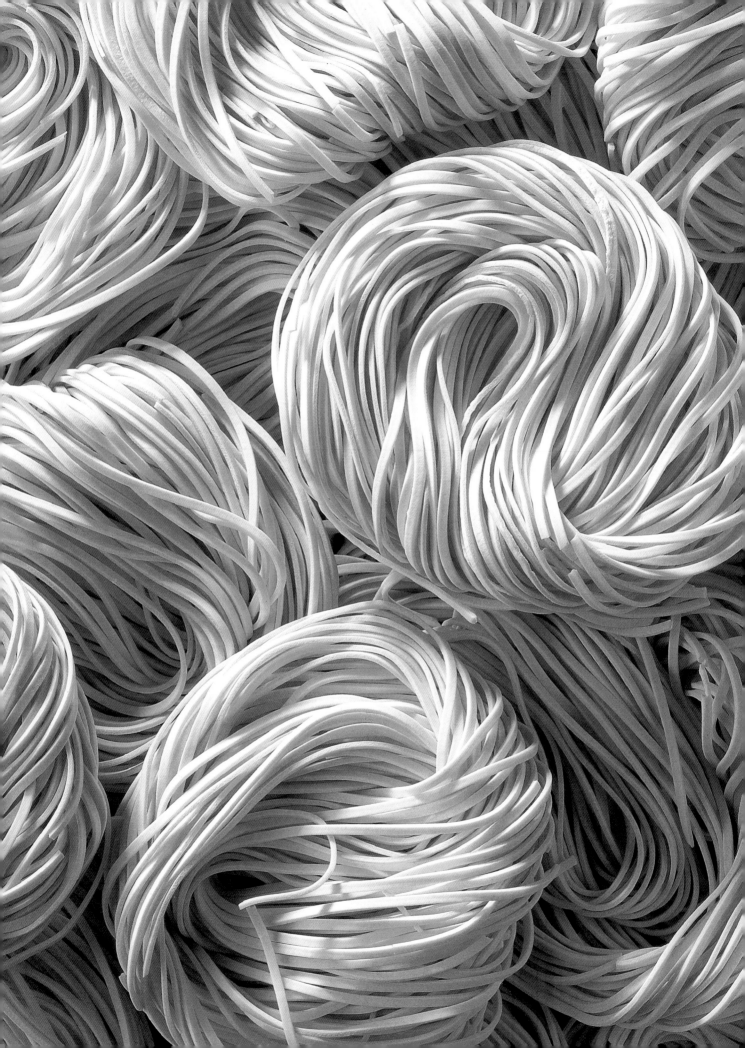

PASTA AND NOODLES

The Italians have been enjoying spaghetti and macaroni since the days of ancient Rome, but it's only in the past decade or so that all manner of pasta have found their way into our kitchens, each one able to assume a dozen or more tantalising guises when sauced and presented. From spicy oriental noodles to the splendidly simple spaghetti tossed with rocket, here is an introduction to the countless possibilities of pasta.

RAVIOLI

For a light texture, the dough for ravioli should be rolled as thinly as possible, but it also needs to be thick enough to remain intact during handling and cooking. Knowledge of the most manageable thickness will come naturally after making it once or twice.

ABOVE: Pumpkin and Herb Ravioli

PUMPKIN AND HERB RAVIOLI

Preparation time: 50 minutes
+ 30 minutes resting
Total cooking time: 1 hour 15 minutes
Serves 6

★ ☆

500 g (1 lb) pumpkin, peeled and cut into chunks
1¾ cups (220 g/7 oz) plain flour
3 eggs, lightly beaten
¼ teaspoon ground nutmeg
15 sage leaves
15 fresh flat-leaf parsley leaves
salt and pepper
125 g (4 oz) butter, melted
60 g (2 oz) freshly grated Parmesan cheese

1 Preheat the oven to moderate 180°C (350°F/Gas 4). Place the pumpkin on an oiled baking tray and bake for 1 hour or until tender; cool. Remove the skin. Place the flour and eggs in a food processor. Process for 30 seconds or until the mixture forms a dough. Transfer to a lightly floured surface and knead for 3 minutes or until the dough is very smooth and elastic.

Cover with a clean cloth and set aside for 30 minutes.

2 Place the pumpkin in a bowl with the nutmeg and mash with a fork. Roll out half the dough to form a rectangle about 2 mm (⅛ inch) thick. Roll out the remaining half to form a rectangle slightly larger than the first.

3 On the first rectangle of dough, place heaped teaspoonsful of the pumpkin mixture in straight rows, at intervals about 5 cm (2 inches) apart. Flatten each pumpkin mound slightly; place one whole sage or parsley leaf on top of each spoonful of pumpkin mixture.

4 Brush lightly between the mounds of filling with water. Place the second sheet of dough on top and then press down gently between the pumpkin mounds to seal. Cut into squares with a knife or a fluted cutter. Bring a large pan of water to the boil and drop in the ravioli a few at a time. Cook for 4 minutes, or until just tender. Drain well. Serve the ravioli sprinkled with salt and pepper and tossed with melted butter and Parmesan cheese.

NOTE: Ravioli can be made several hours in advance. Refrigerate in layers between sheets of greaseproof paper to prevent them sticking together. Cook just before serving.

TAGLIATELLE WITH GREEN OLIVES AND EGGPLANT (AUBERGINE)

Preparation time: 20 minutes
Total cooking time: 20 minutes
Serves 4

500 g (1 lb) tagliatelle or fettucine
1 cup (175 g/5²/₃ oz) green olives
1 large eggplant (aubergine)
2 tablespoons olive oil
2 cloves garlic, crushed
¹/₂ cup (125 ml/4 fl oz) lemon juice
salt and pepper
2 tablespoons chopped fresh parsley
¹/₂ cup (50 g/1²/₃ oz) freshly grated
   Parmesan cheese

1 Add pasta to a large pan of rapidly boiling water and cook until just tender. Drain and return to pan. While pasta is cooking, chop the olives, removing the stones, and cut the eggplant into small cubes.
2 Heat the oil in a heavy-based frying pan. Add the garlic and stir for 30 seconds. Add the eggplant and cook over medium heat, stirring frequently, for 6 minutes or until tender.
3 Add the olives, lemon juice and salt and pepper to the pan. Add the sauce to the pasta and toss. Serve in warmed pasta bowls, sprinkled with parsley and Parmesan cheese.
NOTE: If you prefer, the eggplant can be salted to draw out any bitter juices. Sprinkle the cut eggplant liberally with salt and leave to stand for 30 minutes. Rinse well before using.

FETTUCINE WITH ZUCCHINI (COURGETTE)

Preparation time: 20 minutes
Total cooking time: 15 minutes
Serves 4-6

500 g (1 lb) fettucine
60 g (2 oz) butter
2 cloves garlic, crushed
500 g (1 lb) zucchinis (courgettes), grated
³/₄ cup (75 g/2¹/₂ oz) freshly grated
   Parmesan cheese
1 cup (250 ml/8 fl oz) olive oil
16 medium-sized basil leaves

1 Cook the pasta in a large pan of rapidly boiling water until just tender. Drain and return to pan. While pasta is cooking, heat butter in a deep, heavy-based pan over low heat until the butter is foaming. Add garlic and cook for 1 minute. Add the zucchinis and cook, stirring occasionally, for 1–2 minutes or until softened.
2 Add the zucchini sauce and Parmesan cheese to the pasta and toss well.
3 To make basil leaves crisp, heat oil in a small pan, add 2 leaves at a time and cook 1 minute or until crisp. Remove with a slotted spoon; drain on paper towels. Repeat with remaining basil leaves. Divide pasta between warmed serving bowls, garnish with basil leaves. Serve.

RIBBON NOODLES
Ribbon or flat noodles come in various widths. Tagliatelle and fettucine are fairly similar and can be interchanged in recipes. Tagliatelle is traditionally the wider of the two. Pappardelle is wider still, while tagliolini is the narrowest.

LEFT: Tagliatelle with Green Olives and Eggplant
ABOVE: Fettucine with Zucchini

RICOTTA

Ricotta is an unripened Italian cheese made from the whey left over when full-fat cheeses are made. The albumen in the whey coagulates on heating. Ricotta has a delicate, smooth flavour and is very suitable for cooking with pasta. It can be sweetened with sugar and is often used in fruit tarts or puddings. Ricotta has just the right moisture content to make it perfect in cooked cheesecakes.

ABOVE: Pasta with Ricotta, Chilli and Herbs

PASTA WITH RICOTTA, CHILLI AND HERBS

Preparation time: 25 minutes
Total cooking time: 25 minutes
Serves 4

500 g (1 lb) spiral pasta or penne
1/4 cup (60 ml/2 fl oz) olive oil
3 cloves garlic, crushed
2 teaspoons very finely chopped fresh red chilli
1 cup (20 g/2/3 oz) fresh flat-leaf parsley leaves, roughly chopped
1/2 cup (25 g/3/4 oz) fresh basil leaves, shredded
1/2 cup (15 g/1/2 oz) fresh oregano leaves, roughly chopped
salt and pepper
200 g (6 1/2 oz) fresh ricotta cheese, cut into small cubes

1 Add the pasta to a large pan of rapidly boiling water; cook until just tender. Drain, return to pan. When pasta is almost cooked, heat oil in a non-stick heavy-based frying pan. Add garlic and chillies to pan and stir for 1 minute over low heat.
2 Add the oil mixture, parsley, basil, oregano, salt and pepper to the pasta. Toss well until the mixture coats the pasta thoroughly. Gently fold in the ricotta cubes and serve immediately.

FETTUCINE ALFREDO

Preparation time: 10 minutes
Total cooking time: 15 minutes
Serves 4-6

500 g (1 lb) fettucine
100 g (3 1/3 oz) butter
1 1/2 cups (150 g/4 3/4 oz) freshly grated Parmesan cheese
1 1/4 cups (315 ml/10 fl oz) cream
3 tablespoons chopped fresh parsley
salt and pepper

1 Add the pasta to a large pan of rapidly boiling water and cook until just tender. Drain in a colander and return to pan.
2 While the pasta is cooking, heat the butter in a medium pan over low heat. Add the Parmesan and cream and bring to the boil, stirring regularly.
3 Add the parsley, salt and pepper, and stir to combine. Add the sauce to the pasta and toss well. Serve immediately.
NOTE: This dish will serve eight as a first course. Garnish with extra grated Parmesan cheese if you like.

BUCATINI WITH FARMHOUSE SAUCE

Preparation time: 20 minutes
Total cooking time: 25 minutes
Serves 4-6

☆

2 tablespoons olive oil
250 g (8 oz) mushrooms
1 medium eggplant (aubergine)
2 cloves garlic, crushed
825 g (1 lb 11 oz) canned tomatoes
500 g (1 lb) bucatini or spaghetti
salt and pepper
3 tablespoons chopped fresh parsley

1 Heat the olive oil in a medium heavy-based pan. Wipe the mushrooms with paper towels and then slice them. Chop the eggplant into small cubes.
2 Add the mushrooms, cubes of eggplant and the garlic to the pan and cook, stirring, for 4 minutes. Add the undrained, crushed tomatoes; cover the pan and simmer for 15 minutes.
3 While the sauce is cooking, add the pasta to a large pan of rapidly boiling water and cook until just tender. Drain the pasta well and then return it to the pan. Season the sauce with salt and pepper. Add the chopped parsley to the pan and stir through. Add the sauce to the pasta and toss until well distributed. Serve immediately in warmed pasta bowls.

NOTE: If the pasta is cooked before you are ready to serve it, you can prevent it sticking together by adding a little olive oil after draining and tossing the oil through the pasta.

FAST TOMATO AND HERB PASTA

ADD 1½ cups (135 g/4½ oz) of pasta bows or penne to a large pan of boiling water. Cook over medium heat for about 5 minutes or until almost cooked. Turn off heat and leave the lid on—pasta will continue cooking. Whisk together 3 tablespoons each of olive oil and balsamic vinegar, a squeeze of lemon juice, a little soft brown sugar, 1–2 cloves crushed garlic, salt and freshly ground black pepper. Drain pasta well and toss dressing through. Stir in 1 large chopped ripe tomato, some sliced cucumber and about 1 cup (60 g/2 oz) of combined chopped parsley, basil, coriander and lemon thyme. Mix well and serve immediately with shaved Parmesan cheese. This is also delicious with fresh blanched vegetables, such as asparagus, broccoli, snow or sugar snap peas, or beans. Serves 2–4.

BUCATINI
Bucatini is a narrow, spaghetti-like noodle that is hollow like a drinking straw. A slightly wider version, called Bucatoni, is also available.

ABOVE: Bucatini with Farmhouse Sauce

ingredients evenly. Serve in warmed pasta bowls with shavings of Parmesan cheese. If serving as a first course, this dish will be sufficient for eight.

BLUE CHEESE TAGLIATELLE

Preparation time: 15 minutes
Total cooking time: 20 minutes
Serves 6

★

30 g (1 oz) butter
2 zucchinis (courgettes), sliced
1 clove garlic, crushed
100 ml (3 1/2 fl oz) white wine
100 g (3 1/3 oz) blue cheese, crumbled
300 ml (9 1/2 fl oz) cream
pinch black pepper
500 g (1 lb) white or green tagliatelle
2–3 tablespoons freshly grated
    Parmesan cheese
chopped fresh parsley, to garnish

1 Melt the butter in a frying pan. Add the zucchinis and garlic and cook until the zucchinis are tender. Stir in the wine, cheese, cream and pepper. Simmer for 10 minutes.
2 Add the tagliatelle to a large pan of rapidly boiling water and cook for 6–8 minutes, until tender. Drain, rinse under warm water, drain again.
3 Return the pasta to the pan. Add the sauce and toss through the pasta for a few minutes over low heat. Serve sprinkled with Parmesan and parsley.

TAGLIATELLE WITH ASPARAGUS AND HERBS

Preparation time: 15 minutes
Total cooking time: 15 minutes
Serves 4-6

★

500 g (1 lb) tagliatelle
155 g (5 oz) asparagus
40 g (1 1/3 oz) butter
1 tablespoon chopped fresh parsley
1 tablespoon chopped fresh basil
1 1/4 cups (315 ml/10 fl oz) cream
salt and pepper
1/2 cup (50 g/1 2/3 oz) freshly grated
    Parmesan cheese

1 Cook the pasta in a large pan of rapidly boiling water until just tender. Drain and return to the pan. While the pasta is cooking, cut the asparagus spears into short pieces.
2 Heat the butter in a medium pan, add the asparagus and stir over medium heat for 2 minutes or until just tender. Add the chopped parsley and basil, cream, salt and pepper. Cook for 2 minutes.
3 Add the Parmesan cheese to the pan and stir well. When thoroughly mixed, add to the warm pasta in the pan and toss gently to distribute

ABOVE: Tagliatelle with Asparagus and Herbs

FAST PASTA WITH MUSHROOMS AND MASCARPONE

HEAT ABOUT 30 g (1 oz) butter in a non-stick frying pan. Add 10 medium thinly sliced flat or field mushrooms. Cook over medium heat until soft and golden. Stir in 1–2 cloves crushed garlic and 125 g (4 oz) mascarpone. Stir over low heat until cheese is melted and smooth. Stir in a little cream if mixture is too thick. Season with salt and pepper, add some chopped fresh parsley. Toss through 250 g (8 oz) hot, freshly cooked and drained pasta and serve immediately. Serves 2.

SPAGHETTI WITH FRESH TOMATO SAUCE

Preparation time: 15 minutes + refrigeration
Total cooking time: 10–15 minutes
Serves 4

4 spring onions
4 firm, ripe tomatoes
8 stuffed green olives
2 tablespoons capers
2 cloves garlic, crushed
1/2 teaspoon dried oregano
4 tablespoons chopped fresh parsley
1/3 cup (80 ml/2 3/4 fl oz) olive oil
500 g (1 lb) thin spaghetti

1 Chop the spring onions finely. Cut the tomatoes into small pieces. Chop the olives and capers. Place all ingredients, except pasta, in a bowl; mix well. Cover and refrigerate for at least 2 hours.
2 Add the pasta to a large pan of rapidly boiling water and cook until tender. Drain the pasta and return it to the pan.
3 Add the cold sauce to the hot pasta and mix well. As a variation, add 1/2 cup (30 g/1 oz) of fresh basil leaves.

CHEESE TORTELLINI WITH NUTTY HERB SAUCE

Preparation time: 15 minutes
Total cooking time: 15 minutes
Serves 4-6

500 g (1 lb) ricotta-filled fresh or dried tortellini or ravioli
100 g (3 1/3 oz) walnuts
60 g (2 oz) butter
2/3 cup (100 g/3 1/3 oz) pine nuts
2 tablespoons chopped fresh parsley
2 teaspoons fresh thyme
salt and pepper
1/4 cup (60 g/2 oz) fresh ricotta cheese
1/4 cup (60 ml/2 fl oz) cream

1 Add the pasta to a large pan of rapidly boiling water and cook until just tender. Drain and return to the pan.
2 Chop walnuts into small pieces. While pasta is cooking, heat butter in a heavy-based pan over medium heat until foaming. Add walnuts and pine nuts and stir for 5 minutes or until golden brown. Add the parsley, thyme, salt and pepper.
3 Beat the ricotta with the cream. Add the sauce to the pasta and toss well to combine. Top with a dollop of ricotta cream. Serve immediately.
NOTE: For the best flavour, use fresh herbs wherever possible when making pasta sauces.

THYME

Thyme (*Thymus vulgaris*), is a tiny-leafed but tough herb that has an affinity with eggplant (aubergine), zucchini (courgette) and pepper (capsicum). Lemon thyme (*Thymus citriodorus*) is superb in stuffing mixes. Thyme is easy to grow in a sunny corner of even the smallest garden and it's well worth the effort— home-dried or frozen thyme is far superior to commercially powdered or dried products. To dry thyme, hang bunches in a warm place, then rub the leaves off and store in an airtight jar.

ABOVE: Spaghetti with Fresh Tomato Sauce
BELOW: Cheese Tortellini with Nutty Herb Sauce

SPAGHETTI WITH PRIMAVERA SAUCE

Preparation time: 25 minutes
Total cooking time: 15 minutes
Serves 4-6

★

500 g (1 lb) spaghetti
155 g (5 oz) fresh asparagus
1 cup (175 g/5²/₃ oz) frozen broad beans
40 g (1¹/₃ oz) butter
1 celery stick, sliced
1 cup (155 g/5 oz) frozen green peas
1¹/₄ cups (315 ml/10 fl oz) cream
¹/₂ cup (50 g/1²/₃ oz) freshly grated
    Parmesan cheese
salt and pepper

1 Add the spaghetti to a pan of rapidly boiling water and cook until just tender. Drain and return to the pan.
2 While the spaghetti is cooking, cut the asparagus into small pieces. Bring a medium pan of water to the boil, add the asparagus and cook for 2 minutes. Using a slotted spoon, remove from pan and plunge into cold water.
3 Plunge the broad beans into a pan of boiling water. Remove at once and cool in cold water. Drain and allow to cool completely. Peel the skin from the beans.

4 Heat the butter in a heavy-based frying pan. Add the celery and stir for 2 minutes. Add the peas and cream and cook for another 3 minutes. Add the asparagus, broad beans, Parmesan, salt and pepper and bring to the boil; cook for 1 minute. Add the sauce to the spaghetti and toss to combine. Serve spaghetti immediately in warmed pasta bowls.
NOTE: Use different vegetables, such as leeks, zucchinis (courgettes) and sugar snap peas, and add some fresh chopped dill or basil if you like.

TORTELLINI WITH MUSHROOM SAUCE

Preparation time: 40 minutes
    + 30 minutes resting
Total cooking time: 35–40 minutes
Serves 4

★★

Pasta

2 cups (250 g/9 oz) plain flour
pinch salt
3 eggs
1 tablespoon olive oil
¹/₄ cup (60 ml/2 fl oz) water

Filling

125 g (4 oz) packet frozen spinach, thawed,
    excess liquid removed
¹/₂ cup 125 g (4 oz) ricotta cheese
2 tablespoons freshly grated Parmesan cheese
1 egg, beaten
salt and freshly ground black pepper

Sauce

1 tablespoon olive oil
1 clove garlic, crushed
125 g (4 oz) mushrooms, sliced
1 cup (250 ml/8 fl oz) cream
3 tablespoons freshly grated Parmesan cheese
salt and freshly ground black pepper

1 To make Pasta: Sift the flour and salt onto a board. Make a well in the centre of the flour. In a jug, whisk together eggs, oil and 1 tablespoon of the water. Add the egg mixture gradually to the flour, working in with your hands until the mixture forms a ball. Add extra water if necessary. Knead on a lightly floured surface for

PARMESAN CHEESE
Parmesan (*parmigiano-reggiano*) belongs to a group of Italian cheeses known as *grana* cheeses. It is an essential ingredient of many of the best and most characteristic northern Italian dishes. When buying Parmesan, make sure it is straw-coloured and brittle. It should never be sweaty, grey, or waxy, and should always smell fresh. Shop-bought ground Parmesan is a poor substitute for the fresh product.

BELOW: Spaghetti with Primavera Sauce

SPAGHETTI SIRACUSANI

Preparation time: 20 minutes
Total cooking time: 25 minutes
Serves 4-6

1 large green pepper (capsicum)
2 tablespoons olive oil
2 cloves garlic, crushed
2 x 425 g (13½ oz) cans tomatoes
½ cup (125 ml/4 fl oz) water
2 medium zucchinis (courgettes), chopped
1 tablespoon capers, chopped
3 tablespoons black olives, pitted and halved
2 tablespoons chopped fresh basil leaves
salt and pepper
500 g (1 lb) spaghetti or linguine
½ cup (50 g/1⅔ oz) freshly grated Parmesan
   cheese, for serving

1 Remove membrane and seeds from green pepper. Slice into thin strips. Heat oil in a large, deep pan. Add garlic, stir for 30 seconds over low heat. Add pepper strips, undrained crushed tomatoes, water, zucchinis, capers and olives. Cook for 20 minutes, stirring occasionally.
2 Add basil, salt and pepper, stir. Meanwhile, add pasta to a large pan of rapidly boiling water; cook until just tender; drain. Serve in warmed bowls, top with sauce and sprinkle with Parmesan.

CAPERS

These little green flower buds develop a wonderful piquancy when pickled. They can be used as a seasoning or a condiment and form an essential part of Italian and Provençal cooking. Two tablespoons of chopped capers can be added to mayonnaise for a sharper taste—this mixture makes up the base of a tartare sauce.

*ABOVE: Tortellini with Mushroom Sauce
BELOW: Spaghetti Siracusani*

5 minutes or until dough is smooth and elastic. Place the dough in a lightly oiled bowl. Cover with plastic wrap and set aside for 30 minutes.
2 To make Filling: In a bowl, combine the drained spinach, ricotta and Parmesan cheeses, egg, salt and pepper. Set aside.
3 To make Sauce: Heat the oil in a frying pan. Add the garlic and stir over low heat for 30 seconds. Add the mushrooms and cook for 3 minutes. Pour in the cream and set aside.
4 Roll the dough out on a lightly floured surface until it is very thin. Using a floured cutter, cut into 5 cm (2 inch) rounds. Spoon about ½ teaspoon of filling in the centre of each round. Brush a little water around the edge of each round. Fold the rounds in half to form a semi-circle. Press the edges together firmly. Wrap each semi-circle around your forefinger to form a ring. Press the ends of the dough together firmly.
5 Cook the tortellini in batches in a large pan of rapidly boiling water for about 8 minutes each batch, until just tender. Drain well and return to the pan. Keep warm.
6 Return sauce to medium heat. Bring to the boil. Reduce heat and simmer for 3 minutes. Add the Parmesan cheese, salt and pepper and stir well. Add the sauce to the tortellini and toss until well combined. Divide the tortellini and sauce between individual warmed serving bowls.

FETTUCINE WITH CREAMY MUSHROOM AND BEAN SAUCE

Preparation time: 20 minutes
Total cooking time: 20 minutes
Serves 4

²/₃ cup (100 g/3¹/₃ oz) pine nuts

280 g (9 oz) fettucine

250 g (8 oz) green beans

2 tablespoons oil

1 onion, chopped

2 cloves garlic, crushed

250 g (8 oz) mushrooms, thinly sliced

¹/₂ cup (125 ml/4 fl oz) white wine

300 ml (9¹/₂ fl oz) cream

¹/₂ cup (125 ml/4 fl oz) vegetable stock

1 egg

3 tablespoons chopped fresh basil

¹/₄ cup (40 g/1¹/₃ oz) sun-dried tomatoes,
   cut into thin strips

salt and freshly ground black pepper

50 g (1²/₃ oz) Parmesan cheese, shaved

1 Place the pine nuts in a small pan. Stir over medium heat until golden. Set aside. Add the

fettucine to a large pan of boiling water and cook until just tender. Drain and keep warm.
2 Trim the tops and tails of beans and cut the beans into long thin strips. Heat the oil in a large heavy-based frying pan. Add the onion and garlic and cook over medium heat for 3 minutes or until softened. Add the mushrooms and cook, stirring, for 1 minute. Add the wine, cream and stock. Bring to the boil, reduce heat and simmer for 10 minutes.
3 Lightly beat the egg in a small bowl. Stirring constantly, add a little cooking liquid. Pour the mixture slowly into the pan, stirring constantly for 30 seconds. Keep the heat low—if the mixture boils, it will curdle. Add the beans, basil, pine nuts and tomatoes and stir until heated through. Season, to taste, with salt and pepper. Divide the pasta between warmed serving plates and spoon the sauce over the top. Garnish with shavings of Parmesan cheese.

GREEN BEANS
There are dozens of varieties of green beans to choose from. Whatever the type, beans should be crisp and bright. Avoid buying any limp or overly matured beans with tough-looking pods: the beans should literally snap when bent. Most beans need topping and tailing and some types still need the strings removed.

ABOVE: Fettucine with Creamy Mushroom and Bean Sauce

SEMOLINA
Semolina is wheat which is at a stage of processing between grain and flour. The finest semolina is used for making Italian gnocchi, while medium-ground semolina is used in a variety of desserts, from milk or fruit puddings to sweet cakes.

SEMOLINA GNOCCHI

Preparation time: 20 minutes
  + 1 hour refrigeration
Total cooking time: 40 minutes
Serves 4

3 cups (750 ml/24 fl oz) milk
1/2 teaspoon ground nutmeg
salt and freshly ground black pepper
2/3 cup (85 g/2 3/4 oz) semolina
1 egg, beaten
1 1/2 cups (150 g/4 3/4 oz) freshly grated
  Parmesan cheese
60 g (2 oz) butter, melted
1/2 cup (125 ml/4 fl oz) thick cream
1/2 cup (75 g/2 1/2 oz) freshly grated
  mozzarella cheese

1 Line a deep 28 x 18 x 3 cm (11 x 7 x 1 1/4 inch) Swiss roll tin with baking paper. Place milk, half the nutmeg, salt and pepper in a medium pan. Bring to the boil. Reduce heat and gradually stir in semolina. Cook, stirring occasionally, for 5–10 minutes or until the semolina is very stiff. Remove from heat. Add the egg and 1 cup of the Parmesan cheese to the semolina mixture; stir to combine. Spread the mixture in prepared tin. Refrigerate for 1 hour or until firm.

2 Preheat the oven to moderate 180°C (350°F/Gas 4). Cut the semolina mixture into rounds using a floured 4 cm (1 1/2 inch) cutter. Arrange the semolina rounds in a greased shallow casserole dish.
3 Pour melted butter over the top, followed by cream. Sprinkle with the combined remaining nutmeg and Parmesan and mozzarella cheeses. Bake for 20–25 minutes or until golden. Serve with mixed salad.

FAST PASTA WITH BREADCRUMB SAUCE

PROCESS 5 SLICES of brown bread in a food processor for 30 seconds to make fine crumbs. Add 500 g (1 lb) spiral pasta or farfalle to a large pan of rapidly boiling water and cook until just tender. Drain, keep warm. While pasta is cooking, heat 1/4 cup (60 ml/2 fl oz) olive oil in a large, heavy-based pan over low heat. Add the breadcrumbs and 3 cloves crushed garlic; stir for 3 minutes or until crisp and golden. Combine the hot pasta, breadcrumbs, 2 tablespoons finely chopped fresh parsley and 1/2 cup (45 g/1 1/2 oz) of freshly grated Pecorino cheese in a large bowl. Add ground black pepper. Toss well and serve immediately. Garnish with fresh herbs, if desired. Serves 4–6.

ABOVE: Semolina Gnocchi

MUSHROOMS A valuable source of

vitamins and fibre, these cultivated fungi are adaptable vegetables, fitting in perfectly

with both light modern dishes and heavier rustic fare, with a flavour all their own.

PESTO-FILLED MUSHROOMS

Place 2 cups (60 g/2 oz) of fresh basil leaves, 3 crushed cloves of garlic, ½ cup (80 g/2⅔ oz) of toasted pine nuts and ½ cup (50 g/1⅔ oz) of grated Parmesan cheese in a food processor and process until smooth. Gradually add ⅓ cup (80 ml/2¾ fl oz) of olive oil and process until all the ingredients are well combined. Remove the stalks from

14 small mushrooms (small enough for finger food) and brush the mushrooms lightly with macadamia nut oil. Cook, fan-side down, on a preheated char-grill or barbecue until the mushrooms are lightly browned. Turn the mushrooms over and spoon a level tablespoonful of the prepared pesto on the top of each mushroom. Serve immediately. Makes 14 filled mushrooms.

GOLDEN MUSHROOM TART

Preheat oven to moderately hot 200°C (400°F/Gas 6). Place a sheet of puff pastry on a non-stick baking tray. Heat 2 tablespoons of oil in a frying pan, add 2 thinly sliced onions and 1 tablespoon of red wine vinegar. Cook 10 minutes or until onions have caramelised. Remove from pan, cool slightly on paper towels. Add 60 g (2 oz) butter and 350 g

(11¼ oz) assorted mushrooms to pan; cook for 5 minutes or until tender. Drain off any excess liquid and cool on paper towels. Season, to taste, with salt and pepper. Cook puff pastry for 10 minutes, then very carefully and quickly spread onions over puff pastry base, leaving a 2 cm (¾ inch) border. Top with mushrooms and sprinkle with fresh marjoram leaves and ¼ cup (25 g/¾ oz) grated Parmesan. Cook for another 10 minutes or until golden. Serves 4.

MUSHROOM YOGHURT DIP

Heat 1 tablespoon of oil in a frying pan, add 2 crushed cloves of garlic and 4 finely chopped spring onions. Cook for 3 minutes. Add 220 g (7 oz) of chopped button mushrooms and cook for 5 minutes or until golden. Remove from heat and drain off any excess liquid.

Transfer mixture to a bowl, stir in 200 g (6½ oz) thick natural yoghurt, 1 teaspoon ground cumin and 2 tablespoons of chopped fresh lemon thyme. Use as a dip with crudités, grissini sticks, corn chips or sliced French bread.

MARINATED MUSHROOMS

Place 1 cup (250 ml/8 fl oz) apple cider vinegar, ½ cup (125 ml/4 fl oz) orange juice, 1 tablespoon coriander seeds, 2 sprigs rosemary and 1 bay leaf in a pan, bring to boil. Add 500 g (1 lb) button mushrooms and simmer for 3 minutes. Remove and spoon into a sterilized jar. Boil liquid until reduced by half. Discard rosemary sprigs and bay leaf and replace with fresh ones. Stir in ⅓ cup (80 ml/ 2¾ fl oz) of olive oil. Pour liquid over mushrooms and seal with a layer of olive oil. Will keep, refrigerated, for one month.

WILD MUSHROOM STUFFING

Heat 60 g (2 oz) butter in a frying pan, add 1 finely chopped onion and cook for 3 minutes or until golden. Add 220 g (7 oz) of mixed mushrooms (oyster, Swiss brown, enoki, button) and cook for 5 minutes. Transfer the mixture to a bowl, add 2 cups (60 g/2 oz) of croutons, 3 tablespoons of chopped fresh herbs, ½ cup (95 g/3¼ oz) cooked brown rice, ¼ cup (60 ml/2 fl oz) milk and 1 lightly beaten egg; mix well. Use the mixture to stuff cooked potatoes, eggplants (aubergines) and peppers (capsicums), or fill omelettes and crepes.

CLOCKWISE, FROM TOP LEFT: Marinated Mushrooms; Mushroom Yoghurt Dip; Pesto-filled Mushrooms; Golden Mushroom Tart; Wild Mushroom Stuffing

Sprinkle with Parmesan cheese and bake, covered, for 20–30 minutes.

NOTE: Chopped fresh herbs can be added to this dish and the combination of vegetables varied, according to taste or availability.

PENNE WITH CREAMY PESTO AND TOMATO

Preparation time: 5 minutes
Total cooking time: 20 minutes
Serves 4

375 g (12 oz) penne
2 teaspoons oil
200 g (6¹/2 oz) mushrooms, sliced
³/4 cup (185 g/6 oz) sour cream
¹/2 cup (125 g/4 oz) ready-made pesto
¹/4 cup (40 g/1¹/3 oz) chopped sun-dried
    tomatoes
freshly ground black pepper

1 Add the pasta to a large pan of rapidly boiling water and cook until just tender; drain.
2 Return the pan to the heat, add the oil and heat. Add the mushrooms to the pan and cook for 4 minutes or until soft and golden. Stir in the sour cream, pesto, tomatoes and pepper. Mix well and cook for 2 minutes or until the sauce is heated through.
3 Return the pasta to the pan and mix well. Cook, stirring, for 1 minute or until heated through. Garnish with extra sliced tomatoes and shredded basil, if you like.

NOTE: Pesto can be bought in jars from supermarkets and delicatessens.

THE HISTORY OF PASTA

It was said that Marco Polo brought pasta to Italy from China in 1295, a rumour which does great disservice to the ancient Italians who had been enjoying it since the days of Imperial Rome. Cicero himself was, apparently, inordinately fond of *laganum*, the flat ribbon pasta we now know as tagliatelle. And, from the middle ages, Tasso's story tells how an innkeeper invented tortellini in the image of Venus' navel. So, if you're a pasta-lover, you're in good company.

ABOVE: Pasta Vegetable Bake
RIGHT: Penne with Creamy Pesto and Tomato

PASTA VEGETABLE BAKE

Preparation time: 20 minutes
Total cooking time: 45–50 minutes
Serves 4

1 tablespoon olive oil
1 large onion, finely chopped
1 clove garlic, crushed
3 medium zucchinis (courgettes), sliced
100 g (3¹/3 oz) button mushrooms, sliced
2 cups (500 g/1 lb) ready-made
    tomato pasta sauce
1 cup (155 g/5 oz) frozen peas
salt and pepper
1¹/2 cups (135 g/4¹/2 oz) dried pasta
    (penne or spiralli)
4 tablespoons freshly grated Parmesan cheese

1 Preheat the oven to slow 150°C (300°F/Gas 2). Heat the oil in a frying pan. Add the onion and garlic to pan, cook over low heat for 4 minutes or until the onions are soft. Add zucchinis and mushrooms, cook for 3 minutes. Add the sauce and peas, cook for 3 minutes. Season with salt and pepper. Remove from heat and set aside.
2 Add pasta to a large pan of rapidly boiling water and cook for 10–12 minutes or until just tender. Drain; add to the vegetables in the pan.
3 Spoon the mixture into a casserole dish.

POTATO GNOCCHI WITH TOMATO SAUCE

Preparation time: 35 minutes
Total cooking time: 45–50 minutes
Serves 4

500 g (1 lb) potatoes, peeled and chopped
2 cups (250 g/8 oz) plain flour, sifted
¼ cup (25 g/¾ oz) freshly grated
   Parmesan cheese
30 g (1 oz) butter or margarine, melted
salt and freshly ground black pepper
freshly grated Parmesan cheese, extra,
   for serving

Tomato Sauce

1 kg (2 lb) tomatoes, peeled and chopped
2 cloves garlic, crushed
½ cup (125 ml/4 fl oz) red wine
3 tablespoons finely chopped fresh basil
salt and freshly ground black pepper

1 Cook the potatoes in a pan of boiling water for 15–20 minutes, or until tender. Drain thoroughly and mash until smooth. Transfer to a bowl and allow to cool slightly. Add the flour, Parmesan cheese, butter, salt and pepper. Using a flat-bladed knife, mix together in a cutting motion, to form a firm dough. Knead briefly on a lightly floured surface until smooth. Do not over-handle the dough, or the finished gnocchi will be tough.

2 Roll heaped teaspoonsful of dough into oval shapes. Indent one side using the back of a fork. Cook the gnocchi in batches in a large pan of rapidly boiling water for 3–5 minutes each batch. The gnocchi will float on the surface when cooked. Drain well and keep warm while cooking the remaining gnocchi. Serve in warmed bowls, with the Tomato Sauce. Sprinkle with the extra grated Parmesan cheese.

3 **To make Tomato Sauce:** In a pan, combine the tomatoes, garlic, wine, basil, salt and pepper. Bring to the boil. Reduce the heat and simmer gently for 15–20 minutes, stirring occasionally, until the sauce reduces and thickens slightly.

BASIL
Basil (*Ocymum basilicum*) has a unique spiciness and aroma and in most recipes it is best used in its fresh form. It should be added to dishes at the end of cooking time, to preserve its flavour. If the leaves are to be chopped, shredded or torn, do so at the last possible minute, as they will blacken when cut.

ABOVE: Potato Gnocchi with Tomato Sauce

low heat, stirring regularly. Add the tomatoes, carrot, parsley, and combined vinegar and wine. Reduce heat and simmer for 25 minutes. Season, to taste with salt and pepper.

3 Five minutes before the sauce is cooked, heat the remaining oil in a medium frying pan, add the walnuts and stir over low heat for 5 minutes.

4 While the sauce is cooking, add the pasta to a large pan of rapidly boiling water and cook until just tender. Drain and return to pan. Add the sauce to the pasta and toss to combine. Serve the pasta and the sauce topped with walnuts and sprinkled with Parmesan cheese.

NOTE: Italians often use egg (Roma) tomatoes for sauces—try them if they are available. You will need 6–8 for this recipe as they are quite small.

HERB AND PEPPER FETTUCINE

Preparation time: 5 minutes
Total cooking time: 18 minutes
Serves 4

500 g (1 lb) fettucine

60 g (2 oz) butter

2 cloves garlic, crushed

2 tablespoons finely chopped fresh sage

2 tablespoons finely chopped fresh basil

2 tablespoons finely chopped fresh oregano

2 teaspoons cracked black pepper

4 tablespoons freshly grated Parmesan cheese

1 Cook the pasta in a large pan of rapidly boiling water until just tender; drain.

2 Return the pan to heat and add the butter. Cook over medium heat for 2 minutes or until foaming. Add garlic, sage, basil, oregano and black pepper.

3 Return the pasta to the pan to thoroughly combine. Cook, stirring, for 2 minutes or until heated through. Serve immediately, sprinkled with Parmesan cheese.

TAGLIATELLE WITH TOMATO AND WALNUT SAUCE

Preparation time: 20 minutes
Total cooking time: 50 minutes
Serves 4-6

4 ripe tomatoes

2 tablespoons oil

1 medium onion, finely chopped

1 celery stick, finely chopped

1 medium carrot, grated

2 tablespoons chopped fresh parsley

1 teaspoon red wine vinegar

1/4 cup (60 ml/2 fl oz) white wine

salt and pepper

3/4 cup (75 g/2 1/2 oz) walnuts, roughly chopped

500 g (1 lb) tagliatelle

4 tablespoons freshly grated Parmesan cheese, for serving

1 Using a sharp knife, mark a small cross on the base of each tomato. Place in a bowl and cover with boiling water for about 2 minutes. Drain and allow to cool. Peel the skin down from the cross and discard. Roughly chop the flesh.

2 Heat half the oil in a large heavy-based pan. Cook the onion and celery for 5 minutes over

COOKING PASTA

To cook pasta perfectly, allow 4 litres of water for each 500 g (1 lb) of dried pasta and use a very large pot. Using plenty of water prevents the pasta sticking together and allows for expansion. Adding salt and oil to the water is a matter of personal preference.

ABOVE: Tagliatelle with Tomato and Walnut Sauce

1 Score a cross with a sharp knife in the base of each tomato. Cover with boiling water and leave for about 2 minutes.

2 Drain the tomatoes and allow to cool. Peel the skin in a downwards motion, away from the cross, and discard the skin.

3 To remove the seeds, cut the tomatoes in half horizontally and use a spoon to scoop them out.

PASTA WITH SUN-DRIED TOMATO PESTO

Preparation time: 15 minutes
Total cooking time: 12 minutes
Serves 6

150 g (4³/4 oz) sun-dried tomatoes in olive oil
¹/2 cup (50 g/1²/3 oz) finely grated
   Parmesan cheese
¹/3 cup (50 g/1²/3 oz) pine nuts
¹/2 cup (25 g/³/4 oz) fresh basil leaves
¹/3 cup (80 ml/2³/4 fl oz) olive oil
500 g (1 lb) spiral pasta
155 g asparagus spears, chopped
250 g cherry tomatoes, halved

1 Drain the sun-dried tomatoes. Place in a food processor with the cheese, pine nuts and basil. Process until finely chopped. With the motor running, slowly pour in the oil.
2 Add the pasta to a large pan of boiling water and cook until tender. Drain well in a colander then place the pasta in a large serving bowl.
3 Add the sun-dried tomato mixture to the hot pasta and toss to combine. Place the asparagus in a heatproof bowl. Cover with boiling water and leave for 2 minutes; drain. Toss through the pasta with the cherry tomatoes.

PASTA WITH PESTO

Preparation time: 10 minutes
Total cooking time: 10 minutes
Serves 4

500 g (1 lb) spinach tagliatelle
2 cups (100 g/3¹/3 oz) tightly packed fresh
   basil leaves
4 cloves garlic, peeled and chopped
¹/3 cup (50 g/1²/3 oz) pine nuts
1 cup (100 g/3¹/3 oz) freshly grated
   Parmesan cheese
³/4 cup (185 ml/6 fl oz) olive oil
salt and pepper

1 Add the tagliatelle to a large pan of rapidly boiling water and cook until tender. Drain well and return pasta to the pan. While the pasta is cooking, process the basil, garlic and pine nuts in a food processor until finely ground. Add the cheese and process until well combined.
2 With motor running, slowly pour the olive oil through the feed tube of food processor. Add enough pesto sauce to the pasta to coat well. Season. Garnish with fresh basil leaves, if desired.
NOTE: As a variation, you can toast ¹/4 cup (40 g/1¹/3 oz) of pine nuts in a dry pan and add to the pasta just before serving.

ABOVE: Pasta with Pesto

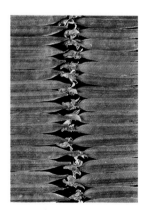

ABOVE: Ricotta-filled Ravioli with Fresh Tomato Sauce (left); Pasta and Vegetable Salad

RICOTTA-FILLED RAVIOLI WITH FRESH TOMATO SAUCE

Preparation time: 35 minutes
  + 30 minutes standing
Total cooking time: 45–50 minutes
Serves 4-6

 ★ ★

Ravioli Dough

1 cup (125 g/4 oz) plain flour
1 egg
1 tablespoon oil
1 teaspoon water

Filling

500 g (1 lb) ricotta cheese
1 tablespoon chopped fresh flat-leaf parsley
1 egg yolk

Sauce

1 tablespoon oil
1 onion, chopped
2 cloves garlic, crushed
1 carrot, chopped
1 kg (2 lb) ripe tomatoes, peeled and chopped
50 g (1²/₃ oz) tomato paste
1 teaspoon soft brown sugar
¹/₂ cup (125 ml/4 fl oz) vegetable stock
1 tablespoon Worcestershire sauce
¹/₂ cup (30 g/1 oz) chopped fresh basil

1 To make Ravioli Dough: Sift the flour into a bowl. Make a well in the centre, add the egg, oil and water and then gradually incorporate into the flour. Turn out onto a lightly floured board, knead until smooth and elastic. Cover and set aside for 30 minutes. While pastry is resting, make the Filling and the Sauce.
2 To make Filling: Combine the ricotta, parsley and egg yolk. Mix well.
3 To make Sauce: Heat the oil in a large heavy-based pan. Add the onion, garlic and carrot. Cook gently for 5–7 minutes. Add the tomatoes, tomato paste, sugar, stock, Worcestershire sauce and basil. Bring to boil, reduce to simmer, cover and cook for 30 minutes. Allow to cool slightly and then process the mixture in a food processor briefly; keep it warm.
4 Halve the dough and re-shape each piece into a smooth ball. Roll out each thinly to a long oblong shape. Place teaspoonsful of filling in mounds at 5 cm (2 inch) intervals in regular lines on one sheet of dough. Brush between mounds with water, place other sheet of dough carefully over top. Press down between filling to seal. Use a pastry wheel or knife to cut into squares.
5 Drop ravioli into a pan of boiling water, cook 8–10 minutes or until tender. Remove ravioli using a slotted spoon, and place into a heated serving dish. Spoon Sauce over and serve.

PASTA AND VEGETABLE SALAD

Preparation time: 15 minutes
Total cooking time: 10 minutes
Serves 4–6 as an accompaniment

250 g (8 oz) bow pasta

250 g (8 oz) broccoli, broken into florets

250 g (8 oz) beans, cut diagonally

125 g (4 oz) snow peas (mange tout), topped
   and tailed

250 g (8 oz) cherry tomatoes

1/3 cup (80 ml/2³/4 fl oz) olive oil

1/4 cup (60 ml/2 fl oz) white wine vinegar

2 teaspoons mustard powder

1 teaspoon turmeric

freshly ground black pepper

snow pea sprouts or herbs,
   to garnish

1 Add the pasta to a large pan of rapidly boiling water and cook until just tender. Drain well and rinse with cold water; set aside.
2 Plunge the broccoli, beans and snow peas into boiling water. Rinse immediately in cold water and set aside. Wash the tomatoes, cut them in half and set aside.
3 Combine olive oil, vinegar, mustard, turmeric and black pepper in a small bowl and beat well with a fork.
4 Place pasta, vegetables and dressing in a bowl; toss well to combine. Place in a serving bowl, top with sprouts or your favourite herbs.

FAST SPAGHETTI WITH ROCKET AND CHILLI

ADD 500 g (1 lb) spaghetti or spaghettini to a large pan of rapidly boiling water and cook until just tender. Drain the spaghetti and return it to the pan. Five minutes before pasta is cooked, heat 2 tablespoons of olive oil in a large heavy-based frying pan. Add 2 teaspoons of chopped chilli and cook for 1 minute over low heat, stirring. Add 450 g (14¹/3 oz) of trimmed rocket and cook for 2–3 minutes or until softened, stirring regularly. Add 1 tablespoon of lemon juice and salt, to taste. Add the rocket mixture to the pasta and toss until combined. Serve immediately. Serves 4–6.

RAVIOLI WITH HERBS

Preparation time: 15 minutes
Total cooking time: 4–6 minutes
Serves 6

2 tablespoons olive oil
1 clove garlic, halved
800 g (1 lb 10 oz) ricotta-filled ravioli
60 g (2 oz) butter, chopped
2 tablespoons chopped fresh parsley
1/3 cup (20 g/²/3 oz) chopped fresh basil
2 tablespoons chopped fresh chives

1 Combine oil and garlic in a small bowl; set aside. Add ravioli to a large pan of rapidly boiling water and cook until tender.
2 Drain ravioli well in a colander and return to pan. Add oil to pasta; discard garlic. Add butter and herbs to ravioli and toss well. As a variation, use fresh coriander instead of parsley. Season with salt and pepper. Sprinkle with Parmesan when serving, if you wish.

SAGE

Sage (*Salvia officinalis*) was once believed to confer wisdom and prolong life. Today the flowers are used as an elegant garnish, while the leaves can be used in stuffings and with many vegetable dishes. When buying sage, keep in mind that the fresh leaves have a more complex, milder flavour than dried sage. The leaves are also used to make an aromatic tea, renowned for its soothing qualities.

*ABOVE: Ravioli
with Herbs*

COOKING AHEAD
If you are cooking for a large crowd, cook the pasta in batches and place in an ovenproof dish. Stir through a little oil, cover the dish with a damp cloth and keep it warm in a slow oven. Alternatively, you can reheat the cooked pasta in a microwave oven.

SWEET AND SOUR NOODLES AND VEGETABLES

Preparation time: 15 minutes
Total cooking time: 15 minutes
Serves 4-6

200 g (6¹/2 oz) thin fresh egg noodles
4 fresh baby corn
¹/4 cup (60 ml/2 fl oz) oil
1 green pepper (capsicum), sliced
1 red pepper (capsicum), sliced
2 celery sticks, sliced diagonally
1 carrot, sliced diagonally
250 g (8 oz) button mushrooms, sliced
3 teaspoons cornflour
2 tablespoons brown vinegar
1 teaspoon chopped fresh chilli
2 teaspoons tomato paste
2 vegetable stock cubes, crumbled
1 teaspoon sesame oil
450 g (14¹/3 oz) canned pineapple pieces
3 spring onions, sliced diagonally

1 Add the noodles to a large pan of boiling water and cook for 3 minutes; drain well. Slice the corn diagonally. Heat the oil in a wok; add the green and red peppers, celery, carrot and mushrooms. Stir over high heat for 5 minutes.
2 Add corn and noodles. Reduce heat to low; cook 2 minutes. Blend cornflour with vinegar in a small bowl until smooth. Add chilli, tomato paste, stock cubes, oil and undrained pineapple pieces to the bowl and stir to combine.
3 Pour pineapple mixture over ingredients in the wok. Stir over medium heat for 5 minutes or until the mixture boils and sauce thickens. Add the spring onions; serve immediately.

FAST CHEESE AND NOODLE OMELETTE

PLACE 85 g (2³/4 oz) instant noodles and contents of flavouring sachet in a bowl. Cover with boiling water, allow to rest for 2–3 minutes or until noodles are soft; drain well. Heat 20–30 g (²/3–1 oz) of butter in a non-stick pan. Add a little chopped red pepper (capsicum) and some sliced onion; cook 1–2 minutes. Add noodles, cook briefly. Pour over 3 lightly beaten eggs. Cook over medium heat for 3–5 minutes, shaking occasionally to prevent sticking. When omelette is almost cooked, sprinkle with about 4 tablespoons grated Cheddar cheese and some chopped fresh herbs. Cook briefly under preheated grill until golden and cooked through. Sprinkle with freshly cracked pepper. Serves 2–4.

ABOVE: Sweet and Sour Noodles and Vegetables

CHILLI SATAY NOODLES

Preparation time: 10 minutes
Total cooking time: 10 minutes
Serves 4-6

500 g (1 lb) thin fresh egg noodles
1 tablespoon oil
1 teaspoon sesame oil
4 tablespoons peanuts, shelled, peeled
2 small red chillies
4 slender eggplants (aubergines), sliced
200 g (6 1/2 oz) sugar snap peas
100 g (3 1/3 oz) bean sprouts
3 tablespoons crunchy peanut butter
1 tablespoon hoi sin sauce
1/3 cup (80 ml/2 3/4 fl oz) coconut milk
2 tablespoons lime juice
1 tablespoon Thai sweet chilli sauce

1 Add the noodles to a large pan of boiling water and cook for 3 minutes. Heat the oils in a wok or pan. Add the peanuts and toss over high heat for 1 minute or until golden. Add the chillies, eggplants and sugar snap peas and cook over high heat for 2 minutes. Reduce the heat to medium and add noodles and sprouts; toss for 1 minute or until combined.
2 Blend the peanut butter, hoi sin sauce, coconut milk, lime juice and chilli sauce until almost smooth. Add to the noodles. Toss over medium heat until the noodles are coated and the sauce is heated.

VEGETARIAN RICE NOODLES

Preparation time: 20 minutes + soaking
Total cooking time: 10 minutes
Serves 4-6

8 dried Chinese mushrooms
250 g (8 oz) dried rice vermicelli noodles
2 tablespoons oil
3 cloves garlic, chopped
4 cm (1 1/2 inch) piece fresh ginger, grated
100 g (3 1/3 oz) fried tofu, cut into
   2.5 cm (1 inch) cubes
1 medium carrot, peeled and cut into fine shreds

100 g (3 1/3 oz) green beans, cut into 3 cm
   (1 1/4 inch) lengths
1/2 red pepper (capsicum), cut into fine strips
2 tablespoons Golden Mountain sauce
1 tablespoon fish sauce (optional)
2 teaspoons soft brown sugar
100 g (3 1/3 oz) bean sprouts
1 cup (75 g/2 1/2 oz) finely shredded cabbage
50 g (1 2/3 oz) bean sprouts, extra, scraggly
   ends removed, to garnish
Thai sweet chilli sauce, for serving

1 Soak the mushrooms in hot water for 20 minutes; drain and slice. Pour boiling water over the noodles and soak them for 1–4 minutes until soft; drain well.
2 Heat a wok or large heavy-based frying pan. Add the oil and when hot add the garlic, ginger and tofu; stir-fry for 1 minute. Add the carrot, beans, red pepper and mushrooms to wok; stir-fry for 2 minutes.
3 Add the sauces and sugar; toss well, cover and steam for 1 minute. Add the noodles, bean sprouts and cabbage; toss, cover and steam for 30 seconds.
4 Arrange the noodles on a serving platter, garnish with bean sprouts and serve with chilli sauce. Serve immediately.
NOTE: Golden Mountain sauce is available from Asian food speciality stores.

NOODLES
To cook fresh Chinese noodles, bring a large quantity of water to the boil—no need to add salt or oil. The Chinese don't like their noodles *al dente*: they should be cooked to just beyond that point. To stop the cooking process, run the noodles under cold water and then toss them in a little oil to prevent them sticking together.

ABOVE: Vegetarian Rice Noodles

CHILLI NOODLE AND CASHEW STIR-FRY

Preparation time: 15 minutes
Total cooking time: 10 minutes
Serves 4

200 g (6¹/2 oz) thin noodles, chopped
¹/4 cup (60 ml/2 fl oz) oil
2 teaspoons chilli oil
3 red chillies, cut in strips
¹/2 cup (80 g/2²/3 oz) unsalted, roasted
   cashew nuts
1 red pepper (capsicum), thinly sliced
2 celery sticks, sliced diagonally
225 g (7¹/4 oz) canned whole baby
   corn, drained
100 g (3¹/3 oz) bean sprouts
2 tablespoons chopped spring onions
1 tablespoon soy sauce
2 tablespoons Thai sweet chilli sauce

1 Add the noodles to a large pan of simmering water and cook until just tender; drain.
2 Heat oils in a wok or pan, add the chillies and cook over medium heat for 1 minute. Add the cashews and toss for 1 minute or until golden.
3 Add the vegetables to the pan and cook over medium heat for 3 minutes or until vegetables are tender. Stir in the noodles and combined sauces. Toss until noodles are heated through and ingredients are combined; serve.

SPRING ONIONS

When buying fresh spring onions, avoid limp or slimy ones and look for crisp stalks and a bright green colour. The larger ones tend to be too strongly flavoured to eat uncooked in salads. If you want to prepare spring onions ahead of time, trim them, wrap them in damp paper towel and then keep them in the refrigerator in a plastic bag. They will stay crisp for up to a week.

CURRY-FLAVOURED NOODLES

Preparation time: 25 minutes
Total cooking time: 10 minutes
Serves 4

250 g (8 oz) thick fresh noodles
¹/4 cup (60 ml/2 fl oz) oil
2 cloves garlic, sliced
1 onion, finely sliced
1 red pepper (capsicum), cut into long,
   thin strips
1 small cucumber, unpeeled, cut into
   thin 4 cm (1¹/2 inch) strips
2 teaspoons mild curry powder
¹/2 cup (125 ml/4 fl oz) vegetable stock
2 teaspoons dry sherry
1 tablespoon soy sauce
¹/2 teaspoon sugar
3 spring onions, sliced diagonally

1 Add the noodles to a large pan of boiling water and cook until just tender; drain.
2 Heat the oil in a wok or pan. Add the garlic, onion and red pepper and stir over medium heat for 3 minutes. Add the cucumber and curry powder and stir over medium heat for another 3 minutes.
3 Add the combined stock, sherry, soy sauce and sugar, stir until the mixture boils. Add the noodles and spring onions, stir over low heat for 3 minutes or until ingredients are well combined and heated through.

ABOVE: Curry-flavoured Noodles
RIGHT: Chilli Noodle and Cashew Stir-fry

NOODLES WITH VEGETABLES AND HERBS

Preparation time: 20 minutes
Total cooking time: 25 minutes
Serves 4-6

30 g (1 oz) butter
1 onion, sliced
1 small red chilli, seeded, cut into strips
1 celery stick, sliced
1 carrot, sliced diagonally
2 tomatoes, peeled
1 tablespoon Taco seasoning mix
2 tablespoons tomato paste
½ cup (125 ml/4 fl oz) red wine
1 bay leaf
½ cup (125 ml/4 fl oz) vegetable stock
2 teaspoons chopped fresh basil
2 teaspoons chopped fresh parsley
375 g (12 oz) thin fresh rice noodles

1 Heat butter and a little oil in a pan. Add onion, chilli, celery and carrot; cook over medium heat 5 minutes. Cut tomatoes into thin wedges and remove seeds. Add seasoning mix, tomatoes, paste, wine, bay leaf and stock to pan; bring to boil. Reduce heat to low, simmer, covered, for 15 minutes, stirring occasionally. Add the herbs to sauce and stir until combined.
2 Cook noodles in a large pan of boiling water until just tender; drain. Toss with sauce to serve.

NOODLES IN BLACK BEAN SAUCE

Preparation time: 10 minutes
Total cooking time: 10–15 minutes
Serves 4

375 g (12 oz) thin fresh egg noodles
1 teaspoon olive oil
1 teaspoon sesame oil
1 tablespoon grated fresh ginger
4 cloves garlic, crushed
1 tablespoon dried, salted black beans, chopped (use Asian variety)
2 tablespoons hoi sin sauce
1 tablespoon black bean sauce
1 tablespoon sugar
½ cup (125 ml/4 fl oz) vegetable stock
230 g (7⅓ oz) canned sliced bamboo shoots, drained
3 spring onions, cut in long slices

1 Add the noodles to a large pan of boiling water and cook until just tender; drain.
2 Heat the oils in a wok or pan. Add the ginger and garlic; stir over low heat for 2 minutes. Add well-rinsed black beans and stir for 2 minutes.
3 Add sauces, sugar and stock to pan. Simmer 5 minutes until slightly reduced and thickened. Add bamboo shoots, spring onions and noodles; stir until heated through and all the ingredients are well combined. Serve immediately.

BLACK BEANS

The black beans called for in Asian recipes are soya beans which have been fermented and salted. They are soft and slightly pulpy, and are usually chopped or crushed to release their pungent flavour. Don't confuse them with the dried black (turtle) beans used in South American cooking.

ABOVE: Noodles with Vegetables and Herbs (left); Noodles in Black Bean Sauce

GRAINS AND PULSES

Spilling out in a cornucopia of fabulous forms—from couscous to red lentils, chickpeas to millet—these wholesome staples are nutritious as well as delicious. When teamed with one another, or with nuts, they provide a diet complete in protein. And they provide the cook with an infinite number of recipe possibilities, inspired by national favourites from all around the world.

ARBORIO RICE

It has large, round pearly grains with a clearly defined hard white core, which, when cooked, remains visible and slightly resistant to the teeth. Arborio has a distinctive aroma and flavour—it is in fact the rice, and not the additions, which make the Northern Italian risotto unique.

CHICKPEA CURRY

Preparation time: 15 minutes
Total cooking time: 40–45 minutes
Serves 4

★

2 onions
4 cloves garlic
1 tablespoon ghee or oil
1 teaspoon chilli powder
1 teaspoon salt
1 teaspoon turmeric
1 teaspoon paprika
1 tablespoon ground cumin
1 tablespoon ground coriander
2 x 440 g (14 oz) cans chickpeas, drained
440 g (14 oz) canned tomato pieces
1 teaspoon garam masala

1 Slice onions finely; crush the garlic. Heat ghee or oil in a medium pan. Add onion and garlic to pan; cook over medium heat, stirring, until soft.
2 Add the chilli powder, salt, turmeric, paprika, cumin and coriander. Stir over heat for 1 minute.
3 Add chickpeas and undrained tomatoes, stir until combined. Simmer, covered, over low heat

ABOVE: Chickpea Curry

20 minutes, stirring occasionally. Stir in garam masala. Simmer, covered, for another 10 minutes.
NOTE: This curry makes a delicious meal wrapped inside chapattis or naan bread.

MUSHROOM RISOTTO

Preparation time: 10 minutes
Total cooking time: 30–35 minutes
Serves 4

★ ★

4 cups (1 litre) vegetable stock
1 cup (250 ml/8 fl oz) white wine
1 tablespoon oil
30 g (1 oz) butter
2 leeks, thinly sliced
250 g (8 oz) field mushrooms, sliced
2 cups (440 g/14 oz) arborio rice
250 g (8 oz) button mushrooms, sliced
2 tablespoons chopped fresh parsley
1/2 cup (50 g/1 2/3 oz) grated Parmesan cheese

1 Bring the stock and wine to the boil in a pan; reduce the heat and keep at a simmer.
2 Heat the oil and butter in a large pan, then add the leeks and cook for 5 minutes or until the

leeks are golden. Add the field mushrooms and cook for 3 minutes. Add the rice to the mushroom mixture and stir until the grains become translucent. Add 1 cup (250 ml/8 fl oz) of the hot liquid to the rice and stir over medium heat until all the liquid is absorbed. Continue to add the hot liquid, ½ cup at a time, stirring until absorbed between each addition. Reserve the final ½ cup of liquid.

3 Stir in the button mushrooms and reserved liquid. Cook, stirring, until the liquid is absorbed and the rice is tender. Stir in parsley and Parmesan cheese. Season with salt and pepper.

VEGETABLE COUSCOUS

Preparation time: 40 minutes
Total cooking time: 30 minutes
Serves 4-6

2 small onions
3 tablespoons olive oil
1 teaspoon turmeric
½ teaspoon chilli powder
2 teaspoons grated fresh ginger
1 cinnamon stick
2 medium carrots, thickly sliced
2 medium parsnips, thickly sliced
1½ cups (375 ml/12 fl oz) vegetable stock
315 g (10 oz) pumpkin, cut into small cubes
250 g (8 oz) cauliflower, cut into
    small florets
2 medium zucchinis (courgettes), cut
    into thick slices
425 g (13½ oz) canned chickpeas, drained
pinch saffron threads
2 tablespoons chopped fresh coriander
2 tablespoons chopped fresh flat-leaf parsley
1¼ cups (230 g/7⅓ oz) instant couscous
1 cup (250 ml/8 oz) boiling water
30 g (1 oz) butter

1 Thinly slice the onions. Heat 2 tablespoons of the oil in a large pan. Add the onions and cook over medium heat for 3 minutes or until the onions are soft, stirring occasionally. Add the turmeric, chilli powder and ginger; cook for another minute, stirring.

2 Add the cinnamon stick, carrots, parsnips and stock to the pan and stir to combine with spices

and onion. Cover and bring to the boil. Reduce heat and simmer, covered, for 5 minutes or until the vegetables are almost tender.

3 Add the pumpkin, cauliflower and zucchinis and simmer for another 10 minutes. Stir in the chickpeas, saffron, coriander and parsley; simmer, uncovered, for 5 minutes. Remove the cinnamon stick.

4 Place the couscous in a bowl and add boiling water. Allow to stand for 2 minutes; add the remaining oil and butter and fluff with a fork. Place a bed of couscous on each serving plate and top with the vegetables.

NOTE: Vegetables may be cooked up to a day in advance and refrigerated. Couscous (available from supermarkets or delicatessens) is best prepared just before serving.

FAST RED LENTIL SOUP

FRY A FINELY chopped onion in a little oil until soft, then add 1 cup (250 g/8 oz) red lentils, 425 g (13½ oz) canned crushed tomatoes and 4 cups (1 litre) of vegetable stock. Bring to the boil; reduce the heat and simmer for 20 minutes, then stir in some chopped basil and serve topped with a small dollop of sour cream. Serves 4.

COUSCOUS

Couscous is made from semolina grain and semolina flour, rolled into tiny pellets. It is a staple in North African cooking, and is traditionally steamed over a pot of stew. The couscous seen most commonly is an 'instant' variety, which only needs to be combined with boiling water and left to stand for a couple of minutes. Butter and oil are then forked through the grains. The name couscous also refers to the whole dish of a stew served over couscous grains.

ABOVE: Vegetable Couscous

1 Soak the chickpeas in water for 4 hours or overnight. Drain and place chickpeas into a food processor. Process for 30 seconds or until chickpeas are finely ground.

2 Add onion, garlic, parsley, coriander, cumin, extra water and baking powder and process for 10 seconds or until mixture is a rough paste. Cover, leave mixture to stand for 30 minutes.

3 **To make Tomato Salsa:** Place all ingredients in a bowl and mix to combine; set aside.

4 Shape heaped tablespoons of felafel mixture into balls. Squeeze out excess liquid using your hands. Heat oil to moderately hot in a deep, heavy-based pan. Gently lower the felafel balls, on a large spoon, into the oil. Cook in batches of 5 at a time, for 3–4 minutes each batch. When balls are well browned, carefully remove from the oil with a large slotted spoon. Drain the felafel well on paper towels.

5 Serve felafel hot or cold on a bed of Tomato Salsa or in some pitta bread with Tomato Salsa and hummus.

NOTE: If the felafel mixture is too wet to form into balls, mix in a small amount of plain flour.

FELAFEL

Felafel has become so popular in Israel that it has almost acquired the status of a national dish. Served in a pocket of pitta bread, with salad and any spicy relish, or with salad and a yoghurt and herb dressing, these crisp little savoury balls made from ground chickpeas make a healthy, wonderful lunch or snack.

ABOVE: Felafel with Tomato Salsa

FELAFEL WITH TOMATO SALSA

Preparation time: 40 minutes + 30 minutes standing + 4 hours soaking
Total cooking time: 20–25 minutes
Serves 6

★ ★

2 cups (440 g/14 oz) chickpeas
3 cups (750 ml/24 fl oz) water
1 small onion, finely chopped
2 cloves garlic, crushed
2 tablespoons chopped fresh parsley
1 tablespoon chopped fresh coriander
2 teaspoons ground cumin
1 tablespoon water, extra
1/2 teaspoon baking powder
oil, for deep-frying

Tomato Salsa

2 medium tomatoes, peeled and finely chopped
1/4 medium Lebanese cucumber, finely chopped
1/2 green pepper (capsicum), finely chopped
2 tablespoons chopped fresh parsley
1 teaspoon sugar
2 teaspoons chilli sauce
1/2 teaspoon ground black pepper
grated rind and juice of 1 lemon

SWEET AND SPICY LENTILS

Preparation time: 10 minutes + overnight soaking
Total cooking time: 35 minutes
Serves 6

★

3/4 cup (140 g/4 1/2 oz) green lentils, soaked overnight
1 small onion, finely chopped
1/2 teaspoon ground cumin
1/2 teaspoon ground cinnamon
4 cloves
1 cup (250 ml/8 fl oz) orange juice
3/4 cup (185 ml/6 fl oz) water

1 Drain the lentils and place them in a medium pan with the onion, cumin, cinnamon, cloves, orange juice and water. Bring to the boil. Reduce heat and simmer, uncovered, stirring occasionally, for about 30 minutes, until liquid has been absorbed and lentils are very soft.

2 Remove cloves and serve lentils hot or cold with your favourite Mexican dish.

MUSHROOM RISOTTO FRITTERS

Preparation time: 20 minutes
+ 1 hour 15 minutes refrigeration
Total cooking time: 35–40 minutes
Serves 4

3 1/4 cups (810 ml/26 fl oz) vegetable stock
1 tablespoon olive oil
20 g (2/3 oz) butter
1 small onion, finely chopped
1 cup (220 g/7 oz) arborio or short-grain rice
150 g (4 3/4 oz) small button mushrooms,
    thinly sliced
1/3 cup (35 g/1 1/4 oz) freshly grated
    Parmesan cheese
oil, for frying

1 Bring stock to boil in a small pan. Reduce heat, cover and simmer slowly until needed. Heat oil and butter in heavy-based pan. Add onion, stir over medium heat for 3 minutes or until softened. Add rice, cook 2 minutes. Add mushrooms, cook for 3 minutes or until soft.
2 Add hot stock 1/2 cup at a time, stirring constantly, until all stock is absorbed. Repeat process, stirring constantly, until all the hot stock has been added and rice is just tender and creamy. (This will take about 20 minutes.) Stir in Parmesan cheese and remove from heat.
3 Transfer mixture to a bowl to cool; refrigerate for at least 1 hour. With wet hands, shape 1/4 cupfuls of mixture into flat rounds. Refrigerate for 15 minutes.

4 Heat about 2.5 cm (1 inch) oil in a non-stick pan. Cook fritters for 3–4 minutes each side, until golden and crisp. Drain on paper towels.

ONION AND PARMESAN PILAF

Preparation time: 5 minutes
Total cooking time: 20–30 minutes
Serves 6

60 g (2 oz) butter
3 onions, chopped
2 cloves garlic, crushed
2 cups (440 g/14 oz) basmati rice
5 cups (1.25 litres) vegetable stock
1 1/2 cups (240 g/7 1/2 oz) shelled peas
1/2 cup (50 g/1 2/3 oz) freshly grated
    Parmesan cheese
1/2 cup (30 g/1 oz) chopped fresh parsley

1 Melt butter in a large pan, add onion and garlic and stir over low heat for 5 minutes or until soft and golden. Add rice and stock, bring to the boil, stir once. Reduce heat to low; simmer, uncovered, for 5 minutes or until almost all the liquid has been absorbed.
2 Add peas, stir until combined. Cover pan, cook over very low heat for 10 minutes or until rice is tender. Stir in Parmesan cheese and parsley, serve.

VEGETABLE STOCK

Most dishes cooked with vegetable stock have more flavour than those simply made with water. When making stock, vegetables should be cleaned but do not need to be peeled. Aromatic vegetables such as leeks, onions, carrots and celery are those most commonly used. Starchy vegetables such as peas and potatoes are not as suitable as they can 'cloud' the stock. Vegetables with a stronger flavour, such as eggplants (aubergines), cabbages or turnips should be avoided. The liquid remaining after cooking mildly-flavoured vegetables also makes a nutritious stock. Vegetable stock can be used in sauces, soups and casseroles.

LEFT: Onion and Parmesan Pilaf
ABOVE: Mushroom Risotto Fritters

TOFU

Tofu has always had a bit of an image problem. We know it's nutritious but not many people actually eat it! Tofu itself is very bland, but lends itself well to marinating and cooking with flavours such as garlic, ginger, soy sauce and chilli. Marinated and fried until crisp on the outside, it can taste every bit as good as something bad for you. If you have tried tofu and not liked it once, try it again—you may be pleasantly suprised.

ABOVE: Wild Rice Pancakes with Tofu and Mushrooms

WILD RICE PANCAKES WITH TOFU AND MUSHROOMS

Preparation time: 25 minutes + 1 hour standing
Total cooking time: approximately 1 hour
Serves 6–12

6 eggs, lightly beaten

3 cups (750 ml/24 fl oz) milk

185 g (6 oz) butter, melted

1 1/2 cups (185 g/6 oz) plain flour

1/2 teaspoon baking powder

2 tablespoons kecap manis

2 tablespoons chopped fresh coriander

2 tablespoons olive oil

2 tablespoons grated fresh ginger

1 fresh red chilli, finely chopped

2 spring onions, finely chopped

1/2 cup (95 g/3 1/4 oz) wild rice, cooked

1 teaspoon sesame oil

1 tablespoon oil

125 g (4 oz) tofu, cut into cubes

315 g (10 oz) mixed fresh mushrooms

2 teaspoons white miso

2 tablespoons soy sauce

1 tablespoon lime juice

2 cloves garlic, crushed

1 Place the eggs, milk and 125 g (4 oz) butter in a large bowl; whisk to combine.
2 Sift the flour and baking powder into a bowl. Gradually whisk the flour into egg mixture. Add kecap manis and coriander; whisk until smooth. Cover and refrigerate for 1 hour.
3 Meanwhile, heat the olive oil in a wok. Add ginger, chilli and spring onions and stir-fry over high heat for 3 minutes. Remove from heat, place in a bowl with wild rice; cover, set aside.
4 Add rice mixture to the pancake mixture and mix well. Heat the remaining butter in a non-stick frying pan, spoon 1/4 cup of the mixture into the pan, tilt the pan so that mixture covers base; cook for 2 minutes, or until the mixture begins to bubble. Turn and cook the other side until golden. Repeat with remaining mixture.
5 Heat oils in a wok. Add the tofu, stir-fry over high heat for 5 minutes, or until tofu is golden. Add mushrooms, miso, soy sauce and lime juice and cook for 4 minutes or until the mixture is heated through. Add the garlic and stir for 1 minute. Serve 2 filled pancakes per person as a first course, or 4 each as a main course.
NOTE: Kecap manis is a thick, dark, sweet, aromatic soy sauce. Traditionally it is flavoured with garlic, star anise, salam leaves and galangal, and sweetened with palm syrup.

Any type of mushroom can be used, for example, button, oyster or enoki.

MUSHROOMS FILLED WITH SPICED QUINOA

Preparation time: 20 minutes
Total cooking time: 40 minutes
Serves 4

1 cup (200 g/6¹/₂ oz) quinoa

2 cups (500 ml/16 fl oz) vegetable stock

1 bay leaf

1 star anise

2 tablespoons oil

3 onions, finely sliced

1 tablespoon ground cumin

1 teaspoon garam marsala

155 g (5 oz) feta cheese, chopped

1 tablespoon chopped fresh mint

2 teaspoons lemon juice

4 large field mushrooms

2 tablespoons olive oil, extra

1 Rinse quinoa under cold water for 5 minutes or until water runs clear; drain well.
2 Place quinoa, vegetable stock, bay leaf and star anise into a heavy-based pan. Bring to boil, reduce heat and simmer for 15 minutes or until quinoa is translucent. Remove from heat and allow to stand for 5 minutes. By this time the stock will be absorbed into the quinoa. Remove bay leaf and star anise.
3 Heat the oil in a large non-stick frying pan. Add onions and cook over medium heat for 10 minutes or until they begin to caramelise.
4 Add the cumin, garam marsala, feta cheese and quinoa. Cook for 3 minutes or until heated through. Remove from heat and stir in the mint and lemon juice.
5 Remove the stalks from the mushrooms, chop the stalks finely and add to quinoa mixture. Brush mushrooms lightly with extra oil, place fan-side down on a preheated char-grill or barbecue. Cook for 3 minutes or until browned (time will vary according to the size of the mushrooms); turn over and fill caps with the quinoa mixture. Cook for 5 minutes or until the mushrooms are tender. Serve hot with salad.
NOTE: Quinoa (pronounced keen-wah) is a grain grown high in the Peruvian Andes. It is favoured by vegetarians and is known as a 'super grain' because of its protein content. Quinoa was considered sacred by the Incas and was used in their religious ceremonies. It is available from health food stores.

AVOCADO AND BLACK BEAN SALAD

Preparation time: 15 minutes + overnight soaking
Total cooking time: approximately 1¹/₂ hours
Serves 4

250 g (8 oz) dried black beans

1 red (Spanish) onion, chopped

4 egg (Roma) tomatoes, chopped

1 red pepper (capsicum), chopped

375 g (12 oz) canned corn kernels, drained

90 g (3 oz) fresh coriander, roughly chopped

2 avocados, peeled and chopped

1 mango, peeled and chopped

150 g (4³/₄ oz) rocket, leaves separated

Dressing

1 clove garlic, crushed

1 small red chilli, finely chopped

2 tablespoons lime juice

¹/₄ cup (60 ml/2 fl oz) olive oil

1 Soak the beans in cold water overnight. Rinse; drain. Place the beans into a large heavy-based pan, cover with water and bring to the boil. Reduce the heat and simmer for 1¹/₂ hours, or until tender. Drain and cool slightly.
2 Place the beans, onion, tomatoes, pepper, corn, coriander, avocado, mango and rocket into a large bowl and toss to combine.
3 To make Dressing: Place all ingredients in a bowl, whisk, pour over the salad and toss.

BLACK BEANS
Black beans are available in dried form from health food stores. Also known as turtle beans, they are an important part of the diet of people in Central and South America, the Caribbean and Mexico. Do not confuse them with Chinese salted or fermented beans.

ABOVE: Avocado and Black Bean Salad

CRISPY LENTIL BALLS

Preparation time: 20 minutes
Total cooking time: 15–20 minutes
Makes about 30

★ ★

1 cup (250 g/8 oz) red lentils
4 spring onions, chopped
2 cloves garlic, crushed
1 teaspoon ground cumin
1 cup (80 g/2 2/3 oz) fresh breadcrumbs
1 cup (125 g/4 oz) grated Cheddar cheese
1 large zucchini (courgette), grated
1 cup (150 g/4 3/4 oz) polenta (cornmeal)
oil, for deep-frying

1 Place the lentils in a medium pan and cover with water. Bring to the boil, reduce heat to low; cover and simmer for 10 minutes or until the lentils are tender. Drain and rinse well under cold water.
2 Combine half the lentils in a food processor or blender with the spring onions and garlic. Process for 10 seconds or until the mixture is pulpy. Transfer to a large bowl and add the remaining lentils, cumin, breadcrumbs, cheese and zucchini. Stir until combined.
3 Using your hands, roll level tablespoons of mixture into balls and toss lightly in polenta.
4 Heat the oil in a heavy-based pan. Gently lower small batches of the balls into moderately hot oil. Cook for 1 minute or until golden brown and crisp. Carefully remove from the oil with tongs or a slotted spoon and drain on paper towels. Repeat the process with the remaining balls. Serve hot.
NOTE: These are delicious served with chutney or yoghurt for dipping.

SPINACH RICE

Preparation time: 5 minutes
Total cooking time: 50 minutes
Serves 4

★

90 g (3 oz) butter
1 cup (200 g/6 1/2 oz) long-grain rice
2 cups (500 ml/16 fl oz) vegetable stock
salt and freshly ground black pepper
2 tablespoons olive oil
2 large onions, finely chopped
250 g (8 oz) frozen chopped spinach, thawed
4 spring onions, chopped

1 Heat butter in a medium heavy-based pan; add the rice and stir over low heat for 10 minutes or until lightly golden.
2 Add stock, salt and pepper. Slowly bring to boil, stirring constantly. Reduce heat and simmer, covered, for 20 minutes. Cover; set aside.
3 Heat the oil in a small pan. Add the onions and stir over medium heat for 5 minutes. Add the spinach, reduce heat and cook, covered, for 5–10 minutes or until the spinach is hot. Add spring onions and stir for 1 minute.
4 Add the spinach mixture to the rice. Stir until just heated through.

ABOVE: Spinach Rice
RIGHT: Crispy Lentil Balls

INDIAN DHAL WITH PITTA TOASTS

Preparation time: 15 minutes
Total cooking time: 20–25 minutes
Serves 4-6

1 1/4 cups (310 g/9 3/4 oz) red lentils

2 tablespoons ghee (clarified butter)

1 medium onion, finely chopped

2 cloves garlic, crushed

1 teaspoon grated fresh ginger

1 teaspoon ground turmeric

1 teaspoon garam masala

2 cups (500 ml/16 fl oz) water

Pitta Toasts

4 rounds of pitta bread

2–3 tablespoons olive oil

1 Place the lentils in a large bowl and cover with water. Remove any floating particles and drain the lentils well.
2 Heat the ghee in a medium pan. Fry the onion for about 3 minutes or until soft. Add the garlic, ginger and spices; cook, stirring for another minute.
3 Add the lentils and water, bring to the boil. Lower the heat and simmer, stirring occasionally, for 15 minutes or until all the water has been absorbed. Watch carefully towards the end of cooking time, as the mixture could burn on the bottom of the pan.
4 Transfer to a serving bowl and serve warm or at room temperature, with Pitta Toasts or with naan or pitta bread.
5 To make Pitta Toasts: Preheat the oven to moderate 180°C (350°F/Gas 4). Cut the pitta bread into wedges and brush lightly with oil. Arrange on an oven tray and cook for 5–7 minutes, until lightly browned and crisp.
NOTE: Oil may be used instead of the ghee if ghee is difficult to obtain. You can also make your own ghee—melt some butter, skim away the white froth on the surface and then pour the clear butter into another container, leaving the white residue behind.

VEGETABLE PILAF

Preparation time: 20 minutes
Total cooking time: 35–40 minutes
Serves 4

1/4 cup (60 ml/2 fl oz) olive oil

1 medium onion, sliced

2 cloves garlic, crushed

2 teaspoons ground cumin

2 teaspoons paprika

1/2 teaspoon allspice

1 1/2 cups (300 g/9 2/3 oz) long-grain rice

1 1/2 cups (375 ml/12 fl oz) vegetable stock

3/4 cup (185 ml/6 fl oz) white wine

3 medium tomatoes, peeled and chopped

155 g (5 oz) button mushrooms, sliced

2 medium zucchinis (courgettes), sliced

155 g (5 oz) broccoli, cut into florets

1 Heat the oil in a large heavy-based pan. Add the onion and cook for 10 minutes over medium heat until golden brown. Add garlic and spices and cook for 1 minute until aromatic.
2 Add rice to pan and stir until well combined. Add vegetable stock, wine, tomatoes and mushrooms and bring to the boil. Reduce heat to low and cover pan with a tight-fitting lid. Simmer for 15 minutes.
3 Add zucchini and broccoli to pan; replace lid and cook for another 5–7 minutes, until vegetables are just tender. Serve immediately.

LENTILS
When buying lentils, look for bright, shiny pulses with no hint of dust, damp or mould. It is important not to buy in bulk as lentils become harder and drier with time. They then take longer to cook and are more likely to break up during cooking. Lentils make excellent purées and soups, and are the easiest to prepare of all the pulses—green lentils require only a few hours soaking and red lentils none at all. Pick over lentils before cooking as they can easily conceal small stones.

ABOVE: Vegetable Pilaf

POLENTA
Its origins unclear—dating back to Ancient Rome or discovered in the New World—and its name used interchangeably with cornmeal, this flour-like staple has found a new identity in the contemporary kitchen.

BASIC POLENTA

Bring 4 cups (1 litre) of water or stock to the boil. Reduce heat and slowly whisk in 1 cup (150 g/4¾ oz) coarse polenta. Continue whisking 5 minutes. Replace whisk with a wooden spoon and stir until spoon can stand and polenta comes away from sides of pan. Stir in 2 tablespoons of softened butter and season with salt and pepper.

MEDITERRANEAN POLENTA FRITTATA

Make polenta as instructed in Basic Polenta recipe. Transfer the mixture to a bowl; add ½ cup (50 g/1⅔ oz) freshly grated Parmesan cheese, 4 finely chopped marinated artichoke hearts, 90 g (3 oz) chopped sun-dried tomatoes, 60 g (2 oz) pitted and chopped niçoise olives, and 1 tablespoon fresh oregano leaves. Spoon the mixture into a lightly greased 30 cm (12 inch) springform (spring-release) pan; spread the mixture evenly over the pan and press down with the back of a spoon. Set aside to cool. Release the frittata from the tin, brush lightly with oil and cook under a preheated grill until just crisp and golden brown. Cut into wedges and serve hot or at room temperature. Serves 6–8.

CHAR-GRILLED POLENTA

Make polenta as directed in the Basic Polenta recipe. Stir in ¼ cup (25 g/ ¾ oz) of freshly grated Parmesan cheese and 1 tablespoon of chopped fresh basil. Spread the mixture over a large pizza tray to form a 2 cm (¾ inch)-thick circle. Set aside to cool. Cut the polenta into wedges. Brush lightly with oil and cook on a preheated char-grill or barbecue for 3 minutes on each side, or until the wedges are crisp. Serve warm as a finger food. Serves 4–6.

POLENTA WITH CHILLI JAM

Serve char-grilled wedges accompanied by a large spoonful of mascarpone cheese, some rocket leaves drizzled with balsamic vinegar, and home-made chilli jam (see page 245) or your favourite spicy tomato relish. Serves 4–6.

POLENTA STICKS WITH ARTICHOKES, FETA AND PEPPERS (CAPSICUMS)

Make polenta as directed in the Basic Polenta recipe. Spread the mixture into a lightly greased 18 cm (7 inch) square pan. Set aside to cool. Cut polenta into 3 cm (1¼ inch)-wide sticks. Brush the sticks lightly with oil and cook under a preheated grill until they are crisp and golden. Serve polenta sticks with quartered marinated artichokes (with stems attached), a round of marinated feta cheese, and strips of roasted red and yellow pepper (capsicum). Serves 4–6.

POLENTA PIZZA

Make polenta as directed in the Basic Polenta recipe. Stir in ½ cup (50 g/ 1⅔ oz) of freshly grated Parmesan cheese. Spread the mixture over the base of a deep 30 cm (12 inch) pizza tray. Set aside to cool. Brush the polenta with oil and bake in a preheated moderately hot 200°C (400°F/Gas 6) oven for 10 minutes. Remove the polenta from the oven and spread 3 tablespoons of pesto sauce over the top, leaving a 1 cm (½ inch) border. Top with some sliced button mushrooms, halved cherry and teardrop tomatoes and 1 sliced green pepper (capsicum). Sprinkle with 125 g (4 oz) grated mozzarella cheese. Bake for 20 minutes or until the cheese is golden. Serves 4.

CLOKWISE, FROM TOP LEFT:
Polenta with Chilli Jam; Char-grilled Polenta; Polenta Sticks with Artichokes, Feta and Peppers; Polenta Pizza; Basic Polenta; Mediterranean Polenta Frittata

1 Boil the stock in a small pan. Reduce heat, cover and keep gently simmering. Heat oil and butter in a medium heavy-based pan. Add onion and stir over medium heat for 3 minutes or until golden; add rice. Reduce heat to low and stir for 3 minutes or until rice is lightly golden. Add a quarter of the stock to the pan. Stir for 5 minutes or until all liquid has been absorbed.

2 Repeat process until all stock has been added and rice is almost tender, stirring constantly. Stir in Parmesan. Remove from heat. Transfer to a bowl to cool; refrigerate for 1 hour.

3 With wet hands, roll 2 tablespoons of rice mixture into a ball. Make an indentation in the ball and press in a cube of mozzarella and a couple of pieces of sun-dried tomato. Reshape the ball to cover indentation, then flatten slightly to a disc shape. Repeat process with remaining mixture. Refrigerate for 15 minutes.

4 Heat oil in a medium heavy-based pan. Gently lower risotto cakes a few at a time into moderately hot oil. Cook for 1–2 minutes or until golden brown. Remove with a slotted spoon and drain on paper towels. Serve risotto cakes with fresh green salad leaves.

ADZUKI BEAN STIR-FRY

Preparation time: 15 minutes + overnight soaking
Total cooking time: 1 hour 15 minutes
Serves 4

☆

1 cup (220 g/7 oz) adzuki beans
1 teaspoon sesame oil
1 tablespoon oil
1 clove garlic, crushed
1 tablespoon grated fresh ginger
3 spring onions, sliced
185 g (6 oz) firm tofu, cut into
    bite-size pieces
125 g (4 oz) shimeji mushrooms, separated
1 red pepper (capsicum), sliced
1 large carrot, sliced
100 g (3 1/3 oz) baby corn
500 g (1 lb) baby bok choy, leaves separated
1 tablespoon oyster sauce
1 tablespoon hoi sin sauce
1/4 cup (60 ml/2 fl oz) salt-reduced soy sauce
1 tablespoon sweet chilli sauce
1 tablespoon lime juice
2 tablespoons chopped fresh coriander

TOMATO AND CHEESE RISOTTO CAKES

Preparation time: 30 minutes
    + 1 hour 15 minutes refrigeration
Total cooking time: 30–40 minutes
Serves 6

☆ ☆

3 1/4 cups (810 ml/26 fl oz) vegetable
    stock
1 tablespoon olive oil
20 g (2/3 oz) butter
1 small onion, finely chopped
1 1/4 cups (275 g/8 3/4 oz) short-grain rice
1/3 cup (35 g/1 1/4 oz) freshly grated
    Parmesan cheese
30 g (1 oz) mozzarella cheese, cut
    into 1 cm (1/2 inch) cubes
30 g (1 oz) sun-dried tomatoes, chopped
oil, for deep-frying
70 g (2 1/3 oz) mixed salad leaves, for serving

ABOVE: Tomato and
Cheese Risotto Cakes

1 Soak adzuki beans in cold water overnight. Rinse and drain well. Place in a large, heavy-based pan, cover with water and bring to the boil. Reduce heat and simmer for 1 hour or until tender; drain.

2 Heat oils in a wok and add the garlic, ginger and spring onions; stir-fry over high heat for 2 minutes. Add tofu and stir-fry for 5 minutes or until golden brown. Add mushrooms, pepper, carrot, corn and bok choy. Stir-fry 3 minutes.

3 Stir in the drained beans, oyster, hoi sin, soy and sweet chilli sauces, lime juice and coriander; cook for 2 minutes, stirring constantly. Serve with steamed rice.

NOTE: Adzuki beans are related to soya beans and are very easily digested. Sometimes referred to as red beans, they are very popular in Japan. Boiled, mashed and mixed with shortening and sugar to form red bean paste, they are used to make many Asian sweets.

LENTIL AND CHICKPEA BURGERS WITH CORIANDER GARLIC CREAM

Preparation time: 30 minutes + refrigeration
Total cooking time: approximately 30 minutes
Makes 10 burgers

1 cup (250 g/8 oz) red lentils
1 tablespoon oil
2 onions, sliced
1 tablespoon tandoori mix powder
425 g (13 1/2 oz) canned chickpeas, drained
1 tablespoon grated fresh ginger
1 egg
3 tablespoons chopped fresh parsley
2 tablespoons chopped fresh coriander
2 1/4 cups (180 g/5 3/4 oz) stale
    breadcrumbs
flour, for dusting

Coriander Garlic Cream

1/2 cup (125 g/4 oz) sour cream
1/2 cup (125 ml/4 fl oz) cream
1 clove garlic, crushed
2 tablespoons chopped fresh coriander
2 tablespoons chopped fresh parsley

1 Prepare and heat barbecue. Bring a large pan of water to the boil. Add the lentils to the boiling water and simmer, uncovered, for 10 minutes or until the lentils are tender. Drain well. Heat the oil in a pan and cook the onions until tender. Add tandoori mix and stir until fragrant. Cool the mixture slightly.

2 Place the chickpeas, half the lentils, ginger, egg and onion mixture in a food processor. Process for 20 seconds or until smooth. Transfer to a bowl. Stir in the remaining lentils, parsley, coriander and breadcrumbs, combine well. Divide the mixture into 10 portions.

3 Shape the portions into round patties. (If the mixture is too soft, refrigerate for 15 minutes or until firm.) Toss the patties in flour and shake off excess. Place the patties on a lightly greased barbecue grill or flatplate. Cook for 3–4 minutes on each side or until browned, turning once. Serve with Coriander Garlic Cream.

4 **To make Coriander Garlic Cream:** Combine the sour cream, cream, garlic and herbs in a bowl and mix well.

NOTE: The patties can be prepared up to 2 days ahead and stored, covered, in the refrigerator. If you prefer, you can cook the patties in a frying pan brushed lightly with oil. The Coriander Garlic Cream can be made up to 3 days in advance. Place in a covered container and store in the refrigerator.

CORIANDER

Coriander (*Coriandrum sativum*) is a useful herb, as all parts of the plant are eaten. The leaves, stems and roots are used in Thai cookery, the leaves are used in Mexican cookery (where it is known as cilantro) and the dried seeds are used whole or ground, particularly in Middle Eastern cookery.

ABOVE: Lentil and Chickpea Burgers with Coriander Garlic Cream

FILO RISOTTO PIE

Preparation time: 45 minutes
Total cooking time: 1 hour 45 minutes
Serves 8

★ ★ ★

2 large red peppers (capsicums)

Risotto

1 cup (250 ml/8 fl oz) white wine
4 cups (1 litre) vegetable stock
2 tablespoons oil
1 clove garlic, crushed
1 leek, sliced
1 fennel bulb, thinly sliced
2 cups (440 g/14 oz) arborio rice
60 g (2 oz) freshly grated Parmesan cheese
10 sheets filo pastry
1/4 cup (60 ml/2 fl oz) olive oil
500 g (1 lb) English spinach, blanched
250 g (8 oz) feta cheese, sliced
1 tablespoon sesame seeds

1 Cut the peppers in half lengthways. Remove the seeds and membrane and then cut into large, flattish pieces. Grill until skin blackens and blisters. Place on a cutting board, cover with a tea towel and allow to cool. Peel the peppers and cut the flesh into smaller pieces.
2 **To make Risotto:** Place wine and stock into a large pan. Bring to the boil and reduce heat.
3 Heat oil and garlic in a large heavy-based pan. Add leek and fennel, cook over medium heat for 5 minutes or until lightly browned. Add rice and stir for 3 minutes or until rice is translucent.
4 Add 1 cup of stock mixture to the rice and stir constantly until liquid is absorbed. Continue adding liquid 1/2 cup at a time, stirring constantly until all the stock mixture has been used and rice is tender. This will take about 40 minutes. Make sure the liquid stays hot as the risotto will become gluggy if it isn't. Remove from the heat, stir in the Parmesan cheese and season with salt and pepper. Set aside until cooled slightly.
5 Brush each sheet of filo with olive oil and fold in half lengthways. Arrange like overlapping spokes on a wheel, in a 23 cm (9 inch) springform (spring-release) pan, with one side of pastry hanging over the side of tin.
6 Spoon half the risotto mixture over the pastry and top with half the red peppers, half the spinach and half the feta cheese. Repeat with the remaining ingredients.

7 Fold pastry over the filling, brush lightly with oil and sprinkle with sesame seeds. Bake for 50 minutes or until the pastry is crisp and golden and the pie is heated through.

MEDITERRANEAN LENTIL SALAD

Preparation time: 20 minutes
+ 4 hours refrigeration
Total cooking time: 20 minutes
Serves 4-6

★

1 large red pepper (capsicum)
1 large yellow pepper (capsicum)
1 cup (250 g/8 oz) red lentils
1 red (Spanish) onion, finely chopped
1 Lebanese cucumber, chopped

Dressing

1/3 cup olive oil
2 tablespoons lemon juice
1 teaspoon ground cumin
2 cloves garlic, crushed
salt and pepper

1 Cut the peppers in half lengthways. Remove the seeds and membrane and then cut into large, flattish pieces. Grill until skin blackens and blisters. Place on a cutting board, cover with a tea towel and allow to cool. Peel the peppers and cut the flesh into 1/2 cm (1/4 inch) strips.
2 Cook the lentils in boiling water for 10 minutes or until tender; do not overcook as they will become mushy. Drain well.
3 Place the peppers, lentils, onion and cucumber into a bowl and toss to combine.
4 **To make Dressing:** Place the olive oil, lemon juice, cumin, garlic, salt and pepper into a small bowl and whisk to combine.
5 Pour Dressing over the salad and mix well. Cover the salad and refrigerate for 4 hours. Allow the salad to return to room temperature before serving.

RICE FOR RISOTTO

Arborio rice is an Italian short-grain rice that was first grown in the Po Valley in the Piedmont region of Italy. It is available at delicatessens and some supermarkets. Other short-grain rices can be substituted but the result will be inferior as a risotto made with arborio rice has a richer, creamier texture.

OPPOSITE PAGE:
Filo Risotto Pie (top);
Mediterranean
Lentil Salad

BROWN RICE TART WITH FRESH TOMATO FILLING

Preparation time: 25 minutes
Total cooking time: approximately 2 hours
Serves 6

Rice Crust

1 cup (200 g/6¹/2 oz) brown rice
1/2 cup (60 g/2 oz) grated Cheddar cheese
1 egg, lightly beaten

Fresh Tomato Filling

6 egg (Roma) tomatoes, halved
6 cloves garlic, unpeeled
1 tablespoon olive oil
freshly ground black pepper
8 sprigs fresh lemon thyme
50 g (1²/3 oz) goats cheese, crumbled
3 eggs, lightly beaten
1/4 cup (60 ml/2 fl oz) milk

1 To make Rice Crust: Cook the rice in plenty of boiling water for 35–40 minutes or until tender; drain and set aside to cool. Preheat the oven to moderately hot 200°C (400°F/Gas 6).

BROWN RICE
Brown rice has more vitamins and minerals than white rice, as it still has its bran layer. To retain the maximum nutrients, it is best to cook rice (white or brown) by the absorption method, as most of the vitamins are water soluble and are lost if the rice is drained.

ABOVE: Brown Rice Tart with Fresh Tomato Filling

Place the rice, cheese and egg into a medium bowl and mix until well combined. Spread the mixture over the base and sides of a lightly greased 25 cm (10 inch) flan tin or quiche dish and bake for 15 minutes.

2 To make Fresh Tomato Filling: Place the tomatoes, cut-side up, and garlic on a non-stick baking tray, brush lightly with oil and sprinkle with pepper. Bake for 30 minutes. Remove from the oven and allow to cool slightly. Remove the skins from the garlic.

3 Reduce oven temperature to moderate 180°C (350°F/Gas 4). Arrange the tomato halves, garlic, lemon thyme and goats cheese over the rice crust.

4 Place the beaten eggs and milk in a bowl and whisk to combine. Pour over the tomatoes. Bake for 1 hour or until set.

NOTE: Goats cheese, also known as chèvre, is available from the speciality cheese section of the supermarket, or from good delicatessens. It has quite a pungent flavour and can be an acquired taste. It will soften when cooked but doesn't become really runny. Feta cheese can be substituted if you prefer.

BEETROOT HUMMUS

Preparation time: 25 minutes
+ overnight soaking
Total cooking time: 1 hour 15 minutes
Serves 8

250 g (8 oz) dried chickpeas
1 large onion, chopped
500 g (1 lb) beetroot
1/2 cup (125 ml/4 fl oz) tahini
   (sesame seed paste)
3 cloves garlic, crushed
1/4 cup (60 ml/2 fl oz) lemon juice
1 tablespoon ground cumin
1/4 cup (60 ml/2 fl oz) olive oil

1 Put the chickpeas in a large bowl, cover with cold water and soak overnight. Drain.
2 Place the chickpeas and onion in a large heavy-based pan, cover with water and bring to the boil. Cook for 1 hour or until chickpeas are very soft. Drain, reserving 1 cup of cooking liquid; allow to cool.
3 Cook the beetroot in a large pan of boiling water until tender. Drain and allow to cool slightly before removing skins.
4 Chop the beetroot and place in a food processor, in batches if necessary. Add the chickpea and onion mixture, tahini, garlic, lemon juice and cumin; process until smooth. Slowly add reserved cooking liquid and olive oil while the machine is running. Process until mixture is thoroughly combined. Drizzle with a little olive oil and serve with Lebanese bread.

TEX MEX CHILLI BEANS

Preparation time: 20 minutes
Total cooking time: 25 minutes
Serves 4

1 tablespoon oil
2 cloves garlic, crushed
2 small fresh red chillies, finely chopped
1 onion, finely chopped
1 green pepper (capsicum), chopped
440 g (14 oz) canned red kidney beans, drained
   and rinsed
440 g (14 oz) canned peeled tomatoes
1/2 cup (125 g/4 oz) ready-made tomato salsa
1 teaspoon soft brown sugar

1 Heat the oil, garlic, chillies and onion in a heavy-based pan and cook over medium heat for 3 minutes or until onion is golden.
2 Add the green pepper, kidney beans, undrained, crushed tomatoes, salsa and sugar. Bring to the boil, reduce heat and simmer, uncovered, for 15 minutes or until the sauce thickens. Chilli Beans can be served with sour cream, guacamole (see page 72) and corn chips.
NOTE: It is said that red kidney beans originated in Mexico approximately 5000 years ago. Red kidney beans contain dietary fibre, iron, potassium, and several B vitamins. Canned chickpeas, drained and rinsed, may be substituted for kidney beans in this recipe if you prefer.

CHICKPEAS

Chickpeas contain dietary fibre, protein, iron, vitamin B1 and potassium. They need to be soaked overnight before being cooked. Canned chickpeas are available and save on soaking and cooking time.

LEFT: Beetroot Hummus
ABOVE: Tex Mex Chilli Beans

SOYA BEANS

The highly nutritious soya bean contains quality vegetable protein as well as dietary fibre and fat. It is one of the world's oldest and most important food crops, and is processed to make soy milk and tofu. The cream-coloured beans, which also come in red and black varieties, can be sprouted to make a crunchy addition to salads, sandwiches and stir-fries.

ABOVE: Almond Sesame Soya Burgers

ALMOND SESAME SOYA BURGERS

Preparation time: 20 minutes
Total cooking time: 3 hours 40 minutes
+ overnight soaking
Makes 10

1 cup (60 g/2 oz) dried soya beans
125 g (4 oz) smoked almonds
1 onion, chopped
1 carrot, grated
1 tablespoon tamari
3 tablespoons rolled oats
1 egg, lightly beaten
3 tablespoons chickpea (besan) flour
1 teaspoon ground cumin
1 teaspoon ground coriander
3 tablespoons sesame seeds
oil, for shallow-frying

1 Soak the soya beans in cold water overnight; rinse and drain well.
2 Place the soya beans in a large heavy-based pan, cover with water and bring to the boil. Reduce the heat and simmer for 3 hours or until the beans are tender. Rinse and drain.
3 Place the soya beans, almonds, onion, carrot and tamari into a food processor and process for 2 minutes or until roughly chopped. Transfer the mixture to a bowl; add oats, egg, chickpea flour, cumin, coriander and sesame seeds; stir to combine.
4 Shape mixture into 10 even-sized patties. Heat the oil in a large frying pan and cook the patties over medium heat for 5 minutes on each side, or until golden and heated through. Burgers are delicious served with a tangy plum and yoghurt sauce, or with a salad and maybe a toasted bun.
NOTE: Canned soya beans may be used instead of dried ones if you are short of time (use 2½ cups/160 g/5¼ oz). Tamari is a rich soy sauce which, unlike regular soy sauce, is brewed without wheat.

FAST BEAN PUREE

RINSE AND DRAIN 800 g (1 lb 9⅔ oz) canned cannellini beans. Place the beans in a food processor bowl with a clove of crushed garlic and a teaspoon of chopped fresh rosemary. Process briefly until the ingredients are combined, then with the motor running add 3 tablespoons of olive oil in a thin stream. When all the oil has been incorporated, season with salt and pepper. Serve at room temperature as a dip with corn chips or toasted pitta bread. Or warm the purée gently in a pan and serve as an accompaniment to roasted or grilled vegetables. Serves 4.

PUFFED MILLET CEREAL

Preparation time: 5 minutes
Total cooking time: 15–20 minutes
Makes approximately 780 g (1 lb 9 oz)

175 g (5²/₃ oz) puffed millet
350 g (11¹/₄ oz) dried fruit and nut mix
90 g (3 oz) unprocessed natural bran
60 g (2 oz) flaked coconut
¹/₂ cup (175 g/5²/₃ oz) honey

1 Preheat the oven to moderate 180°C (350°F/Gas 4). Combine the puffed millet, dried fruit and nut mix, bran and coconut in a large bowl.
2 Heat the honey in a small pan over low heat. Pour the honey over the millet mixture. Stir until well mixed.
3 Spoon cereal into two baking dishes. Bake for 15 minutes, turning the cereal several times during cooking.
NOTE: Puffed millet is available from health food stores. However, puffed corn can be substituted if you can't find puffed millet.

Millet is suitable for people with an allergy to wheat as it is gluten-free. It also has more protein and vitamin B than wheat. Warming the honey slightly before adding it to the cereal makes it easier to mix. Cereal should be stored in an airtight container in a cool dark place.

CRUNCHY NUT MUESLI

Preparation time: 20 minutes
Total cooking time: 25 minutes
Makes 1 kg (2 lb)

500 g (1 lb) rolled oats
125 g (4 oz) bran cereal
1 cup (150 g/4³/₄ oz) pistachio nuts, shelled and roughly chopped
1 cup (160 g/5¹/₄ oz) macadamia nuts, roughly chopped
1 cup (100 g/3¹/₃ oz) pecan nuts, roughly chopped
125 g (4 oz) dried apples, chopped
125 g (4 oz) dried apricots, chopped
¹/₂ cup (125 ml/4 fl oz) maple syrup
1 teaspoon vanilla essence

1 Preheat the oven to moderate 180°C (350°F/Gas 4). Place oats, bran, pistachios, macadamias, pecans, dried apples and dried apricots in a bowl and mix to combine.
2 Place maple syrup and vanilla in a small pan and cook over low heat for 3 minutes or until syrup becomes runny and easy to pour.
3 Pour maple syrup over oat mixture and toss lightly to coat. Divide mixture between two non-stick baking dishes. Bake for 20 minutes or until the muesli is lightly toasted, turning frequently. Allow mixture to cool before transferring to an airtight container.
NOTE: Oats are a good source of protein, B vitamins, calcium and fibre. They are one of the few grains that do not have the bran and germ removed during processing.

MILLET
Millet contains more protein and iron than any other grain. It can be bought in a variety of forms—as grains, flakes or flour—and is gluten-free. Millet flours produce flattish breads and the grains can be made into tasty pilafs and burgers. For those on gluten-free diets, the flakes can be used to make a creamy breakfast porridge.

*ABOVE: Puffed Millet Cereal
BELOW: Crunchy Nut Muesli*

BORLOTTI BEAN MOUSSAKA

Preparation time: 45 minutes + overnight soaking
Total cooking time: 2¼–2½ hours
Serves 6

★★

250 g (8 oz) dried borlotti beans

2 large eggplants (aubergines), sliced

⅓ cup (80 ml/2¾ fl oz) olive oil

1 clove garlic, crushed

1 onion, chopped

125 g (4 oz) button mushrooms, sliced

2 x 440 g (14 oz) cans peeled
   tomatoes, chopped

1 cup (250 ml/8 fl oz) red wine

1 tablespoon tomato paste

1 tablespoon chopped fresh oregano

Topping

1 cup (250 g/8 oz) natural yoghurt

4 eggs, lightly beaten

2 cups (500 ml/16 fl oz) milk

¼ teaspoon ground paprika

½ cup (50 g/1⅔ oz) freshly grated
   Parmesan cheese

½ cup (40 g/1⅓ oz) fresh breadcrumbs

1 Soak the borlotti beans in cold water overnight; rinse and drain well.

2 Place the borlotti beans into a large heavy-based pan, cover with water and bring to the boil. Reduce heat and simmer for 1½ hours or until tender; drain.

3 Meanwhile, sprinkle the eggplant slices with salt and set aside for 30 minutes. Rinse and pat dry. Brush the eggplant slices with a little of the oil and cook under a preheated grill for 3 minutes on each side or until golden. Drain on paper towels.

4 Preheat the oven to moderately hot 200°C (400°F/Gas 6). Heat the remaining oil in a large heavy-based pan; add the garlic and onion and cook over medium heat for 3 minutes or until the onion is golden. Add mushrooms and cook for 3 minutes or until browned. Stir in the tomatoes, wine, tomato paste and oregano; bring to the boil; reduce heat and simmer for 40 minutes or until sauce has thickened.

5 To assemble Moussaka: Spoon the borlotti beans into a large, ovenproof dish, top with tomato sauce and eggplant slices.

6 To make Topping: Place the yoghurt, eggs, milk and paprika into a jug and whisk to combine. Pour over the eggplant and set aside for 10 minutes. Combine the Parmesan and breadcrumbs in a bowl. Sprinkle over the moussaka. Bake for 45–60 minutes or until the moussaka is heated through and top is golden.

BORLOTTI BEANS
Borlotti beans are brown with speckled red markings and are also known as cranberry or Roman beans. They have a distinctive chestnut flavour and a creamy texture. Fresh borlotti beans have a long, burgundy speckled pod and can be purchased in spring and summer.

*ABOVE: Borlotti
Bean Moussaka*

BRAISED LIMA BEANS WITH LEEKS AND PEARS

Preparation time: 30 minutes
  + overnight soaking
Total cooking time: 1 1/2 hours
Serves 4

250 g (8 oz) dried large lima beans
  (butter beans)
2 tablespoons oil
2 cloves garlic, crushed
2 leeks, sliced
1 teaspoon soft brown sugar
2 pears, peeled and cut into thick slices
2 medium tomatoes, peeled, seeded
  and diced
1 teaspoon fennel seeds
1 cup (250 ml/8 fl oz) white wine
2 tablespoons white wine vinegar
155 g (5 oz) asparagus, cut into
  4 cm (1 1/2 inch) lengths
8 small sage leaves
salt and pepper
2 tablespoons pine nuts, toasted

1 Soak lima beans in cold water overnight; rinse and drain well.
2 Place the beans in a heavy-based pan, cover with water and bring to the boil. Reduce heat and simmer for 1 hour; drain.
3 Heat the oil in a large non-stick frying pan. Add the garlic, leeks and brown sugar and cook over medium heat for 10 minutes, or until the leeks begin to caramelise.
4 Add pears, tomatoes, fennel seeds, white wine and wine vinegar; simmer for 10 minutes or until the liquid has reduced by a quarter.
5 Stir in lima beans, asparagus and sage; season with salt and pepper. Cook for 5 minutes or until the asparagus is tender. Sprinkle with toasted pine nuts and serve.
NOTE: Lima beans originated in Peru and are named after the capital, Lima. They have a light buttery flavour and a creamy texture. Lima beans can be small or large: the smaller beans can be white or green, the large are only white.

To toast pine nuts, spread them on an oven tray and place in a preheated moderate 180°C (350°F/Gas 4) oven for about 5 minutes or until golden.

CHILLI POLENTA CAKE

Preparation time: 25 minutes
Total cooking time: 25–30 minutes
Makes one 20 cm (8 inch) cake

1 1/3 cups (165 g/5 1/2 oz) plain flour
1 1/2 teaspoons baking powder
1 teaspoon salt
1 1/4 cups (185 g/6 oz) polenta (cornmeal)
1 cup (125 g/4 oz) grated Cheddar cheese
1 cup (250 g/8 oz) natural yoghurt
1/2 cup (125 ml/4 fl oz) milk
2 eggs
1/2 cup (80 g/2 2/3 oz) chopped red pepper
  (capsicum)
2 teaspoons chopped fresh chilli
60 g (2 oz) unsalted butter

1 Preheat oven to moderately hot 200°C (400°F/Gas 6). Sift flour, baking powder and salt into a large bowl. Mix in polenta and cheese. In a separate bowl, whisk yoghurt, milk, eggs, red pepper and chilli. Heat a 20 cm (8 inch) ovenproof frying pan, then melt butter. Stir butter into yoghurt mixture, then pour all liquid ingredients into dry ingredients. Mix well.
2 Pour into hot pan; cook in the oven for 25–30 minutes or until a skewer comes out clean.

BELOW: Chilli Polenta Cake

CASSEROLES AND BAKES

One-dish courses like these give new meaning to the concept of 'potluck'. No matter how many different ingredients go into the making of a savoury casserole or bake, the finished product is always more delicious than the sum of its parts. Immensely satisfying on its own, or eaten with a loaf of home-made bread, there's little more one could ask for—except to invite a few friends to share the indulgence.

BAKED FETTUCINE

Preparation time: 20 minutes
Total cooking time: 25 minutes
Serves 4

★

500 g (1 lb) spinach fettucine
60 g (2 oz) butter or margarine
1 onion, finely chopped
300 g (9²/₃ oz) sour cream
1 cup (250 ml/8 fl oz) cream
¹/₄ teaspoon ground nutmeg
¹/₂ cup (50 g/1²/₃ oz) freshly grated
   Parmesan cheese
salt and freshly ground black pepper, to taste
1 cup (150 g/4³/₄ oz) freshly grated
   mozzarella cheese

1 Preheat the oven to moderate 180°C (350°F/ Gas 4). Add the fettucine to a large pan of rapidly boiling water and cook until just tender. Drain well and set aside. While the pasta is cooking, melt the butter in a large pan. Add the chopped onion and stir constantly over low heat until the onion is tender. Add the drained fettucine to the pan.
2 Add the sour cream to the pan and toss well, using a spoon and a fork. Simmer, stirring, until the pasta is well coated.
3 Add the cream, nutmeg, half of the Parmesan

ABOVE: Baked Fettucine

cheese, salt and pepper; stir. Pour into a greased casserole dish. Sprinkle with combined mozzarella and remaining Parmesan cheese. Bake for 15 minutes or until the cheese is softened and golden.
NOTE: You can vary this recipe by using plain fettucine or adding chopped fresh herbs such as basil, parsley or thyme. Grated carrot can be stirred in as well. If you like garlic, stir in a crushed clove or two just before the onion is finished cooking.

FAST VEGETABLE STEW

FRY A CHOPPED onion in a medium pan until soft. Add 2 chopped zucchinis (courgettes), 100 g (3¹/₃ oz) of sliced button mushrooms, and 1 chopped red pepper (capsicum). Add 400 g (12²/₃ oz) canned, crushed tomatoes and a splash of balsamic vinegar; cook, covered, over medium heat 10 minutes, or until vegetables are tender. Uncover; cook for 5 minutes, or until mixture has thickened slightly. Season; serve over pasta or rice. Serves 4.
Variation: Mix the stew with 2 cups (350 g/11¹/₄ oz) of cooked pasta, such as spiral or penne, and place in an ovenproof dish. Sprinkle with a mixture of grated cheese and breadcrumbs. Bake in a hot 210°C (415°F/Gas 6–7) oven for about 10 minutes or until golden.

CARROT PESTO BAKE

Preparation time: 45 minutes
  + 30 minutes standing
Total cooking time: 55 minutes
Serves 4

50 g (1²/₃ oz) butter

¹/₂ cup (60 g/2 oz) plain flour

3 cups (750 ml/24 fl oz) milk

²/₃ cup (160 g/5¹/₄ oz) light sour cream

1 teaspoon cracked black pepper

100 g (3¹/₃ oz) Cheddar cheese, grated

4 eggs, lightly beaten

2 tablespoons ready-made pesto

750 g (1¹/₂ lb) carrots, peeled and grated

250 g (8 oz) instant lasagne sheets

50 g (1²/₃ oz) Cheddar cheese, grated, extra

1 Brush a 30 x 20 cm (12 x 8 inch) ovenproof baking dish with melted butter or oil. Heat the butter in a large pan; add the flour. Stir over low heat until mixture is lightly golden and bubbling. Add combined milk, sour cream and pepper gradually to pan, stirring until mixture is smooth between each addition. Stir constantly over medium heat for 5 minutes, or until the mixture boils and thickens. Boil for another minute; remove from heat. Stir in cheese; cool slightly. Gradually add beaten eggs, stirring constantly.

2 Pour a third of the sauce into another bowl to make the topping and set aside. Add the pesto and grated carrot to the remaining sauce, stirring to combine.

3 Preheat the oven to slow 150°C (300°F/ Gas 2). Beginning with one-third of the carrot mixture, alternate layers of carrot mixture with sheets of lasagne in prepared dish. Use three layers of each, finishing with lasagne sheets. Spread reserved sauce evenly over the top. Sprinkle with extra cheese. Set aside for 15 minutes before cooking to allow the pasta to soften. Bake for 40 minutes or until sauce has set and is golden.

4 Remove from the oven; cover and set aside for 15 minutes prior to serving—this will ensure that it will slice cleanly and more easily. Serve with a crisp green salad.

FAST PUMPKIN GRATIN

PREHEAT OVEN to moderately hot 200°C (400°F/Gas 6). Grate 400 g (12²/₃ oz) of butternut pumpkin and spread into a small, shallow ovenproof dish. Pour 1 cup (250 ml/8 fl oz) of cream over pumpkin and stir through. In a small bowl, combine ¹/₂ cup (40 g/1¹/₃ oz) of fresh breadcrumbs, 4 tablespoons of finely grated cheese and ¹/₂ teaspoon of nutmeg. Sprinkle this mixture over top of pumpkin and cream; bake for about 20 minutes. Serves 4.

PESTO
Pesto Genovese is the classic basil pesto and is a simple combination of basil leaves, pine nuts, freshly grated Parmesan cheese, garlic cloves, olive oil, and salt and pepper. All pestos are highly flavoured and should be used sparingly, to complement rather than overwhelm the foods they accompany. In Italian the word *pesto* means 'pounded': the traditional method of making pesto being to grind the ingredients with a mortar and pestle.

ABOVE: Carrot Pesto Bake

HUNGARIAN CASSEROLE

Preparation time: 30 minutes
Total cooking time: 30 minutes
Serves 4-6

4 large potatoes
1 tablespoon olive oil
30 g (1 oz) butter
1 medium onion, chopped
1 red and 1 green pepper (capsicum),
    roughly chopped
440 g (14 oz) can chopped tomatoes
1 cup (250 ml/8 fl oz) vegetable stock
2 teaspoons caraway seeds
2 teaspoons paprika
salt and freshly ground black pepper

Crispy Croutons

1 cup (250 ml/8 fl oz) oil
4 slices white bread, crusts removed and
    cut into small cubes

1 Peel the potatoes; cut into large chunks. Heat the oil and butter in a large heavy-based pan; cook the potatoes over medium heat, turning regularly, until crisp on the edges.
2 Add the onion and red and green peppers; cook for 5 minutes. Add tomatoes with juice, vegetable stock, caraway seeds and paprika. Season to taste with salt and pepper. Simmer, uncovered, for 10 minutes or until potatoes are tender. Serve with Crispy Croutons.
3 To make Croutons: Heat oil in a frying pan over medium heat. Cook croutons, turning often, for 2 minutes or until golden brown and crisp. Drain on kitchen paper.

MEXICAN TOMATO BAKE

Preparation time: 25 minutes
Total cooking time: 30 minutes
Serves 4-6

2 tablespoons oil
2 red (Spanish) onions, chopped
2 cloves garlic, crushed
6 ripe tomatoes, peeled and chopped
1 green pepper (capsicum), seeded and chopped
1 tablespoon red wine vinegar
1 teaspoon sugar
1/2 teaspoon ground chilli powder
375 g (12 oz) canned corn kernels, drained
125 g (4 oz) plain corn chips
1 1/4 cups (155 g/5 oz) grated Cheddar cheese
1 cup (250 g/8 oz) sour cream

1 Preheat oven to warm 160°C (315°F/Gas 2–3). Heat oil in a medium pan. Add onions and garlic; cook over medium heat for 3 minutes. Add tomatoes, pepper, vinegar, sugar and chilli.

RIGHT: Hungarian Casserole

Cook, uncovered, for 6–7 minutes or until tomatoes are soft and liquid has evaporated. Stir in corn kernels over heat for 3 minutes.

2 Arrange layers of corn chips, sauce and cheese in a casserole dish, finishing with cheese layer.

3 Spread with sour cream. Bake, uncovered, for 15 minutes. Sprinkle with chopped chives.

WINTER VEGETABLE CASSEROLE

Preparation time: 15 minutes
Total cooking time: 40 minutes
Serves 4

2 medium potatoes
1 medium parsnip
200 g (6¹/2 oz) pumpkin
30 g (1 oz) butter
1 tablespoon flour
1¹/2 cups (375 ml/12 fl oz) milk
¹/2 teaspoon ground nutmeg
salt and freshly ground black pepper, to taste

Crumble Topping

1 cup (80 g/2²/3 oz) fresh breadcrumbs
100 g (3¹/3 oz) roasted cashew nuts, roughly chopped
30 g (1 oz) butter

1 Peel potatoes, parsnip and pumpkin; cut the pumpkin into large bite-sized pieces and potato and parsnip into smaller pieces. Cook vegetables in a large pan of boiling water for 8 minutes or until just tender. Drain and then arrange cooked vegetables in base of a large, deep ovenproof dish.

2 Melt butter in a pan over low heat. Add flour and cook, stirring constantly, for 1 minute. Remove from the heat and gradually stir in milk. Return pan to heat, bring mixture to the boil, stirring constantly, until thickened; boil for another minute. Add the nutmeg and salt and pepper; pour sauce over the vegetables. Preheat the oven to moderate 180°C (350°F/Gas 4).

3 To make Crumble Topping: Combine the breadcrumbs and cashews. Sprinkle them over the vegetables. Dot the crumble topping with butter; bake for 30 minutes or until golden. Garnish with cress, if desired.

MEXICAN CUISINE
When the Spanish conquered Mexico more than 400 years ago they not only found gold, but also corn, beans, chillies, tomatoes, avocados, potatoes, squash, zucchini and a wealth of new fruits and spices—including pineapples, papayas, peanuts, cocoa and vanilla. The sophistication and excitement of the Aztec and Mayan Indian dishes sent the chefs of Europe running to their kitchens and today Mexican food is enjoyed worldwide.

*ABOVE: Mexican Tomato Bake
LEFT: Winter Vegetable Casserole*

BAKED CHEESE AND SPINACH CANNELLONI

Preparation time: 40 minutes
Total cooking time: I hour 20 minutes
Serves 4

Tomato Sauce

2 tablespoons olive oil

I large onion, finely chopped

2 cloves garlic, finely chopped

3 x 400 g (12²/3 oz) cans tomatoes, roughly chopped

2 sprigs fresh rosemary

2 bay leaves

2 tablespoons tomato paste

salt and pepper

500 g (1 lb) English spinach

150 g (4³/4 oz) feta cheese, crumbled

150 g (4³/4 oz) ricotta cheese

¹/2 cup (50 g/1²/3 oz) freshly grated Parmesan cheese

2 tablespoons finely chopped fresh mint leaves

2 eggs, lightly beaten

2 tablespoons pine nuts, toasted

salt and pepper

16 instant cannelloni tubes

200 g (6¹/2 oz) mozzarella cheese, finely grated

I **To make Tomato Sauce:** Heat the olive oil in a large pan. Add the onions and garlic; cook over medium heat until the onions are soft. Add the tomatoes, herbs and tomato paste; mix thoroughly. Bring to the boil, reduce heat and simmer for 25–30 minutes until the sauce is thick. Season, to taste. Remove the bay leaves and rosemary sprigs and discard them.

2 Preheat the oven to moderately hot 200°C (400°F/Gas 6). Wash and remove the stems from the spinach. Steam or microwave until just wilted. Drain thoroughly and chop roughly. Combine the spinach with the cheeses, mint, beaten eggs, pine nuts, salt and pepper. Mix thoroughly. Using a small spoon or knife, carefully fill the cannelloni tubes.

3 Spoon some Tomato Sauce over the base of a large, shallow baking dish. Arrange cannelloni shells on top. Cover with remaining Tomato Sauce and mozzarella. Bake for 30–40 minutes until top is golden and pasta is tender.

POTATO CAKE

Preparation time: 20 minutes
Total cooking time: I hour 5 minutes
Serves 4-6

8 medium potatoes

30 g (1 oz) butter

2 tablespoons olive oil

I clove garlic, crushed

¹/2 teaspoon ground pepper

2 cups (200 g/6¹/2 oz) dried breadcrumbs

I cup (125 g/4 oz) grated Cheddar cheese

¹/2 cup (50 g/1²/3 oz) freshly grated Parmesan cheese

I Preheat oven to moderate 180°C (350°F/Gas 4). Brush a deep 20 cm (8 inch) springform (spring-release) tin with melted butter. Line base and side with greased paper. Peel potatoes; slice thinly.

2 Heat butter and oil; add garlic and pepper. Overlap some potato slices in the base of tin. Brush with butter mixture. Sprinkle with some of the combined breadcrumbs and cheeses. Continue layering, ending with cheese. Press down firmly. Bake for 1 hour.

BAY LEAVES

The bay (*Laurus nobilis*) is an evergreen shrub with an ancient history. Also called laurel, it is native to the Mediterranean area. The ancient Greeks gave bay or laurel wreaths to winners of Olympic Games, poets and heroes. Bay leaves have an exquisite flavour, the pungency of which increases with the amount used and the cooking time. Burning a few leaves on a baking sheet or saucer removes kitchen smells.

ABOVE: Potato Cake

ROASTED VEGETABLE LASAGNE

Preparation time: 50 minutes
Total cooking time: 1 hour
Serves 6

★★★

Marinade

1/2 cup (125 ml/4 fl oz) olive oil
2 tablespoons red wine vinegar
1 tablespoon finely chopped capers
1 tablespoon finely chopped parsley
1 clove garlic, finely chopped
1 teaspoon tomato paste
salt and pepper

1 red pepper (capsicum)
1 large eggplant (aubergine), sliced lengthways,
    salted, rinsed and well-drained
2 large zucchinis (courgettes), sliced
    thinly lengthways
400 g (12²/3 oz) sweet potato, peeled and
    sliced thinly lengthways
6 egg (Roma) tomatoes, quartered
375 g (12 oz) fresh lasagne sheets

1/3 cup (90 g/3 oz) good-quality pesto
300 g (9²/3 oz) bocconcini, finely sliced
olive oil
1 cup (100 g/3¹/3 oz) freshly grated
    Parmesan cheese

1 Preheat the oven to moderately hot 200°C (400°F/Gas 6). Combine marinade ingredients in a bowl and whisk thoroughly.
2 Cut red pepper in half lengthways. Remove seeds and membrane and cut into large, flattish pieces. Grill until skin blackens and blisters. Place on a cutting board, cover with a tea towel; allow to cool. Peel, discard skin and cut flesh into thick strips. Place red pepper and remaining vegetables in large baking dish; coat with half the marinade. Bake for 15 minutes, turn and coat again with remaining marinade. Cook for another 15 minutes.
3 Cut the pasta into 24 sheets, each 10 x 16 cm (about 4 x 6¹/2 inches). Make 6 individual stacks in the following order: pasta, zucchini and sweet potato, 2 teaspoons pesto and bocconcini slices, pasta, eggplant and red pepper, pasta, tomatoes, 2 teaspoons pesto and bocconcini slices, pasta. Transfer the stacks to greased baking dish. Brush the tops with olive oil and sprinkle with grated Parmesan cheese. Bake for 15–20 minutes or until heated through and tender.

FLAVOURED VINEGARS
Wine vinegars are, in general, the mildest and most versatile of the vinegar family. The name is derived from the French *vinaigre*, meaning soured wine. Wine vinegars can be successfully flavoured with fresh herbs such as tarragon, basil, mint and thyme. Put a few sprigs of your chosen herb in a sterilised bottle, pour in the vinegar, seal and leave for three weeks. Strain the vinegar and return to a sterilised bottle with one small fresh sprig of the herb for identification. Never use garlic to flavour bottles of vinegar or oil—it can react badly and cause food poisoning.

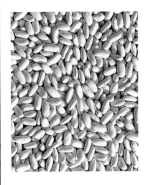

ABOVE: Roasted Vegetable Lasagne

SAVOY CABBAGE

Savoy Cabbage is one of the prettiest cabbages and, with its green, ruffled and deeply veined leaves, it is perfectly suited to recipes for stuffed cabbage leaves. When buying any variety of cabbage, choose those with firm, heavy heads and a bright, fresh colour. The leaves of the Savoy will be loose but they should never be limp.

ABOVE: Spicy Cabbage Rolls

SPICY CABBAGE ROLLS

Preparation time: 40 minutes
Total cooking time: 30 minutes
Serves 6

★

6 large green cabbage leaves

Filling

2 teaspoons olive oil
4 spring onions, finely chopped
1 clove garlic, crushed
2 tablespoons tomato paste
1/2 cup (75 g/2 1/2 oz) currants
2 tablespoons slivered almonds
1 teaspoon cumin seeds
1/2 teaspoon ground cinnamon
2 tablespoons finely chopped
   fresh parsley
2 1/2 cups (470 g/15 oz) cooked
   long-grain rice
1 cup (250 ml/8 fl oz) vegetable stock

Yoghurt Sauce

3/4 cup (185 g/6 oz) plain yoghurt
1 teaspoon ground cumin
1 tablespoon finely chopped fresh mint

1 Preheat the oven to moderately hot 190°C (375°F/Gas 5). Brush a deep ovenproof dish with melted butter or oil.
2 Blanch the cabbage leaves in boiling water for 10 seconds or until they are soft and pliable. Drain; remove and discard the hard stalk from the leaves. Set leaves aside.
3 To make Filling: Heat the oil in a large pan. Add the spring onions and garlic and cook over medium heat for 30 seconds. Add the tomato paste, currants, almonds, cumin seeds, cinnamon, parsley and rice; stir until well combined. Remove from heat and cool slightly.
4 Place 3 tablespoons of filling on the edge of one cabbage leaf. Roll into a neat parcel, folding in the edges while rolling. Repeat with the remaining filling and leaves. Place the cabbage parcels, flap-side down, in prepared dish and pour the stock over them. Invert an ovenproof plate on top of the cabbage parcels to prevent them from falling apart. Cover with a lid or foil; bake for 20–25 minutes or until heated through.
5 To make Yoghurt Sauce: Mix together the yoghurt, cumin and mint in a bowl. Serve the cabbage rolls warm or cold with Yoghurt Sauce.
NOTE: Make the Yoghurt Sauce just before serving. If the leaves are difficult to remove from cabbage, boil the whole cabbage in enough water to cover, for about 3–4 minutes. Remove and cool slightly. The leaves should separate easily.

GOLDEN NUGGET SOUFFLES

Preparation time: 20 minutes
Total cooking time: 1 hour 40 minutes
Serves 4

☆

4 golden nugget pumpkins
60 g (2 oz) butter
3 tablespoons plain flour
2/3 cup (170 ml/5 1/2 fl oz) milk
3 eggs, separated
1/2 cup (65 g/2 1/4 oz) grated Gruyère cheese

1 Preheat oven to hot 210°C (415°F/Gas 6–7).
Cut the tops from each pumpkin and scoop out
all the seeds and fibre. Place the pumpkins in an
ovenproof dish; cover the dish with foil; bake
for 1 hour. Remove pumpkins from the dish;
invert onto a wire rack to drain away any liquid.
2 Using a metal spoon, scoop most of the
softened flesh from the pumpkins, leaving a little
behind to support the skin. Mash the pumpkin
flesh in a bowl and set aside to cool.
3 Melt the butter in a small pan; add the flour
and stir for 1 minute, or until golden and
bubbling. Add milk gradually, stirring until
smooth between each addition. Stir constantly
over medium heat until mixture thickens; cook
for another minute, then remove from heat. Stir
the egg yolks and cheese into the milk mixture;

add the pumpkin and mix together until smooth
and creamy. Season with salt and pepper.
4 Beat the egg whites with electric beaters until
stiff peaks form; fold whites into pumpkin
mixture with a metal spoon. Make sure the egg
white is mixed in thoroughly so that no white
streaks are visible but, at the same time, fold in
gently and quickly, to retain the volume.
5 Spoon mixture into pumpkin shells, filling to
just below the rim. Don't overfill or pumpkins
will overflow while cooking. If there is any filling
remaining, bake it in a small ramekin at the same
time the pumpkins are baked. Place filled
pumpkins in a baking dish; bake 20–25 minutes,
or until puffed and golden. Serve immediately.

FAST CREAMY POLENTA

POLENTA IS an excellent, easy to prepare
accompaniment to casseroles. In a medium
heavy-based pan, bring 1 1/3 cups
(350 ml/11 fl oz) of vegetable stock and
1 cup (250 ml/8 fl oz) of water to the boil.
Add 1 cup (150 g/4 3/4 oz) of polenta
(cornmeal) and stir constantly for 10 minutes
over medium-low heat. The mixture will
become very thick. Remove from the heat
and stir in 1/3 cup (80 ml/2 3/4 fl oz) of cream
and 30 g (1 oz) of butter. If appropriate to
the dish, use 1/2 cup (50 g/1 2/3 oz) Parmesan
cheese instead of the butter. Serves 2–4.

OREGANO

Oregano was used by the
Greeks in its wild form of
rigani. The name is literally
translated as 'joy of the
mountains' and the warm,
heady scent of the wild
herb can be found in the
traditional Greek salad of
feta, tomato, olives and
onion. Today there are
many varieties of oregano,
one of the best being
Origanum heracleoticum.
This is the Greek variety
and retains the native
characteristics in its sharp
bite and aroma.

*ABOVE: Golden
Nugget Soufflés*

SPICY CHICKPEA AND VEGETABLE CASSEROLE

Preparation time: 25 minutes
  + overnight soaking
Total cooking time: 1 hour 30 minutes
Serves 4

1½ cups (330 g/10½ oz) dried chickpeas
2 tablespoons oil
1 large onion, chopped
1 clove garlic, crushed
3 teaspoons ground cumin
½ teaspoon chilli powder
½ teaspoon allspice
425 g (13½ oz) canned peeled
  tomatoes, crushed
1½ cups (375 ml/12 fl oz) vegetable stock
300 g (9⅔ oz) pumpkin, cut into large cubes
150 g (4¾ oz) green beans, topped
  and tailed
200 g (6½ oz) button squash, quartered
2 tablespoons tomato paste
1 teaspoon dried oregano

1 Place the chickpeas in a large bowl; cover with cold water and soak overnight; drain.
2 Heat the oil in a large pan; add the onions and garlic and stir-fry for 2 minutes or until tender. Add the cumin, chilli powder and allspice; stir-fry for 1 minute. Add the chickpeas, tomatoes and stock to the pan. Bring to the boil; reduce heat and simmer, covered, for 1 hour, stirring occasionally.
3 Add the pumpkin, beans, squash, tomato paste and oregano. Stir to combine. Simmer, covered, for another 15 minutes. Remove the lid from the pan and simmer, uncovered, for another 10 minutes to reduce and thicken sauce slightly.
NOTE: A quick way to soak chickpeas is to place them in a large pan and cover with cold water. Bring to the boil; remove from heat and soak for two hours. If you are in a hurry, substitute canned chickpeas. Drain and rinse thoroughly before use.

LAYERED POTATO AND APPLE BAKE

Preparation time: 30 minutes
Total cooking time: 45 minutes
Serves 6

2 large potatoes
3 medium green apples
1 medium onion
½ cup (60 g/2 oz) finely grated
  Cheddar cheese
1 cup (250 ml/8 fl oz) cream
¼ teaspoon ground nutmeg
freshly ground black pepper

1 Preheat the oven to moderate 180°C (350°F/Gas 4). Brush a large, shallow ovenproof dish with melted butter or oil. Peel the potatoes and cut into thin slices. Peel, core and quarter the apples. Cut into thin slices. Slice the peeled onion into very fine rings.
2 Layer the potatoes, apples and onions in the prepared dish, ending with a layer of potatoes. Sprinkle evenly with cheese. Pour the cream over the top, covering as evenly as possible.
3 Sprinkle with nutmeg and black pepper, to taste. Bake for 45 minutes or until golden brown. Remove from the oven and allow to stand for 5 minutes before serving.
NOTE: To prevent potatoes and apples browning before assembling dish, place in a bowl of cold water with a squeeze of lemon juice. Drain and pat dry with paper towels before using.

FAST EGGPLANT (AUBERGINE) BAKE

SLICE 6 BABY eggplants (aubergines) lengthways; dust lightly with flour and fry in some oil until golden brown; drain on paper towels. Lay in a shallow ovenproof dish and cover with ½ cup (125 g/ 4 oz) of good-quality ready-made tomato pasta sauce. Sprinkle with 1 cup (150 g/ 4¾ oz) grated mozzarella and ¼ cup (25 g/¾ oz) of grated Parmesan cheese. Season with freshly ground black pepper and bake in a moderate 180°C (350°F/ Gas 4) oven for 15 minutes or until top is golden and bubbling. Serve with a strongly-flavoured salad, such as rocket dressed with olive oil and lemon juice. Serves 2.

CUMIN

Cumin (*Cuminum cyminum*) has an earthy, warm flavour. Commonly used in curries, it also flavours a variety of other dishes. In Spain it is the traditional seasoning for chickpeas and is also used in vegetable and rice dishes. Cumin seeds need lengthy cooking and are therefore often sold in powdered form. This effectively preserves the flavour and makes it easier to add the right amount.

OPPOSITE PAGE: Layered Potato and Apple Bake (top); Spicy Chickpea and Vegetable Casserole

1 To trim asparagus, bend the stem end of each spear. They will snap where any woodiness begins. Tie the spears into a bundle.

2 Place the asparagus, tips upwards, into a pan of boiling water. Cook for 2–3 minutes, then lift the asparagus out with tongs. Dip the tips briefly into the boiling water.

ABOVE: Stuffed Pumpkins

STUFFED PUMPKINS

Preparation time: 25 minutes
Total cooking time: 50 minutes
Makes 4

4 medium golden nugget pumpkins
1/4 cup (60 ml/2 fl oz) water
1/2 cup (95 g/3 1/4 oz) cooked rice
2 teaspoons curry paste
1 tablespoon finely chopped fresh coriander
1 green apple, finely chopped
1 small zucchini (courgette), finely chopped
1 small carrot, finely chopped
60 g (2 oz) button mushrooms, thinly sliced
155 g (5 oz) asparagus spears, chopped
2 teaspoons currants
1/4 teaspoon garam masala
60 g (2 oz) butter, melted

1 Preheat oven to hot 210°C (415°F/Gas 6–7). Cut top off each pumpkin; set aside. Scoop out seeds and discard. Arrange pumpkins in medium ovenproof dish; replace tops. Add water to dish and cover firmly with foil; bake for 30 minutes. Remove from oven; remove pumpkins; drain water and brush dish with melted butter or oil.
2 Combine rice, curry paste, coriander, apple, zucchini, carrot, mushrooms, asparagus, currants, garam masala and butter in a medium bowl; mix well. Spoon rice and vegetable mixture into the pumpkin cavities. Top with lids. Return to prepared dish and cover with foil. Bake pumpkins for 20 minutes or until just cooked.

CAULIFLOWER AND PASTA BAKE WITH CROUTON TOPPING

Preparation time: 25 minutes
Total cooking time: 1 hour
Serves 6

150 g (4 3/4 oz) short pasta (such as penne)
600 g (1 1/4 lb) cauliflower, cut into florets
2 tablespoons olive oil
2 red (Spanish) onions, chopped
2 cloves garlic, finely chopped
80 g (2 2/3 oz) butter
4 tablespoons plain flour
4 cups (1 litre) milk
2 cups (200 g/6 1/2 oz) freshly grated
  Parmesan cheese
1/2 cup (30 g/1 oz) firmly packed
  shredded fresh basil
5 slices of day-old bread, crusts removed
50 g (1 2/3 oz) butter, melted

1 Preheat the oven to moderate 180°C (350°F/Gas 4). Cook the pasta in rapidly boiling water until tender; drain. Steam the cauliflower until just tender. Heat the olive oil in a frying pan. Fry the onions and garlic over medium heat until the onions are soft. Combine in a bowl with the cauliflower.

2 Melt the butter in a large pan. Blend in the flour and cook, stirring constantly, for 1 minute. Gradually whisk in the milk. Stir constantly until the mixture boils and thickens. Remove from the heat and stir through 1¼ cups (125 g/4 oz) of the grated Parmesan cheese and the basil. Add the cauliflower, pasta and onions to the sauce; mix thoroughly.

3 Spoon the cauliflower mixture into a large ovenproof dish. Cut the bread into large cubes. Toss the cubes in melted butter and then scatter them over the cauliflower mixture. Sprinkle with the remaining Parmesan cheese. Bake for 35–40 minutes until the top is golden.

FENNEL CRUMBLE

Preparation time: 25 minutes
Total cooking time: 40 minutes
Serves 6

2 fennel bulbs
¼ cup (60 ml/2 fl oz) plus 2 tablespoons
   lemon juice
salt and freshly ground black pepper
1 tablespoon honey
1 tablespoon plain flour
1¼ cups (315 ml/10 fl oz) cream

Crumble Topping

¾ cup (75 g/2½ oz) rolled oats
½ cup (60 g/2 oz) plain flour
1 cup (110 g/3⅔ oz) black rye breadcrumbs,
   (made from 3 slices bread)
60 g (2 oz) butter
1 clove garlic, crushed

1 Preheat the oven to moderate 180°C (350°F/Gas 4). Brush a large ovenproof serving dish with melted butter or oil. Trim fennel and cut into thin slices. Wash and drain well. Bring a large pan of water to boil. Add ¼ cup (60 ml/ 2 fl oz) lemon juice and fennel slices. Cook over medium heat for 3 minutes. Drain; rinse under cold water.

2 Place the fennel in a large bowl. Add the extra lemon juice with the black pepper and honey; toss to combine. Sprinkle with the flour. Spoon into the prepared dish and pour the cream over the top.

3 **To make Crumble Topping:** Combine the oats, flour and breadcrumbs. Heat the butter in a small pan, add the garlic and cook 30 seconds. Pour over the dry ingredients and mix well. Sprinkle the crumble over the fennel. Bake for 20–30 minutes or until fennel is tender and crumble is browned.

NOTE: White or wholemeal breadcrumbs can be used in place of rye bread. Fennel has an aniseed flavour. Blanching it before use softens the texture slightly and reduces the strong flavour.

FAST COUSCOUS

COUSCOUS IS a simple and delicious way to soak up the casserole juices. Put 1 cup (185 g/6 oz) of instant couscous in a large heatproof bowl and add ¾ cup (185 ml/ 6 fl oz) of boiling water. Leave the couscous to stand for about 3–5 minutes. Stir through 30 g (1 oz) butter with a fork, until the butter has melted and the grains have fluffed up. Season with salt and pepper or some fresh herbs of your choice. To add extra flavour, stir through a little crushed garlic that has been sautéed in some butter or oil. Serves 2.

FENNEL
Add fennel to soups or sauces, and roasted or marinated vegetables, for a light aniseed flavour. Fennel resembles a short, bulbous celery plant. The leaves can be used in salads and stuffings and the raw bulb cooked as a vegetable, or served thinly sliced as part of an antipasto platter.

ABOVE: Fennel Crumble

Brush with melted butter or oil. Cut each eggplant into 6 slices lengthways. Sprinkle with salt; set aside for 30 minutes. Rinse under cold water; drain. Pat dry with paper towels.

2 Place the eggplants on a cold grill tray. Brush with oil. Cook under medium–high heat for 5 minutes or until golden brown on each side. Drain on paper towels. Trim the woody ends from the asparagus. Steam or microwave until just tender. Cut 6 asparagus into 5 cm (2 inch) lengths; set aside. Finely chop the remaining asparagus. Heat the butter in a medium pan. Add the spring onions and cook over medium-high heat for 1 minute. Stir in the flour. Add the milk gradually to the pan, stirring until the mixture is smooth. Stir constantly over medium heat for 5 minutes or until the mixture boils and thickens; boil for another minute.

3 Add cheese, lemon juice, salt and pepper, yolk and chopped asparagus. Mix well and remove from the heat. Place 6 eggplant slices on the prepared tray. Spread the asparagus filling evenly over each eggplant slice. Top with the remaining eggplant slices.

4 To make Soufflé Topping: Using electric beaters, beat egg white in a small, clean bowl until stiff peaks form. Spread egg white evenly over eggplant. Sprinkle with the cheese and decorate with remaining asparagus. Bake for 15 minutes until cheese is melted and topping set.

BAKED EGGPLANT (AUBERGINE) AND ASPARAGUS SANDWICH

Preparation time: 45 minutes
  + 30 minutes standing
Total cooking time: 40 minutes
Serves 6

2 medium eggplants (aubergines)
1 tablespoon olive oil
155 g (5 oz) asparagus
50 g (1²/₃ oz) butter
¹/₃ cup (40 g/1¹/₃ oz) finely chopped spring onions
¹/₂ cup (60 g/2 oz) plain flour
1 cup (250 ml/8 fl oz) milk
3 tablespoons grated Romano cheese
1 tablespoon lemon juice
salt and freshly ground black pepper
1 egg yolk

Soufflé Topping

1 egg white
3 tablespoons grated Romano cheese

ABOVE: Baked Eggplant and Asparagus Sandwich

1 Preheat the oven to moderate 180°C (350°F/Gas 4). Line an oven tray with foil.

MUSHROOM LASAGNE

Preparation time: 20 minutes
Total cooking time: 1 hour
Serves 6

250 g (8 oz) packet instant lasagne sheets
1¹/₄ cups (310 g/9³/₄ oz) ready-made pasta sauce
2 tablespoons oil
2 cloves garlic, crushed
4 spring onions, sliced
500 g (1 lb) button mushrooms
2 tablespoons chopped fresh basil leaves
250 g (8 oz) ricotta cheese, crumbled
¹/₂ cup (50 g/1²/₃ oz) freshly grated Parmesan cheese
¹/₂ teaspoon ground nutmeg
155 g (5 oz) rocket
¹/₂ cup (60 g/2 oz) grated Cheddar cheese
¹/₂ cup (75 g/2¹/₂ oz) grated mozzarella cheese

1 Preheat the oven to moderately hot 200°C (400°F/Gas 6). Divide the lasagne sheets into three equal portions. Spread 3 tablespoons of the pasta sauce into the base of a large, rectangular ovenproof dish; top with a layer of lasagne sheets.
2 Heat the oil in a frying pan, add the garlic and spring onions and cook for 3 minutes. Add the mushrooms and cook for another 5 minutes. Remove from the heat and stir in the basil.
3 Spread half of the mushroom mixture in a layer on the pasta sheets, then top with half of the ricotta cheese. Sprinkle with half of the Parmesan cheese, nutmeg and rocket. Layer the second portion of lasagne sheets on top, then half of the remaining pasta sauce.
4 Repeat the top layer with the remaining ingredients, finishing with pasta sauce. Scatter the Cheddar and Mozzarella cheeses over the top and bake for 40–50 minutes until the lasagne is tender and the topping is golden.

EGGPLANT (AUBERGINE) AND TOMATO BAKE

Preparation time: 20 minutes
  + 20 minutes standing
Total cooking time: 1 hour 15 minutes
Serves 6

2 large eggplants (aubergines)
1/4 cup (60 ml/2 fl oz) olive oil
2 large onions, chopped
1 teaspoon ground cumin
1 cup (250 ml/8 fl oz) good-quality white wine
800 g (1 lb 10 oz) canned tomatoes, crushed
2 cloves garlic, crushed
2 red chillies, finely chopped (optional)
1/2 cup (75 g/2 1/2 oz) currants
3 tablespoons chopped fresh coriander

1 Preheat the oven to hot 210°C (415°F/ Gas 6–7). Cut the eggplants into 2 cm (3/4 inch) thick rounds. Place on a tray and sprinkle generously with salt. Set aside for 20 minutes.
2 Heat 2 tablespoons of oil in a large pan. Add the onions and cook over medium heat for 5 minutes or until softened. Add the cumin and stir for 1 minute. Add the wine. Bring to boil; reduce heat and simmer for 10 minutes, or until the mixture has reduced by three-quarters. Add the tomatoes. Bring to the boil; reduce the heat and cook for 10 minutes. Add the garlic, chillies

and currants. Simmer for 5 minutes; remove from the heat. Rinse the eggplant slices and squeeze them dry using paper towels. Heat the remaining oil in a large frying pan. Fry the eggplant slices over medium heat for 3–4 minutes. Drain on paper towels.
3 Layer the eggplant slices and tomato mixture in a large ovenproof dish, sprinkle fresh coriander between each layer. Finish with a layer of eggplant. Bake for 30 minutes. Serve with pasta.

FAST OVEN FRIES

LEAVE THE SKINS on Desiree potatoes and cut them into thin chips. Preheat the oven to very hot 230°C (450°F/Gas 8). Lightly grease a baking sheet with olive oil. Spread the chips over the baking sheet and drizzle with a little more olive oil. Bake for 20–25 minutes, or until crisp, turning only once during the cooking time. Serve immediately, while still hot.

EGGPLANT (AUBERGINE)
When buying eggplants look for firm, glossy fruit that are neither wrinkled nor patchy and feel heavy and solid. If it is soft, the eggplant is old and will be bitter; if hard it is under-ripe. If it yields slightly to pressure, then it is perfect. Store eggplants for four or five days in a plastic bag in the refrigerator.

ABOVE: Eggplant and Tomato Bake

SALADS

If your idea of a salad is a few chopped-up lettuce leaves topped with slices of cucumber and tomato wedges, then read on. Vegetarian food really comes into its own with the salad: raw, roasted, even steamed vegetables, partnered with your choice of nut, grain or pulse, then dressed or simply drizzled with extra virgin olive oil—the possibilities are only limited by your imagination.

BURGHUL

Burghul or bulgur is cracked wheat that has been hulled, steamed and dried, a process that makes the grain softer and easier to cook and gives it a lighter texture. Burghul has a nutty flavour and is most often seen in the Lebanese salad, tabouli.

ABOVE: Farfalle Salad with Sun-dried Tomatoes and Spinach

FARFALLE SALAD WITH SUN-DRIED TOMATOES AND SPINACH

Preparation time: 20 minutes
Total cooking time: 12 minutes
Serves 4-6

★

500 g (1 lb) farfalle (butterfly pasta) or spiral pasta
3 spring onions
60 g (2 oz) sun-dried tomatoes, cut into strips
500 g (1 lb) English spinach, stalks trimmed and leaves shredded
4 tablespoons toasted pine nuts
1 tablespoon chopped fresh oregano

Dressing

1/4 cup (60 ml/2 fl oz) olive oil
1 teaspoon chopped fresh chilli
1 clove garlic, crushed
salt and pepper

1 Add the pasta to a large pan of rapidly boiling water and cook until just tender. Drain the pasta and rinse well under cold water. Transfer to a large salad bowl.

2 Trim the spring onions and chop finely. Add to the pasta with the tomatoes, spinach, pine nuts and oregano.

3 To make Dressing: Combine the oil, chilli, garlic, salt and pepper in a small screw-top jar and shake until well combined. Pour the dressing over the top of the salad; toss well and serve immediately.

FAST PEPPER (CAPSICUM) SALAD

ROAST OR CHAR-GRILL 1 large red, 1 large green and 1 large yellow pepper (capsicum). Cover with a tea towel; allow to cool before peeling away skin. Cut the peppers into thick strips. Place in a bowl with 1 tablespoon of olive oil, 2 tablespoons of green peppercorns and 155 g (5 oz) marinated Kalamata olives. Stir through 2 tablespoons of chopped fresh mint and 1 tablespoon of raspberry vinegar. Serve on a bed of rocket leaves. Serves 4–6.

MIXED HERBED TABOULI

Preparation time: 20 minutes
  + 15 minutes standing
Total cooking time: Nil
Serves 8

³/4 cup (130 g/4¹/4 oz) burghul
³/4 cup (185 ml/6 fl oz) water
150 g (4³/4 oz) fresh flat-leaf parsley
30 g (1 oz) fresh chives
2¹/2 cups (75 g/2¹/2 oz) fresh basil leaves
¹/2 cup (10 g/¹/3 oz) fresh mint leaves
4 spring onions, finely chopped
3 medium tomatoes, chopped
¹/3 cup (80 ml/2³/4 fl oz) lemon juice
¹/4 cup (60 ml/2 fl oz) olive oil

1 Combine the burghul and water in a medium bowl. Allow to stand for 15 minutes or until all the water has been absorbed.
2 Remove large stalks from the parsley and discard them. Wash and dry the other herbs thoroughly. Chop well with a large sharp knife or in a food processor. (If using a food processor, take care not to over-process.)
3 Place the burghul, parsley, chives, basil, mint, spring onions, tomatoes, lemon juice and oil in a serving bowl and toss well to combine. Refrigerate until required.

HERBED FETA SALAD

Preparation time: 20 minutes + 30 minutes
Total cooking time: 10 minutes
Serves 6–8

2 slices thick white bread
200 g (6¹/2 oz) feta cheese
1 clove garlic, crushed
1 tablespoon finely chopped fresh marjoram
1 tablespoon finely chopped fresh chives
1 tablespoon finely chopped fresh basil
2 tablespoons white wine vinegar
¹/3 cup (80 ml/2³/4 fl oz) olive oil
1 red coral lettuce
1 butter, coral or oak-leaf lettuce

1 Preheat oven to moderate 180°C (350°F/ Gas 4). Remove crusts from bread and cut bread into cubes. Place on an oven tray in a single layer; bake for 10 minutes, or until crisp and lightly golden; cool completely.
2 Cut feta into small cubes; place in a bowl. Combine garlic, marjoram, chives, basil, vinegar and oil in small screw-top jar and shake for 30 seconds. Pour over feta and cover with plastic wrap. Leave for at least 30 minutes, stirring occasionally. Wash and dry lettuces. Tear leaves into pieces and place in a bowl. Add feta with dressing, and bread cubes; toss.

*ABOVE: Mixed Herb Tabouli
BELOW: Herbed Feta Salad*

Combine salad greens, green pepper and lemon zest in a large serving bowl.

2 To make Dressing: Whisk all ingredients in a small mixing bowl for 2 minutes or until well combined. Pour dressing over salad and toss to combine. Serve chilled.

NOTE: Make dressing and salad just before serving. Choose a selection of your favourite salad greens for this recipe. This is delicious served in summer with a chilled frascati or a light red wine.

WARM LENTIL AND RICE SALAD

Preparation time: 15 minutes
Total cooking time: 40 minutes
Serves 6

1 cup (185 g/6 oz) green lentils
1 cup (200 g/6½ oz) Basmati rice
4 large red (Spanish) onions, finely sliced
4 cloves garlic, crushed
1 cup (250 ml/8 fl oz) olive oil
45 g (1½ oz) butter
2 teaspoons ground cinnamon
2 teaspoons ground sweet paprika
2 teaspoons ground cumin
2 teaspoons ground coriander
3 spring onions, chopped
freshly ground black pepper

1 Cook the lentils and rice in separate pans of water until the grains are just tender; drain.
2 Meanwhile, cook the onions and garlic in oil and butter for 30 minutes, over low heat, until very soft.
3 Stir in the cinnamon, paprika, cumin and coriander and cook for a few minutes longer.
4 Combine the onion and spice mixture with well-drained rice and lentils. Stir in the chopped spring onions until combined and add ground pepper, to taste. Serve warm.

NOTE: Do not use red lentils for this recipe as they become mushy very quickly and do not retain their shape. It is not necessary to soak the lentils prior to cooking, but they need to be rinsed thoroughly.

BASMATI RICE
Basmati rice is a narrow long-grain rice with a silky texture, grown in the foothills of the Himalayas. Before basmati rice is cooked, it should always be washed to remove any dust and grit. Its delicate flavour makes it the ideal accompaniment for spicy Indian dishes.

ABOVE: Garden Salad

GARDEN SALAD

Preparation time: 15 minutes
Total cooking time: Nil
Serves 4-6

1 green oak-leaf lettuce
150 g (4¾ oz) rocket
1 small radicchio lettuce
1 large green pepper (capsicum), cut into thin strips
zest of 1 lemon

Dressing

2 tablespoons roughly chopped fresh coriander
¼ cup (60 ml/2 fl oz) lemon juice
2 teaspoons soft brown sugar
2 tablespoons olive oil
1 clove garlic, crushed (optional)

1 Wash and dry the salad greens thoroughly; tear into bite-size pieces.

FETA
Feta was originally made from ewes milk by shepherds in the mountain regions of Greece near Athens. Fresh feta is crumbly and dripping with the whey (liquid) in which it is ripened. When it matures it becomes dry and acquires a salty bite. We are most familiar with it as an ingredient of the traditional Greek salad.

SOUTH-WESTERN BEAN SALAD

Preparation time: 20 minutes
+ overnight soaking
Total cooking time: 50 minutes
Serves 4-6

1 cup (220 g/7 oz) dried black beans
1 cup (200 g/6 1/2 oz) white cannellini beans
1 medium red (Spanish) onion
1 medium red pepper (capsicum)
270 g (8 2/3 oz) canned corn kernels, drained
3 tablespoons chopped fresh coriander
1 clove garlic, crushed
1/2 teaspoon ground cumin
1/2 teaspoon French mustard
2 tablespoons red wine vinegar
1/4 cup (60 ml/2 fl oz) olive oil
salt and pepper

1 Soak the beans in separate bowls in cold water overnight. Drain the beans; place them in separate pans and cover with water. Bring both pans of water to the boil, reduce heat and simmer for 45 minutes or until tender. Drain, rinse and allow to cool.
2 Chop the onion and red pepper. Place in a bowl and add the beans, corn and coriander. Stir until well combined.
3 Combine the garlic, cumin, mustard and vinegar in a small jug; gradually whisk in the oil. Season lightly with salt and pepper. Pour over the bean mixture and toss lightly to combine.
NOTE: South-Western Bean Salad can be made up to a day in advance. It is a great dish to serve at a barbecue or take on a picnic, as it can be made ahead of time and will carry well. Black beans are also known as turtle beans and are available at good delicatessens. They are not to be confused with Chinese black beans.

FAST MELON SALAD

CUT A LARGE honeydew melon into slices and arrange on a large platter. Scatter 2 cups (60 g/4 oz) of thoroughly washed watercress sprigs (the leaves can harbour a lot of grit) over the top. Arrange on top, 2 sliced avocados, 1 thinly sliced large red pepper (capsicum), 220 g (7 oz) of marinated feta cheese that has been broken into large chunks, and 90 g (3 oz) of marinated niçoise olives. Make a dressing by putting 1/4 cup (60 ml/2 fl oz) olive oil, 2 tablespoons of white wine vinegar and 1 teaspoon Dijon mustard in a screw-top jar. Shake until well combined and drizzle over the salad. Serves 4–6.

ABOVE: South-Western Bean Salad

PEARS

Buy pears when they are slightly underripe and allow them to ripen at room temperature until there is a little 'give' at the stalk end. Beware of an oozing softness at the blossom end as this indicates trouble within. Once ripe, they will keep for a day or two in the refrigerator but, if serving pears on a fruit platter or as a dessert, allow them to return to room temperature for the full flavour to be appreciated. Williams and Comice pears are best suited to desserts. Asian pears such as the Chinese and the Tientsin Ya add a crisp texture to fruit and vegetable salads; they should be used while firm.

BELOW: Spinach and Avocado Salad with Warm Mustard Vinaigrette

SPINACH AND AVOCADO SALAD WITH WARM MUSTARD VINAIGRETTE

Preparation time: 15 minutes
Total cooking time: 2 minutes
Serves 8

30 English spinach leaves (90 g/3 oz)
1 red or green curly-leafed lettuce
2 medium avocados
3 tablespoons olive oil
2 teaspoons sesame seeds
1 tablespoon lemon juice
2 teaspoons wholegrain mustard

1 Wash and thoroughly dry the spinach and lettuce leaves. Tear leaves into bite-size pieces. Place in a large serving bowl.
2 Peel the avocados and cut into thin slices. Scatter over the leaves. Heat 1 tablespoon of oil in a small pan. Add the sesame seeds and cook over low heat until they just start to turn golden. Remove from the heat immediately and allow to cool slightly.
3 Add the lemon juice, remaining oil and mustard to the pan and stir to combine. While still warm, pour over the salad and toss gently to coat leaves. Salad is best served immediately.

FAST PASTA SALAD

COOK 250 g (8 oz) of pasta spirals in a large pan of boiling water until tender. Drain the spirals well and return to the pan. Stir through a little olive oil to prevent the pasta sticking, then add 4 tablespoons of ready-made pesto and toss until evenly combined. Transfer to a serving bowl to cool, then add 150 g (4¾ oz) of quartered cherry tomatoes and ½ cup (75 g/2½ oz) of chopped black olives. Serve at room temperature. Serves 4.

SPROUT AND PEAR SALAD WITH SESAME DRESSING

Preparation time: 30 minutes
Total cooking time: Nil
Serves 6

250 g (8 oz) snow pea (mange tout) sprouts
250 g (8 oz) fresh bean sprouts
30 g (1 oz) fresh chives
100 g (3⅓ oz) snow peas (mange tout)
1 celery stick
2 firm pears, not green
fresh coriander sprigs
sesame seeds, for garnish

Sesame Dressing

2 tablespoons soy sauce
1 teaspoon sesame oil
1 tablespoon soft brown sugar
2 tablespoons peanut oil
1 tablespoon rice vinegar

1 Wash and drain the snow pea sprouts. Remove the brown tips from the bean sprouts. Cut the chives into 4 cm (1½ inch) lengths and cut the snow peas and celery into thin matchstick strips. Peel and core the pears. Cut them into thin strips, slightly wider than the celery and snow peas. Place in a bowl and cover with water to prevent discoloration.
2 To make Sesame Dressing: Combine all the ingredients in a small screw-top jar and shake them well.
3 Drain the pears. Combine all salad ingredients and the coriander sprigs in a large serving bowl. Pour the dressing over and toss lightly. Sprinkle with sesame seeds and serve immediately.

WATERCRESS SALAD

Preparation time: 35 minutes
Total cooking time: Nil
Serves 4-6

500 g (1 lb) watercress
3 celery sticks
1 cucumber
3 medium oranges
1 red (Spanish) onion, thinly sliced and
  separated into rings
³/4 cup (35 g/1 ¼ oz) chopped fresh chives
¹/2 cup (60 g/2 oz) chopped pecans or walnuts

Dressing

¹/4 cup (60 ml/2 fl oz) olive oil
¹/4 cup (60 ml/2 fl oz) lemon juice
2 teaspoons grated orange rind
1 teaspoon seeded mustard
freshly ground black pepper
1 tablespoon honey

1 To make Salad: Wash and drain all vegetables. Break the watercress into small sprigs, discarding the coarser stems. Cut the celery into thin 5 cm (2 inch) long sticks. Peel, halve and seed the cucumber and cut into thin slices. Peel the oranges, remove all the white pith and cut the oranges into segments between the membrane. Refrigerate until needed.
2 To make Dressing: Combine oil, juice, rind, mustard, pepper and honey in a screw-top jar. Shake vigorously to combine.
3 Combine all the salad ingredients except nuts in a serving bowl. Pour dressing over and toss. Sprinkle with pecans or walnuts.

WATERCRESS

When buying watercress, the darker and larger the leaves, the better the cress. Watercress does not keep well but will stay freshest if it is completely submerged in water and stored in the refrigerator. Sprigs of watercress look beautiful in green salads, and its slightly peppery flavour adds contrast. It also makes an excellent garnish for cold soups.

ABOVE: Sprout and Pear Salad with Sesame Dressing
LEFT: Watercress Salad

177

OLIVES

Round or oblong, plump or wrinkled, black, green or brown, marinated with chillies and herbs, pureéd into a luscious tapenade or simply eaten on their own, olives seem to encapsulate the essence of the Mediterranean.

MARINATED LEMON AND GARLIC OLIVES

Rinse and drain 500 g (1 lb) brined Kalamata olives. Make a small incision in the side of each olive to allow the marinade to penetrate thoroughly. Layer the olives in a sterilised jar with fine strips of lemon rind, 3 finely sliced cloves of garlic, 1 tablespoon of coriander seeds and 2 bay leaves. Pour over ¼ cup (60 ml/2 fl oz) of balsamic vinegar and cover the olives with extra virgin olive oil. Seal the jar and set aside in a cool dark place to marinate for one week. Serve these olives as part of an antipasto platter.

CHILLI-SPICED BABY OLIVES WITH HERBS

Rinse and drain 500 g (1 lb) brined Niçoise olives. Layer in a sterilised jar with 4 halved small red chillies, a few thinly cut slices of lime, 1 teaspoon chilli flakes, 2 finely sliced cloves of garlic and several sprigs of your favourite herbs.

Combine 2 tablespoons lime juice with 2 tablespoons tarragon vinegar, 1 cup of (250 ml/8 fl oz) extra virgin olive and a few crushed peppercorns; pour over olives. Add extra oil to cover if needed. Seal and leave to marinate in a cool, dark place for 1 week.

OLIVE AND TOMATO TAPENADE

Place 155 g (5 oz) of pitted and roughly chopped marinated Niçoise olives in a food processor. Add 2 finely chopped spring onions, 60 g (2 oz) of drained capers, 60 g (2 oz) of chopped sun-dried tomatoes and 60 g (2 oz) of chopped sun-dried peppers (capsicums). Process for 10 seconds or until all ingredients are roughly chopped—do not overprocess or mixture will turn to a paste. Transfer to a

bowl, fold in 2 finely chopped egg (Roma) tomatoes, 1 tablespoon of chopped fresh parsley and 1 tablespoon of olive oil. Season with salt and pepper. Serve with crackers or toast.

OLIVE SALSA

Put 250 g (8 oz) chopped marinated green olives and 90 g (3 oz) chopped marinated black olives in a bowl. Add 1 finely chopped red (Spanish) onion, 1 chopped yellow pepper (capsicum), 4 chopped egg (Roma) tomatoes and 3 tablespoons chopped fresh basil; toss. Whisk 1 crushed clove of garlic, 2 finely chopped red chillies, 1 tablespoon each orange juice and lemon juice and ¼ cup (60 ml/2 fl oz) olive oil. Pour over olive mixture; cover and refrigerate. Serve at room temperature.

BRUSCHETTA WITH OLIVES, BOCCONCINI AND TOMATOES

Cut wood-fired bread into 1 cm (½ inch) thick slices, brush each slice lightly with olive oil and cook under a preheated grill or char-grill until golden on both sides. Top with a thick slice of egg (Roma) tomato, thin slices of bocconcini, a slice of gherkin, a basil leaf, and some finely chopped marinated black olives. Drizzle with olive oil and sprinkle with cracked black pepper to serve.

CLOKWISE, FROM TOP LEFT: Bruschetta with Olives, Bocconcini and Tomatoes; Olive Salsa; Marinated Lemon and Garlic Olives; Olive and Tomato Tapenade; Chilli-spiced Baby Olives with Herbs

PREPARING SNOW PEAS

1 Pull any threads from the tails of the snow peas, then snap off the tops.

2 Pull the tops down to remove the string from the side.

SNOW PEAS

Snow peas, also known as mange tout, are harvested when the peas are still immature. When buying snow peas, look for small ones; once the peas are round, the pod will be stringy and too tough to be eaten. As with other peas, beans and sweet corn, snow peas start converting their sugar into starch from the moment they are picked. This process subtly alters their taste and they should be eaten as soon as possible after purchase.

ABOVE: Snow Pea Salad

SNOW PEA SALAD
(MANGE TOUT SALAD)

Preparation time: 25 minutes
Total cooking time: 5 minutes
Serves 4-6

200 g (6¹/2 oz) snow peas (mange tout), sliced diagonally
1 large red pepper (capsicum), sliced
4 leaves oak leaf lettuce
5 leaves green coral lettuce
250 g (8 oz) cherry tomatoes
60 g (2 oz) watercress sprigs
Parmesan cheese, to serve

Garlic Croutons

3 slices white bread
¹/4 cup (60 ml/2 fl oz) olive oil
1 clove garlic, crushed

Dressing

2 tablespoons olive oil
1 tablespoon mayonnaise
1 tablespoon sour cream
2 tablespoons lemon juice
1 teaspoon soft brown sugar
cracked black pepper

1 Wash the lettuce and tomatoes. Combine the snow peas, red pepper, watercress, lettuces and tomatoes in a large bowl.
2 To make Garlic Croutons: Remove the crusts from the bread slices. Cut the bread into 1 cm (¹/2 inch) squares. Heat the olive oil in small, heavy-based pan and add the crushed garlic. Stir in the prepared bread cubes and cook until golden and crisp. Remove from the heat and leave to drain well on paper towels.
3 To make Dressing: Whisk all the ingredients in a small bowl for 2 minutes or until combined. Just before serving, pour the dressing over the salad, stirring until well combined. Top with the Garlic Croutons and thin shavings of Parmesan cheese.
NOTE: Use a vegetable peeler to make thin shavings of Parmesan cheese.

FAST SPINACH SALAD

IN A LARGE bowl, mix together 2 tablespoons olive oil, 1 crushed clove garlic, 2 teaspoons white wine vinegar and a little black pepper. Add 100 g (3¹/3 oz) thinly sliced mushrooms and stir to coat well. Put 300 g (9²/3 oz) torn English spinach leaves in a salad bowl. Add mushrooms and dressing and 2 sliced hard-boiled eggs. Toss well. Crumble 100 g (3¹/3 oz) feta cheese over the top. Serves 2–4.

PEARS WITH BRIE AND PECANS

Preparation time: 15 minutes
Total cooking time: Nil
Serves 4

200 g (6½ oz) brie cheese, at room
    temperature
3 medium pears
1 butter or mignonette lettuce
4 tablespoons finely chopped pecans

Vinaigrette Dressing

3 tablespoons oil
1 tablespoon tarragon vinegar

1 Cut the brie into thin wedges. Do not peel
the pears, but cut them into quarters; remove
the cores and slice the pears thinly. Wash and
dry the lettuce thoroughly, then separate the
leaves and arrange on individual serving plates.
Top with the brie and pears.
2 To make Vinaigrette Dressing: Place the oil
and vinegar in a small screw-top jar and shake
well. Drizzle the dressing over the salad and
sprinkle with pecans. Serve immediately.
NOTE: Camembert can be used instead of brie
in this recipe. Ripe brie or camembert give the
best flavour. Make sure that the cheese is at
room temperature to serve.

WARM BEAN SALAD

Preparation time: 10 minutes
Total cooking time: 8 minutes
Serves 4

2 tablespoons olive oil
1 medium onion, finely chopped
1 clove garlic, crushed
1 small red pepper (capsicum), cut into
    short strips
90 g (3 oz) green beans
60 g (2 oz) button mushrooms, sliced
1 tablespoon balsamic vinegar
440 g (14 oz) canned mixed beans
chopped fresh parsley, for serving

1 Heat half the oil in a medium pan. Add the
onions and cook for 2 minutes over medium
heat. Add the garlic, red pepper, green beans,
mushrooms and vinegar. Cook for another
5 minutes, stirring occasionally.
2 Thoroughly rinse and drain the mixed beans.
Add to the vegetables with the remaining oil and
stir until just warmed through. Sprinkle with
chopped parsley for serving.

BRIE
It was at the Congress
of Vienna in 1815, when
delegates, establishing the
boundaries of Europe after
the Battle of Waterloo,
pronounced Brie 'the king
of cheeses'. Since then it
has gained a world-wide
reputation and following.
When brie is perfectly ripe
it will ooze slightly at
room temperature. It has
a lovely warm, creamy
flavour best experienced
from the whole cheese,
rather than in the form of
a packaged wedge.

*LEFT: Pears with Brie
and Pecans
ABOVE: Warm
Bean Salad*

CURLY ENDIVE AND BLUE CHEESE SALAD

Preparation time: 15 minutes
Total cooking time: 5 minutes
Serves 6

3 slices bread
3 tablespoons oil
30 g (1 oz) butter
1 curly endive
125 g (4 oz) blue cheese
2 tablespoons olive oil
3 teaspoons white wine vinegar
2 tablespoons chopped fresh chives

1 To make croutons, remove crusts from bread and cut into small squares. Heat oil and butter in a frying pan until bubbling and add bread. Cook, tossing frequently, for 3 minutes or until golden. Drain on paper towels.
2 Wash and dry the endive thoroughly. Place the leaves in a serving bowl and crumble cheese over the top.
3 Place the oil and vinegar in a small screw-top jar and shake well. Drizzle the dressing over the salad, add the chives and croutons and toss. Serve immediately.

RED CABBAGE SALAD

Preparation time: 15 minutes
Total cooking time: Nil
Serves 6

155 g (5 oz) red cabbage, finely shredded
125 g (4 oz) green cabbage, finely shredded
2 spring onions, finely chopped
3 tablespoons olive oil
2 teaspoons white wine vinegar
1/2 teaspoon French mustard
1 teaspoon caraway seeds

1 Combine the red and green cabbage and spring onions in a serving bowl.
2 Place the oil, vinegar, mustard and caraway seeds in a small screw-top jar and shake well.
3 Pour the dressing over the salad, toss lightly to combine and serve immediately.

GREEN BEAN SALAD

Preparation time: 15 minutes
Total cooking time: 15 minutes
Serves 4

280 g (9 oz) green beans
1 tablespoon olive oil
2 teaspoons lemon juice
1 tablespoon pine nuts
1/3 cup (80 ml/2 3/4 fl oz) tomato juice
1 clove garlic, crushed
few drops Tabasco sauce

1 Top and tail beans; place in a pan of boiling water. Boil for 1 minute, drain and plunge into iced water; drain well; toss with oil and lemon juice. Preheat oven to moderate 180°C (350°F/ Gas 4). Spread nuts on a foil-covered oven tray and cook for 5 minutes. Do not allow to burn.
2 Combine tomato juice, garlic and Tabasco in a small pan. Bring to boil; simmer, uncovered, over low heat for 8 minutes or until reduced by half. Allow to cool. Arrange beans on a serving plate; pour tomato mixture over. Sprinkle with nuts.

SPINACH AND NUT SALAD

Preparation time: 15 minutes
Total cooking time: 2 minutes
Serves 4

30 English spinach leaves (about 90 g/3 oz)
250 g (8 oz) young green beans, chopped
1/2 medium onion, finely sliced
1/3 cup (90 g/3 oz) plain yoghurt
1 tablespoon lemon juice
1 tablespoon shredded fresh mint
4 tablespoons chopped walnuts, toasted
fresh mint leaves, to serve
red pepper (capsicum) curls, to serve

1 Rinse the spinach in cold water. Cover the beans with boiling water, leave 2 minutes. Drain; pat spinach and beans dry with paper towels; cool.
2 Arrange spinach, beans and onion on a serving plate. Mix yoghurt, lemon juice and mint in a bowl. Pour over the salad, sprinkle with walnuts and garnish with mint leaves and red pepper.

BLUE CHEESE
Blue cheeses happened first by accident, but the penicillin moulds that give cheese blue veins have since been identified and isolated, and blue varieties are now manufactured by most cheese-producing countries. Blue cheese can be anything from golden yellow to chalk white, but should be flecked with blue mould throughout. The only thing a blue cheese should never be is brown and clouded.

OPPOSITE PAGE, FROM TOP: Green Bean Salad; Red Cabbage Salad; Curly Endive and Blue Cheese Salad

1 Chop the tomato and cut the cucumber into rounds. Thinly slice the radishes and onion, and cut the feta cheese into small cubes.

2 Combine the prepared tomato, cucumber, radishes, onion, feta and olives in a serving bowl. Drizzle with the combined lemon juice, olive oil and oregano. Serve on a bed of coral lettuce, if you like.

CABBAGE WITH CRISP-FRIED ONION

Preparation time: 20 minutes
Total cooking time: Nil
Serves 4-6

1/2 medium Chinese or Savoy cabbage
1/2 cup (35 g/1 1/4 oz) crisp-fried onion
1/4 cup (25 g/3/4 oz) crisp-fried garlic
1/2 red pepper (capsicum), cut into very
   fine strips
3 tablespoons fresh mint leaves, shredded
1/3 cup (80 ml/2 3/4 fl oz) coconut milk
1 tablespoon fish sauce (optional)
1 teaspoon soft brown sugar
2 fresh red chillies, finely sliced
lime wedges, for serving

1 Finely shred the cabbage. Arrange on a serving platter and sprinkle the crisp-fried onions and garlic, red pepper and mint over the top.

2 Combine the coconut milk, fish sauce and brown sugar in a small bowl and mix well. Pour over the salad. Sprinkle with chillies and serve with lime wedges.

NOTE: Crisp-fried onion and crisp-fried garlic are available in jars from Asian food shops. They are commonly used in Thai cookery, as a garnish for salads, soups and noodle dishes. You can make your own at home by finely slicing peeled onion and garlic and cooking over low heat in oil, stirring regularly until crisp and golden brown. Drain well and allow to cool before seasoning with salt. This should be done when you are ready to serve.

GREEK SALAD

Preparation time: 15 minutes
Total cooking time: Nil
Serves 4

1 large tomato
1 medium Lebanese cucumber
2 radishes
1 small onion
100 g (3 1/3 oz) feta cheese
1/4 cup (45 g/1 1/2 oz) pitted black olives
2 tablespoons lemon juice
3 tablespoons olive oil
1/2 teaspoon dried oregano leaves

ABOVE: Greek Salad

WILD AND BROWN RICE SALAD

Preparation time: 20 minutes
Total cooking time: 40 minutes
Serves 6

1/2 cup (95 g/3 1/4 oz) wild rice
1 cup (200 g/6 1/2 oz) brown rice
1 medium red (Spanish) onion
1 small red pepper (capsicum)
2 celery sticks
2 tablespoons chopped fresh parsley
4 tablespoons chopped pecans

Dressing
1/4 cup (60 ml/2 fl oz) orange juice
1/4 cup (60 ml/2 fl oz) lemon juice
1 teaspoon finely grated orange rind
1 teaspoon finely grated lemon rind
1/3 cup (80 ml/2 3/4 oz) olive oil

1 Cook the wild rice in a pan of boiling water for 30–40 minutes until just tender. Drain well and then allow to cool completely. Meanwhile, boil the brown rice for 25–30 minutes, drain well and allow it to cool.
2 Chop the onion and red pepper finely. Cut the celery into thin slices. Combine in a bowl with the parsley and the cooked rices. Place the pecans in a dry frying pan and stir over medium heat for 2–3 minutes until lightly toasted. Transfer to a plate to cool.
3 To make Dressing: Place the orange and lemon juices, rinds and the olive oil in a small screw-top jar and then shake well to combine.
4 Pour the dressing over the salad and gently fold through. Add the pecans and gently mix through. Serve with pitta or crusty bread, if desired.

COLESLAW

Preparation time: 25 minutes
Total cooking time: Nil
Serves 4

155 g (5 oz) green cabbage
155 g (5 oz) red cabbage
2 medium carrots
3 spring onions
1/4 cup (60 g/2 oz) mayonnaise
1 tablespoon white wine vinegar
1/2 teaspoon French mustard
salt and pepper

1 Finely shred the cabbages, grate the carrots and finely chop the spring onions. Combine in a large bowl and toss together until well mixed.
2 Whisk together the mayonnaise, vinegar and mustard, and season with salt and pepper. Toss through the salad.

WILD RICE
Wild rice, despite its name, is not a rice at all but the seed of an aquatic grass native to North America, where it was traditionally harvested by the American Indians. A slightly different variety is grown in Asia. True wild rice is hard to find and is often very expensive, but worth it for the wonderful flavour. Cultivated types grown for the commercial market have less taste but are also less expensive. Be careful when preparing, as overcooking wild rice will diminish its flavour.

ABOVE: Wild and Brown Rice Salad

185

PEANUTS

The peanut is native to South America and, surprisingly, is not a nut but a legume. Raw peanuts taste faintly like green beans. Peanuts can be tossed in a little hot oil and salt, then toasted in a moderate oven.

CUCUMBER SALAD WITH PEANUTS AND CHILLI

Preparation time: 25 minutes + 45 minutes marinating
Total cooking time: Nil
Serves 4-6

3 medium cucumbers
2 tablespoons white vinegar
2 teaspoons white sugar
1–2 tablespoons sweet chilli sauce
12 French shallots, chopped
1/2 cup (15 g/1/2 oz) fresh coriander leaves
185 g (6 oz) roasted peanuts, chopped
2 tablespoons crisp fried garlic
1 tablespoon fish sauce (optional)

1 Peel the cucumber, cut in half lengthways, scoop out the seeds and slice thinly.
2 Combine the vinegar and sugar in a small bowl and stir until sugar has dissolved. Transfer to a large bowl and add cucumber, vinegar mixture, chilli sauce, shallots and coriander leaves. Allow to marinate for 45 minutes.
3 Just before serving, sprinkle with peanuts, fried garlic and fish sauce.
NOTE: If French shallots are unavailable, use red (Spanish) onions.

HERBED POTATO SALAD

Preparation time: 15 minutes
Total cooking time: 10–15 minutes
Serves 4

650 g (1 lb 5 oz) red-skinned potatoes
1 red (Spanish) onion
1 tablespoon chopped fresh mint
1 tablespoon chopped fresh parsley
1 tablespoon chopped fresh chives
4 tablespoons mayonnaise
4 tablespoons plain yoghurt

1 Scrub the potatoes (do not peel) and cut into cubes. Cook in a large pan of boiling water until just tender, drain and cool completely. Finely slice the onion.
2 Place the potatoes, onion and herbs in a large bowl. Combine the mayonnaise and yoghurt, then gently mix through to coat the potato, taking care not to break it up too much. Serve at room temperature.
NOTE: You will get best results from a good-quality whole egg mayonnaise (home-made is even better).

ABOVE: Cucumber Salad with Peanuts and Chilli

CHICKPEA AND OLIVE SALAD

Preparation time: 20 minutes
+ overnight soaking
Total cooking time: 25 minutes
Serves 6

1¹/₂ cups (330 g/10¹/₂ oz) dried chickpeas
1 small Lebanese cucumber
2 medium tomatoes
1 small red (Spanish) onion
3 tablespoons chopped fresh parsley
¹/₂ cup (60 g/2 oz) pitted black olives
1 tablespoon lemon juice
3 tablespoons olive oil
1 clove garlic, crushed
1 teaspoon honey

1 Place the chickpeas in a large bowl and cover with cold water. Leave to soak overnight. Drain the chickpeas, place in a pan, cover with fresh water and cook for 25 minutes or until just tender. Drain and allow to cool.
2 Cut the cucumber in half lengthways, scoop out seeds and cut into 1 cm (¹/₂ inch) slices. Cut the tomatoes into cubes roughly the same size as the chickpeas, and chop onion finely. Combine the chickpeas, cucumber, tomato, onion, parsley and olives in a serving bowl.
3 Place the lemon juice, oil, garlic and honey in a small screw-top jar and shake well. Pour the dressing over the salad and toss lightly to combine. Serve at room temperature.

TOFU SALAD

Preparation time: 20 minutes
+ 1 hour marinating
Total cooking time: Nil
Serves 4

2 teaspoons Thai sweet chilli sauce
¹/₂ teaspoon grated fresh ginger
1 clove garlic, crushed
2 teaspoons soy sauce
2 tablespoons oil
250 g (8 oz) firm tofu
105 g (3¹/₂ oz) snow peas (mange tout), cut
into 3 cm (1¹/₄ inch) lengths
2 small carrots, cut into matchsticks
105 g (3¹/₂ oz) red cabbage, finely shredded
2 tablespoons chopped peanuts

1 Place the chilli sauce, ginger, garlic, soy sauce and oil in a small screw-top jar and shake well. Cut the tofu into 2 cm (³/₄ inch) cubes. Place the tofu in a medium bowl, pour the marinade over and stir. Cover with plastic wrap and refrigerate for 1 hour.
2 Place the snow peas in a small pan, pour boiling water over and leave to stand for 1 minute, then drain and plunge into iced water. Drain well.
3 Add the snow peas, carrots and cabbage to tofu and toss lightly to combine. Transfer to a serving bowl or individual plates, sprinkle with peanuts and serve immediately.

BELOW: Chickpea and Olive Salad (top); Tofu Salad

1 Preheat oven to moderate 180°C (350°F/ Gas 4). Brush lavash with oil, and sprinkle lightly with paprika. Cut in half lengthways, then across into 16 strips. Place on a baking tray and bake for 5 minutes or until golden. Cool on a rack.
2 Wash and dry lettuce thoroughly. Combine chives with cottage cheese. Arrange with other ingredients on individual plates, with four lavash crisps on the side. Serve immediately.
NOTE: Lavash is rectangular flat bread. It is available from supermarkets.

NACHOS SALAD

Preparation time: 20 minutes
Total cooking time: Nil
Serves 4

440 g (14 oz) canned red kidney beans
1 large tomato, cut into cubes
1/2 cup (125 g/4 oz) bottled mild salsa
280 g (9 oz) packet plain corn chips
8 lettuce leaves, shredded
1 small avocado, sliced
20 g (2/3 oz) Cheddar cheese, grated

1 Empty the beans into a colander or strainer and rinse under running water. Drain well and combine with the tomato and salsa.
2 Arrange a bed of corn chips on each plate and top with lettuce, bean mixture and avocado. Sprinkle with the grated cheese and serve.

COTTAGE CHEESE

Cottage cheese originated in America and is made from the curds of skimmed milk. Its low fat content makes it a popular dieter's choice. Cottage cheese goes well with fruit salad, while creamed cottage cheese is excellent in cooking.

ABOVE, FROM TOP:
Penne Salad with
Sun-dried Tomatoes;
Nachos Salad; Cottage
Cheese Salad

COTTAGE CHEESE SALAD

Preparation time: 20 minutes
Total cooking time: 5 minutes
Serves 4

1 sheet lavash bread
2 teaspoons canola oil
mild paprika, to sprinkle
16 red oak leaf lettuce leaves
2 tablespoons chopped fresh chives
500 g (1 lb) cottage cheese
200 g (6 1/2 oz) red grapes
1 medium carrot, grated
3 tablespoons alfalfa sprouts

PENNE SALAD WITH SUN-DRIED TOMATOES

Preparation time: 20 minutes
Total cooking time: 10 minutes
Serves 6

500 g (1 lb) penne pasta
1 tablespoon olive oil
150 g (4 3/4 oz) sun-dried tomatoes, drained
1/2 cup (25 g/3/4 oz) fresh basil leaves
1/2 cup (70 g/2 1/3 oz) black pitted olives, halved
2 tablespoons olive oil, extra
2 teaspoons white wine vinegar
1 clove garlic, cut in half
60 g (2 oz) Parmesan, shaved

1 Cook pasta in a large pan of boiling water until just tender. Drain and rinse under cold water; drain again. Place in a large serving bowl and combine with oil to prevent sticking.
2 Thinly slice sun-dried tomatoes. Mix basil leaves and tomatoes into pasta with the olives.
3 Place the extra oil, vinegar and garlic in a small screw-top jar and shake well. Leave for 5 minutes then discard garlic. Shake dressing again and then pour over salad. Stir gently to combine. Garnish with shavings of Parmesan and serve immediately.

CITRUS WALNUT SALAD

Preparation time: 20 minutes
Total cooking time: Nil
Serves 8

★

2 oranges
2 grapefruit
125 g (4 oz) sugar snap peas
75 g (2¹/₂ oz) rocket, leaves torn
¹/₂ oak leaf lettuce, leaves torn
1 large Lebanese cucumber, sliced
¹/₃ cup (40 g/1¹/₃ oz) walnut pieces

Walnut Dressing
2 tablespoons walnut oil
2 tablespoons oil
2 teaspoons tarragon vinegar
2 teaspoons seeded mustard
1 teaspoon sweet chilli sauce

1 Peel the oranges and grapefruit, removing all the white pith. Cut the fruit into segments between the membrane, removing the seeds. Cover the sugar snap peas with boiling water and leave to stand for 2 minutes. Plunge the peas into iced water. Drain and pat dry with sheets of paper towel. Combine the fruit, peas, rocket, lettuce, cucumber and walnut pieces in a large bowl.
2 To make Walnut Dressing: Combine all the ingredients in a screw-top jar and shake well.
3 Pour the dressing over the salad ingredients and toss until combined.

SPICY POTATO SALAD

Preparation time: 15 minutes
Total cooking time: 20 minutes
Serves 6

★

500 g (1 lb) baby new potatoes, halved
250 g (8 oz) green beans, trimmed, tailed and halved diagonally

Dressing
¹/₄ cup (60 ml/2 fl oz) olive oil
2 red chillies, seeded and sliced
1 clove garlic, crushed
¹/₄ cup (15 g/¹/₂ oz) chopped fresh coriander
1 tablespoon red wine vinegar
¹/₂ teaspoon caraway seeds

1 Cook the potatoes in a large pan of gently simmering water for 20 minutes, or until tender but still firm; drain and set aside. Blanch beans in boiling water for 2 minutes or until bright green and just tender; drain beans and set aside.
2 To make Dressing: Whisk all ingredients in a small bowl for 2 minutes or until well combined. Pour the dressing over the combined beans and potatoes and serve immediately or the salad will discolour.

CARAWAY SEEDS
Caraway seeds (*Carum carvi*) are renowned for their digestive properties and are rich in mineral salts and proteins. When chewed, the seeds help get rid of the smell of garlic and are also said to stimulate the appetite. Most commonly seen in heavy rye bread, caraway seeds are also used when making seed bread. A little bowl of caraway seeds is a great accompaniment for strong cheeses such as Munster and Livarot.

ABOVE: Citrus Walnut Salad

VEGETABLES ON THE SIDE

Accompaniments, maybe—but good-quality, well-prepared vegetables take on a special identity when playing foil to your main course and complementing the theme of the meal. So many varieties, a plethora 'now in-season', a hundred colours, shapes and tastes: the only dilemma you'll have at the greengrocer is deciding which to choose.

GHEE

Ghee is the fat most used in Indian cooking and in many Arab countries, where it is known as *samna*. Its strong, sweet flavour is produced by clarifying butter and then discarding the white froth and whey. Flavourings are often added: in India, cumin seeds, bay leaves, cloves and ginger; and in the Middle East, oregano, thyme and other herbs.

ABOVE: Potato and Pea Curry

POTATO AND PEA CURRY

Preparation time: 20 minutes
Total cooking time: 35 minutes
Serves 4

750 g (1 1/2 b) potatoes, peeled
2 teaspoons brown mustard seeds
2 tablespoons ghee or oil
2 onions, sliced
2 cloves garlic, crushed
2 teaspoons grated fresh ginger
1 teaspoon turmeric
salt and pepper
1/2 teaspoon chilli powder
1 teaspoon ground cumin
1 teaspoon garam masala
1/2 cup (125 ml/4 fl oz) water
2/3 cup (110 g/3 2/3 oz) fresh or frozen peas
2 tablespoons chopped fresh mint

1 Cut the potatoes into large cubes. Heat the mustard seeds in a large dry pan until they start to pop. Add the ghee, onions, garlic and ginger and cook, stirring, until soft. Add the turmeric, salt, pepper, chilli, cumin, garam masala and potatoes. Stir until the potatoes are coated.
2 Add the water and simmer, covered, for 15–20 minutes, or until the potatoes are just tender. Add the peas and stir; simmer, covered, for 3–5 minutes, or until the potatoes are cooked and the liquid is absorbed. Stir in the mint and serve hot or warm.

ROSTI

Preparation time: 10 minutes
+ refrigeration
Total cooking time: 45 minutes
Serves 4

6 medium potatoes (750 g/1 1/2 lb)
salt and freshly ground black pepper
60 g (2 oz) butter

1 Place the potatoes in a large pan of boiling water and cook until just tender. Drain, cool and peel. Cover and refrigerate overnight. Grate potatoes, add salt and pepper to taste.
2 Heat half the butter in a medium heavy-based frying pan; when sizzling, add the potatoes and press down to form a level, thin layer. Cook over medium to low heat for 15–20 minutes or until the potatoes are crusty and golden brown on the underside, taking care not to burn them. Shake the pan to prevent sticking. Place a large plate over the pan and invert Rosti onto it.
3 Heat the remaining butter in the pan, slide the Rosti back into the pan and cook for another

15–20 minutes until the other side is crisp and golden. Serve at once, cut into wedges, with a fresh green salad.

EGGPLANT (AUBERGINE) WITH TOMATO HERB SAUCE

Preparation time: 30 minutes
Total cooking time: 40 minutes
Serves 4

6–8 slender eggplants (aubergines)
olive oil, for frying, plus 2 tablespoons, extra
2 cloves garlic, crushed
I onion, chopped
I red pepper (capsicum), seeded and
    chopped
2 ripe tomatoes, chopped
1/2 cup (125 ml/4 fl oz) vegetable stock
I teaspoon finely chopped fresh thyme
I teaspoon finely chopped fresh marjoram
2 teaspoons finely chopped fresh oregano
I teaspoon sugar
3–4 teaspoons white wine vinegar
3 tablespoons small black olives
salt and pepper
1/4 cup (7 g/1/4 oz) fresh basil leaves, shredded

I Cut the eggplants in half lengthways. Pour enough oil into a large frying pan to cover the base. Heat until the oil is almost smoking. Fry the eggplants in batches over medium-high heat for 2–3 minutes on each side, or until golden brown. Remove from the pan with tongs and drain on paper towels. Add more oil, if necessary, to cook each batch. Cover the eggplants and keep them warm.
2 Heat the extra oil in a pan and add the garlic and onion. Stir over medium heat for 2–3 minutes. Add the red pepper and tomatoes and cook, stirring, for 1–2 minutes or until just softened.
3 Add the stock to the pan. Bring to the boil, reduce heat and simmer, stirring occasionally, for 5–10 minutes or until the liquid reduces and thickens. Stir in the thyme, marjoram, oregano, sugar and vinegar. Cook for another 3–4 minutes. Stir in the olives; season with salt and pepper. Serve the warm eggplants topped with the tomato sauce and the shredded basil.
NOTE: The tomato mixture can be made a day ahead, without the herbs. Add herbs when reheating—this helps to retain the colour and will ensure the flavour does not become bitter.

THYME
Thyme (*Thymus vulgaris*) is one of the essential herbs of Mediterranean cooking. It has its best flavour when in flower and, though it dries well, it is best to cook with fresh thyme whenever possible. When buying dried thyme, be aware that powdery leaves indicate the herb is older and will have less flavour and fragrance. Buy dried thyme in small quantities as stale herbs spoil a dish.

ABOVE: Eggplant with Tomato Herb Sauce

CHIVES

Chives are one of the four classic *fines herbes*—the perfectly balanced quartet of chives, chervil, parsley and tarragon. Chives range in flavour from mild to strong, according to size. The larger ones have the most onion-like taste.

STUFFED ZUCCHINI (COURGETTE) BLOSSOMS

Preparation time: 35 minutes
Total cooking time: 20 minutes
Serves 4

★ ★

1/2 cup (125 g/4 oz) ricotta cheese
1/2 cup (60 g/2 oz) finely grated
   Cheddar or mozzarella cheese
2 tablespoons fresh chopped chives
12 zucchini (courgette) blossoms
1/3 cup (40 g/1 1/3 oz) plain flour

Batter
1 cup (125 g/4 oz) plain flour
1 egg, lightly beaten
3/4 cup (185 ml/6 fl oz) iced water
oil, for deep-frying

Tomato Sauce
1 tablespoon olive oil
1 small onion, finely chopped

1 clove garlic, crushed
425 g (13 1/2 oz) canned, crushed tomatoes
1/2 teaspoon dried oregano

1 Combine the ricotta, Cheddar or mozzarella, and the chives in a small bowl.
2 Gently open out the zucchini blossoms; remove stamens and spoon in the cheese mixture. Close up the blossoms and twist the ends to seal. Dust lightly with the flour and shake off the excess.
3 To make Batter: Place the flour in a medium bowl; make a well in centre. Add the egg and water; beat until all the liquid is incorporated and the batter is free of lumps.
4 Heat the oil in a large pan until moderately hot. Using tongs, dip each blossom into the batter and then lower into the oil. Fry the blossoms until just golden; drain on paper towels. Serve immediately with Tomato Sauce.
5 To make Tomato Sauce: Heat the oil in a small pan and add the onions. Cook over medium heat for 3 minutes, until the onions are soft. Add the garlic and cook for another minute. Add the tomatoes and the oregano and stir to combine. Bring mixture to the boil, reduce heat and simmer gently for 10 minutes. Serve hot.
NOTE: Small zucchini blossoms often have a baby zucchini still attached to them. Larger blossoms are sometimes available without the zucchini.

BELOW: Stuffed Zucchini Blossoms

BAKED ROOT VEGETABLES WITH SWEET GINGER GLAZE

Preparation time: 25 minutes
Total cooking time: 1 hour 10 minutes
Serves 4-6

★

150 g (4 3/4 oz) sweet potato
1 medium potato
1 medium carrot
1 medium parsnip
1 medium turnip
2 tablespoons olive oil
60 g (2 oz) butter
2 tablespoons caster sugar
1 tablespoon finely grated fresh ginger
1/4 cup (60 ml/2 fl oz) water

1 Preheat oven to hot 210°C (415°F/Gas 6–7). Brush a large baking tray with oil.

2 Peel the sweet potato, potato, carrot, parsnip and turnip and cut into sticks about 5 cm (2 inches) long and 1 cm (½ inch) thick.

3 Place the vegetables in a single layer on the prepared baking tray and brush them all over with olive oil. Bake for 1 hour or until golden.

4 Melt the butter in a small pan. Add the sugar and stir over low heat until the sugar has dissolved. Add the grated ginger and the water and stir to combine. Bring to the boil, reduce heat to low and simmer, uncovered, for 5 minutes or until the mixture has reduced and thickened slightly. Pour the glaze over the baked vegetables; toss to coat and return the tray to the oven for another 5 minutes. Serve immediately, with steamed green vegetables if you like.

FAST PAN-FRIED ASPARAGUS

TRIM THE ENDS from 155 g (5 oz) of asparagus spears (try to choose young, slim spears for this recipe). Heat 1 tablespoon of oil and 20 g (⅔ oz) of butter in a frying pan, add the asparagus and cook for 3–4 minutes, turning frequently to cook all sides. The asparagus will turn bright green, then begin to brown in patches. Add a couple of teaspoons of lemon juice at the end of cooking time; toss through and serve immediately. Serves 2–4.

SAUTEED ROSEMARY POTATOES

Preparation time: 15–20 minutes
Total cooking time: 35 minutes
Serves 4–6

✫

750 g (1 ½ lb) baby new potatoes
30 g (1 oz) butter
2 tablespoons olive oil
black pepper
2 cloves garlic, crushed
1 tablespoon finely chopped fresh rosemary
1 teaspoon coarse rock or sea salt
½ teaspoon cracked black pepper

1 Wash the potatoes, pat dry with paper towels. Cut in half. Lightly boil or steam potatoes until they are just tender. Drain; cool slightly.

2 Heat the butter and oil in a large heavy-based frying pan. When the mixture is foaming, add the potatoes and season with pepper. Cook over medium heat for 5–10 minutes or until golden and crisp, tossing regularly to ensure that the potatoes are evenly coloured.

3 Stir in the garlic, rosemary and salt. Cook for 1 minute or until well coated. Add the cracked pepper and mix well. Serve hot or warm.

NOTE: Fresh thyme would work nicely in this recipe, as would fresh parsley.

SALT

Salt, or sodium chloride, has been used as a food preservative and seasoning since ancient times. One of its most valuable properties is its ability to draw the moisture from foods. This is why we often chop up eggplant (aubergine) and leave it covered in salt before cooking—the salt draws out the bitter juice.

ABOVE: Baked Root Vegetables with Sweet Ginger Glaze BELOW: Sautéed Rosemary Potatoes

SUGAR PEAS AND CARROTS IN LIME BUTTER

Preparation time: 15 minutes
Total cooking time: 10 minutes
Serves 4

125 g (4 oz) carrots
125 g (4 oz) sugar snap peas
60 g (2 oz) butter
2 cloves garlic, crushed
1 tablespoon lime juice (and rind from 1 lime, to make zest for garnish)
1/2 teaspoon soft brown sugar

1 Peel the carrots and cut into thin diagonal slices. Wash and string the sugar snap peas. Heat the butter in a large heavy-based frying pan. Add the garlic, cook over low heat for 1 minute. Add the lime juice and sugar. Cook, stirring over low heat, until sugar has completely dissolved.
2 Add the carrots and peas and cook over medium heat for 2–3 minutes or until just cooked. Serve hot. Garnish with lime zest.
3 To make lime zest, peel lime rind into long strips using a vegetable peeler. Remove all white pith. Cut into long thin strips with a sharp knife.
NOTE: Snow peas (mange tout) or green beans can be used in place of sugar snap peas. Baby carrots also make an attractive addition to this recipe—leave a portion of the green tops on. If limes are unavailable, substitute lemon juice and zest. This dish can be adapted to make a light salad—replace the butter with 2 tablespoons of olive oil and cook according to the recipe. Cool to room temperature and sprinkle with finely chopped cashews or toasted pine nuts.

POTATO CAKES WITH APPLE SAUCE

Preparation time: 20 minutes
Total cooking time: 30 minutes
Serves 4

4 cups (620 g/1 lb 4 2/3 oz) finely grated potato
1 large onion, finely chopped
2 teaspoons celery or fennel seeds
3 tablespoons plain flour
2 eggs, beaten
salt and freshly ground black pepper
oil, for frying
1 cup (250 ml/8 fl oz) ready-made apple sauce

JUICING LIMES
To obtain the maximum amount of juice from fresh limes, place them in the microwave oven on High for 30 seconds. This softens the fruit and allows the juice to be more easily squeezed out.

1 Squeeze the excess liquid from the potatoes. Combine the potatoes, onions, celery or fennel seeds, flour, beaten eggs, salt and pepper in a large bowl; stir until just mixed.
2 Heat 2 cm (3/4 inch) of oil in a large heavy-based frying pan. Form 2 heaped tablespoons of mixture at a time into flat cakes. Cook the cakes for 3 minutes on each side or until golden brown and cooked through. Serve immediately with apple sauce.
NOTE: Squeezing the excess liquid from grated potato helps to prevent the oil from spitting during frying. Canned, puréed baby apple makes a good apple sauce.

ABOVE: Potato Cakes with Apple Sauce RIGHT: Sugar Peas and Carrots in Lime Butter

SPRING ONION AND CELERY BUNDLES

Preparation time: 20 minutes
Total cooking time: 10 minutes
Serves 6

4 celery sticks
24 spring onions
30 g (1 oz) butter
1 teaspoon celery seeds
1 tablespoon honey
1/2 cup (125 ml/4 fl oz) vegetable stock
1 teaspoon soy sauce
1 teaspoon cornflour
1 teaspoon water

1 Cut the celery into 10 cm (4 inch) lengths, then into strips the same thickness as spring onions. Cut the root from the spring onions. Cut the spring onions into 10 cm (4 inch) lengths. Reserve spring onion tops for ties. Plunge spring onion tops into boiling water for 30 seconds or until they are bright green, then plunge immediately into iced water. Drain and pat dry with paper towels.
2 Combine the spring onions and celery sticks. Divide into six bundles. Tie each bundle firmly with a spring onion top.
3 Heat butter in a frying pan. Fry the bundles quickly over medium-high heat for 1 minute on each side. Remove from pan. Add celery seeds and cook for 30 seconds. Add honey, stock, soy sauce, and blended cornflour and water. Bring to the boil, reduce heat, stirring continuously. Add the spring onion and celery bundles. Simmer gently for 7 minutes, or until bundles are just tender. Serve immediately with cooking liquid.
NOTE: This is a very attractive way to serve vegetables. Try it with bundles of carrot and zucchini sticks, asparagus, pumpkin and parsnip or any vegetable combination that takes about the same amount of cooking.

POTATO CURRY WITH SESAME SEEDS

Preparation time: 20 minutes
Total cooking time: 20 minutes
Serves 4

4 large potatoes
1 tablespoon oil
1 teaspoon cumin seeds
1 teaspoon coriander seeds
2 teaspoons mustard seeds
2 tablespoons sesame seeds
1/2 teaspoon turmeric
1 teaspoon chopped fresh chilli
2 teaspoons finely grated lemon rind
2 tablespoons lemon juice
salt and pepper

1 Boil, steam or microwave the potatoes until tender. Cool, peel and chop. Heat the oil in a large heavy-based pan over medium heat. Cook the cumin, coriander and mustard seeds for 1 minute, stirring constantly.
2 Add the sesame seeds; cook for 1–2 minutes, stirring until golden. Add the turmeric, chillies, potatoes, lemon rind and juice. Stir until well combined and heated through. Season, to taste, with salt and pepper.

ABOVE: Potato Curry with Sesame Seeds

CUTTING AND PEELING AVOCADOS

1 To cut an avocado in half, insert a knife in until it is just touching the stone and cut all the way around. Twist the two halves in opposite directions and gently pull apart.

2 Embed the knife into the stone, twist and pull out.

3 Gently pull away the skin with your fingers.

ABOVE: Mexican-style Vegetables

MEXICAN-STYLE VEGETABLES

Preparation time: 30 minutes
+ 2 hours refrigeration
Total cooking time: 50 minutes
Serves 4–6

Polenta

1¹/₃ cups (350 ml/11 fl oz) vegetable stock

1 cup (250 ml/8 fl oz) water

1 cup (150 g/4³/₄ oz) polenta (cornmeal)

¹/₂ cup (50 g/1²/₃ oz) freshly grated
   Parmesan cheese

2 tablespoons olive oil

1 large green pepper (capsicum)

1 large red pepper (capsicum)

3 medium tomatoes

6 green button squash

6 yellow button squash

1 cob fresh corn

1 tablespoon oil

1 medium onion, sliced

1 tablespoon ground cumin

¹/₂ teaspoon chilli powder

2 tablespoons chopped fresh
   coriander (optional)

salt and freshly ground black pepper

1 Brush a 20 cm (8 inch) round springform (spring–release) tin with oil.

2 **To make Polenta:** Place the stock and water in a medium pan and bring to the boil. Add the polenta and stir to combine; stir constantly for 10 minutes or until very thick. (Polenta must be stirred for the time given, otherwise it will be gritty.) Remove from the heat and stir in the Parmesan. Spread the mixture into the prepared tin; smooth the surface. Refrigerate for 2 hours. Turn out, cut into six wedges. Brush one side with olive oil, cook under a preheated grill for 5 minutes or until edges are browned. Repeat with other side.

3 Cut the green and red peppers into small squares; chop the tomatoes, cut the squash into quarters and cut the corn into 2 cm (³/₄ inch) slices, then in quarters.

4 Heat the oil in a large pan. Cook the onion over medium heat for 5 minutes or until soft. Stir in the cumin and chilli powder; cook for 1 minute. Add the vegetables. Bring to the boil and reduce heat. Simmer, covered, over low heat for 30 minutes or until the vegetables are tender, stirring occasionally. Stir in the coriander, if using. Add salt and pepper. Serve with polenta wedges.

NOTE: Vegetables can be cooked up to one day ahead. Polenta can be cooked one day ahead. Grill just before serving. A little crushed garlic can be added to the olive oil before brushing.

PUMPKIN WITH CHILLI AND AVOCADO

Preparation time: 20 minutes
Total cooking time: 10 minutes
Serves 6

750 g (1 1/2 lb) pumpkin
2 tablespoons olive oil
1 tablespoon chopped fresh coriander leaves
1 tablespoon chopped fresh mint
2 teaspoons sweet chilli sauce
1 small red (Spanish) onion, finely chopped
2 teaspoons balsamic vinegar
1 teaspoon soft brown sugar
1 large avocado

1 Scrape the seeds from the inside of the pumpkin. Cut the pumpkin into slices. Remove the skin. Cook in a large pan of simmering water until tender but still firm. Remove from heat; drain well.
2 Mix oil, coriander, mint, chilli sauce, onion, vinegar and sugar in a small bowl. Cut the avocado in half. Remove the seed using a sharp-bladed knife. Peel and discard the skin from the avocado. Cut the avocado flesh in thin slices.
3 Combine the warm pumpkin and avocado in a serving bowl. Gently toss the coriander dressing through. Serve immediately.
NOTE: Assemble this dish just before serving. The dressing can be made up several hours in advance. Store, covered, in the refrigerator. Add one small red chilli, finely chopped, to the dressing if you want a spicier flavour.

VEGETABLE CURRY

Preparation time: 25 minutes
Total cooking time: 20–25 minutes
Serves 4-6

1 tablespoon brown mustard seeds
2 tablespoons ghee or oil
2 onions, chopped
4 tablespoons mild curry paste
400 g (12 2/3 oz) canned tomatoes
1/2 cup (125 g/4 oz) plain yoghurt
1 cup (250 ml/8 fl oz) coconut milk
2 carrots, sliced
220 g (7 oz) cauliflower florets
2 slender eggplants (aubergines), sliced
220 g (7 oz) green beans, halved
155 g (5 oz) broccoli florets
2 zucchinis (courgettes), sliced
90 g (3 oz) baby button mushrooms, halved
salt

1 Place the mustard seeds in a dry pan and heat until they start to pop. Add the ghee or oil and onions to the pan; cook, stirring, until the onions are just soft. Add the curry paste and stir for 1 minute until the mixture is fragrant.
2 Add the tomatoes, yoghurt and coconut milk; stir over low heat until combined. Add the carrots and simmer, uncovered, for 5 minutes.
3 Add the cauliflower and eggplants; simmer for 5 minutes. Stir in the remaining ingredients; simmer, uncovered, for 10–12 minutes. Serve hot with steamed rice.

COCONUT MILK
Coconut milk is fundamental to Asian cooking and is made, not from the liquid inside the coconut, but from the juice of the grated and pressed coconut flesh. The first extraction, which is the coconut cream, is very thick. The milk comes from a second pressing. Coconut milk is available in cans, tetra packs, or in powdered form.

LEFT: Pumpkin with Chilli and Avocado
ABOVE: Vegetable Curry

VEGETABLE PUREES

These versatile mixtures can double as dips and pasta sauces, and are fabulous as

fillings for pancakes and omelettes—but never forget how great they are on their own.

JERUSALEM ARTICHOKE PUREE
Place 1 kg (2 lb) peeled Jerusalem artichokes and 2 sliced cloves of garlic in a pan, cover with cold water and bring to boil. Cook until artichokes are tender. Process artichokes and garlic in food processor with 60 g (2 oz) butter until smooth, gradually adding ¼ cup (60 ml/2 fl oz) extra virgin olive oil.

Season with salt and pepper, drizzle with olive oil and sprinkle with sweet paprika.

PARSNIP AND LEEK PUREE
Cook 1 thinly sliced leek and 3 large peeled and chopped parsnips in a pan of boiling salted water until tender. Drain well, purée in blender or food processor. Place purée in a pan, add 2 tablespoons

chopped fresh chives, 30 g (1 oz) butter, and salt and pepper, to taste. Cook until the purée is heated through. Remove from the heat and stir through about 3 tablespoons of crème fraîche.

ASPARAGUS PUREE
Heat 30 g (1 oz) butter and 1 tablespoon oil in a pan, add 3 chopped spring onions

and 315 g (10 oz) of young, thin chopped asparagus; cook for 3 minutes. Add ½ cup (125 ml/4 fl oz) vegetable stock and ½ cup (125 ml/4 fl oz) cream, cover and simmer until tender. Remove the vegetables from the liquid and process until smooth. Bring liquid to boil and reduce by one quarter. Return purée to pan, stir in 1 tablespoon grated Parmesan cheese. Cook over medium heat for 5 minutes or until the purée thickens slightly. Season with salt and pepper. If the asparagus is stringy, the purée should be passed through a sieve.

RED PEPPER (CAPSICUM) PUREE
Grill 3 large red peppers (capsicums) until the skin blisters and blackens. Place peppers in a plastic bag, cool slightly, then peel, remove seeds and roughly

chop the flesh. Place the peppers in a food processor, add 4 chopped spring onions, 2 crushed cloves of garlic and 2 finely chopped small red chillies. Process until smooth, transfer to a pan and stir in 2 tablespoons fish sauce (optional), 2 tablespoons lime juice and 2 tablespoons chopped fresh coriander. Cook over medium heat for 5 minutes, or until thickened slightly.

ROAST TOMATO AND CHICKPEA PUREE
Soak 250 g (8 oz) dried chickpeas in cold water overnight. Cook the chickpeas in boiling salted water with 1 chopped onion and 1 bay leaf for 1½ hours or until tender. Drain, remove the bay leaf and reserve ¼ cup (60 ml/2 fl oz) of liquid. Cut 4 egg (Roma) tomatoes in

halves, sprinkle with sea salt and drizzle with olive oil. Bake in a preheated moderately hot 200°C (400°F/Gas 6) oven for 30–40 minutes or until the tomatoes are very tender. Allow the tomatoes and chickpeas to cool a little, place in a food processor, then add 2 crushed cloves of garlic, 2 tablespoons of lime juice, 1 teaspoon sugar, ¼ cup (60 ml/2 fl oz) of olive oil and the reserved liquid; process until smooth. Stir through 2 tablespoons of chopped fresh basil and 1 tablespoon of freshly grated Parmesan cheese.

CLOCKWISE, FROM TOP LEFT: Parsnip and Leek Purée; Asparagus Purée; Red Pepper Purée; Jerusalem Artichoke Purée; Roast Tomato and Chickpea Purée

ROASTING PEPPERS
(CAPSICUMS)

1 Discard the seeds and membrane from the peppers and cut the flesh into large flattish pieces.

2 Put under a hot grill, skin-side-up, until the skin is black and blistered. Cover with a tea towel (or put in a plastic bag) and set aside.

3 When the peppers are cool enough to handle, peel away and discard the skins. The roasted flesh will be sweeter than the raw.

OPPOSITE PAGE:
Marinated Barbecued
Vegetables

MARINATED BARBECUED VEGETABLES

Preparation time: 40 minutes
+ 1 hour marinating
Total cooking time: 5 minutes
Serves 4–6

3 small slender eggplants (aubergines)
2 small red peppers (capsicums)
3 medium zucchinis (courgettes)
6 medium mushrooms

Marinade

1/4 cup (60 ml/2 fl oz) olive oil
1/4 cup (60 ml/2 fl oz) lemon juice
1/4 cup (7 g/1/4 oz) shredded fresh basil leaves
1 clove garlic, crushed

1 Cut the eggplants into diagonal slices. Place on a tray in a single layer, sprinkle with salt and let stand for 15 minutes. Rinse thoroughly and pat dry with paper towels. Trim the red peppers, remove the seeds and membrane and cut into long, wide pieces. Cut the zucchinis into diagonal slices. Trim each mushroom stalk so that it is level with the cap. Place all the vegetables in a large, shallow non-metal dish.
2 To make Marinade: Place the oil, juice, basil and garlic in a small screw-top jar. Shake vigorously until well combined. Pour the marinade over the vegetables and stir gently. Store, covered with plastic wrap, in the refrigerator for 1 hour, stirring occasionally. Prepare and heat the barbecue.
3 Place the vegetables on a hot, lightly greased barbecue grill or flatplate. Cook pieces over the hottest part of the fire for 2 minutes on each side. Transfer to a serving dish once browned. Brush the vegetables frequently with any remaining marinade while cooking.
NOTE: Vegetables can be marinated for up to 2 hours. Take them out of the refrigerator 15 minutes before cooking. This dish can be served warm or at room temperature. Serve any leftovers with thick slices of crusty bread or individual bread rolls. Other herbs, such as parsley, rosemary or thyme, can be added to the marinade. The marinade also makes a great salad dressing.

HASSELBACK POTATOES

Preparation time: 20 minutes
Total cooking time: 45 minutes
Serves 6

8 medium potatoes (about 1.5 kg/3 lb), peeled and cut in halves
60 g (2 oz) butter, melted
1 tablespoon fresh white breadcrumbs
2/3 cup (85 g/2¾ oz) grated Cheddar cheese
1/2 teaspoon ground sweet paprika

1 Preheat oven to hot 210°C (415°F/Gas 6–7). Brush a shallow ovenproof dish with melted butter or oil.
2 Place each potato cut-side down on a board. Using a small, sharp knife, make thin slices into the potatoes, taking care not to cut right through. Place the potatoes, sliced side up, in the prepared dish. Brush with the melted butter. Bake the potatoes for 30 minutes, brushing occasionally with butter.
3 Sprinkle with the combined fresh breadcrumbs, grated cheese and paprika; bake for another 15 minutes or until golden brown. Serve immediately.

FAST HERBED CABBAGE

SHRED 440 g (14 oz) of cabbage finely. You can use green or red cabbage, or a combination of both. Melt 30 g (1 oz) of butter in a pan with a lid, add the cabbage and toss to combine with the butter. Put the lid on the pan and 'steam' the cabbage over low heat for about 5 minutes, until tender. Remove the lid and lift the cabbage with tongs from time to time to cook it evenly. Stir through 4 tablespoons finely shredded basil and serve immediately. Season to taste with salt and freshly ground black pepper. Serves 2.

FAST HERBED POTATOES

COOK 12 small new potatoes in a pan of boiling water until just tender. Drain and return to the pan. Add about 30 g (1 oz) butter and 1 tablespoon each of chopped fresh chives and fresh lemon thyme leaves. Cover with a lid; shake over low heat until the butter has melted; season. Serves 4.

potato into cubes. Add the coconut milk and water to the wok. Bring to the boil; reduce heat and simmer, uncovered, for 5 minutes. Add the sweet potato to the wok; cook for 6 minutes.
2 Add the eggplant and kaffir lime leaves to the wok; cook for 10 minutes, or until the vegetables are very tender, stirring occasionally.
3 Add the fish sauce, lime juice and rind, and sugar to the wok. Toss until well combined with the vegetables. Sprinkle with some fresh coriander leaves. You can garnish the curry with extra kaffir lime leaves, if you wish. Serve with steamed rice.

THAI CURRY PASTE

Preparation time: 10 minutes
Total cooking time: 3 minutes
Makes approximately 1 cup

1 tablespoon coriander seeds
2 teaspoons cumin seeds
2 teaspoons dried shrimp paste
1 teaspoon black peppercorns
1 teaspoon ground nutmeg
12 large red or green chillies
1 cup (135 g/4¹/₂ oz) French shallots, chopped
2 tablespoons oil
4 stems lemon grass (white part only),
   finely chopped
10 cloves garlic, chopped
2 tablespoons fresh coriander roots, chopped
2 tablespoons fresh coriander stems, chopped
6 kaffir lime leaves, chopped
2 teaspoons grated lime rind
2 teaspoons salt

1 Toast the coriander and cumin seeds in a dry frying pan for 2–3 minutes, then grind finely.
2 Wrap the shrimp paste in foil and cook under a hot grill for 3 minutes—turn the package twice, using tongs.
3 Process everything together until smooth. Refrigerate in an airtight container for up to 3 weeks.
NOTE: Some recipes in this book call for red or green curry paste. Use this recipe to make your own or buy it in jars from the supermarket.

THAI CURRY PASTE
Red and green curry pastes are fundamental flavour bases for Thai curries, but are equally useful for flavouring soups, fried rice, pasta, home-fried potatoes and scrambled eggs. Red curry paste has fresh red chillies as its base, while green curry paste uses fresh green chillies. If home-made, these pastes will keep their bite for up to 3 weeks if refrigerated.

GREEN VEGETABLE CURRY WITH SWEET POTATO AND EGGPLANT (AUBERGINE)

Preparation time: 25 minutes
Total cooking time: 30 minutes
Serves 4-6

1 tablespoon oil
1 medium onion, chopped
1–2 tablespoons green curry paste
1 medium sweet potato
1¹/₂ cups (375 ml/12 fl oz) coconut milk
1 cup (250 ml/8 fl oz) water
1 medium eggplant, quartered and sliced
6 kaffir lime leaves
2 tablespoons fish sauce (optional)
2 tablespoons lime juice
2 teaspoons lime rind
2 teaspoons soft brown sugar
fresh coriander leaves

ABOVE: Green
Vegetable Curry
with Sweet Potato
and Eggplant

1 Heat the oil in a large wok or frying pan. Add the onion and curry paste to the wok and stir for 3 minutes over medium heat. Cut the sweet

BABY BAKED POTATOES

Preparation time: 20 minutes + 1 hour standing
Total cooking time: 30 minutes
Serves 6

★

750 g (1½ lb) baby potatoes
2 tablespoons olive oil
2 tablespoons fresh thyme leaves
2 teaspoons crushed sea salt

1 Wash the potatoes thoroughly under cold water. Cut any large ones in half so that they are all a uniform size for even cooking. Boil, steam or microwave the potatoes until they are just tender. (Potatoes should remain whole and intact.) Drain and lightly pat them dry with paper towels.
2 Place the potatoes in a large bowl; add the oil and thyme. Toss gently to coat the potatoes and set aside for 1 hour. Preheat the oven to moderate 180°C (350°F/Gas 4).
3 Place the potatoes in a lightly oiled baking dish. Bake for 20 minutes, turning frequently and brushing with the remaining oil and thyme mixture, until golden brown. Place in a serving bowl and sprinkle with salt. Garnish with extra thyme sprigs, if desired.

SPICY STEAMED CORN COBS

Preparation time: 25 minutes
Total cooking time: 10–20 minutes
Serves 4

★

4 corn cobs or 15 baby corn cobs
5 cm (2 inch) piece fresh ginger, grated
3 cloves garlic, chopped
1–3 teaspoons chopped fresh red chillies
2 teaspoons green peppercorns, crushed
2 tablespoons water
2 tablespoons fish sauce (optional)

1 Remove the husks and all the silk threads from the corn cobs. In a bowl, place the ginger, garlic, chillies, peppercorns and water; mix well.
2 Roll each cob in the spice mixture and place in a steaming basket, lined with banana leaves or baking paper.
3 Place the basket over a wok or pan of boiling water, cover and steam for 10–20 minutes (depending on the size of the corn), or until the corn is tender; drain. Sprinkle with fish sauce and serve immediately.
NOTE: Bamboo steaming baskets are inexpensive to buy and very handy for steaming vegetables. Always line the base to prevent food falling through. Baby corn cobs are available from speciality fruit and vegetable shops.

SEA SALT
Sea salt, sometimes called *gros sel*, is produced from sea water evaporated in bays or from salt marshes. For flavour, sea salt is difficult to surpass. It can be bought as coarse granules, to be used in a grinder, or as fine grains or flakes.

*LEFT: Baby Baked Potatoes
ABOVE: Spicy Steamed Corn Cobs*

RED VEGETABLE CURRY

Preparation time: 25 minutes
Total cooking time: 25–30 minutes
Serves 4

★

1 tablespoon oil
1 medium onion, chopped
1–2 tablespoons red curry paste
1½ cups (375 ml/12 fl oz) coconut milk
1 cup (250 ml/8 fl oz) water
2 medium potatoes, chopped
220 g (7 oz) cauliflower florets
6 fresh kaffir lime leaves
155 g (5 oz) snake beans, cut into
    short pieces
½ red pepper (capsicum), cut into strips
10 fresh baby corn, cut in half lengthways
1 tablespoon green peppercorns,
    roughly chopped
¼ cup (20 g/⅔ oz) fresh basil leaves,
    roughly chopped
2 tablespoons fish sauce (optional)
1 tablespoon lime juice
2 teaspoons soft brown sugar
½ cup (15 g/½ oz) fresh coriander leaves

1 Heat the oil in a large wok or frying pan. Cook the onions and curry paste for 4 minutes over medium heat, stirring.

2 Add the coconut milk and water, bring to the boil and simmer, uncovered, for 5 minutes. Add the potatoes, cauliflower and lime leaves and simmer for 7 minutes. Add the snake beans, red pepper strips, corn and peppercorns; cook for 5 minutes or until the vegetables are tender.
3 Add the basil, sauce, juice and sugar. Sprinkle with coriander leaves. Serve with steamed rice.
NOTE: If fresh baby corn are not available use canned baby corn and add just before serving.

FENNEL, TOMATO AND WHITE BEAN STEW

Preparation time: 25 minutes
Total cooking time: 1 hour 15 minutes
Serves 4-6

★

5 tomatoes, peeled seeded and chopped
2 leeks, washed and sliced
2 cloves garlic, finely chopped
1 large fennel bulb, washed, halved,
    cored and sliced
3 tablespoons extra virgin olive oil
¼ cup (60 ml/2 fl oz) Pernod
2 fresh bay leaves
5 sprigs fresh thyme
salt and freshly ground black pepper
500 g (1 lb) Desiree potatoes, peeled and
    cut into large chunks
400 g (12⅔ oz) canned cannellini beans,
    rinsed and drained
1 cup (250 ml/8 fl oz) vegetable stock
1 cup (250 ml/8 fl oz) white wine
½ cup (125 g/4 oz) ready-made pesto,
    for serving

1 Preheat the oven to moderate 180°C (350°F/Gas 4). In a large ovenproof dish combine the first nine ingredients. Mix well. (This should preferably be done well ahead of time to allow the flavours to develop.)
2 Cover the dish and bake for 30 minutes. Remove from the oven; add the potatoes, beans, stock and wine. Mix well and cover. Bake for another 35–45 minutes or until the potatoes are cooked through. Remove the bay leaves and thyme and discard them. Serve in warmed bowls, with a spoonful of pesto.

KAFFIR LIME LEAVES
Both the fruit and the leaves of this Southeast Asian tree are highly aromatic. The leaves are used in Asian cooking in much the same way as bay leaves in European dishes. Fresh leaves are available from good greengrocers; dried leaves, which still have a strong flavour, can be bought at health food shops and speciality Asian food stores.

BELOW: Red Vegetable Curry

WRINKLED POTATOES WITH MOJO SAUCE

Preparation time: 20 minutes
Total cooking time: 20–25 minutes
Serves 4-6

18 baby potatoes
1 tablespoon olive oil
2 teaspoons salt

Mojo Sauce

2 cloves garlic
1 teaspoon cumin seeds
1 teaspoon ground sweet paprika
1/3 cup (80 ml/2 3/4 fl oz) olive oil
2 tablespoons white wine vinegar
1 tablespoon hot water

1 Preheat oven to hot 210°C (415°F/Gas 6–7). Place potatoes in a single layer in a baking dish. Pour oil over and shake to distribute evenly. Sprinkle the salt evenly over the potatoes.

2 Bake for 20–25 minutes or until the potatoes are golden brown and slightly wrinkled. Shake the pan twice during cooking time.

3 **To make Mojo Sauce:** Place the garlic, cumin and paprika in a food processor and blend for 1 minute. With the motor running, add the oil slowly in a thin stream, blending until all the oil is added. Add the vinegar and hot water, blend for another minute.

4 Serve the potatoes hot accompanied by a spoonful of Mojo Sauce.

RATATOUILLE

Preparation time: 20 minutes
Total cooking time: 25–30 minutes
Serves 4

2 tablespoons olive oil
2 medium onions, cut in wedges
2 medium zucchinis (courgettes), cut in thick sticks
1 small red pepper (capsicum), cut in squares
1 small green pepper (capsicum), cut in squares
1 small yellow pepper (capsicum), cut in squares
2 cloves garlic, crushed
1 medium eggplant (aubergine), halved
440 g (14 oz) canned tomatoes, crushed
1/2 teaspoon dried basil or oregano leaves
freshly ground black pepper
fresh parsley sprigs (optional)

1 Heat the oil in a large, heavy-based pan and cook the onions over medium heat for 4 minutes or until soft. Add the zucchinis, peppers and garlic, stir for 3 minutes.

2 Cut the eggplant in chunks and add to the pan with the tomatoes, basil or oregano and pepper; bring to boil. Reduce the heat to simmer and cook, covered, for 15–20 minutes or until the vegetables are tender. Sprinkle the parsley over the top and serve with crusty bread.

PARSLEY

Parsley (*Petroselinum crispum*), is the veritable powerhouse of the herb world. It is packed with vitamins A, B complex, C and E, and the minerals iron and calcium. Parsley is said to ease digestion, as well as clear the complexion, regulate the functioning of the intestines and prevent the formation of gallstones. It is the principal element of *bouquet garni*—a bunch of mixed herbs added to stocks and soups, to give a depth of background flavour.

ABOVE: Wrinkled Potatoes with Mojo Sauce BELOW: Ratatouille

CANDIED SWEET POTATO

Preparation time: 10 minutes
Total cooking time: 45–60 minutes
Serves 6

800 g (1 lb 10 oz) orange sweet potato
90 g (3 oz) butter
1/2 cup (95 g/3 1/4 oz) soft brown sugar
1 tablespoon lemon juice
1/2 cup (125 ml/4 fl oz) orange juice
1 cinnamon stick
2 teaspoons grated lemon rind

1 Preheat the oven to moderate 180°C (350°F/Gas 4). Peel the sweet potatoes and cut into thick rounds. Arrange the rounds in an ovenproof dish, pour melted butter over the top.
2 Add the sugar, lemon and orange juices and the cinnamon stick.
3 Cover with a lid or aluminium foil and bake for about 30 minutes. Uncover and stir the mixture gently; remove the cinnamon stick, sprinkle the lemon rind over the top and cook, uncovered, for another 15–30 minutes until the top is slightly crisp.
NOTE: Candied sweet potato is a dish traditionally served at Thanksgiving in America as an accompaniment. There are as many versions as there are cooks.

SWEET POTATO

Sweet potato, sometimes known as kumera and often erroneously as yam, is not a potato at all. It *is* a tuber, however, and starchy, like potato. Sweet potato can be cooked any way you would cook ordinary potato.

COMBINATION VEGETABLE STEW

Preparation time: 15 minutes
Total cooking time: 10–15 minutes
Serves 4-6

2 teaspoons olive oil
1 small onion, thinly sliced
1/4 cup (60 g/2 oz) tomato paste
1/4 teaspoon chilli powder
1 teaspoon cumin seeds
1/2 cup (125 ml/4 fl oz) tomato juice
1 cup (250 ml/8 fl oz) vegetable stock
440 g (14 oz) canned tomatoes, crushed
2 small carrots, sliced
2 medium zucchinis (courgettes), halved
    and cut into chunks
20 green beans, topped and tailed
315 g (10 oz) cauliflower, cut into small florets

1 Heat the oil in a large pan. Add the onions, tomato paste, chilli, cumin seeds and tomato juice. Stir until well combined.
2 Add the stock and crushed tomatoes. Bring to the boil. Reduce the heat. Add the remaining vegetables. Simmer, uncovered, until soft. Serve with fresh tortillas.

ABOVE: Combination Vegetable Stew
RIGHT: Candied Sweet Potato

BROAD BEANS WITH PEAS AND ARTICHOKES

Preparation time: 15 minutes
Total cooking time: 15 minutes
Serves 4-6

2 medium onions
2 tablespoons fresh dill
1 tablespoon fresh mint leaves
1/4 cup (60 ml/2 fl oz) olive oil
250 g (8 oz) frozen broad beans, rinsed and drained
1/2 cup (125 ml/4 fl oz) water
2 tablespoons lemon juice
250 g (8 oz) frozen peas
400 g (12²/3 oz) canned artichoke hearts, drained, cut in half
4 spring onions, chopped
salt and freshly ground black pepper

1 Slice the onions into rings. Finely chop the dill and mint.
2 Heat the oil in a large pan. Add the onions. Stir over low heat for 5 minutes or until soft and golden.
3 Add the beans, water and lemon juice to the pan. Bring to the boil, reduce the heat and simmer, covered, for 5 minutes.
4 Add the peas, artichoke hearts and herbs. Simmer, covered, for 5 minutes, or until the peas are just tender, but not soft. Remove from the heat, stir in the spring onions, salt and pepper. Serve warm or at room temperature.

BEANS WITH TOMATOES

Preparation time: 15 minutes
Total cooking time: 20 minutes
Serves 6

500 g (1 lb) green beans
440 g (14 oz) canned tomatoes
2 tablespoons olive oil
1 large onion, chopped
1 clove garlic, crushed
2 teaspoons sugar
2 tablespoons red wine vinegar
1 tablespoon chopped fresh basil
3 tablespoons chopped olives (optional)
ground pepper
basil leaves, to garnish

1 Trim the tops and tails from the beans and cut the beans in half. Cook in boiling water for 3 minutes; drain and rinse in cold water to refresh colour. Set aside. Chop the tomatoes, reserving the juice.
2 Heat the oil in a pan; add the onion and garlic and cook, stirring, until onion starts to brown. Sprinkle the sugar over the onions and cook until it caramelises. Add the vinegar; cook for 1 minute. Add the tomatoes and juice, fresh basil, olives and pepper. Simmer, uncovered, for 5 minutes.
3 Add the beans and simmer until warmed through. Serve garnished with basil leaves.

ORGANIC VEGETABLES
Some people may find the label 'organic' on foods quite confusing. It means that the fruit or vegetables are grown without the use of any chemical fertilizers or pesticides. There are strict regulations governing the labelling of such produce for sale, so you can be assured that they really are chemical-free. They may be slightly more expensive, as organic vegetables are more labour intensive for the grower, but are preferred by people concerned about the possible ill effects of chemicals on their health and the environment.

*ABOVE: Broad Beans with Peas and Artichokes
LEFT: Beans with Tomatoes*

HOME-MADE YOGHURT

To make yoghurt, use 500 ml (16 fl oz) of either skim or full-cream milk. Put the milk in a pan, bring to the boil until the froth rises and then reduce the heat and simmer gently for at least 2 minutes. Leave to cool until lukewarm, about 43–44°C (110–115°F). Blend about 2 tablespoons of natural yoghurt with a little of the warm milk and then stir into the rest of the milk. Pour the mixture into either a warmed Pyrex bowl or sterilised jars and then seal tightly. You may need to stand the bowl or jars in a pan of hot tap water and wrap a blanket or towel around the pan. Leave this in a warm place for at least 6 hours, or until cooled and set. Refrigerate the yoghurt for about 2 hours before using. For a thicker, creamier yoghurt, blend 1–2 tablespoons of milk powder with the milk before heating.

SPICY EGGPLANT (AUBERGINE) SLICES

Preparation time: 15 minutes
+ 15 minutes standing
Total cooking time: 15 minutes
Serves 4-6

2 medium eggplants (aubergines)
salt
1/3 cup (40 g/1 1/3 oz) plain flour
2 teaspoons ground cumin
2 teaspoons ground coriander
1 teaspoon chilli powder
oil, for frying
1/2 cup (125 g/4 oz) plain yoghurt
1 tablespoon chopped fresh mint

1 Cut the eggplants into 1 cm (1/2 inch) slices. Arrange in a single layer on a tray and cover well with salt. Allow to stand for 15 minutes, then rinse and pat dry thoroughly with paper towels.
2 Sift the flour and spices onto a plate. Dust the eggplant slices with flour mixture; shake off any excess. Heat about 2 cm (3/4 inch) oil in a heavy-based pan. Cook the eggplant slices a few at a time, for 2–3 minutes each side or until golden. Drain on paper towels. Combine the yoghurt and mint. Serve with the warm eggplant.

GOLDEN ROAST VEGETABLES

Preparation time: 15 minutes
Total cooking time: 1 hour
Serves 6

6 medium potatoes
90 g (3 oz) butter, melted
1/4 cup (60 ml/2 fl oz) olive oil
6 small onions
750 g (1 1/2 lb) pumpkin, peeled
6 baby carrots

1 Preheat oven to hot 210°C (415°F/Gas 6–7). Peel and wash the potatoes, cut them in half. Boil the potatoes for 5 minutes; drain. Pat dry with paper towels. Using the prongs of a fork, scrape the potatoes to form a rough surface.
2 Place the potatoes in a shallow baking dish; brush liberally with combined butter and oil. Bake for 20 minutes.
3 Meanwhile, peel the onions and trim the bases flat. Cut the pumpkin into 6 even-sized pieces and trim the tops of the carrots. Add to the potatoes in the dish; brush with butter mixture in the baking dish. Bake for 20 minutes, brush again and bake for another 15 minutes.

ABOVE: Spicy Eggplant Slices

VEGETABLES IN COCONUT MILK

Preparation time: 20 minutes
Total cooking time: 15 minutes
Serves 4

2 tablespoons oil

2 cloves garlic, chopped

5 cm (2 inches) fresh ginger, grated

2 teaspoons fresh green peppercorns (optional)

1 medium eggplant (aubergine), diced

1 small sweet potato, diced

2 teaspoons water

100 g (3¹/₃ oz) green beans, cut into 5 cm
   (2 inch) pieces

750 g (1¹/₂ lb) asparagus, cut into 5 cm
   (2 inch) pieces

¹/₂ cup (125 ml/4 fl oz) coconut milk

2 teaspoons fish sauce (optional)

2 cups (100 g/3¹/₃ oz) English spinach leaves

¹/₂ cup (15 g/1¹/₂ oz) fresh basil leaves

1 Heat oil in a wok or heavy-based frying pan. Add garlic, ginger and peppercorns and cook for 30 seconds. Add the eggplant, sweet potato and water; cook for 5 minutes over medium heat, stirring frequently. Add beans, cover and steam for 4 minutes, shaking to prevent sticking.

2 Add the asparagus and coconut milk to the wok and cook for 3 minutes or until the asparagus is just tender. Add the fish sauce, spinach and basil; toss until the spinach and basil soften slightly.

FAST GRILLED MUSHROOMS

REMOVE STEMS from large flat field mushrooms (allow one per person) and wipe tops with paper towels. Lay the mushrooms upturned on a foil-lined grill tray; brush with olive oil. Use an oil infused with herbs, garlic or chilli, if you like. Cook slowly under low heat for about 5 minutes, until the mushrooms are tender and juicy, brushing with more olive oil occasionally. Season with salt and pepper.

FAST GARLIC CREAM MUSHROOMS

HEAT 30 g (1 oz) butter in a medium pan. Add 250 g (8 oz) sliced button mushrooms and 2 cloves crushed garlic. Stir over medium heat 3–5 minutes until mushrooms are soft. Turn heat to high, add 1 cup (250 ml/8 fl oz) cream; bring to boil. Reduce to a simmer for 3 minutes until cream has thickened slightly. Add 1 tablespoon chopped parsley and then season, to taste. Serves 2.

PREPARING DRIED MUSHROOMS

1 Put the dried mushrooms in a heatproof bowl and cover with boiling water. Leave them to soak for about 10 minutes.

2 When the water has cooled, squeeze out all the excess moisture from the mushrooms, which should be swollen and rehydrated.

3 Slice the mushrooms finely, or prepare them as directed in the recipe.

ABOVE: Vegetables in Coconut Milk

STIR-FRIES

Stir-frying means dinner in a snap. Quick and easy, it's one of the best ways to ensure that vegetables, once cooked, retain their natural colour, full flavour and crisp texture. Very little nutritional value is lost when you stir-fry, and it's a brilliant solution to the age-old quandary of what to do with those few random vegetables in the crisper. Combine your own choice of vegetables to make a unique, great-tasting meal.

Stir-fry over medium heat for 1 minute. Add the broccoli, peppers, mushrooms and olives. Stir-fry for another 2 minutes or until the vegetables are a bright colour and just tender.
3 Combine the soy sauce, honey and chilli sauce in a bowl and mix well. Pour the sauce over the vegetables and toss lightly to combine. Sprinkle with the sesame seeds and serve immediately.

PEPPERED STIR-FRIED SNAKE BEANS

Preparation time: 20 minutes
Total cooking time: 8 minutes
Serves 4

☆

1 tablespoon drained, canned green peppercorns
1/2 cup (15 g/1/2 oz) fresh coriander leaves
 and chopped stems
1 tablespoon oil
2 cloves garlic, chopped
220 g (7 oz) snake beans, cut into
 4 cm (11/2 inch) lengths
155 g/5 oz asparagus, cut into 4 cm
 (11/2 inch) lengths
1 teaspoon soft brown sugar
2 teaspoons water
1 tablespoon fish sauce (optional)
1 teaspoon chopped fresh red or green
 chillies (optional)

1 Finely crush the peppercorns. Chop the coriander leaves and mix in a bowl with the stems and peppercorns.

WHAT TO SPROUT

Many beans and seeds can be sprouted successfully. Here are a few of the most common beans and seeds for sprouting:
- mung beans
- soya beans
- chickpeas
- adzuki beans
- lentils
- alfalfa seeds
- fenugreek seeds
Experiment with sprouting different types of beans and seeds and then include them raw in salads or toss a handful into stir-fries at the last minute.

VEGETABLE STIR-FRY

Preparation time: 15 minutes
Total cooking time: 5–10 minutes
Serves 4

☆

1 tablespoon sesame seeds
2 spring onions
250 g (8 oz) broccoli
1 medium red pepper (capsicum)
1 medium yellow pepper (capsicum)
150 g (43/4 oz) button mushrooms
1 tablespoon oil
1 teaspoon sesame oil
1 clove garlic, crushed
2 teaspoons grated fresh ginger
1/4 cup (45 g/11/2 oz) black olives
1 tablespoon soy sauce
1 tablespoon honey
1 tablespoon sweet chilli sauce

1 Place the sesame seeds on an oven tray and cook under a hot grill until golden; set aside until needed. Finely slice the spring onions and cut the broccoli into small florets. Cut the peppers in half, remove and discard the seeds and membrane and cut the flesh into thin strips. Cut the mushrooms in half.
2 Heat the oils in a wok or large frying pan. Add the garlic, ginger and spring onions.

*ABOVE: Vegetable Stir-fry
RIGHT: Peppered Stir-fried Snake Beans*

DAY ONE
Place the beans in a jar and fill with cold water. Cover the jar with muslin or a clean stocking, secure with a rubber band and leave to soak overnight.

DAY TWO
Drain the water from the jar, fill with clean water and drain again. Store in a cool, dark place.

DAY THREE
Repeat the rinsing and draining procedure twice a day. Make sure that the beans are well drained, as any remaining water could cause them to rot.

DAY FOUR
The beans should be well sprouted by now. Transfer the jar to a light place for the last half-day. Rinse again; refrigerate for up to 1 week.

---

2 Heat oil in a wok or frying pan. Add peppercorn mixture, garlic, beans, asparagus and sugar; stir-fry for 30 seconds over medium heat.
3 Add the water, cover and steam for 2 minutes or until the vegetables are just tender. Season with fish sauce; sprinkle with chillies and serve immediately.
NOTE: Snake beans have a delicious crisp texture. However, if they are not available, green beans may be substituted.

GOLDEN FRIED EGGPLANT (AUBERGINE) AND CABBAGE

Preparation time: 20 minutes
Total cooking time: 5 minutes
Serves 4

☆

2 tablespoons oil
3 spring onions, chopped
3 cloves garlic, chopped
1 tablespoon soft brown sugar
2 medium eggplants (aubergines), cut
   into wedges
2 teaspoons Golden Mountain sauce
1/4 Chinese cabbage, shredded
2 tablespoons lime juice
2 teaspoons fish sauce (optional)
1 chilli, finely sliced

1 Heat oil in a wok or large frying pan. Add onions and garlic and stir for 1 minute over medium heat.
2 Add the sugar and eggplant wedges to the wok and stir-fry for 3 minutes, or until the eggplant is golden brown.
3 Add the Golden Mountain sauce, cabbage and lime juice to the wok. Toss, then cover and steam for 30 seconds or until the cabbage softens slightly. Add the fish sauce and stir through. Serve immediately sprinkled with sliced chilli.
NOTE: Thai eggplants are purple or have purple and white stripes, and come in a range of sizes. Some may be as small as a tiny pea, others the size of a golf ball or shaped like a small zucchini (courgette). Any of these may be used for this recipe, but make sure to alter the cooking time to suit the size of the eggplant. Golden Mountain sauce is an essential ingredient in Thai cooking. Buy it at Asian food stores.

FAST SPICED CORN

DRAIN 425 g (13½ oz) canned baby corn and pat dry with paper towels. Heat 1 tablespoon of oil in a wok. Add a crushed clove of garlic, 1 teaspoon of chopped red chilli and ½ teaspoon ground cumin; stir-fry for about 30 seconds. Add the corn and stir-fry for 3 minutes or until heated through. Serve immediately. Serves 2–4.
Note: Spicy corn is so quick to make, it is an excellent last-minute accompaniment to a meal where a little added zest is needed.

ABOVE: Golden Fried Eggplant and Cabbage

TOFU AND TEMPEH

Rich in protein and carbohydrates, these by-products of the soya bean have been a vital part of the Oriental diet for centuries, contributing substance to vegetable dishes.

SPICY TEMPEH SALAD
Preheat the oven to moderately hot 200°C (400°F/Gas 6). Place 250 g (8 oz) of spicy tempeh, cut into fine strips, on a non-stick baking tray. Brush the tempeh strips lightly with sesame oil and bake for 20 minutes. Place the tempeh into a bowl with 4 cups (400 g/12⅔ oz) of julienned vegetables (use carrots, snow peas/mange tout, red pepper/capsicum and spring onions). Add 2 cups (150 g/4¾ oz) of shredded red cabbage, 2 tablespoons of toasted sesame seeds and 125 g (4 oz) of crispy fried Chinese noodles. To make the dressing, whisk together 2 crushed cloves of garlic, 1 tablespoon of sweet chilli sauce, 2 tablespoons of lime juice and ¼ cup (60 ml/2 fl oz) of oil. Pour the dressing over the salad and toss to combine. Serves 4–6.

STEAMED TEMPEH WITH ASIAN GREENS
Line a large bamboo steamer with a combination of Asian greens (bok choy, cabbage, broccoli and coriander leaves).

Top with some carrot strips, finely sliced oyster mushrooms and 250 g (8 oz) spicy tempeh cut into bite-sized pieces. Cover the bamboo steamer and place it in a wok one-quarter full of water. Steam for 7 minutes, add a few snow peas (mange tout) and steam for another 3 minutes or until the greens are tender and the tempeh is heated through. To make the sauce, combine ½ cup (125 ml/4 fl oz) of sweet chilli sauce with ¼ cup (60 ml/2 fl oz) of soy sauce. Serve the greens topped with vegetables and tempeh and drizzled with sauce. Serves 4–6.

SESAME TOFU BITES

Rinse and cut 500 g (1 lb) of firm tofu into 2.5 cm (1 inch) cubes. Place the tofu in a shallow dish with 2 crushed cloves of garlic, 2 tablespoons of grated fresh ginger, 1 tablespoon of soft brown sugar and ⅓ cup (80 ml/2¾ fl oz) of salt-reduced soy sauce. Cover and refrigerate for about 2 hours and then drain well. Combine 1 cup (155 g/5 oz) of sesame seeds, 1 tablespoon of cornflour and 2 tablespoons of wholemeal plain flour in a large mixing bowl. Add the tofu cubes and toss to coat in the sesame-flour mixture. Heat ¼ cup (60 ml/2 fl oz) of oil in a frying pan. Add the tofu in batches and cook until golden. Drain on paper towels. To make a chilli dipping sauce, place 2 tablespoons of sweet chilli sauce, 2 tablespoons of lime juice, 2 tablespoons of chopped fresh coriander and 200 g (6½ oz) of thick natural yoghurt in a small bowl and stir well to combine. Serves 4.

VEGETABLE TOFU KEBABS

Thread 375 g (12 oz) of firm tofu, cut into cubes, and some cherry tomatoes, button mushrooms, bay leaves and green pepper (capsicum), cubed, onto large bamboo or metal skewers. Brush lightly with a mixture of ¼ cup (60 ml/2 fl oz) of pineapple juice, 1 tablespoon of Teriyaki marinade and 1 tablespoon of chopped fresh mint. Cook on a preheated char-grill or barbecue, basting frequently until the vegetables are tender. Serves 4.

CLOCKWISE, FROM TOP LEFT:
Sesame Tofu Bites; Vegetable Tofu Kebabs; Steamed Tempeh with Asian Greens; Spicy Tempeh Salad

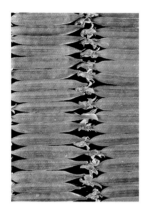

SESAME OIL

The wonder of sesame oil is that it not only lends its uniquely nutty flavour to a dish, but it enlivens the other flavours as well. There are various types of sesame oil, which range from the thick, brown oil made from roasted sesame seeds and used by the Chinese for seasoning rather than frying, to the pale yellowish oil used in Indian and Middle Eastern dishes.

ABOVE: Tofu and Vegetables

TOFU AND VEGETABLES

Preparation time: 25–30 minutes
Total cooking time: 20 minutes
Serves 4-6

★

125 g (4 oz) rice vermicelli

3/4 cup (185 ml/6 fl oz) oil

1 tablespoon soy sauce

1 tablespoon sherry

1 tablespoon oyster sauce (optional)

1/2 cup (125 ml/4 fl oz) vegetable stock

2 teaspoons cornflour

2 teaspoons water

1 tablespoon oil, extra

1 clove garlic, crushed

1 teaspoon grated fresh ginger

375 g (12 oz) firm tofu, cut into small cubes

2 medium carrots, cut into matchsticks

250 g (8 oz) snow peas (mange tout), trimmed

4 spring onions, finely sliced

425 g (13 1/2 oz) canned straw mushrooms, drained

1 Break the vermicelli into short lengths. Heat half the oil in a wok. Cook the vermicelli in batches in the wok over medium heat until crisp, adding more oil when necessary. Drain on paper towels.

2 Combine the soy sauce, sherry, oyster sauce and stock in a small bowl. Blend the cornflour with the water in a small bowl.

3 Heat the wok; add the extra oil and the garlic and ginger and cook over high heat for 1 minute. Add the tofu and stir-fry for 3 minutes. Remove the tofu from the wok. Add the carrots and snow peas to the wok and stir-fry for 1 minute. Add the combined sauces and vegetable stock; cover and cook for another 3 minutes, or until the vegetables are just cooked.

4 Return the tofu to the wok. Add the spring onions, mushrooms and blended cornflour. Stir until the sauce has thickened, then remove from the heat. Serve with the crisp vermicelli.

SNOW PEAS (MANGE TOUT) WITH RED PEPPER (CAPSICUM)

Preparation time: 15–20 minutes
Total cooking time: 7 minutes
Serves 4

1 large onion, peeled
185 g (6 oz) snow peas (mange tout)
1 tablespoon oil
1 tablespoon grated fresh ginger
1 red pepper (capsicum), cut into strips
1 small clove garlic, crushed
1 tablespoon oyster sauce (optional)
1 teaspoon sugar
pinch salt
1 tablespoon water

1 Cut the onion in half and slice thinly in rings. Remove ends and threads from the snow peas.
2 Heat the oil in a frying pan or wok. Add the onion, ginger and red pepper and stir-fry over high heat 4–5 minutes or until the vegetables are just tender. Add the garlic and snow peas and stir-fry for 2 minutes, or until the snow peas become bright green.
3 Add the oyster sauce, sugar, salt and water to the pan and mix through. Serve immediately.

THAI COCONUT VEGETABLES

Preparation time: 15–20 minutes
Total cooking time: 15 minutes
Serves 4-6

1 tablespoon oil
2 small onions, peeled, cut in wedges
1 teaspoon ground cumin
150 g (4¾ oz) cauliflower florets
1 medium red pepper (capsicum), chopped
2 celery sticks, sliced diagonally
1½ cups (185 g/6 oz) grated pumpkin
1 cup (250 ml/8 fl oz) coconut milk
1 cup (250 ml/8 fl oz) vegetable stock
1 tablespoon sweet chilli sauce
150 g (4¾ oz) green beans
1 tablespoon finely chopped fresh coriander

1 Heat oil in a frying pan or wok. Add onion and cumin and stir-fry over medium heat for 2 minutes, or until the onion is golden.
2 Add cauliflower and stir-fry over high heat for 2 minutes. Add red pepper, celery and pumpkin and stir-fry over high heat for 2 minutes, or until vegetables have begun to soften.
3 Add coconut milk, stock and chilli sauce and bring to boil. Reduce heat and cook, uncovered, for 8 minutes, or until the vegetables are almost tender. Trim tops and tails from beans and cut beans in half. Add to pan with coriander, cook another 2 minutes or until beans are just tender. Serve with steamed rice.

TEMPEH

Tempeh is similar to tofu in that it is made from the soya bean. Unlike tofu, however, tempeh, like miso and soy sauce, is a fermented product. Tempeh is made by adding a culture to the cooked soya beans. It is then compressed into firm blocks. Tempeh is often available marinated in a mixture of spices, as it is very bland in itself.

ABOVE: Snow Peas with Red Pepper
BELOW: Thai Coconut Vegetables

ALMOND AND BROCCOLI STIR-FRY

Preparation time: 10 minutes
Total cooking time: 5 minutes
Serves 4

1 teaspoon coriander seeds
500 g (1 lb) broccoli
3 tablespoons olive oil
2 tablespoons slivered almonds
1 clove garlic, crushed
1 teaspoon finely shredded fresh ginger
2 tablespoons red wine vinegar
1 tablespoon soy sauce
2 teaspoons sesame oil
1 teaspoon toasted sesame seeds

1 Lightly crush the coriander seeds with a mortar and pestle or with a rolling pin. Cut the broccoli into small florets.
2 Heat the oil in a wok or a large heavy-based frying pan. Add the coriander seeds and almonds. Stir quickly over medium heat for 1 minute or until the almonds are golden.
3 Add the garlic, ginger and broccoli to the pan. Stir-fry over high heat for 2 minutes. Remove the pan from the heat. Pour the combined vinegar, sauce and oil into the pan. Toss until the broccoli is well coated. Serve immediately, sprinkled with toasted sesame seeds.
NOTE: This dish may be prepared up to two hours ahead. Cook just before serving.

CHINESE VEGETABLES WITH GINGER

Preparation time: 10–15 minutes
Total cooking time: 5 minutes
Serves 4

1 tablespoon oil
3 teaspoons grated fresh ginger
4 spring onions, sliced
230 g (7⅓ oz) canned water chestnuts, drained and sliced
425 g (13½ oz) canned baby corn, drained
1 cup (45 g/1½ oz) finely sliced Chinese cabbage
125 g (4 oz) bean sprouts, tails removed
1 tablespoon soy sauce
1–2 tablespoons oyster sauce (optional)
2 teaspoons sesame oil

1 Heat the oil in a heavy-based pan or wok and add the ginger and spring onion. Stir-fry over high heat for 1 minute. Add the water chestnuts and baby corn; stir-fry for 30 seconds.
2 Add the cabbage, bean sprouts and sauces; stir-fry for 1 minute. Stir in the sesame oil and toss well. Serve immediately.

GINGER

Ginger (*Zingiber officinale*) is a rhizome (underground stem). Buy firm pieces without any soft spots and make sure they aren't spongy when squeezed. The longer ginger has grown before harvesting, the more fibrous it is—this can make it difficult to cut finely, but it will be hotter and more flavoursome. Ginger can be kept for a week on the counter, and longer in the refrigerator. Wrap in paper towel to absorb moisture and then place in a plastic bag.

ABOVE: Chinese Vegetables with Ginger

FAST STIR-FRIED ASIAN GREENS

WASH AND DRY 500 g (1 lb) of bok choy or choy sum, or a combination of both. Cut the stems and leaves into manageable pieces, about 5 cm (2 inches) long. Heat 1 tablespoon of peanut oil in a wok; add 1 crushed clove of garlic and a teaspoon of finely grated fresh ginger and cook for a few seconds. Add the greens and stir-fry for 1–2 minutes, until just tender; add 2 teaspoons of soy sauce (and a teaspoon of sesame oil if you like) and toss to combine. Serve immediately. Serves 4.
Note: Chinese green vegetables cooked in this manner turn bright green—they look irresistible and are very nutritious.

STIR-FRIED ASPARAGUS WITH SESAME SEEDS

Preparation time: 10 minutes
Total cooking time: 6 minutes
Serves 4

1 tablespoon sesame seeds
2 tablespoons oil
1 clove garlic, finely chopped
1 teaspoon grated fresh ginger
750 g (1 1/2 lb) asparagus, trimmed and cut
   into 5 cm (2 inch) pieces
1/2 teaspoon pepper
1/2 teaspoon sugar
2 teaspoons sesame oil
1 tablespoon soy sauce

1 Heat a wok or frying pan; add the sesame seeds and stir-fry over high heat for 2 minutes or until golden. Remove from wok and set aside.
2 Heat the oil in the wok and add the garlic, ginger and asparagus. Stir-fry over high heat for 3 minutes or until almost tender. Sprinkle the vegetables with pepper and add the sugar. Stir-fry over high heat for 1 minute.
3 Sprinkle with the sesame oil, soy sauce and sesame seeds and serve immediately.

STIR-FRIED MUSHROOMS

Preparation time: 10–15 minutes
Total cooking time: 5 minutes
Serves 4

1 tablespoon oil
2.5 cm (1 inch) piece of galangal, finely sliced
2 cloves garlic, chopped
2 red chillies, finely sliced
200 g (6 1/2 oz) button mushrooms, halved
100 g (3 1/3 oz) oyster mushrooms, halved
1 tablespoon fish sauce (optional)
1 teaspoon Golden Mountain sauce
1/2 cup (30 g/1 oz) chopped fresh basil

1 Heat the oil in a wok or frying pan. Add the galangal, garlic and chillies to the wok and stir-fry for 2 minutes. Add the button mushrooms and stir-fry for another 2 minutes. Add the oyster mushrooms and stir-fry for approximately 30 seconds, tossing constantly until the mushrooms begin to soften.
2 Add the fish sauce, Golden Mountain sauce and basil and toss well to combine. Serve immediately with main courses and steamed rice.
NOTE: Other varieties of mushroom may be used in this recipe. Galangal is available from Asian speciality food stores.

GOLDEN MOUNTAIN SAUCE
This thin, salty, spicy sauce is available from Asian speciality shops. It is made from soya beans and looks like fish sauce or soy sauce, but has a completely different flavour. It is often used in Thai dishes and can be used as a substitute for fish sauce.

ABOVE: Stir-fried Asparagus with Sesame Seeds
BELOW: Stir-fried Mushrooms

over medium heat for 30 seconds, stirring constantly. Add the beans, spring onions and broccoli, then stir-fry for 3 minutes.

3 Add the red peppers and stir-fry for another 2 minutes. Add the bok choy and stir-fry for 1 minute. Stir in the sesame oil and the soy sauce and toss until well combined with the vegetables. Transfer to a serving dish and serve immediately. Serve with steamed rice.

NOTE: It is important not to overcook vegetables when stir-frying. Use the minimum amount of oil and cook over medium-high heat, stirring and tossing the vegetables constantly. They will soften slightly but should never be cooked to a limp and greasy state. Add the leafy green vegetables last when stir-frying, and cook only until the leaves have just softened. Cutting vegetables into thin, even-sized pieces on the diagonal helps them to cook quickly.

THAI STIR-FRIED VEGETABLES

Preparation time: 25 minutes
Total cooking time: 5 minutes
Serves 4

1 tablespoon oil
4 cloves garlic, chopped
3 stems lemon grass (white part only), finely chopped
2 teaspoons chopped fresh red chillies
2 celery sticks, cut into short pieces
100 g (3¹/₃ oz) beans, cut into short pieces
155 g (5 oz) asparagus, cut into short pieces
¹/₂ red pepper (capsicum), cut into thin short pieces
2 tablespoons fish sauce (optional)
2–6 teaspoons sweet chilli sauce
1 teaspoon Golden Mountain sauce
100 g (3¹/₃ oz) bean sprouts
¹/₂ cup (80 g/2²/₃ oz) roasted peanuts, chopped (optional)
¹/₂ cup (15 g/¹/₂ oz) fresh coriander leaves

1 Heat the oil in a wok or large frying pan. Add the garlic and lemon grass and cook for 1 minute. Add chilli, celery and beans and stir-fry for 1 minute.

LEMON GRASS
Lemon grass (*Cymbopogon citratus*), gives dishes a balm-like flavour that is difficult to define. Lemon grass is easily grown and can be bought fresh from the greengrocers. It is a fibrous, woody stalk and usually only the bulb-like base is used. Dried lemon grass is a useful substitute and can be used to make a refreshing herbal tea.

ABOVE: Chinese-style Stir-fried Vegetables

CHINESE-STYLE STIR-FRIED VEGETABLES

Preparation time: 15 minutes
Total cooking time: 7 minutes
Serves 4

300 g (9²/₃ oz) baby bok choy
100 g (3¹/₃ oz) snake beans
2 spring onions
150 g (4³/₄ oz) broccoli
1 medium red pepper (capsicum)
2 tablespoons oil
2 cloves garlic, crushed
2 teaspoons grated fresh ginger
1 tablespoon sesame oil
2 teaspoons soy sauce

1 Wash and trim the thick stalks from the bok choy, and then cut the leaves into wide strips. Slice the snake beans into 5 cm (2 inch) lengths and the spring onions diagonally. Cut the broccoli into small florets and the red pepper into diamonds about 2.5 cm (1 inch) wide.
2 Heat the oil in a large heavy-based frying pan or wok. Add the garlic and ginger and cook

SHIITAKE AND OYSTER MUSHROOMS

One of the most popular of Chinese mushrooms, shiitakes can be eaten dried or fresh. In Asia, they are preferred dried and are grown for this purpose. The best shiitake have thick caps with white fissures. Shiitake have a rich, smoky flavour and are available both wild and cultivated. Oyster mushrooms grow on dead trees and have long been cultivated in Asia for their subtle flavour, reminiscent of the sea. They need careful cooking as they can be tough, but they make wonderful additions to casseroles and can be stir-fried, grilled, or deep-fried in a tempura batter.

2 Add the asparagus and red pepper and toss well; cover and steam for 1 minute. Add the fish sauce, chilli sauce, Golden Mountain sauce and bean sprouts to the wok and toss well.

3 Arrange on a serving platter; scatter peanuts and coriander over the top and serve at once.

NOTE: Use any vegetable in season, such as broccoli, baby corn or snow peas (mange tout).

ORIENTAL MUSHROOM STIR-FRY

Preparation time: 35 minutes
Total cooking time: 10 minutes
Serves 4

250 g (8 oz) hokkein noodles

1 teaspoon sesame oil

1 tablespoon peanut oil

2 cloves garlic, crushed

2 tablespoons grated fresh ginger

6 spring onions, sliced

1 red pepper (capsicum), sliced

200 g (6½ oz) oyster mushrooms

200 g (6½ oz) shiitake mushrooms, sliced

1 cup (125 g/4 oz) chopped fresh
   garlic chives

3 tablespoons roasted cashews

2 tablespoons kecap manis

3 tablespoons salt-reduced soy sauce

1 Soak the hokkein noodles in boiling water for 2 minutes; drain and set them aside.

2 Heat the sesame oil and peanut oil in a wok. Add the garlic, ginger and spring onions. Stir-fry over high heat for 2 minutes. Add the red pepper and all the mushrooms and stir-fry over high heat for 3 minutes or until the mushrooms are golden brown.

3 Stir in the drained noodles. Add the chives, cashews, kecap manis and soy sauce. Stir-fry for 3 minutes or until the noodles are coated in sauce mixture.

NOTE: Kecap manis is an Indonesian sweet soy sauce, and is readily available from specialist stores and some supermarkets.

FAST SAUTEED VEGETABLES WITH SWEET SOY

HEAT 1–2 teaspoons of sesame oil and 2 teaspoons of olive oil in a large frying pan or wok, swirling to coat the base of the pan. Toss in 200 g (6½ oz) of small broccoli florets and stir-fry for about 2 minutes. Add 150 g (4¾ oz) of finely shredded cabbage and 90 g (3 oz) of sugar snap peas to the pan. Toss with the broccoli for about 2–3 minutes over medium heat or until the vegetables are just cooked. Drizzle a little sweet soy (kecap manis) or soy sauce and some honey, to taste, over the vegetables. Toss well to combine and serve immediately. Serves 2–4.

ABOVE: Oriental Mushroom Stir-fry

SAVOURY BREADS MUFFINS AND SCONES

Few things enhance a cook's reputation as much as fresh, home-made bread. Serve onion and parmesan scones warm from the oven with a stockpot of soup on a cold winter's night, or focaccia for lunch on a sunny patio. These savoury breads fulfil their aromatic promise for any occasion, compelling everyone who bites into one with the same thought: 'More, please!'

SOURDOUGH

Historically, sourdough was made in areas where fresh yeast was scarce. Its flavour is produced by a starter combination of flour and water (or milk) that has been left to ferment before being added to the dough. The character of the starter differs depending on the climate of the region in which it is made. To make sourdough bread, a portion of the starter is combined with other ingredients and the bread is finished like any other. Flour and water are added to the remaining starter which is kept to leaven more batches of dough.

ABOVE: Sourdough Rye Bread

SOURDOUGH RYE BREAD

Preparation time: 50 minutes
+ 1 hour 30 minutes rising + 1–3 days standing
Total cooking time: 40 minutes
Makes 2 loaves

 ✷ ✷

Sourdough Starter

7 g (1/4 oz) sachet dried yeast
1 teaspoon caster sugar
2 cups (200 g/6 1/2 oz) rye flour
1 3/4 cups (440 ml/14 fl oz) warm water

Bread Dough

1 cup (100 g/3 1/3 oz) rye flour
4 1/2 cups (560 g/1 lb 2 oz) unbleached
   plain flour
1/4 cup (45 g/1 1/2 oz) soft brown sugar
3 teaspoons caraway seeds
2 teaspoons salt
7 g (1/4 oz) sachet dried yeast, extra
1 cup (250 ml/8 fl oz) warm water, extra
1/4 cup (60 ml/2 fl oz) oil

1 To make Sourdough Starter: Combine yeast, sugar, rye flour and warm water in a medium bowl. Cover with plastic wrap and set aside overnight at room temperature to sour. For a stronger flavour, leave for up to 3 days.

2 To make Bread Dough: Brush a large baking tray with oil or melted butter. In a large bowl, combine the rye flour, 3 1/2 cups (440 g/14 oz) of the plain flour, sugar, seeds and salt. Dissolve the yeast in warm water. Make a well in the centre of the flour mixture; add sourdough starter, dissolved yeast and oil. Mix, using a wooden spoon, then hands, until the dough forms a rough, slightly sticky ball which leaves the side of the bowl. Add some of the remaining flour, if necessary—you may not need to use it all.

3 Turn onto a lightly floured surface. Knead for 10 minutes or until smooth and elastic. Incorporate the remaining flour, if needed. Place the dough in a large, lightly oiled bowl. Leave, covered with plastic wrap, in a warm place for 45 minutes or until well risen. Punch down and knead for 1 minute. Divide into two even-sized portions. Shape into round or oblong loaves; place on tray. Sprinkle with rye flour; use end of wooden spoon handle to punch holes 2 cm (3/4 inch) deep in the top, or make three slashes. Leave, covered with plastic wrap, in a warm place for 45 minutes, or until the dough is well risen. Sprinkle with extra flour. Bake in a preheated moderate 180°C (350°F/Gas 4) oven for 40 minutes or until a skewer inserted in the centre comes out clean. Cool on a wire rack.

TRADITIONAL CORN BREAD

Preparation time: 15 minutes
Total cooking time: 25 minutes
Makes one 20 cm loaf

1 cup (150 g/4 3/4 oz) polenta (cornmeal)
2 tablespoons caster sugar
1 cup (125 g/4 oz) plain flour
2 teaspoons baking powder
1/2 teaspoon bicarbonate of soda
1/2 teaspoon salt
1 egg, lightly beaten
1 cup (250 ml/8 fl oz) buttermilk
60 g (2 oz) butter, melted

1 Preheat the oven to hot 210°C (415°F/Gas 6–7). Brush a 20 cm (8 inch) square cake tin with oil or melted butter, and line the base with baking paper. Place the polenta and sugar in a large bowl. Add the sifted flour, baking powder, soda and salt and mix thoroughly.
2 Combine the beaten egg, buttermilk and melted butter in a large jug. Stir the mixture quickly into dry ingredients. Stir only until the ingredients are moistened.
3 Pour the mixture into the prepared tin and smooth the surface. Bake for 20–25 minutes, or until a skewer inserted in the centre comes out clean. Place on a wire rack and leave to cool for 10 minutes before turning out. Cut into squares and serve warm.
NOTE: This is best eaten on day of baking. For successful results, use fine to medium cornmeal, available from most health food stores.

MALT BREAD

Preparation time: 45 minutes + 1 hour
50 minutes standing
Total cooking time: 40 minutes
Makes 1 loaf

1 cup (250 ml/8 fl oz) lukewarm water
7 g (1/4 oz) sachet dried yeast
1 teaspoon sugar
2 cups (300 g/9 2/3 oz) plain wholemeal flour
1 cup (125 g/4 oz) plain flour
2 teaspoons ground cinnamon
1/2 cup (60 g/2 oz) raisins

30 g (1 oz) butter, melted
1 tablespoon treacle
1 tablespoon liquid malt extract, plus
1/2 teaspoon
1 tablespoon hot milk

1 Brush a 21 x 14 x 7 cm (8 1/2 x 5 1/2 x 2 3/4 inch) loaf tin with oil; line the base with baking paper. Combine the water, yeast and sugar in a small bowl. Cover with plastic wrap and set aside in a warm place for 10 minutes or until foamy. Sift the flours and cinnamon into a large bowl; add raisins and stir. Make a well in the centre. Add melted butter, treacle, tablespoon of malt extract and the yeast mixture.
2 Using a knife, mix to a soft dough. Turn onto lightly floured surface; knead 10 minutes or until smooth. Shape into a ball and place in a lightly oiled bowl. Set aside, covered with plastic wrap, in a warm place for 1 hour or until well risen. Punch down. Knead 3 minutes or until smooth.
3 Roll into a 20 cm (8 inch) square and then roll up. Place in tin, with the seam underneath, and set aside, covered with plastic wrap, in a warm place for 40 minutes or until well risen.
4 Preheat oven to moderate 180°C (350°F/ Gas 4). Brush with combined milk and remaining malt. Bake for 40 minutes or until a skewer comes out clean. Set aside for 3 minutes in tin before transferring to a wire rack to cool.

BUTTERMILK
Home-made buttermilk is the rather tart liquid whey left over from churning cream to make butter. Commercial buttermilk is widely available and is used mostly in soda breads, pancakes and biscuits. Buttermilk adds flavour and its acidity reacts with bicarbonate of soda to release gas which makes the dough or batter light. The commercial variety has a smoother consistency, reflecting the fact that it is made by adding a bacterial culture to low-fat or skim milk.

ABOVE: Malt Bread

3 Turn the dough onto a lightly floured surface and knead until smooth. Divide dough into two. Place on prepared trays and press out into a circle approximately 2.5 cm (1 inch) thick. Score each with a knife into 8 wedges, cutting lightly into the top of the bread. Dust lightly with flour. Bake for 20–25 minutes, or until a deep golden colour and sounds hollow when tapped on the base. Serve warm with butter.

GRISSINI

Preparation time: 40 minutes
+ 25 minutes standing
Total cooking time: 30 minutes
Makes 18

⭐

7 g (¹/₄ oz) sachet dried yeast
¹/₂ cup (125 ml/4 fl oz) warm water
²/₃ cup (170 ml/5¹/₂ fl oz) milk
60 g (2 oz) butter
1 tablespoon caster sugar
4 cups (500 g/1 lb) unbleached plain flour
1 teaspoon salt
rock salt, sesame or poppy seeds, to coat

1 Brush 3 baking trays with melted butter or oil. Dissolve yeast in warm water in a small bowl. Cover with plastic wrap, then leave in a warm place for 5 minutes or until frothy. In a small pan heat the milk, butter and sugar until the mixture is just warm and the butter has melted.
2 Place 3¹/₂ cups (435 g/13³/₄ oz) of the flour and the salt in a large bowl. Add yeast and milk mixture and mix thoroughly until well combined. Add enough of the remaining flour to make a soft dough. Turn onto a lightly floured surface and knead for 10 minutes, or until dough is smooth and elastic. Divide into 18 even-sized pieces.
3 Roll each piece to the thickness of a pencil and to a length of about 30 cm (12 inches). Preheat the oven to hot 210°C (415°F/Gas 6–7). Place lengths of dough 3 cm (1¹/₄ inches) apart on baking trays. Cover with plastic wrap and leave for 20 minutes.
4 Brush dough with cold water and sprinkle with rock salt or seeds. Bake 15–20 minutes or until golden. Remove from oven, cool on wire rack. Reduce oven to moderate 180°C (350°F/Gas 4). Return grissini to trays, and bake for another 5–10 minutes, or until dried out and crisp. Serve with soups, salads, dips and pre-dinner drinks.

LEMON PEPPER BREAD

Preparation time: 20 minutes
Total cooking time: 25 minutes
Serves 8

⭐

2 cups (250 g/8 oz) self-raising flour
1 teaspoon salt
2 teaspoons lemon pepper, or 1 teaspoon
    grated lemon rind and 2 teaspoons
    black pepper
45 g (1¹/₂ oz) butter, chopped
1 tablespoon chopped fresh chives
³/₄ cup (90 g/3 oz) grated Cheddar cheese
2 teaspoons white vinegar
³/₄ cup (185 ml/6 fl oz) milk

1 Preheat the oven to hot 210°C (415°F/Gas 6–7). Brush two oven trays with melted butter or oil. Sift the flour and salt into a large bowl and add the lemon pepper, or lemon rind and pepper. Using your fingertips, rub in the butter until the mixture resembles coarse breadcrumbs. Stir in the chives and cheese.
2 Stir vinegar into milk (it should look slightly curdled). Add to flour mixture and mix to a soft dough, adding more milk if dough is too stiff.

ABOVE: Lemon Pepper Bread

FOCACCIA

Preparation time: 50 minutes + 2 hours standing
Total cooking time: 25 minutes
Makes 1 flat loaf

★ ★

7 g (¼ oz) sachet dried yeast

1 cup (250 g/8 fl oz) warm water

1 teaspoon caster sugar

2 tablespoons olive oil

3¼ cups (405 g/12¾ oz) unbleached plain flour

1 tablespoon full cream milk powder

½ teaspoon salt

Topping

1 tablespoon olive oil

1–2 cloves garlic, crushed

12 black olives

fresh rosemary sprigs

1 teaspoon dried oregano

1–2 teaspoons coarse sea salt

 Brush a 28 x 18 cm (11 x 7 inch) rectangular tin with oil or melted butter. Combine yeast, water and sugar in a large bowl; stir to dissolve yeast. Cover with plastic wrap and leave in a warm place about 10 minutes or until frothy; add oil. Sift 3 cups (375 g/12 oz) of the flour, milk powder and salt onto yeast mixture. Beat with a wooden spoon until well combined. Add enough of the remaining flour (you may not need to use it all) to form a soft dough and then turn onto a lightly floured surface.

2 Knead 10 minutes or until dough is smooth and elastic. Place in a large, lightly oiled bowl; brush surface with oil. Cover with plastic wrap and leave in a warm place 1 hour or until well risen. Punch down; knead 1 minute. Roll into a 28 x 18 cm (11 x 7 inch) rectangle and place in tin. Cover with plastic wrap and leave to rise in a warm place for 20 minutes. Using the handle of a wooden spoon, press dough all over at regular intervals to form indents 1 cm (½ inch) deep. Cover with plastic wrap and set aside for a further 30 minutes or until well risen. Preheat the oven to moderate 180°C (350°F/Gas 4).

3 To make Topping: Brush combined olive oil and garlic over surface of bread. Top with olives and rosemary sprigs and then sprinkle with oregano and salt.

4 Bake for 20–25 minutes or until golden and crisp. Cut into large squares and serve warm. Leftover Focaccia can be toasted, if you like.

OLIVE OIL

The best, and also the most expensive, olive oil is cold-pressed virgin olive oil. This is produced from the first pressing of high-grade fruit at a low temperature. The oil from the next pressing is 'virgin' olive oil. Subsequent pressings will produce a blander oil with a less distinct flavour and paler colour. 'Light' olive oil refers to the colour and flavour, not to the amount of fat or kilojoules.

ABOVE: Focaccia

CHAPATTIS

Preparation time: 40 minutes + standing time
Total cooking time: 40 minutes
Makes 20

2¹/₂ cups (310 g/9³/₄ oz) fine wholemeal flour
1 teaspoon salt
1 tablespoon oil
1 cup (250 ml/8 fl oz) warm water
¹/₂ cup (60 g/2 oz) fine wholemeal flour, extra

1 Place the flour and salt in a large mixing bowl; make a well in the centre. Add the oil and water all at once and use a wooden spoon, then your hands, to mix to a firm dough.
2 Turn onto a lightly floured surface and knead for 15 minutes. Do not incorporate the extra flour at this stage. Form dough into a smooth ball and place in a bowl. Cover with plastic wrap and set aside for at least 2 hours. The dough can be left overnight, if desired.
3 Divide the dough into 20 even-sized pieces. Form each piece into a smooth ball. With the aid of the extra flour, roll each ball into a thin, pancake-sized circle. Cover each chapatti with floured plastic wrap and leave to rest while rolling the remaining dough.
4 Heat a heavy-based frying pan until hot. Cook each chapatti for 1 minute, then turn and cook the other side for another minute. Adjust the heat so that the dough browns but does not burn. While the chapatti is cooking, press the edges with a folded tea towel. This will help bubbles to form and make the chapatti lighter.
5 Stack and wrap the cooked chapattis in a clean tea towel to keep them warm and soft. Serve immediately with curry and vegetable dishes.
NOTE: Fine wholemeal flour, often referred to as Roti flour, is available from most health food shops. Plain wholemeal flour can be used instead, but the chapattis may be a little denser.

TORTILLAS

Preparation time: 30 minutes
Total cooking time: 20 minutes
Makes 16

1¹/₂ cups (185 g/6 oz) plain flour, sifted
1 cup (150 g/4³/₄ oz) maize meal, sifted
1 cup (250 ml/8 fl oz) warm water

1 Combine the flour and maize meal in a large bowl. Make a well in the centre and then gradually add the warm water. Using a knife, mix to a firm dough. Turn out onto a lightly floured surface. Knead the dough for 3 minutes or until smooth.
2 Divide the dough into 16 portions. Roll out one portion on a lightly floured surface to a 20 cm (8 inch) round. Set aside, cover with plastic wrap and repeat with remaining portions.
3 Heat a dry heavy-based frying pan or flatplate. Place one tortilla in the pan. When the edges begin to curl slightly, turn and cook the other side. A few seconds each side is ample cooking time. If residual flour begins to burn in the pan, wipe it out with paper towels.
NOTE: Maize meal is a flour made from corn kernels. The texture varies and this recipe requires a finely ground one. It is not to be confused with polenta or cornmeal which will not work in this recipe. Tortillas (pronounced tor-tee-yah) will remain fresh for a week in an airtight container. Warm quickly in the oven or microwave. Stale tortillas can be torn into bite-sized pieces and fried in oil until crisp.

CHAPATTIS
Chapattis are a form of Indian unleavened bread made from a finely ground wholemeal flour called atta. Traditionally they are cooked in two stages: first the dough is browned in the pan and then it is toasted directly over the fire, the steam creating moist, puffed pockets in the centre. Chapattis are eaten hot with Indian savoury dishes and curries.

FAST BEER BREAD ROLLS

PROCESS 3¹/₄ cups (405 g/12³/₄ oz) plain flour, 3 teaspoons baking powder, 1 teaspoon salt, 1 tablespoon sugar and 50 g (1²/₃ oz) chopped butter until crumbly. Add 1¹/₂ cups (375 ml/12 fl oz) beer and process in bursts to form a soft dough. Turn out onto a well-floured surface and knead until smooth, adding extra flour if needed. Divide into four balls, place on greased oven trays and flatten slightly. Brush with a little water and slash tops with a knife. Bake in a preheated hot 210°C (415°F/Gas 6-7) oven for 10 minutes. Reduce to moderate 180°C (350°F/Gas 4) and bake for about 10 minutes, or until cooked. Cool on a wire rack. Serve with butter. Makes 4 rolls.

OPPOSITE PAGE:
Chapattis (top); Tortillas

CHEESES
Everyone loves cheese, and the creative touches added to this selection of popular fresh cheeses dress them up just enough to turn a nearly perfect natural food into a perfectly delectable course on its own.

ASHED HERB GOATS CHEESE
Place 4 sprigs each of sage, rosemary, thyme and marjoram in a small pan. Cover and cook the herbs over medium heat for 20 minutes without removing the lid. Transfer blackened herbs to a food processor and finely chop. Remove four 100 g (3⅓ oz) goats cheese logs or rounds from their packages and pat dry on paper towels. Coat the goats cheese in the ashed herbs, cover with plastic wrap and refrigerate overnight.

MARINATED GRILLED GARLIC HALOUMI
Pat 500 g (1 lb) haloumi cheese dry on paper towels. Cut haloumi into thick slices and place in a shallow dish; add 2 finely sliced cloves of garlic, 2 tablespoons of chopped fresh basil, 1 teaspoon lime juice, 60 g (2 oz) sliced sun-dried tomatoes and 1 cup (250 ml/ 8 fl oz) olive oil. Cover and leave to marinate overnight. Remove haloumi and tomatoes from marinade and arrange on top of slices of wood-fired bread; cook under a preheated grill on high until cheese is soft and golden brown. Drizzle with lime juice and sprinkle with freshly ground black pepper.

FETA CHEESE AND SUN-DRIED TOMATOES IN OIL

Pat dry 350 g (11¼ oz) feta cheese with paper towels. Cut into cubes. Sprinkle 1 tablespoon each cracked black pepper and dried oregano leaves and 1 teaspoon coriander seeds over base of a sterilised 3-cup (750 ml/24 fl oz) jar. Arrange the feta, 4 small fresh red chillies, several sprigs of rosemary and 125 g (4 oz) sun-dried tomatoes in a jar. Cover with olive oil, seal tightly and refrigerate. This will keep, refrigerated, for 1–2 months.

BAKED RICOTTA CHEESE

Drain 500 g (1 lb) ricotta cheese through muslin over a bowl for 3 hours. Mix the ricotta and 3 lightly beaten egg whites in a bowl. Spoon into a loaf tin and press down firmly. Drizzle with ½ cup (125 ml/4 fl oz) of olive oil and sprinkle with 1 tablespoon of sweet paprika, 1 teaspoon of ground cumin and freshly ground black pepper. Bake in a preheated moderate 180°C (350°F/ Gas 4) oven for 40 minutes or until golden brown. Cool slightly, remove from the tin and spoon over pan juices. Serve sliced with wood-fired bread and an antipasto platter.

PESTO HERB SPREAD

Place 500 g (1 lb) cream cheese and 1 tablespoon of ready-made pesto into a food processor and process until smooth. Add 30 g (1 oz) of chopped fresh chives and 3 tablespoons of chopped fresh coriander and process until combined. Spoon mixture into a 20 cm (8 inch) round cake tin lined with plastic wrap. Cover and refrigerate for 3 hours or until firm. Remove from tin and coat with chopped smoked almonds. Serve with crackers, sun-dried tomatoes and olives.

ALMOND RICOTTA CREAM WITH FRESH FRUITS AND BERRIES

Combine 250 g (8 oz) ricotta cheese, 1 tablespoon of thick cream, 100 g (3⅓ oz) ground almonds, 200 g (6½ oz) of vanilla fromage frais, 4 tablespoons of caster sugar and 1 teaspoon of vanilla essence in a bowl. Spoon into a double layer of muslin, tie ends together and suspend over a bowl in a cool place overnight. Turn out onto a plate; serve with fresh fruits and berries.

CLOKWISE, FROM TOP LEFT:
Marinated Grilled Garlic Haloumi; Feta Cheese and Sun-dried Tomatoes in Oil; Ashed Herb Goats Cheese; Pesto Herb Spread; Baked Ricotta Cheese; Almond Ricotta Cream with Fruits and Berries

233

2 Combine egg, milk, Tabasco and oil in a separate bowl. Add egg mixture, pepper, corn and parsley all at once to dry ingredients. Stir quickly with a wooden spoon or rubber spatula until all ingredients are just moistened. (Do not over-mix—batter should be quite lumpy.)
3 Spoon into tin. Bake 20 minutes or until golden. Remove from oven, loosen with a knife but leave in tin 2 minutes; cool on a wire rack.

SPICY VEGETABLE MUFFINS

Preparation time: 20 minutes
Total cooking time: 25 minutes
Makes 12

2 cups (250 g/8 oz) self-raising flour
3 teaspoons curry powder
salt and freshly ground black pepper
1/2 cup (80 g/2 2/3 oz) grated carrot
1/2 cup (60 g/2 oz) grated orange sweet potato
1 cup (125 g/4 oz) grated Cheddar cheese
90 g (3 oz) butter, melted
1 egg, lightly beaten
3/4 cup (185 ml/6 fl oz) milk

1 Preheat oven to moderate 180°C (350°F/Gas 4). Brush a 12-hole muffin tin with oil or melted butter. Sift the flour, curry powder, salt and pepper into a bowl. Add the carrot, sweet potato and cheese and mix through with your fingertips until ingredients are evenly combined. Make a well in the centre.

FREEZING MUFFINS

Muffins are undoubtedly best eaten warm from the oven on the day they are baked, but they can also be frozen for up to three months. Either put them in an airtight container, or wrap each one separately in foil. They do not need to be thawed—simply reheat in a moderate 180°C (350°F/Gas 4) oven for about 10 minutes.

ABOVE: Pepper and Corn Muffins
RIGHT: Spicy Vegetable Muffins

PEPPER (CAPSICUM) AND CORN MUFFINS

Preparation time: 15 minutes
Total cooking time: 20 minutes
Makes 12

1 cup (125 g/4 oz) plain flour
1/4 teaspoon salt
1 tablespoon baking powder
1 cup (150 g/4 3/4 oz) fine polenta (cornmeal)
1 tablespoon caster sugar
1 egg
2/3 cup (170 ml/5 1/2 fl oz) milk
1/4 teaspoon Tabasco sauce (optional)
1/4 cup (60 ml/2 fl oz) oil
1/2 red pepper (capsicum), finely chopped
440 g (14 oz) canned corn kernels, drained
3 tablespoons finely chopped fresh parsley

1 Preheat the oven to hot 210°C (415°F/Gas 6–7). Brush a 12-hole muffin tin with oil or melted butter. Sift flour, salt and baking powder into a large bowl. Add the polenta and sugar. Stir thoroughly until all the ingredients are well mixed. Make a well in the centre of the mixture.

PECANS
Pecans are native to the United States and were widely used in American Indian cooking. Now their most renowned use is in that American favourite, the pecan pie, but they are also often used in stuffing for the Thanksgiving turkey. Their flavour is somewhat similar to that of the walnut, but the pecan is oilier. It is, in fact, one of the oiliest nuts we eat, with 70 per cent oil content being quite usual.

2 Add the combined butter, egg and milk all at once. Using a wooden spoon, stir until the ingredients are just combined. (Do not over-mix—batter should be quite lumpy.)

3 Spoon batter into tin. Bake for 25 minutes or until puffed and golden, then loosen with a knife and leave in the tin for 2 minutes before turning out onto a wire rack to cool.

ZUCCHINI (COURGETTE) AND CARROT MUFFINS

Preparation time: 20 minutes
Total cooking time: 20 minutes
Makes 12

☆

2 medium zucchinis (courgettes)
2 carrots, peeled
2 cups (250 g/8 oz) self-raising flour
pinch salt
1 teaspoon ground cinnamon
1/2 teaspoon ground nutmeg
1/2 cup (60 g/2 oz) chopped pecans
2 eggs
1 cup (250 ml/8 fl oz) milk
90 g (3 oz) butter, melted

1 Preheat the oven to hot 210°C (415°F/Gas 6–7). Brush a 12-hole muffin tin with melted butter or oil. Grate the zucchinis and carrots. Sift the flour, salt, cinnamon and nutmeg into a large bowl. Add the carrot, zucchini and chopped pecans. Stir thoroughly until all the ingredients are well combined.

2 Combine the eggs, milk and melted butter in a separate bowl and whisk well until combined.

3 Make a well in the centre of the flour mixture; add the egg mixture all at once. Mix quickly with a fork or rubber spatula until all the ingredients are just moistened. (Do not over-mix; the batter should be quite lumpy.)

4 Spoon the batter evenly into the prepared tin. Bake for 15–20 minutes or until golden. Loosen the muffins with a flat-bladed knife or spatula and leave in the tin for 2 minutes, before turning out onto a wire rack to cool.

ABOVE: Zucchini and Carrot Muffins

CHEDDAR CHEESE

Cheddar, which is probably Britain's best-known cheese, originated in the small Somerset town from which it takes its name. One of Cheddar's best qualities is its adaptability: it can be served as a dessert cheese but also melts well enough to make it good for cooking. Cheddar can be bought in various strengths, ranging from mild to strong and well matured. Try different Cheddars to find one that suits your taste.

ABOVE: Mini Onion and Parmesan Scones

MINI ONION AND PARMESAN SCONES

Preparation time: 25 minutes
Total cooking time: 12 minutes
Makes 24

30 g (1 oz) butter
1 small onion, finely chopped
2 cups (250 g/8 oz) self-raising flour, sifted
pinch salt
1/2 cup (50 g/1²/3 oz) finely shredded
    Parmesan cheese
1/2 cup (125 ml/4 oz) milk
1/2 cup (125 ml/4 oz) water
cayenne pepper, for sprinkling

1 Preheat the oven to hot 210°C (415°F/Gas 6–7). Brush an oven tray with melted butter or oil. Melt the butter in a small pan; add onions and cook, over low heat, for 2–3 minutes or until soft; cool slightly.
2 Combine the flour, salt and Parmesan cheese in a bowl. Make a well in the centre; add onions and almost all the combined milk and water. Mix lightly, with a flat-bladed knife, to a soft dough, adding more liquid if necessary.

3 Knead dough briefly on a lightly floured surface until smooth and press out to 2 cm (3/4 inch) thickness. Cut dough into rounds with a floured 3 cm (1¼ inch) plain round cutter. Place rounds on prepared tray and sprinkle each lightly with cayenne pepper. Cook for 10–12 minutes until golden brown.
NOTE: Treat scone dough with a light touch. Cut the liquid in with a knife and then take care not to over-knead or you'll have tough scones.

CHEESE AND CHIVE SCONES

Preparation time: 20 minutes
Total cooking time: 12 minutes
Makes 9

2 cups (250 g/8 oz) self-raising flour
pinch salt
30 g (1 oz) butter, chopped
1/2 cup (60 g/2 oz) grated Cheddar cheese
3 tablespoons shredded Parmesan cheese
2 tablespoons chopped chives
1/2 cup (125 ml/4 fl oz) milk
1/2 cup (125 ml/4 fl oz) water
3 tablespoons grated Cheddar cheese, extra

ROSEMARY
Rosemary's Latin name, *Rosmarinus officinalis*, translates rather poetically as 'dew of the sea' and the herb's strong aroma and piney taste are indeed reminiscent of the dry Mediterranean hillsides. Rosemary should be used with discretion, as its distinctive flavour can easily overpower others.

1 Preheat the oven to hot 210°C (415°F/Gas 6–7). Brush an oven tray with melted butter or oil. Sift the flour and salt into bowl. Rub in the butter using your fingertips. Stir in the cheeses and the chives. Make a well in the centre; add the milk and almost all of the water. Mix lightly with a flat-bladed knife to form a soft dough, adding more liquid if necessary.

2 Knead the dough briefly on a lightly floured surface until smooth. Press out the dough to 2 cm (¾ inch) thickness. Using a floured 5 cm (2 inch) plain round cutter, cut rounds from dough. Place the rounds on prepared tray and sprinkle with extra cheese. Cook for 12 minutes or until cheese is golden.

POTATO AND OLIVE SCONES

Preparation time: 25 minutes
Total cooking time: 15 minutes
Makes 15

250 g (8 oz) potatoes, peeled and chopped
½ cup (125 ml/4 fl oz) milk
freshly ground black pepper
2 cups (250 g/8 oz) self-raising flour
30 g (1 oz) butter, chopped
3 tablespoons black olives, pitted
   and chopped
3–4 teaspoons chopped fresh rosemary
½ cup (125 ml/4 fl oz) water
milk, extra, for glazing

1 Preheat the oven to hot 210°C (415°F/ Gas 6–7). Brush an oven tray with melted butter or oil. Boil or microwave the potatoes until tender. Mash the potatoes with the milk and season with pepper.

2 Sift the flour into a large bowl; add the butter and rub in, using fingertips. Add the olives and rosemary and stir until just combined. Make a well in the centre; add the mashed potato and almost all of the water. Mix with a flat-bladed knife to a soft dough, adding more liquid if necessary.

3 Knead the dough briefly on a lightly floured surface until smooth. Press out to a thickness of 2 cm (¾ inch). Using a floured 5 cm (2 inch) plain round cutter, cut rounds from the dough and place them on the prepared tray. Brush the tops with extra milk and cook for 10–15 minutes until the scones are golden brown. Serve hot or cold with butter.

NOTE: The saltiness of the olives means that no extra salt needs to be added to this dough.

ABOVE: Potato and Olive Scones

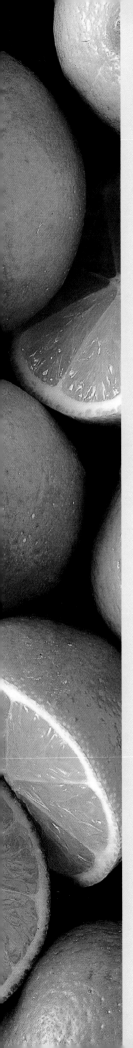

SAUCES DRESSINGS AND CONDIMENTS

Made to enhance both the taste and presentation of a dish, the list of sauces, dressings and condiments is virtually endless, with variations of old favourites appearing with each new cooking trend. But, traditional or innovative, they all have a common purpose: elevating a simple food into the realm of the fantastic.

SAUCES FOR COURSES
Vegetables are delicious served with a sauce. Try artichokes or asparagus with Aïoli, Hollandaise or Mayonnaise; broccoli or cauliflower with a Classic White or Cheese Sauce; potatoes with Blue Cheese Dressing or Aïoli; and tomatoes with Vinaigrette, Herb Vinaigrette or a Vinaigrette made with balsamic vinegar.

CLASSIC WHITE SAUCE (BECHAMEL)

Preparation time: 15 minutes
Total cooking time: 10 minutes
Makes about 250 ml (8 fl oz)

1 cup (250 ml/8 fl oz) milk
1 slice of onion
1 bay leaf
6 peppercorns
30 g (1 oz) butter
1 tablespoon plain flour
salt and white pepper

1 Combine milk, onion, bay leaf and peppercorns in a small pan. Bring to the boil; remove the pan from heat and set aside to infuse for 10 minutes. Strain the milk and discard all the flavourings.
2 Melt the butter in a small pan and add the flour. Stir over medium heat for 1 minute, or until the mixture is golden and bubbling. Remove from heat, add milk very slowly, a little at a time, and stir between each addition until mixture is completely smooth. When all the milk has been added, return to heat, keep stirring over medium heat until mixture boils and thickens.

ABOVE: Cheese Sauce (with vegetables)

3 Boil for another minute and remove from the heat. Season with salt and white pepper.
NOTE: Infusing the milk with onion, bay leaves and peppercorns adds flavour. Plain milk may be used, particularly if adding other flavourings.

VARIATION
■ **Parsley sauce:** Add 3 tablespoons finely chopped fresh parsley to the finished sauce and stir to combine. Other fresh herbs such as chives, dill or tarragon may be added, or try different combinations of your favourite herbs.

CHEESE SAUCE (MORNAY)

Preparation time: 10 minutes
Total cooking time: 10 minutes
Makes about 250 ml (8 fl oz)

30 g (1 oz) butter
1 tablespoon plain flour
1 1/3 cups (350 ml/11 fl oz) milk
1/2 cup (60 g/2 oz) finely grated Cheddar cheese
1/4 teaspoon mustard powder
salt and pepper

1 Melt the butter in a small pan, add flour. Stir for 1 minute over medium heat until the mixture is golden and bubbling. Remove from heat, add the milk very slowly, a little at a time, and stir between each addition until mixture is completely smooth. When all the milk has been added, return to the heat and stir over medium heat until mixture boils and thickens.

2 Boil for 1 minute more and remove from heat. Add cheese and mustard powder. Stir until cheese has melted and sauce is smooth. Season.

BASIC HOLLANDAISE

Preparation time: 5 minutes
Total cooking time: 10 minutes
Makes about 315 ml (10 fl oz)

175 g (5 2/3 oz) butter
2 tablespoons water
4 egg yolks
1 tablespoon lemon juice
salt and white pepper

1 Melt the butter in a small pan. Skim any froth from the top and discard; cool the melted butter.

Combine water and egg yolks in another small pan. Using a wire whisk, beat for about 30 seconds until the mixture is pale and creamy.

2 Place the pan over very low heat and continue whisking for 3 minutes or until thick and foamy; remove from the heat. (Make sure the pan does not get too hot or you will end up with scrambled eggs.)

3 Add the cooled butter slowly, a little at a time at first, whisking well between each addition. Keep adding the butter in a thin stream, whisking continuously, until all the butter has been used. Try to avoid using the milky white whey in the bottom of the pan, but don't worry if a little gets in. Stir in the lemon juice and season with salt and white pepper.

VARIATION

■ **Processor method:** Use the same quantities of ingredients as for making basic hollandaise, but place the yolks, water and juice in a food processor and blend for 10 seconds. Melt the butter; skim off the froth. With the motor running, add the melted hot butter to the processor in a thin stream. Transfer to a bowl and season, to taste.

■ **Orange Hollandaise (Maltaise):** Replace the tablespoon of lemon juice with 2 tablespoons of orange juice. (Strain through a fine sieve to remove any pulp before measuring.)

MICROWAVE HOLLANDAISE

Hollandaise Sauce can also be whipped up quickly in the microwave oven. Melt 200 g (6 1/2 oz) butter in a microwave-proof jug for 1 minute. Beat 3 egg yolks and 2 tablespoons of lemon juice together in a microwave bowl and add the melted butter, stirring well. Cook on medium heat for 1 minute 20 seconds, stopping to stir the sauce every 20 seconds. The sauce should be well-thickened.

ABOVE: Basic Hollandaise (with asparagus)

3 Bring to the boil, reduce heat and simmer, uncovered, for about 15 minutes or until the sauce has thickened slightly. Season, to taste. **NOTE:** This will keep, covered, for up to 2 days in the refrigerator, or freeze for up to 2 months. Reheat in a pan or in the microwave. Serve hot over pasta, or use as a pizza sauce.

BASIC VINAIGRETTE
(FRENCH DRESSING)

Preparation time: 3 minutes
Total cooking time: Nil
Makes about 125 ml (4 fl oz)

2 tablespoons white wine vinegar
1/3 cup (80 ml/2³/₄ fl oz) light olive oil
1 teaspoon French mustard
salt and white pepper

1 Place the vinegar, olive oil and French mustard in a small screw-top jar. Shake until all the ingredients are combined. Season, to taste, with salt and white pepper.

VARIATION
■ **Herb Vinaigrette:** Use a herb-infused vinegar instead of plain vinegar in the basic recipe. Or add 1 tablespoon finely chopped fresh herbs.

BLUE CHEESE DRESSING

Preparation time: 5 minutes
Total cooking time: Nil
Makes about 250 ml (8 fl oz)

1/2 cup (125 g/4 oz) whole egg mayonnaise
1/4 cup (60 ml/2 fl oz) thick cream
1 teaspoon white wine vinegar
1 tablespoon finely chopped fresh chives
50 g (1²/₃ oz) blue cheese

1 Combine the mayonnaise, cream, wine vinegar and chopped chives in a small bowl.
2 Crumble the blue cheese into the mayonnaise mixture and gently stir through. Cover and refrigerate for up to 3 days. Serve over cooked asparagus or boiled small potatoes, on jacket potatoes or with a green salad.

TOMATO SAUCE

Preparation time: 15 minutes
Total cooking time: 20 minutes
Serves 4

1.5 kg (3 lb) large ripe tomatoes
1 tablespoon olive oil
1 medium onion, finely chopped
2 cloves garlic, crushed
1 teaspoon dried oregano leaves
2 tablespoons tomato paste
1 teaspoon sugar
salt and pepper

1 Mark a small cross on the base (opposite stem end) of each tomato. Place in a small bowl and cover with boiling water for 2 minutes; drain and cool. Peel the skin down from the cross and discard. Finely chop the flesh.
2 Heat the oil in a medium pan. Add the onion and cook, stirring, over medium heat 3 minutes or until soft. Add garlic and cook for 1 minute. Add tomato, oregano, tomato paste and sugar.

MUSTARD SEEDS
There are three types of mustard seeds—black, brown and yellow. Black mustard seeds have the strongest flavour, but are unable to withstand mechanised harvesting processes, so have largely been replaced in prepared mustards by the milder brown seeds.

ABOVE: Tomato Sauce (with pasta)

BASIC MAYONNAISE

Preparation time: 10 minutes
Total cooking time: Nil
Makes about 250 ml (8 fl oz)

2 egg yolks
1 teaspoon Dijon mustard
4 teaspoons lemon juice
1 cup (250 ml/8 fl oz) light olive oil
salt and white pepper

1 Place egg yolks in a medium bowl. Add mustard and 2 teaspoons of the lemon juice; whisk for 30 seconds until light and creamy.
2 Add olive oil, about a teaspoon at a time, whisking continuously. Increase the amount of oil as the mayonnaise thickens. When all the oil has been added, stir in the remaining 2 teaspoons lemon juice; season with salt and white pepper.

VARIATION

■ **Processor method:** Process the yolks, mustard and juice in a food processor for 10 seconds. With the motor running, add the oil in a slow, thin stream until combined. Transfer to a bowl and season, to taste.

THOUSAND ISLAND DRESSING

Preparation time: 10 minutes
Total cooking time: Nil
Makes about 350 ml (11 fl oz)

1 cup (250 g/8 oz) whole egg mayonnaise
2–3 tablespoons chilli sauce
1 pimento, finely chopped, or 1/3 cup
   (50 g/1 2/3 oz) finely chopped olives
1 tablespoon grated onion
2 tablespoons finely chopped green
   pepper (capsicum)
milk (optional)

1 Combine mayonnaise, chilli sauce, pimento, onion and green pepper in a bowl; mix well.
2 Add a little milk for a thinner consistency. Allow dressing to stand for at least 2 hours before use. Refrigerate, covered, for up to 3 days.

AÏOLI (GARLIC MAYONNAISE)

Preparation time: 10 minutes
Total cooking time: Nil
Makes about 250 ml (8 fl oz)

2 egg yolks
3 large cloves garlic, crushed
4 teaspoons lemon juice
1 cup (250 ml/8 fl oz) light olive oil
salt and white pepper

1 Place the egg yolks in a medium bowl. Add the garlic and 2 teaspoons of the lemon juice; whisk for 30 seconds until light and creamy.
2 Add the olive oil, about a teaspoonful at a time, whisking continuously. Increase the amount of oil as the mayonnaise thickens. When all the oil has been added, stir in the remaining 2 teaspoonsful of lemon juice and season, to taste, with salt and white pepper.

ABOVE: Aïoli (with char-grilled vegetables)

243

HARISSA

Preparation time: 25 minutes + soaking
Total cooking time: 1–2 minutes
Makes about 250 ml (8 fl oz)

250 g/8 oz fresh or dried birds-eye chillies
  (or any small red chillies)
1 tablespoon caraway seeds
1 tablespoon coriander seeds
2 teaspoons cumin seeds
4–6 cloves garlic, peeled
1 tablespoon dried mint
1 teaspoon salt
1/2 cup (125 ml/4 fl oz) extra-virgin olive oil

1 Wearing rubber gloves, remove stems of chillies, split in half, remove seeds and soften in hot water for 5 minutes (if using fresh chillies, or 30 minutes if using dried).
2 While the chillies are soaking, dry-fry caraway, coriander and cumin in a pan until seeds become aromatic, about 1–2 minutes. Drain chillies and place in a food processor. Add seeds, garlic, mint and salt to food processor and, slowly adding the olive oil, process until a smooth, thick paste forms.
NOTE: Refrigerate sauce, covered, up to 2 weeks. Serve at room temperature as an accompaniment to Moroccan foods such as couscous, or stir into soups and stews for extra spice.

CUCUMBER RAITA

Preparation time: 5 minutes
Total cooking time: 1 minute
Serves 2–4

2 Lebanese cucumbers, peeled and finely chopped
1 cup (250 g/8 oz) plain yoghurt
1 teaspoon ground cumin
1/2 teaspoon grated fresh ginger
salt and freshly ground black pepper
paprika

1 Combine cucumbers with yoghurt in a bowl. Fry cumin in a dry pan for 1 minute until fragrant, then add to yoghurt mixture with the ginger. Season with salt and pepper.
2 Place in a bowl and dust with a little paprika. Serve chilled. Refrigerate for up to 2 days.

BASIL PESTO

Preparation time: 10 minutes
Total cooking time: Nil
Makes about 250 ml (8 fl oz)

250 g/8 oz fresh basil
1/3 cup (50 g/1 2/3 oz) toasted pine nuts
2 cloves garlic, crushed
1/3 cup (35 g/1 1/4 oz) finely grated
  Parmesan cheese
1/3 cup (80 ml/2 3/4 fl oz) olive oil
salt and pepper

1 Remove basil leaves from the stalks. Wash and dry the leaves and place them in a food processor with the pine nuts, garlic and Parmesan cheese. Process until finely chopped.
2 With the motor running, add the olive oil in a thin stream and process until well combined. Season, to taste, with salt and pepper.
NOTE: To toast pine nuts, either place in a small pan and stir over low heat until golden; or grill until golden, stirring to prevent burning.

GARLIC
The intensity of garlic when used as a flavouring depends on how it is prepared. Whole garlic added to soups or sauces and cooked slowly will be mild; finely minced garlic will be strong and pungent, as its oils are released in the mashing; and whole or half cloves of garlic can be used to flavour cooking oil (the cloves are removed from the hot oil to leave a subtle garlic flavour).

ABOVE: Basil Pesto (with pasta)

CORIANDER CHUTNEY

Preparation time: 15 minutes
Total cooking time: Nil
Makes about 250 ml (8 fl oz)

90 g (3 oz) fresh coriander (leaves,
   stems and roots)
3 tablespoons desiccated coconut
1 tablespoon soft brown sugar
1 teaspoon salt
1 tablespoon grated fresh ginger
1 small onion, chopped
2 tablespoons lemon juice
1–2 small green chillies

1 Wash, dry and roughly chop all parts of the
fresh coriander. Place in a food processor with
the coconut, brown sugar, salt, ginger, onion
and lemon juice.
2 Remove the seeds from the chillies. Roughly
chop the chillies and add to the bowl; process
for about 1 minute or until finely chopped.
Serve chilled. Store, covered, in the refrigerator
for up to 2 days.

SPICY TOMATO SALSA

Preparation time: 15 minutes
Total cooking time: 2–3 minutes
Makes about 375 ml (12 fl oz)

1 red serrano or jalapeño chilli
3 medium ripe tomatoes, finely chopped
1 small red (Spanish) onion, finely chopped
3 tablespoons chopped fresh coriander leaves
2 tablespoons lime juice

1 Roast the chilli by holding over a gas flame
(using tongs or a fork), or cooking under a hot
grill, until the skin is blackened and blistered.
Cover with a tea towel, leave to cool, then peel
away the skin. Cut chilli in half and scrape out
the seeds; discard seeds. Finely chop the flesh.
2 Combine all the ingredients in a bowl and
leave to stand for 30 minutes to allow all the
flavours to combine. Salsa will keep for up to
3 days in the refrigerator.

CHILLI JAM

Preparation time: 25 minutes
Total cooking time: 35 minutes
Makes about 250 ml (8 fl oz)

12 red jalapeño chillies
2 medium ripe tomatoes
1 small onion, finely chopped
1 green apple, finely grated
1/2 cup (125 ml/4 fl oz) red wine vinegar
1/2 cup (125 g/4 oz) sugar

1 Cut the chillies in half lengthways; remove
and discard the seeds. Lay the chillies, cut side
down, on an oven tray and place under a hot
grill until the skin is black. Cover with a tea
towel; allow to cool.
2 Cut a small cross in the base (opposite stem
end) of the tomatoes. Place in a small bowl,
cover with boiling water and set aside for
2 minutes. Drain and cool. Peel skin from the
chillies and tomatoes; chop the flesh finely.
3 Combine the onion, apple, vinegar and sugar
with the tomatoes and chillies in a medium pan.
Stir until sugar has dissolved; bring to the boil.
Reduce heat and simmer for 30 minutes. Store,
covered, in the refrigerator for up to a month.
NOTE: Chilli jam can be used sparingly as a
relish with cheese, or added to soups and stews
for extra spice.

COCONUTS
When harvested, coconuts
are covered in a pliable
green shell, their flesh is
soft and moist and they
are filled with juice. When
they mature, the shell
hardens and the outer
green husk is removed to
reveal the brown fibrous
shell. Weight is the most
important factor, when
choosing a coconut—the
heavier the nut, the juicier
it will be. Make sure the
'eyes' look dry and there
is no smell of mould.

*BELOW: Chilli Jam
(with cheeses and
char-grilled vegetables)*

VANILLA

Vanilla comes from the seed pod of a tropical climbing orchid. This pod is usually referred to as a bean, which it resembles. To use, the whole bean is split lengthways to release the tiny seeds contained inside. It can then be used to infuse milk or custard, or buried in sugar to impart its flavour. It is available in a liquid form, known as extract or essence, which can vary in strength. A good guide to the quality of the essence is its price—the best quality is expensive, but strong, and needs only to be used in small amounts.

HOT CHOCOLATE SAUCE

Preparation time: 5 minutes
Total cooking time: 20 minutes
Makes about 315 ml (10 fl oz)

200 g (6 1/2 oz) dark chocolate, chopped
3/4 cup (185 ml/6 fl oz) water
1 tablespoon caster sugar
1/2 teaspoon vanilla essence
1/4 cup (60 ml/2 fl oz) cream
10 g (1/3 oz) butter
1 tablespoon rum or brandy, optional

1 Stir the chocolate, water and sugar in a medium heatproof bowl over a small pan of simmering water until chocolate has melted. Continue cooking over low heat 15 minutes, stirring occasionally.
2 Remove from the heat and stir in the vanilla, cream, butter, and rum or brandy, if using. Serve.
NOTE: Store for up to 2 weeks in a screw-top jar. Sauce will thicken on refrigeration, but can be reheated gently to serve. Serve hot over ice cream or as a sauce for profiteroles, waffles and pancakes.

CREME ANGLAISE

Preparation time: 5 minutes
Total cooking time: 10 minutes
Serves 4-6

3 egg yolks
2 tablespoons caster sugar
1 1/2 cups (375 ml/12 fl oz) milk
1/2 teaspoon vanilla essence

1 Whisk the yolks and sugar in a bowl for 2 minutes or until light and creamy. Heat the milk in a small pan until almost boiling; pour onto egg mixture, stirring constantly.
2 Return the mixture to the pan and stir over low heat for about 5 minutes or until it has slightly thickened. Do not allow to boil or the custard will curdle. Remove from heat and stir in vanilla essence; transfer to a jug to serve.
NOTE: This sauce is best made 30 minutes before serving. Cover surface with plastic wrap to prevent a skin forming. Serve as you would any custard, with poached fruit and puddings.

BUTTERSCOTCH SAUCE

Preparation time: 5 minutes
Total cooking time: 15 minutes
Makes about 375 ml (12 fl oz)

125 g (4 oz) butter
1/2 cup (95 g/1 1/4 oz) soft brown sugar
2 tablespoons golden syrup
1/2 cup (125 ml/4 fl oz) cream
1 teaspoon vanilla essence

1 Combine the butter and sugar in a medium pan. Stir over low heat until the butter has melted and the sugar has dissolved. Bring mixture to the boil.
2 Add the golden syrup and cream. Reduce heat and simmer for 10 minutes, or until the sauce has thickened slightly. Remove from the heat and add the vanilla. Serve hot or cold. This mixture will thicken on standing. Serve spooned over ice cream, and with waffles or pancakes.

BERRY COULIS

Preparation time: 8 minutes
Total cooking time: Nil
Makes about 250–375 ml (8–12 fl oz)

250 g (8 oz) strawberries, raspberries or blackberries
2–4 tablespoons icing sugar
1 tablespoon lemon juice
1–2 tablespoons Cointreau or Grand Marnier (optional)

1 Hull the strawberries. Place the berries in a blender or food processor. Add the icing sugar and lemon juice; blend or process until smooth.
2 Add Cointreau or Grand Marnier, to taste. This sauce will keep, covered and refrigerated, for up to 3 days. Serve it with fresh and cooked whole fruit, tartlets and ice cream or cream.
NOTE: Use fresh or frozen fruit—frozen berries are available from some supermarkets. Sieve the fruit if a smooth sauce is required. For Mango Coulis, use 2 mangoes, peeled, seeded and puréed, or frozen mango purée. Proceed as above.

OPPOSITE PAGE: CLOCKWISE, FROM TOP LEFT: Hot Chocolate Sauce; Crème Anglaise; Berry Coulis; Butterscotch Sauce

DESSERTS

Sweet pies, warm sticky puddings, home-made mousses and soufflés—even the printed words start the taste buds tingling. And that's nothing compared to the sight, aroma and taste of a seductively luscious sweet course presented at the end of a meal (who said anything about being full?). The ideas in this sensational selection are just as thrilling for the cook, too, because they're all from the 'to die for' rather than the 'too hard' recipe box.

CHOCOLATE

The Aztecs of Mexico used the beans of the cacao tree to make a drink, but it was the Spanish explorer Cortez who first brought them to Europe in 1528. For a long time, the Spanish tried to keep the existence of chocolate a secret, and were so successful that Dutch and English pirates would throw the beans overboard if they were captured as part of a cargo. London's first chocolate shop opened in 1657 but high customs duty kept chocolate a luxury for the fashionable rich until the nineteenth century.

ABOVE: Blueberry Cheesecake

BLUEBERRY CHEESECAKE

Preparation time: 40 minutes + refrigeration
Total cooking time: 45–50 minutes
Serves 8–10

125 g (4 oz) butter
1 cup (100 g/3^1/3 oz) rolled oats
100 g (3^1/3 oz) wheatmeal biscuits, finely crushed
2 tablespoons soft brown sugar

Filling

375 g (12 oz) light cream cheese
100 g (3^1/3 oz) fresh ricotta cheese
^{1}/3 cup (90 g/3 oz) caster sugar
^{1}/2 cup (125 g/4 oz) sour cream
2 eggs
1 tablespoon finely grated orange rind
1 tablespoon plain flour

Topping

250 g (8 oz) fresh blueberries
^{3}/4 cup (240 g/7^1/2 oz) spreadable blackberry
  fruit or conserve
^{1}/4 cup (60 ml/2 fl oz) cherry brandy

1 Brush a 20 cm (8 inch) round deep springform tin with melted butter or oil and line the base with non-stick baking paper. Melt the butter in a pan, add the oats and biscuit crumbs and mix well. Stir in the sugar. Press half the biscuit mixture into the base of the tin and gradually press the remainder around the sides, using a glass to firm it into place, but not all the way up to the rim. Refrigerate for 10–15 minutes. Preheat oven to moderate 180°C (350°F/Gas 4).

2 **To make Filling:** Beat the cream cheese, ricotta, sugar and sour cream with electric beaters until smooth. Beat in the eggs, orange rind and flour until smooth. Put the tin on a flat oven tray to catch any drips, pour the filling into the crust and bake for 40–45 minutes, or until the filling is just set. Remove from the oven but leave in the tin to cool.

3 **To make Topping:** Scatter the blueberries on top of the cheesecake. Sieve the spreadable fruit or conserve into a small pan with the brandy. Stir over medium heat until smooth and then simmer for 2–3 minutes. Carefully brush over the blueberries. Refrigerate for several hours or overnight, until well chilled.

CHOCOLATE HAZELNUT OMELETTE

Preparation time: 20 minutes
Total cooking time: 15 minutes
Serves 4

3 tablespoons finely chopped hazelnuts

60 g (2 oz) dark chocolate, roughly chopped

4 egg yolks

3 tablespoons caster sugar

5 egg whites

salt

30 g (1 oz) unsalted butter

1 tablespoon cocoa powder

1 Stir hazelnuts in a dry pan over medium heat until golden. Set aside.

2 Place the chocolate in a small heatproof bowl over a pan of simmering water. Stir until melted. Allow to cool slightly.

3 Using electric beaters, beat the egg yolks and sugar for 1 minute or until thick. Add the melted chocolate and beat well.

4 Beat the whites with a pinch of salt until stiff peaks form. Fold a third at a time into chocolate mixture. Fold through the hazelnuts. Preheat grill.

5 Melt the butter in a medium frying pan. When butter is foaming pour in the chocolate mixture. Swirl pan until mixture evenly covers base. Cook over low heat for 1–2 minutes or until set half-way through and bubbles have formed on top. Place under grill, cook until golden. Divide into 4 wedges and place on serving plates. Dust with sifted cocoa. Serve with vanilla ice cream and fresh or frozen berries.

RICH CHOCOLATE SELF-SAUCING PUDDING

Preparation time: 20 minutes
Total cooking time: 45–50 minutes
Serves 6

1¹/₂ cups (185 g/6 oz) self-raising flour

¹/₄ cup (30 g/1 oz) cocoa powder

³/₄ cup (185 g/6 oz) caster sugar

90 g (3 oz) butter, melted

³/₄ cup (185 ml/6 fl oz) milk

2 eggs, lightly beaten

Sauce

1¹/₂ cups (375 ml/12 fl oz) milk

1 cup (250 ml/8 fl oz) water

185 g (6 oz) dark chocolate, chopped

1 Preheat oven to moderate 180°C (350°F/Gas 4). Brush a 9-cup capacity deep ovenproof dish with oil or melted butter.

2 Sift flour and cocoa into a large bowl; add sugar, make a well in the centre. Add butter and combined milk and eggs. Using a wooden spoon, stir until just combined and smooth; do not over-beat. Pour into prepared dish.

3 To make Sauce: Place the milk, water and chocolate in a small pan; stir over low heat until melted and smooth. Pour slowly over the pudding mixture. Bake for 45–50 minutes, until firm to the touch. Serve with cream or ice cream and fresh fruit, if desired.

COOKING WITH CHOCOLATE

When chocolate is called for in a recipe, buy a good-quality 'cooking chocolate'. Compound chocolate, which has extra vegetable fats added, sets much more quickly than cooking chocolate and is best when used for making things such as chocolate decorations.

LEFT: Chocolate Hazelnut Omelette
ABOVE: Rich Chocolate Self-saucing Pudding

1 Preheat oven to warm 160°C (315 F/Gas 2–3). Brush four 185 ml (6 fl oz) ramekins with oil or melted butter. Place cream, milk and vanilla bean in small pan. Stir over low heat until almost boiling. Remove from heat; cool. Remove vanilla bean and cut in half. Scrape out inside of one half of bean (save the other half for later use) and add the seeds to the milk mixture.

2 Beat the eggs, yolks and caster sugar in a small bowl and gradually add the cream mixture. Pour into the prepared ramekins. Stand the ramekins in a baking dish and pour in enough hot water to come halfway up the sides of the ramekins. Place a piece of foil lightly over baking dish to cover the ramekins.

3 Bake for 45 minutes, or until the custard is set and a knife comes out clean when inserted into the centre. Remove the ramekins from the water bath and set aside to cool. Refrigerate for several hours or overnight.

4 Preheat the grill to high heat. Sprinkle the combined brown sugar and cinnamon over the top of each custard. Place the custards under the grill until tops are dark brown and bubbling. Remove from the grill and refrigerate for 5 minutes before serving.

NOTE: As a variation, add a spoonful of blueberries to the bottom of each ramekin and top with custard before baking. This custard is also delicious served with fresh berries.

PEACH BAKLAVA

Preparation time: 40 minutes
Total cooking time: 20–25 minutes
Serves 8

★ ★

6 sheets filo pastry
60 g (2 oz) butter, melted
2/3 cup (85 g/2 3/4 oz) slivered almonds
1 1/2 teaspoons ground cinnamon
1/2 cup (95 g/3 1/4 oz) soft brown sugar
3/4 cup (185 ml/6 fl oz) orange juice, strained
4 peaches
icing sugar, for dusting

1 Preheat the oven to moderate 180°C (350°F/Gas 4). Cut each sheet of pastry into 8 squares. Line eight 1-cup muffin tins with 3 layers of filo pastry, brush the pieces with melted butter to stick them together and overlap the sheets at angles.

PERFECT BRULEES

A perfect crème brûlée (literally 'burnt cream' in French) should have a crisp caramelised crust over a creamy custard. To create the best crust, always use a grill with a gas flame—this provides the instant high heat needed to caramelise the sugar. Extreme as it may sound, professional cooks use a small blowtorch, available from hardware stores.

ABOVE: Vanilla Bean Custard Brûlée

VANILLA BEAN CUSTARD BRULEE

Preparation time: 10 minutes
+ 3 hours refrigeration
Total cooking time: 55 minutes
Serves 4

★ ★

1 cup (250 ml/8 fl oz) cream
1 cup (250 ml/8 fl oz) milk
1 whole vanilla bean
2 eggs
2 egg yolks
1/4 cup (60 g/2 oz) caster sugar
1/3 cup (60 g/2 oz) soft brown sugar
1/2 teaspoon ground cinnamon

1 Score a small cross in the base of each peach. Put in a heatproof bowl, cover with boiling water and leave for 2 minutes.

2 Remove from hot water and plunge into cold water to cool quickly. Peel the skin away from the cross.

2 Combine the almonds, cinnamon and half the sugar in a small bowl. Sprinkle over the bases then cover with the 3 final squares of filo pastry brushed with butter. Bake for 10–15 minutes.

3 Meanwhile, dissolve the remaining sugar in the orange juice, bring to the boil, reduce the heat and simmer. Halve the peaches and slice thinly, add to the syrup and stir gently to coat the fruit. Simmer for 2–3 minutes; lift from the pan with a slotted spoon. Arrange the peaches on the pastries, dust with icing sugar and serve with clotted cream or ice cream.

NOTE: Peaches can be peeled if you like. Tinned peaches can be used instead of fresh.

1 Peel apples, remove cores and cut apples into quarters. Place water, juice, sugar, cloves and mint in a pan. Stir over low heat without boiling until sugar dissolves. Bring to the boil.

2 Add apples to pan. Cook over low heat with lid tilted to let steam escape, for 10 minutes or until apples are soft but not breaking up. Add basil. Remove from heat, set aside until cold.

3 Carefully remove apples and place in a bowl; pour syrup through a sieve over top of apples. Serve chilled with berries and cream or yoghurt.

*ABOVE: Peach Baklava
BELOW: Poached Apples with Cloves, Mint and Basil*

POACHED APPLES WITH CLOVES, MINT AND BASIL

Preparation time: 15 minutes
Total cooking time: 30 minutes
Serves 4

4 large or 6 small green apples
2 1/2 cups (600 ml/20 fl oz) water
2 tablespoons lemon juice
1/2 cup (125 g/4 oz) sugar
4 whole cloves
4 sprigs fresh mint
6 leaves fresh basil
cream or yoghurt, for serving

SCENTED GERANIUMS
Geraniums are wonderful in both the kitchen and the garden. There are up to 50 different scented varieties in a multitude of colours and textures. Their leaves can be used in teas, biscuits, muffins and cakes and they are great in finger bowls—just lightly crush the lemon-scented leaves in water.

ABOVE: Vanilla Almond Biscotti with Geranium Cream

VANILLA ALMOND BISCOTTI WITH GERANIUM CREAM

Preparation time: 1 hour + overnight standing
Total cooking time: 1 hour
Serves 6–8

★ ★

1/2 cup (125 g/4 oz) caster sugar
2 tablespoons caster sugar, extra
1 vanilla bean, split in half
3 rose-scented geranium leaves

Biscotti

125 g (4 oz) blanched almonds
3 egg whites
3/4 cup (90 g/3 oz) plain flour

Geranium Cream

1 cup (250 ml/8 fl oz) cream
1/2 cup (125 ml/4 fl oz) thick (double) cream
selection of fruits in season: grapes, kiwi fruit,
    strawberries, blueberries, blackberries,
    raspberries or mulberries

1 Preheat oven to moderate 180°C (350 F/Gas 4). Place each measure of caster sugar into a separate screw-top jar. Add vanilla bean to the 1/2 cup of sugar and geranium leaves to the 2 tablespoons of sugar. Shake each jar for 10 seconds, then set aside for at least 2 hours to allow flavours to develop.
2 **To make Biscotti:** Brush a 26 x 8 x 4.5 cm (10 1/2 x 3 x 1 3/4 inch) bar tin with oil or melted butter; line the base and sides with baking paper. Spread the blanched almonds on a baking tray and bake in the oven for 4 minutes or until the nuts are lightly golden; cool.
3 Place the egg whites in a clean, dry bowl. Using electric beaters, beat until stiff peaks form. Gradually add the vanilla-scented sugar, beating constantly until the mixture is thick and glossy and the sugar has dissolved.
4 Transfer the mixture to a large bowl. Add the sifted flour and almonds. Using a metal spoon, gently fold the ingredients together. Spread into the prepared tin and smooth the surface. Bake for 25 minutes; remove from oven and allow to cool completely in the tin. Turn the loaf out and then wrap in aluminium foil. Refrigerate overnight.
5 Preheat the oven to warm 160°C (315°F/Gas 2–3). Brush two baking trays with oil or melted butter. Using a sharp serrated knife, cut the cooked loaf into 5 mm (1/4 inch) slices.

Arrange the slices on the baking trays; bake for 30 minutes or until lightly golden and crisp.

6 To make Geranium Cream: Using electric beaters, beat the geranium-flavoured sugar with cream until firm peaks form. Using a metal spoon, fold into thick cream. Trim fruits and serve with biscotti and cream. Vanilla Almond Biscotti will keep for up to 2 weeks in an airtight container. Fruits and cream are best prepared on the day of serving. Vanilla and geranium sugars can be prepared up to 2 weeks in advance.

NOTE: This dessert can be served on individual plates but would make an attractive platter for a party or buffet. Vanilla Almond Biscotti are also delicious served plain, as an accompaniment to coffee. As a variation, other nuts can be used instead of almonds. Roasted hazelnuts or pistachios are particularly delicious.

PEACH CHARLOTTES WITH MELBA SAUCE

Preparation time: 30 minutes
  + 20 minutes standing
Total cooking time: 40 minutes
Serves 4

★★

1 cup (250 g/8 oz) sugar
4 cups (1 litre) water
6 medium peaches
1/3 cup (80 ml/2 3/4 fl oz) peach liqueur
2 loaves brioche
100 g (3 1/3 oz) butter, melted
1/2 cup (160 g/5 1/4 oz) apricot jam, warmed
  and sieved

Melba Sauce

315 g (10 oz) fresh or thawed frozen raspberries
2 tablespoons icing sugar

1 Preheat the oven to moderate 180°C (350°F/Gas 4). Brush four 1-cup capacity ovenproof ramekins or moulds with melted butter. Combine the sugar and water in large, heavy-based pan. Stir over medium heat until the sugar completely dissolves. Bring to the boil, reduce heat slightly and add the whole peaches. Simmer, covered for 20 minutes. Drain and cool. Peel the skins and slice the flesh thickly. Place in a bowl, sprinkle with liqueur and set aside for 20 minutes.

2 Cut the brioche into 1 cm (1/2 inch) thick slices; remove the crusts. With a scone-cutter, cut rounds to fit the tops and bases of each dish. Cut the remaining slices into 2 cm (3/4 inch) wide fingers and trim to fit the height of the dish. Dip the first round into melted butter and place in the base of the dish. Dip brioche fingers into melted butter and press around the sides of dish, overlapping slightly. Line all the dishes in this manner.

3 Fill the lined dishes evenly with peach slices and top with the last round of brioche dipped in melted butter. Press to seal. Place the dishes on a baking tray and bake for 20 minutes. Turn onto serving plates, brush with jam and pour Melba Sauce alongside. Serve with fresh berries, if desired.

4 To make Melba Sauce: Process the berries in a food processor and add icing sugar, to taste. Push through a fine sieve.

NOTE: The peaches can be cooked, the dishes lined with brioche and the sauce made, up to 6 hours ahead. Refrigerate the charlottes, then fill and bake them close to serving time.

ABOVE: Peach Charlottes with Melba Sauce

SUMMER FRUITS Fresh flowers

everywhere, long balmy days, the first swim of the year, plus the promise of rich, ripe

stone fruit and berries just around the corner—what better time of year than summer?

RASPBERRY FOOL

Beat 1¼ cups (315 ml/10 fl oz) of cream until soft peaks form, add ⅓ cup (40 g/1⅓ oz) of sifted icing sugar and beat until just combined. Lightly crush 250 g (8 oz) of fresh raspberries with a fork. Fold crushed berries through cream; refrigerate for up to 2 hours. To serve, spoon into dessert glasses and accompany with brandy snaps or wafers.

MANGO ICE CREAM

Heat 1¼ cups (315 ml/10 fl oz) of cream until it just comes to the boil; remove from the heat. Whisk 4 egg yolks in a heatproof bowl with ¾ cup (185 g/ 6 oz) caster sugar until thick and pale. Gradually add hot cream to the egg mixture, whisking constantly. Return all this to the pan and stir over very low heat for about 5 minutes until the

mixture thickens slightly. Be careful not to let it boil or it will curdle. Pour the mixture into a clean bowl and set aside to cool, stirring occasionally. Peel 2 large mangoes, remove stone and purée the flesh in blender. Stir into the cooled custard; pour into a shallow metal tray. Cover, freeze until firm. Transfer to a bowl, beat with electric beaters until smooth. Return to tray, freeze until firm.

NECTARINE TARTS

Preheat the oven to moderately hot 200°C (400°F/Gas 6) and brush a flat oven tray with melted butter. Cut a sheet of thawed frozen puff pastry into four squares. Brush all over with melted butter and dust generously with icing sugar. Arrange thick slices of nectarine diagonally across the pastry, then fold two corners over and seal in the centre. Brush the pastry parcels again with melted butter and place them on the prepared tray. Bake for 20 minutes or until golden. Dust with more icing sugar, and serve warm with thick cream.

FRESH FRUIT WITH BUTTERSCOTCH MASCARPONE

Combine 60 g (2 oz) of butter, ½ cup (95 g/3¼ oz) of soft brown sugar and 1 cup (250 ml/8 fl oz) of cream in a

small pan. Stir over low heat until the mixture is melted and smooth and bring to the boil. Reduce the heat and simmer for about 3 minutes. Choose a selection of seasonal fruits such as berries, figs, plums, apricots, peaches or starfruit and serve with dollops of mascarpone or cream. (Also delicious with fresh ricotta.) Drizzle the butterscotch over the fruit or mascarpone. Serve immediately.

CHERRY GRATIN

Remove the stems and stones from 500 g (1 lb) of cherries and arrange the cherries in a shallow heatproof dish. Combine ½ cup (125 ml/4 fl oz) of cream and ½ cup (125 ml/4 fl oz) of thick (double) cream in a pan and heat the mixture until it just boils. Whisk 2 egg yolks together with 2 tablespoons caster sugar in a medium heatproof bowl until thick and

pale. Pour in the hot cream gradually, whisking until combined. Return the mixture to the pan and stir over very low heat for about 5 minutes, until it thickens. Make sure that the mixture does not boil. Cool slightly, then pour over the cherries. To prepare ahead of time, you can refrigerate gratin for up to 4 hours at this stage. To serve, sprinkle 2 tablespoons of soft brown sugar evenly over the surface and cook under a hot grill until the top is browned and just bubbling. Sprinkle with icing sugar just before serving.

CLOKWISE, FROM TOP LEFT:
Nectarine Tarts; Fresh Fruit with
Butterscotch Mascarpone; Raspberry
Fool; Cherry Gratin; Mango Ice Cream

257

dish on a large oven tray and bake for 20–25 minutes or until the soufflé is well-risen and cooked through. Cut the collars from the dishes and serve the soufflés immediately, sprinkled with sifted icing sugar.

STICKY DATE PUDDING

Preparation time: 35 minutes
Total cooking time: 55 minutes
Serves 6-8

200 g (6¹/2 oz) dates, pitted and chopped
I cup (250 ml/8 fl oz) water
I teaspoon bicarbonate of soda
100 g (3¹/3 oz) butter
²/3 cup (160 g/5¹/4 oz) caster sugar
2 eggs, lightly beaten
I teaspoon vanilla essence
1¹/2 cups (185 g/6 oz) self-raising flour

Sauce

I cup (185 g/6 oz) soft brown sugar
¹/2 cup (125 ml/4 fl oz) cream
100 g (3¹/3 oz) butter

I Preheat the oven to moderate 180°C (350°F/Gas 4). Brush a 20 cm (8 inch) square

HOT PASSIONFRUIT SOUFFLE

Preparation time: 20 minutes
Total cooking time: 20–25 minutes
Serves 4

2 egg yolks
¹/2 cup (125 g/4 oz) passionfruit pulp
(about 6 passionfruit)
2 tablespoons lemon juice
³/4 cup (90 g/3 oz) icing sugar
6 egg whites
icing sugar, for decorating

I Preheat oven to hot 210°C (415°F/Gas 6–7). Place a collar of baking paper to come about 3 cm above the sides of 4 small ramekins. Tie securely with string. Lightly grease base and side of ramekins (including the paper) and sprinkle with caster sugar; shake out excess.
2 Combine yolks, pulp, lemon juice and half the icing sugar in a large bowl. Whisk until well combined. With electric beaters, beat egg whites in a large bowl until soft peaks form. Gradually add the remaining icing sugar, beating well after each addition.
3 Using a large metal spoon, fold the egg white mixture in batches through the passionfruit mixture. Spoon into dishes. Using a flat-bladed knife, cut through the mixture in a circular motion 2 cm (³/4 inch) from the edge. Place the

ABOVE: Hot
Passionfruit Soufflé
RIGHT: Sticky
Date Pudding

cake tin with oil or melted butter. Line the base with baking paper. Combine the dates and water in a small pan. Bring to the boil and remove from heat. Stir in soda and set aside to cool to room temperature.

2 Using electric beaters, beat the butter and sugar in a small bowl until light and creamy. Add the eggs gradually, beating thoroughly after each addition. Add the essence and beat until combined. Transfer to a large bowl.

3 Using a metal spoon, fold in the flour and dates with the liquid and stir until just combined—do not over-beat. Pour into prepared tin and bake for 50 minutes, until a skewer comes out clean when inserted into centre of pudding. Leave in tin for 10 minutes before turning out.

4 To make Sauce: Combine sugar, cream and butter in a small pan; stir until butter melts and sugar dissolves. Bring to boil, reduce heat and simmer for 2 minutes. Cut the pudding into wedges and place on serving plates. Pour hot sauce over. Serve immediately, with extra cream and raspberries, if desired.

APPLE PIE

Preparation time: 40 minutes
  + 20 minutes refrigeration
Total cooking time: 55 minutes
Serves 6

1 1/4 cups (155 g/5 oz) plain flour
1/4 cup (30 g/1 oz) icing sugar
90 g (3 oz) butter, cut into pieces
2 egg yolks, lightly beaten
1 tablespoon iced water

Filling

12 cooking apples
50 g (1 2/3 oz) butter
1/4 cup (45 g/1 1/2 oz) soft brown sugar
1 teaspoon cinnamon
1 teaspoon mixed spice
1 egg white
1 teaspoon caster sugar

1 Preheat oven to hot 210°C (415°F/Gas 6–7). Brush the rim of a 23 cm (9 inch) pie dish with melted butter. Sift flour and sugar into a large bowl; add the butter. Rub the butter into the flour with your fingertips until the mixture is

fine and crumbly. Add the yolks and mix with a knife to a firm dough, adding a little water if necessary. Turn onto a lightly floured surface and press together until smooth.

2 Roll the pastry out on baking paper to a 25 cm (10 inch) round, cut 1 cm (1/2 inch) wide strips from the edge, cover rim of dish. Cover dish and remaining pastry with plastic wrap; refrigerate for 20 minutes.

3 Peel and core apples, cut each into 8 slices. Melt butter in large non-stick frying pan and add brown sugar and spices. Stir over medium heat until sugar dissolves; add apples, toss to coat with butter mixture. Cook, covered, for 10 minutes, turning occasionally, until apples are soft but still hold their shape. Remove the lid and cook for another 5 minutes, until liquid is reduced; cool.

4 Place cooled apple and any liquid into the pie dish. Place pastry over fruit, pressing lightly onto the rim. Trim the edges, pinch together to seal. Decorate with trimmings. Brush with egg white and sprinkle with sugar. Bake for 40 minutes, until golden. Serve warm with custard.

APPLES

When a recipe calls for apples, choose a variety that will maintain its shape and flavour during cooking. Tart apples with a high percentage of acidic tannin cope best with sautéeing, poaching or baking, while dessert apples, which have a sweet taste and are wonderful raw, tend to lose their shape and become very watery when baked. The ever-versatile Granny Smith apple is ideal for cooking, as it remains firm, and is also tasty enough to eat raw.

ABOVE: Apple Pie

MERINGUES

Apparently, Napoleon so loved these concoctions of whipped egg whites and sugar that he named them after the small Swiss town of Meringen where they were served to him. When cooking, it is important to use a very low oven setting so that the meringue, with its high sugar content, doesn't burn but just dries out. For perfect meringues, bake for the specified time, then turn off the oven, prop open the door with a wooden spoon and leave them inside until the oven is completely cold.

ABOVE: Strawberry Meringue Stacks

STRAWBERRY MERINGUE STACKS

Preparation time: 25 minutes
Total cooking time: 40 minutes
Serves 6

★★

4 egg whites
1 cup (250 g/8 oz) caster sugar
500 g (1 lb) strawberries, hulled
1¼ cups (315 ml/10 fl oz) cream, whipped

1 Preheat oven to slow 150°C (300°F/Gas 2). Brush two 32 x 28 cm (13 x 11 inch) oven trays with melted butter or oil. Cut non-stick baking paper to fit trays. Using an 8 cm (3 inch) round cutter as a guide, mark 12 circles onto paper, and place pencil-side down on trays.
2 Place egg whites in a medium, clean dry bowl. Using electric beaters, beat until soft peaks form. Add the sugar gradually, beating constantly until mixture is thick and glossy and all the sugar has dissolved. Spread meringue into rounds on the prepared trays. Bake for 40 minutes then turn off heat and allow meringues to cool in oven.
3 Place half the strawberries into a food processor or blender and blend until completely liquid. Slice the remaining strawberries and fold through whipped cream. To serve, sandwich two meringue rounds together with cream

mixture and place on each plate. Pour some strawberry sauce around base of the meringue.
NOTE: The meringues can be made up to two days in advance and stored in an airtight container. Strawberry sauce can be made up to one day ahead. Make the strawberry cream mixture up to two hours in advance. Store the sauce and cream, covered, in the refrigerator. After assembling, serve immediately. If you prefer a sweeter sauce, a little caster sugar can be added. Garnish with strawberry leaves to serve, if you wish.

FAST CARAMEL, NUT AND BANANA PARFAIT

PLACE 100 g (3⅓ oz) butter, ½ cup (95 g/3¼ oz) of soft brown sugar, 2 tablespoons of golden syrup, ¼ cup (60 g/2 oz) of sour cream and 1 cup (250 ml/8 fl oz) of cream in a pan and whisk over low heat until all the sugar is dissolved. Simmer gently, without stirring, for 5 minutes (be careful it doesn't boil over) and remove from heat. When bubbles have subsided, stir in ½ cup (160 g/5¼ oz) condensed milk. Allow to cool slightly. Layer sliced banana, scoops of vanilla ice cream, crushed pecans and warm caramel sauce in dessert glasses. Drizzle a little chocolate liqueur over the top of each parfait if you like. Serves 4–6.

1 Using a sharp knife, cut through the flesh down either side of the stone.

2 Score the flesh in a criss-cross pattern.

3 Invert the halves to push out the flesh.

MARINATED FIGS WITH RASPBERRY SAUCE

Preparation time: 20 minutes + standing
Total cooking time: 5–10 minutes
Serves 4

6 fresh figs, halved
1¼ cups (315 ml/10 fl oz) dessert wine
1 cinnamon stick
1 tablespoon soft brown sugar
315 g (10 oz) fresh raspberries
¼ cup (60 g/2 oz) caster sugar
1 teaspoon lemon juice
½ cup (110 g/3²/₃ oz) mascarpone

1 Place figs in a glass or ceramic bowl. Combine wine, cinnamon and sugar in a small pan and warm over low heat. When sugar has dissolved, pour over figs. Cover; allow to stand for 2 hours.
2 Set aside a few raspberries for garnishing, if you wish, and blend the rest with the caster sugar in a food processor. Sieve, then stir in the lemon juice.
3 Drain the figs; strain and reserve the marinade. Grill the figs until golden. Pour a little raspberry sauce onto each dessert plate (enough to cover the base). Arrange 3 fig halves on each plate and serve with a spoonful of mascarpone.

CITRUS DELICIOUS

Preparation time: 25 minutes
Total cooking time: 1 hour
Serves 4

½ cup (60 g/2 oz) self-raising flour
1 cup (250 g/8 oz) caster sugar
2 teaspoons grated orange rind
⅓ cup (80 ml/2¾ fl oz) orange juice
½ cup (125 ml/4 fl oz) lemon juice
125 g (4 oz) butter, melted
1 cup (250 ml/8 fl oz) milk
3 eggs, separated

1 Preheat oven to moderate 180°C (350°F/Gas 4). Lightly grease a 6-cup ovenproof dish with melted butter or oil. Sift flour into a large bowl. Add sugar; stir until combined. Mix orange rind and juice in bowl with lemon juice, butter, milk and yolks; whisk lightly with a fork until smooth. Add to flour mixture, stir to combine.
2 Beat egg whites in a small bowl with electric beaters until stiff peaks form. Using a metal spoon, fold gently into flour mixture. Pour into dish. Place dish in a deep baking dish. Pour enough hot water into baking dish to come halfway up sides. Bake for 1 hour or until firm in centre. Remove dish from water and serve.

ABOVE: Marinated Figs with Raspberry Sauce

PUMPKIN PIE

Preparation time: 30 minutes
+ 30 minutes standing
Total cooking time: 1 hour 15 minutes
Serves 8

★★

1¼ cups (155 g/5 oz) plain flour
100 g (3⅓ oz) butter, chopped
2 teaspoons caster sugar
4 tablespoons chilled water
1 egg yolk, lightly beaten, mixed with
   1 tablespoon milk, for glazing

Filling

2 eggs, lightly beaten
¾ cup (140 g/4⅔ oz) soft brown sugar

BELOW: Pumpkin Pie

500 g (1 lb) pumpkin, cooked, mashed
   and cooled
⅓ cup (80 ml/2¾ fl oz) cream
1 tablespoon sweet sherry
1 teaspoon ground cinnamon
½ teaspoon ground nutmeg
½ teaspoon ground ginger

1 Sift the flour into a large bowl and add chopped butter. Using your fingertips, rub the butter into the flour for 2 minutes or until the mixture is fine and crumbly. Stir in the caster sugar. Add almost all the liquid and mix to a firm dough, adding more liquid if necessary. Turn onto a lightly floured surface and press together for 1 minute or until smooth.
2 Roll out the pastry, on a sheet of baking paper, until it is large enough to cover the base and side of a 23 cm (9 inch) diameter pie dish. Line the dish with pastry, trim away excess and crimp the edges. Roll out the pastry trimmings to a thickness of 2 mm (¼ inch). Using a sharp knife, cut out leaf shapes of different sizes. Score vein markings onto the leaves. Refrigerate the pastry-lined dish and the leaf shapes for about 20 minutes.
3 Cut a sheet of greaseproof paper to cover the pastry-lined dish. Spread a layer of dried beans or rice over the paper. Bake for 10 minutes, remove from oven and discard paper and beans or rice. Return the pastry to the oven for 10 minutes or until lightly golden. Meanwhile, place the leaves on an oven tray lined with baking paper, brush with egg glaze and bake for 10–15 minutes, until golden; set aside to cool.
4 To make Filling: Preheat the oven to moderate 180°C (350°F/Gas 4). Whisk the eggs and sugar in a large bowl. Add the cooled pumpkin, cream, sweet sherry and spices and stir to combine thoroughly. Pour the mixture into the pastry shell, smooth the surface with the back of a spoon and bake for 40 minutes or until set. If the pastry edge begins to brown too much during cooking, cover the edge with foil. Allow the pie to cool to room temperature and place the leaves on top of the filling. Serve with cream or ice cream, if desired.
NOTE: As an alternative to using the pastry trimmings to make the decoration, you can use a sheet of ready-rolled puff pastry. Cut out some leaf shapes, brush with egg white and bake on a tray, in a moderate 180°C (350°F/Gas 4) oven, until puffed and golden, about 10–15 minutes.

MINI TOFFEE PUFFS WITH LIQUEUR CREAM

Preparation time: 30 minutes
Total cooking time: 30 minutes
Serves 4-6

★★

30 g (1 oz) butter
1/4 cup (60 ml/2 fl oz) water
1/4 cup (30 g/1 oz) plain flour
1 egg, lightly beaten

Liqueur Cream

1/2 cup (125 ml/4 fl oz) cream
1 tablespoon Grand Marnier

Toffee

1 cup (250 g/8 oz) caster sugar
1/3 cup (80 ml/2¾ fl oz) water

1 Preheat oven to hot 220°C (425°F/Gas 7). Line an oven tray with baking paper. Combine the butter and water in a small pan. Stir over low heat until the butter is melted and the mixture just boils. Remove from heat and add the flour all at once. Using a wooden spoon, beat mixture until smooth. Return to heat and beat until mixture thickens and comes away from the side of the pan. Remove from heat; cool slightly. Transfer to a small bowl. Using electric beaters, add the egg gradually, beating until the mixture is thick and glossy.

2 Drop teaspoonsful of mixture about 4 cm (1½ inches) apart on prepared tray. Bake for 10 minutes, reduce heat to moderate 180°C (350°F/Gas 4) and bake for another 5–10 minutes, or until golden and well puffed. Pierce the side of each puff to release steam. Turn off oven, return puffs to the oven to dry out the inside; allow to cool.

3 **To make Liqueur Cream:** Using electric beaters, beat cream until soft peaks form. Add Grand Marnier and beat until just combined. Place cream in a piping bag fitted with a small plain nozzle. Pipe into puffs.

4 **To make Toffee:** Combine sugar and water in a small pan. Stir over low heat until sugar dissolves, brushing down sides of pan occasionally. Bring to boil, reduce heat and simmer until golden. Quickly spoon over the puffs and allow to set.

NOTE: The puffs can be made up to 6 hours in advance; store in an airtight container. Fill and coat with toffee within 1 hour of serving.

CHOCOLATE MOUSSE

Preparation time: 20 minutes
Total cooking time: 2 minutes
  + 2 hours refrigeration
Serves 4

★★

250 g (8 oz) dark chocolate
3 eggs
1/4 cup (60 g/2 oz) caster sugar
2 teaspoons dark rum
1 cup (250 ml/8 fl oz) cream, whipped
  to soft peaks

1 Place chocolate in a small heatproof bowl; stir over a pan of simmering water until chocolate has melted and mixture is smooth. Allow to cool.

2 Using electric beaters, beat the eggs and sugar in a small bowl for 5 minutes or until thick, pale and increased in volume.

3 Transfer mixture to a large bowl. Using a metal spoon, fold melted chocolate and rum into egg mixture; fold in whipped cream. Work quickly and lightly until mixture is just combined.

4 Spoon into four 1-cup capacity ramekins or dessert glasses. Refrigerate 2 hours or until set.

CHOCOLATE LEAVES

Choose a selection of non-toxic leaves (roses or ivy are good) with prominent veins on the underside. Don't pick furry leaves, as the fibres stick to the chocolate and leave it with a dull finish. Melt a little chocolate and paint it generously over the underside of the leaf with a fine brush. Leave to set, then peel away the leaf. If the coating of chocolate is too thin, it will break.

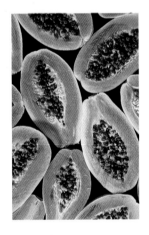

ABOVE: Mini Toffee Puffs with Liqueur Cream

ABOVE: Blueberry Pie

2 Turn the dough out onto a sheet of baking paper and press together until smooth. Roll out to a circle about 30 cm (12 inches) in diameter and cover with plastic wrap. Refrigerate for 10 minutes. Place blueberries in a bowl and sprinkle sugar, rind and cinnamon over the top.
3 Place the dough (still on baking paper) onto an oven tray. Brush the centre lightly with egg white. Pile blueberry mixture onto dough in a circle 20 cm (8 inches) in diameter; fold edges of the pastry over the filling. Bake for 30–35 minutes or until golden. Dust the top with icing sugar and serve.

CHOC-CHIP TOFU ICE CREAM

Preparation time: 20 minutes + freezing
Total cooking time: Nil
Serves 4

500 g (1 lb) silken tofu
¼ cup (60 ml/2 fl oz) maple syrup
2 tablespoons honey
3 tablespoons macadamia nut oil
1 cup (250 ml/8 fl oz) soy milk
1 cup (250 ml/8 fl oz) thickened cream
220 g (7 oz) macadamia nuts, roasted and
  roughly chopped
125 g (4 oz) dark chocolate, roughly chopped

1 Soak the tofu in hot water for 2 minutes. Plunge the tofu into iced water and allow to stand for 2 minutes; drain. Place the tofu, maple syrup, honey and macadamia nut oil in a food processor and process until smooth. Gradually add the soy milk and cream and process until the mixture is thick and creamy.
2 Transfer the mixture to a large freezer container or metal tin. Fold in macadamia nuts and chocolate. Cover with a lid or with foil and place in the freezer.
3 Gently stir the ice-cream when it is starting to freeze around the edges. Repeat the process, partially freezing and stirring twice more, then allow to freeze thoroughly.
NOTE: Make sure you use silken tofu, which is very soft, rather than firm tofu for this recipe. The silken tofu has a pleasant, creamy texture.

BLUEBERRIES

The blueberry is a truly all-American fruit. The small, dark, purplish-blue berries are collected from an evergreen shrub, with North America producing some 75 per cent of the world's entire crop. The wild berry is generally felt to be superior to the larger, sweeter, cultivated fruit—an opinion obviously shared by the Alaskan voles (small rodents) whose teeth are stained blue throughout the entire berry season.

BLUEBERRY PIE

Preparation time: 20 minutes
  + 10 minutes refrigeration
Total cooking time: 30–35 minutes
Serves 4

1½ cups (185 g/6 oz) plain flour
125 g (4 oz) butter, chopped
½ cup (60 g/2 oz) icing sugar
¼ cup (60 ml/2 fl oz) lemon juice
500 g (1 lb) fresh blueberries
3 tablespoons icing sugar, extra
1 teaspoon finely grated lemon rind
½ teaspoon ground cinnamon
1 egg white, lightly beaten

1 Preheat the oven to moderate 180°C (350°F/Gas 4). Place the flour, butter and icing sugar in a food processor. Process for 15 seconds or until fine and crumbly. Add almost all the juice and process briefly until the mixture comes together, adding more juice if necessary.

PAVLOVA ROLL WITH RASPBERRY COULIS

Preparation time: 25 minutes
Total cooking time: 15 minutes
Serves 8–10

★ ★

4 egg whites
1 cup (250 g/8 oz) caster sugar
1 teaspoon cornflour
2 teaspoons lemon juice or vinegar
2/3 cup (170 ml/5 1/2 fl oz) cream, whipped
1/4 cup (55 g/1 3/4 oz) chopped fresh berries

Raspberry Coulis

2 tablespoons brandy
250 g (8 oz) fresh raspberries, washed
   and hulled
1 tablespoon icing sugar

 Brush a 25 x 30 cm (10 x 12 inch) Swiss roll tin with oil and line with non-stick baking paper extending up 2 sides. Preheat the oven to moderate 180°C (350°F/Gas 4). Beat the egg whites into soft peaks. Gradually add 3/4 cup sugar and beat until thick and glossy. Combine 1 tablespoon sugar with the cornflour. Fold into the meringue with the lemon juice or vinegar. Spoon into the tin and smooth. Bake for 12–15 minutes until springy.

2 Put a large sheet of baking paper on top of a tea towel and generously sprinkle with the rest of the sugar. Turn the pavlova onto this, peel off the lining paper and leave for 3 minutes. Roll up pavlova from the long side using the tea towel to assist; cool. Fold berries into whipped cream.

3 Unroll the pavlova, fill with the cream mixture and re-roll without the tea towel and baking paper. Transfer to a plate and refrigerate.

4 To make Raspberry Coulis: Put the brandy, raspberries and icing sugar in a food processor and process until well blended. Serve Pavlova Roll in slices with Raspberry Coulis.

NOTE: If you prefer, a thick fruit purée may be used to fill the roll.

FAST SILKEN TOFU WITH BERRIES AND MAPLE SYRUP

DRAIN AND CUT 500 g (1 lb) silken tofu into bite-size pieces. Divide between four bowls. Top with mulberries, blueberries and strawberries. Drizzle with maple syrup and serve with almond biscotti. Serves 4.

CASTER SUGAR

Caster sugar is used in cooking because its finer granules dissolve quickly. If you are caught without any in your store cupboard, make your own by simply whizzing some sugar cubes or granulated sugar in a food processor until powdery.

ABOVE: Pavlova Roll with Raspberry Coulis

CAKES PASTRIES AND SWEET MUFFINS

Remember the creamy sponges and sweet-smelling scones that came out of the oven on rainy Saturday afternoons when you were a child? Baking is one of the family traditions that deserves to be kept alive and well, even in these fast-paced times. These recipes fulfil the brief, and more, by including a few extra servings of the best of the flavours of today.

NUTMEG DATE CAKE

Preparation time: 25 minutes
Total cooking time: 55 minutes
Serves 8–10

2 cups (375 g/12 oz) soft brown sugar, plus
   2 tablespoons
2 cups (250 g/8 oz) plain flour
2 teaspoons baking powder
125 g (4 oz) cold butter, chopped
1 teaspoon bicarbonate soda
¾ cup (185 ml/6 fl oz) milk
2 eggs, beaten
1½ teaspoons grated fresh nutmeg
375 g (12 oz) dried dates, roughly chopped
icing sugar, for dusting
whipped cream, for serving

1 Preheat the oven to moderate 180°C
(350°F/Gas 4). Brush a 22 cm (8¾ inch)
springform (spring-release) pan with melted
butter or oil; line the base with baking paper.
2 Process the 2 cups of brown sugar with the
flour and baking powder in a food processor for
10 seconds. Add butter; process for another
10 seconds until the mixture resembles fine
crumbs. Press half the mixture into the base of
the prepared tin.

3 Dissolve the soda in the milk; add the eggs
and nutmeg and whisk. Pour the mixture into
the remaining brown sugar and flour mixture
and process for another 10 seconds. Pour into
the cake tin and scatter half the dates over the
top. Bake for 55 minutes. Remove the cake
from the oven and cool in tin for 10 minutes.
Remove from tin and cool on a wire rack.
4 Place the remaining dates on top of the cake,
sprinkle with the extra brown sugar and place
under a very hot grill for about 1 minute, or
until the sugar begins to melt; cool. Dust the top
with icing sugar and serve with cream.

FAST CHOCOLATE FUDGE COOKIES

PREHEAT THE OVEN to moderate 180°C
(350°F/Gas 4). Sift ¾ cup (90 g/3 oz) of
plain flour and ½ cup (60 g/2 oz) of self-
raising flour into a large bowl; stir in 1 cup
(125 g/4 oz) of chopped walnuts and ½ cup
(90 g/3 oz) of choc bits. Make a well in the
centre of the dry ingredients; add 125 g
(4 oz) of melted butter, 200 g (6½ oz) of
melted dark chocolate, 2 tablespoons of
golden syrup and 2 lightly beaten eggs. Stir
until combined. Drop level tablespoonsful
onto a greased oven tray. Leave about 4 cm
(1½ inches) between each cookie to allow
for spreading. Bake 12 minutes, transfer to a
wire rack to cool. Makes about 30.

NUTMEG

Because nutmeg loses its
flavour so quickly, ideally
you should buy whole
nutmegs and grate them as
required. Nutmeg graters
are available from department stores and speciality
kitchen shops. The spice is
used in both sweet and
savoury dishes, and most
commonly those based on
cream, milk or eggs.
Freshly grated nutmeg is
an essential topping for a
traditional eggnog.

*ABOVE: Nutmeg
Date Cake*

FRESH PINEAPPLE
When buying pineapple, look for fruit that is fully ripe. A ripe pineapple should be pale yellow, have no soft patches, and you should be able to pull the central leaves easily from the top. An unripe fruit that has no fragrance and is dark green will be extremely tart—it should be left out of the refrigerator to ripen for a couple of days. Small pineapples often have more flavour than the larger specimens.

PINEAPPLE AND BANANA CAKE

Preparation time: 40 minutes
Total cooking time: 1 hour
Serves 8–10

2 medium bananas, mashed
1/2 cup (130 g/4 1/4 oz) drained crushed pineapple
1 1/4 cups (310 g/9 3/4 oz) caster sugar
1 2/3 cups (200 g/6 1/2 oz) self-raising flour
2 teaspoons ground cinnamon
2/3 cup (170 ml/5 1/2 fl oz) oil
1/4 cup (60 ml/2 fl oz) pineapple juice
2 eggs

Icing

250 g (8 oz) cream cheese
1 1/2 cups (185 g/6 oz) icing sugar
1 small mango, thinly sliced

1 Preheat the oven to moderate 180°C (350°F/Gas 4). Brush a 23 cm (9 inch) round cake tin with melted butter or oil and line the base and side with baking paper.

2 Place the bananas, pineapple and sugar in a large bowl. Add the sifted flour and cinnamon; using a wooden spoon, stir to combine.

3 Whisk the oil, pineapple juice and eggs together and add to the banana mixture. Stir until the ingredients are combined and the mixture is smooth.

4 Pour into the prepared tin, smooth the surface and bake for 1 hour, or until a skewer comes out clean when inserted into the centre of cake. Leave in the tin for 10 minutes; turn onto a wire rack to cool.

5 **To make Icing:** Using electric beaters, beat the cream cheese and icing sugar until light and fluffy. Using a serrated knife, cut the cake in half horizontally. Spread a third of the icing over the bottom layer of the cake and arrange the mango slices over the icing. Replace the top layer and cover the top of the cake with the remaining icing. Decorate with pieces of glacé pineapple, if desired.

NOTE: This cake will keep for up to 4 days in an airtight container. Refrigerate during hot weather. Tinned mango, thinly sliced pineapple or pawpaw may be used in the filling.

ABOVE: Pineapple and Banana Cake

PEANUT CHOC-CHIP MUFFINS

Preparation time: 15 minutes
Total cooking time: 20–25 minutes
Makes 12

★

2 cups (250 g/8 oz) self-raising flour
1/3 cup (80 g/2²/3 oz) raw sugar
1¹/2 cups (240 g/7¹/2 oz) dark choc bits
1 egg
1 cup (250 g/8 oz) crunchy peanut butter
2 tablespoons strawberry jam
60 g (2 oz) butter, melted
1 cup (250 ml/8 fl oz) milk
icing sugar, for dusting

1 Preheat oven to moderate 180°C (350°F/Gas 4). Brush a 12-hole standard size muffin tin with melted butter or oil.
2 Sift flour into a large bowl. Add sugar and choc bits; make a well in centre. Add combined egg, peanut butter, jam, butter and milk. Stir until just combined. (Do not overbeat.)
3 Spoon evenly into muffin cups. Bake for 20–25 minutes or until a skewer comes out clean when inserted in the centre. Loosen muffins in the pan and leave for 10 minutes before turning onto a wire rack to cool. Dust with icing sugar.

GLACE FRUIT
Glacé fruit is fruit that has been preserved in a sugar syrup. It is moist and sticky on the inside and, because of a final dipping in a strong syrup, the surface has a glazed appearance.

FLOURLESS CHOCOLATE FRUIT AND NUT CAKE

Preparation time: 40 minutes
Total cooking time: 1 hour
Serves 8–10

★

5 egg whites
3/4 cup (185 g/6 oz) caster sugar
100 g (3¹/3 oz) glacé apricots, chopped
100 g (3¹/3 oz) glacé figs, chopped
80 g (2²/3 oz) glacé ginger, chopped
250 g (8 oz) blanched almonds, finely chopped
250 g (8 oz) dark cooking chocolate, chopped
60 g (2 oz) dark cooking chocolate, melted
1¹/2 cups (375 ml/12 fl oz) cream

OPPOSITE PAGE; Peanut Choc-Chip Muffins (top); Flourless Chocolate Fruit and Nut Cake

1 Preheat oven to slow 150°C (300°F/Gas 2). Brush a deep 24 cm (9¹/2 inch) round springform

(spring-release) pan with melted butter or oil. Line base and side with baking paper.
2 Using electric beaters, beat egg whites until soft peaks form. Gradually add sugar, beating well after each addition; beat until sugar has dissolved and the mixture is thick and glossy.
3 Using a metal spoon, fold in fruits, ginger, almonds, and both the chopped and melted chocolate. Stir until just combined. Spread in tin and bake for 1 hour or until a skewer comes out clean when inserted in centre. Leave in tin for 15 minutes before removing. Cool on a wire rack. When completely cooled, whip cream until stiff peaks form. Using a piping bag with a plain nozzle, pipe swirls of cream on top of the cake. Decorate with chocolate leaves, if desired.

STICKY ALMOND CAKE

Preparation time: 30 minutes
Total cooking time: 50 minutes
Serves 8–10

★ ★

4 eggs
3/4 cup (185 g/6 oz) caster sugar
2 teaspoons grated orange rind
90 g (3 oz) butter, melted
1/4 cup (60 ml/2 fl oz) cream
3/4 cup (90 g/3 oz) self-raising flour

Almond Topping

2 cups (185 g/6 oz) flaked almonds
90 g (3 oz) butter
1/3 cup (90 g/3 oz) caster sugar
1/4 cup (60 ml/2 fl oz) cream
2 tablespoons honey
1/2 teaspoon ground mixed spice

1 Preheat oven to moderate 180°C (350°F/Gas 4). Grease a deep 23 cm (9 inch) round springform (spring-release) pan; line with baking paper.
2 Using electric beaters, beat eggs and sugar in a large bowl until thick and pale. Using a metal spoon, fold in orange rind, butter and cream. Fold in sifted flour. Pour into tin and bake for 40 minutes, or until firm in the centre.
3 To make Almond Topping: Combine almonds, butter, sugar, cream, honey and spice in a pan. Stir over medium heat until boiling. Spread over cake and bake another 10 minutes or until topping is golden. Cool in tin for 10 minutes before transferring to serving plate.

STRAWBERRIES

Strawberries as we know them today are, in fact, a hybrid variety. They were developed by crossing the American Virginian strawberries, which were large in size but lacking in flavour, with Chilean fruit which had a particularly intense flavour. With this cross the modern berry was born and since then hundreds of new varieties have appeared. When you choose strawberries, don't be seduced by the biggest and brightest—those with the most intense perfume have the best flavour.

ABOVE: Orange Berry Sponge

ORANGE BERRY SPONGE

Preparation time: 1 hour
Total cooking time: 45 minutes
Serves 8–10

★ ★ ★

1/2 cup (60 g/2 oz) plain flour
1/4 cup (30 g/1 oz) cornflour
1 teaspoon baking powder
1/4 cup (60 ml/2 fl oz) milk
50 g (12/3 oz) butter
3/4 cup (185 g/6 oz) caster sugar
3 eggs
3 egg yolks
1 teaspoon finely grated orange rind
11/2 cups (375 ml/12 fl oz) cream
3–4 teaspoons icing sugar
1–2 tablespoons Grand Marnier
250 g (8 oz) strawberries, hulled and sliced
250 g (8 oz) blueberries
2 tablespoons flaked almonds, toasted
icing sugar, for dusting

1 Preheat the oven to moderate 180°C (350°F/Gas 4). Brush a 30 x 20 cm (12 x 8 inch) shallow cake tin with melted butter or oil. Line the base and sides with baking paper extending 3 cm (1¼ inches) over each edge. Sift the flours and baking powder twice onto a sheet of greaseproof paper. Place milk and butter in pan. Stir over medium heat until butter has melted. (Take care not to boil mixture, but keep it hot.)
2 Place the sugar, eggs and yolks in a large heatproof bowl. Stand the bowl over a pan of simmering water. Using electric beaters, beat the mixture over heat until pale yellow, thick and glossy and increased in volume. Remove bowl from heat. Stir in rind until well combined.
3 Using a metal spoon, fold in a third of the flour at a time. Fold in the hot butter mixture and stir until just smooth. (Do not over-mix. It is important to keep as much volume as possible in the mixture.) Spoon the mixture into the prepared tin. Bake for 25–30 minutes or until springy to touch. Leave in the tin to cool.
4 Turn the cake out onto a flat work surface. Using a sharp serrated knife, trim away any dark patches. Cut the cake into three even rectangles, around 10 x 20 cm (4 x 8 inches) each.

5 Beat the cream and icing sugar with electric beaters until stiff peaks form. Stir in the Grand Marnier.

6 Spread one quarter of the cream mixture over one layer of cake. Top with a third of the berries. Add a second layer of cake; press down lightly. Repeat the process with cream and berries, reserving some berries for the top and finishing with the third cake layer. Spread the remaining cream evenly over the top and sides of the cake. Decorate the cake with the remaining berries and toasted flaked almonds. Dust the cake lightly with icing sugar.

NOTE: To toast almonds, scatter on an oven tray lined with baking paper. Place in a preheated moderate 180°C (350°F/Gas 4) oven for 5–10 minutes. Do not use frozen or canned berries in this recipe as they are too soggy. If blueberries are unavailable, substitute any berry in season, such as blackberries, or omit the second berry variety entirely, if you prefer.

CHOCOLATE CARROT SLICE

Preparation time: 20 minutes
Total cooking time: 30 minutes
Makes 32

1 cup (125 g/4 oz) self-raising flour
1 teaspoon ground cinnamon
3/4 cup (185 g/6 oz) caster sugar
1/2 cup (80 g/2 2/3 oz) finely grated carrot
1 cup (185 g/6 oz) mixed dried fruit
1/2 cup (90 g/3 oz) choc bits
1/3 cup (30 g/1 oz) desiccated coconut
2 eggs, lightly beaten
90 g (3 oz) unsalted butter, melted
1/3 cup (40 g/1 1/3 oz) chopped walnuts

Cream Cheese Frosting

125 g (4 oz) cream cheese
30 g (1 oz) unsalted butter
1 1/2 cups (185 g/6 oz) icing sugar, sifted
1 teaspoon hot water

1 Preheat the oven to moderate 180°C (350°F/Gas 4). Brush a shallow 23 cm (9 inch) square cake tin with melted butter or oil and line the base and sides with baking paper.

2 Sift the flour and cinnamon into a large bowl. Add the caster sugar, grated carrot, mixed fruit, choc bits and coconut and stir until just combined. Add the beaten eggs and butter and then stir until combined.

3 Spread the mixture evenly into the prepared tin and smooth the surface. Bake for 30 minutes or until golden. Cool the cake in the tin and turn out onto a flat surface.

4 To make Cream Cheese Frosting: Using electric beaters, beat the cream cheese and butter in a small bowl until smooth. Add the icing sugar and beat for 2 minutes or until the mixture is light and fluffy. Add the water and beat until well combined.

5 Spread the slice with frosting using a flat-bladed knife and sprinkle with walnuts. Cut into 16 squares, then cut each square into triangles.

NOTE: This slice can be frozen for up to two months. The topping may be sprinkled with grated chocolate, if desired.

CREAM CHEESE

Cream cheese is made from whole milk, or a combination of whole milk and cream. Not only for spreading on bread, it is very useful as a base for dips and icings. For subtle flavouring, press scented leaves or herbs into cream cheese and wrap in plastic overnight. Discard the leaves and the cheese will be lightly perfumed.

ABOVE: Chocolate Carrot Slice

ICINGS AND FROSTINGS

Sweet or piquant, cooked or uncooked, toppings like these help to convert an

unadorned home-made muffin or a simple sweet slice to an outstanding event.

EASY BUTTER CREAM
Using electric beaters, beat 80 g (2²⁄₃ oz) of soft butter with ½ cup (60 g/2 oz) of icing sugar. Flavourings, such as 2 teaspoons of finely grated orange rind, 60 g (2 oz) of melted and cooled chocolate, or a few drops of your favourite flavoured essence and some complementary food colouring, can be added if you wish.

CHOCOLATE ICING
Combine 30 g (1 oz) of melted butter, 2 tablespoons of hot water and 2 tablespoons of sifted cocoa powder in a bowl and stir the mixture until it forms a smooth paste. Add 1 cup (125 g/4 oz) of sifted icing sugar and stir until the ingredients are well combined and the mixture is quite smooth.

HONEY MOCK CREAM
Using electric beaters, beat 125 g (4 oz) butter with ⅓ cup (90 g/3 oz) of caster sugar and 2 tablespoons of honey until the mixture is light and creamy. Pour cold water onto the mixture, swirl around and pour off. Beat again for 2 minutes, then swirl water over the mixture and pour it off again. Repeat this process four more times until the

mixture is white and creamy and the sugar has completely dissolved. This cream is a delicious topping for spiced cakes or cupcakes.

CITRUS GLACE ICING

Combine 1 cup (125 g/4 oz) of sifted icing sugar, 10 g (1/3 oz) of unsalted butter and 1 teaspoon finely grated citrus rind in a small heatproof bowl. Add sufficient juice (about 1–2 tablespoons) to make a firm paste. Stand the bowl over a pan of simmering water and stir until the icing is smooth and glossy; remove from heat. Spread onto cake or biscuits with a long palette knife. Orange, lemon or lime rind and juice can be used.

SOFT CITRUS ICING

Make a deliciously simple glacé icing by combining 1¼ cups (155 g/5 oz) sifted icing sugar, 30 g (1 oz) softened butter, a little grated citrus rind and enough hot water to mix to a thick, smooth paste. Spread over cake. This mixture is easy to work with as it doesn't set quickly. The same mixture can also be heated in a small bowl over simmering water. Work quickly with this method, using a hot, wet knife for spreading, as the icing will set very quickly.

CREAM CHEESE FROSTING

Chop 185 g (6 oz) cream cheese into small cubes and, using electric beaters, beat until smooth. Add 1/3 cup (40 g/ 1⅓ oz) sifted icing sugar and a couple of teaspoons of lemon juice and beat until well combined. Add a little more juice, to taste, if you like but don't make the frosting too runny. This is an excellent topping for carrot or banana cakes.

CHOCOLATE GANACHE

Combine 100 g (3⅓ oz) of chopped dark chocolate, 60 g (2 oz) unsalted butter and a tablespoon of cream in a heatproof bowl. Stand bowl over a pan of simmering water; stir until the mixture is melted and smooth. This mixture can be cooled slightly and poured while still liquid over a very smooth cake. (If the top surface is rough, turn the cake upside down and use the base as the top.) Ganache can also be cooled until it is spreadable, or cooled and then beaten to make a lighter, fluffier topping.

CLOKWISE, FROM TOP LEFT: Citrus Glacé Icing; Chocolate Ganache; Chocolate Icing (with whipped cream and chocolate lattice); Honey Mock Cream; Soft Citrus Icing; Easy Butter Cream; Cream Cheese Frosting

COFFEE LIQUEUR GATEAU

Preparation time: 1 hour + 1 hour refrigeration
Total cooking time: 40–50 minutes
Serves 8–10

⭐ ⭐ ⭐

125 g (4 oz) brazil nuts
100 g (3¹/₃ oz) blanched almonds
80 g (2²/₃ oz) hazelnuts
2 tablespoons plain flour
³/₄ cup (185 g/6 oz) caster sugar
7 egg whites
¹/₄ cup (60 ml/2 fl oz) Tia Maria or Kahlua
small chocolate buttons, for decoration
sifted icing sugar, for dusting

Coffee Cream

200 g (6¹/₂ oz) butter
150 g (4³/₄ oz) dark chocolate, melted
2–3 teaspoons icing sugar
2 teaspoons warm water
3–4 teaspoons instant coffee powder

1 Preheat oven to moderate 180°C (350°F/Gas 4). Brush a deep 20 cm (8 inch) round tin with melted butter or oil. Line base and side with baking paper. Place nuts on an oven tray. Bake for 5–10 minutes or until golden. Rub the nuts vigorously in a clean tea towel to remove hazelnut skins. Grind the nuts finely in food processor.
2 Transfer the nuts to a large bowl; add flour and ¹/₂ cup (125g/4 oz) of the sugar; mix well. Using electric beaters, beat egg whites in a large bowl until soft peaks form. Gradually add the remaining sugar, beating until thick and glossy and the sugar is dissolved. Using a metal spoon, fold nut mixture into egg mixture a third at a time. Spoon into the tin; smooth surface. Bake for 35–40 minutes or until springy to the touch. Leave the cake in the tin to cool completely.
3 To make Coffee Cream: Beat butter in a small bowl with electric beaters until light and creamy. Gradually pour in melted chocolate, beating until well combined. Add icing sugar and combined water and coffee powder; beat until smooth.
4 To assemble Gateau: Turn cake onto a flat working surface. Using a sharp serrated knife, carefully cut it horizontally into three layers. Use top layer of cake as base of gateau. Brush first layer with half the liqueur. Spread with one-fifth of the Coffee Cream.
5 Place a second cake layer on top. Brush with rest of liqueur and spread with a quarter of remaining Coffee Cream. Top with final layer. Spread top and sides with rest of Coffee Cream. Decorate top with chocolate buttons; dust with icing sugar. Refrigerate for 1 hour or until firm.

CHOCOLATE BUTTONS

Small chocolate buttons can be made at home with 150 g (4³/₄ oz) of melted chocolate melts. Line two trays with baking paper. Place half the chocolate in a small paper icing bag. Seal the end of the bag, then snip off the tip. Pipe small chocolate buttons onto trays. Tap the trays lightly on the bench to flatten the buttons. Allow to set, then peel off the paper and use the buttons to decorate cakes.

ABOVE: Coffee Liqueur Gateau

PREPARING ALMONDS
Some recipes call for blanched almonds, which simply means almonds with the skins removed. These are available in packets already blanched, or you can do it yourself. Cover the almonds with boiling water and leave for 30 seconds, then drain and remove the skins by rubbing the nuts between your fingers or in a tea towel. When decorating cakes, use toasted rather than raw nuts for the best flavour. Spread them in a single layer on an oven tray and then bake at moderate 180°C (350°F/ Gas 4) for 5–10 minutes, until lightly golden. Cool and use as desired.

BANANA CAKE

Preparation time: 25 minutes
Total cooking time: 1 hour
Makes one 20 cm (8 inch) round cake

★

125 g (4 oz) butter
1/2 cup (125 g/4 oz) caster sugar
2 eggs, lightly beaten
1 teaspoon vanilla essence
4 medium ripe bananas, mashed
1 teaspoon bicarbonate of soda
1/2 cup (125 ml/4 fl oz) milk
2 cups (250 g/8 oz) self-raising flour

Butter Frosting

125 g (4 oz) butter
3/4 cup (90 g/3 oz) icing sugar
1 tablespoon lemon juice
1/4 cup (15 g/1/2 oz) flaked coconut, toasted

1 Preheat the oven to moderate 180°C (350°F/Gas 4). Brush a 20 cm (8 inch) round cake tin with oil or melted butter and line the base with baking paper. Using electric beaters, beat butter and sugar in a small bowl until light and creamy. Add the eggs gradually, beating thoroughly after each addition. Add the essence and mashed banana and beat until combined.

2 Transfer the mixture to a large bowl. Dissolve the soda in the milk. Using a metal spoon, fold in the sifted flour alternately with the milk. Stir until all the ingredients are just combined and the mixture is smooth. Spoon into the prepared tin; smooth the surface. Bake for 1 hour or until a skewer comes out clean when inserted into the centre of cake. Leave in the tin for 10 minutes before turning onto a wire rack to cool.

3 **To make Frosting:** Using electric beaters, beat the butter, icing sugar and lemon juice until smooth and creamy. Spread onto the cooled cake, sprinkle with toasted coconut flakes.

NOTE: Very ripe bananas are best for this recipe as they have the most developed flavour. Decorate with untoasted coconut, if you prefer.

ABOVE: Banana Cake

fork until just combined. (Do not overbeat—batter should look quite lumpy.)

2 Spoon the mixture into the tin. Bake for 12–15 minutes or until firm. Loosen the muffins with a knife before turning out onto a wire rack to cool.

NOTE: For a delicious topping, combine 50 g (1²/₃ oz) chocolate, 1 tablespoon cream and 10 g (¹/₃ oz) butter in a pan; stir over low heat until smooth. Refrigerate until firm, then pipe or spoon over muffins. Sprinkle with icing sugar.

STRAWBERRY AND PASSIONFRUIT MUFFINS

Preparation time: 20 minutes
Total cooking time: 10–15 minutes
Makes 12

★

1³/₄ cups (215 g/6³/₄ oz) self-raising flour
pinch salt
1 teaspoon baking powder
¹/₂ teaspoon bicarbonate of soda
¹/₄ cup (60 g/2 oz) caster sugar
1 cup (175 g/5²/₃ oz) chopped fresh
  strawberries
¹/₂ cup (125 g/4 oz) canned (or fresh)
  passionfruit pulp
1 egg
³/₄ cup (185 ml/6 fl oz) milk
60 g (2 oz) butter, melted

STORING MUFFINS
Muffins are best eaten on the day they are made. However, they may be frozen for up to 3 months. Allow the muffins to cool completely, then seal them in an airtight freezer bag. When ready to use, thaw the muffins at room temperature, then either serve as they are or warm them in a moderate oven.

DOUBLE CHOC MUFFINS

Preparation time: 15 minutes
Total cooking time: 12–15 minutes
Makes 6 large muffins

★

2 cups (250 g/8 oz) plain flour
2¹/₂ teaspoons baking powder
¹/₄ cup (30 g/1 oz) cocoa powder
2 tablespoons caster sugar
1 cup (175 g/5²/₃ oz) dark choc bits
1 egg, lightly beaten
¹/₂ cup (125 g/4 oz) sour cream
³/₄ cup (185 ml/6 fl oz) milk
90 g (3 oz) butter, melted

1 Preheat the oven to moderate 180°C (350°F/Gas 4). Brush a 6-hole large muffin tin with melted butter or oil. Sift the flour, baking powder and cocoa into a large mixing bowl. Add the sugar and the choc bits and stir to mix through. Make a well in the centre of the mixture. Add the combined egg, sour cream, milk and melted butter all at once and stir with a

*ABOVE: Double
Choc Muffins
RIGHT: Strawberry and
Passionfruit Muffins*

MUFFIN TINS
These muffins were made in American-style non-stick muffin tins, found in department stores or large supermarkets. They are available in 6- or 12-hole trays, and the holes range through three sizes—mini, standard and large. These recipes use the standard size, unless otherwise indicated. Even though the tins are 'non-stick', it is advisable to lightly grease them, at least on the base, as the sugar content of some muffins can cause them to stick.

1 Preheat the oven to hot 210°C (415°F/ Gas 6–7). Brush a 12-hole muffin tin with melted butter or oil.

2 Sift the flour, salt, baking powder, soda and sugar into a bowl. Add the strawberries and stir to combine. Make a well in the centre.

3 Add the passionfruit pulp and the combined egg and milk. Pour the melted butter into the flour mixture all at once and lightly stir with a fork until just combined. (Do not overbeat; the batter should be quite lumpy.)

4 Spoon the mixture into the prepared tins and bake for 10–15 minutes, or until golden brown. Loosen the muffins with a flat-bladed knife or spatula and turn out onto a wire rack to cool. Top with softened, sweetened cream cheese or whipped cream and fresh strawberry halves and sprinkle with icing sugar, if desired.

BLUEBERRY MUFFINS

Preparation time: 20 minutes
Total cooking time: 20 minutes
Makes 6 large muffins

3 cups (375 g/12 oz) plain flour
1 tablespoon baking powder
3/4 cup (140 g/4²/3 oz) soft brown sugar
125 g (4 oz) butter, melted
2 eggs, lightly beaten
1 cup (250 ml/8 fl oz) milk
1 cup (155 g/5 oz) blueberries
icing sugar, for sprinkling

1 Preheat oven to hot 210°C (415°F/Gas 6–7). Brush a 6-hole large muffin tin with melted butter or oil. Sift flour and baking powder into a large bowl. Stir in sugar; make a well in centre.

2 Add combined melted butter, eggs and milk all at once; stir until just blended. (Do not overmix; the batter should look quite lumpy.)

3 Fold in blueberries thoroughly but lightly. Spoon batter into tin. Bake 20 minutes or until golden brown. Loosen with a knife and transfer to a wire rack to cool. Sprinkle with icing sugar.

ABOVE: Blueberry Muffins

SCONES

Plain scones are delicious and very simple to make, but it is equally easy to throw in a handful of extra ingredients. Sultanas, currants or raisins are traditional favourites, but you can also use chopped mixed peel, or even finely chopped dried apricots or peaches. Make savoury scones by adding grated cheese or chopped fresh herbs to the basic mixture.

SCONES

Preparation time: 20 minutes
Total cooking time: 10–12 minutes
Makes 12

2 cups (250 g/8 oz) self-raising flour
pinch salt (optional—see Note)
30 g (1 oz) butter, cut into small pieces
1/2 cup (125 ml/4 fl oz) milk
1/3 cup (80 ml/2 3/4 fl oz) water
milk, extra, for glazing

1 Preheat the oven to hot 210°C (415°F/ Gas 6–7). Brush an oven tray with melted butter or oil. Sift the flour and salt (if using) into a bowl. Add the chopped butter and rub in lightly using your fingertips.
2 Make a well in the centre of the flour. Add almost all of the combined milk and water. Mix with a flat-bladed knife to a soft dough, adding more liquid if necessary.
3 Turn the dough onto a lightly floured surface (use self-raising flour). Knead the dough briefly and lightly until smooth. Press or roll out the dough to form a round 1.5 cm (5/8 inch) thick.

4 Cut the dough into rounds using a floured round 5 cm (2 inch) cutter. Place the rounds on the prepared tray; glaze with milk. Bake the scones for 10–12 minutes or until golden brown. Serve with jam and whipped cream.
NOTE: Use a light touch when kneading scones or they may turn out heavy and tough—the dough needs very little handling. It is usual to add a pinch of salt to the mixture when making scones, even the sweet ones, to enhance the flavour.

FAST LEMON SHORTBREADS

PREHEAT THE OVEN to moderate 180°C (350°F/Gas 4). Place 1 cup (125 g/4 oz) of plain flour, 1 tablespoon of rice flour, 100 g (3 1/3 oz) of chopped cold butter and 1/2 teaspoon finely grated lemon rind into a food processor. Add about 1 tablespoon of lemon juice; process briefly until combined. Turn out onto a lightly floured surface, roll out to a thickness of 5 mm (1/4 inch). Cut out desired shapes, place on a baking tray covered with baking paper. Bake for 10–12 minutes, until pale golden. Cool on a wire rack. Makes about 20.

ABOVE: Scones

APPLE STRUDEL

Preparation time: 20 minutes
Total cooking time: 25–30 minutes
Makes 2 strudels

4 green cooking apples
30 g (1 oz) butter
2 tablespoons orange juice
1 tablespoon honey
1/4 cup (60 g/2 oz) sugar
1/2 cup (60 g/2 oz) sultanas
2 sheets ready-rolled puff pastry
1/4 cup (45 g/1 1/2 oz) ground almonds
1 egg, lightly beaten
2 tablespoons soft brown sugar
1 teaspoon ground cinnamon

1 Preheat the oven to hot 220°C (425°F/ Gas 7). Brush two oven trays lightly with melted butter or oil. Peel, core and thinly slice the apples. Heat the butter in a medium pan; add the apples and cook for 2 minutes until lightly golden. Add the orange juice, honey, sugar and sultanas. Stir over medium heat until the sugar dissolves and the apples are just tender.

Transfer the mixture to a bowl and leave until completely cooled.

2 Place a sheet of the pastry on a flat work surface. Fold it in half; and make small cuts in the folded edge of the pastry at 2 cm (3/4 inch) intervals. Open out the pastry and sprinkle with half of the ground almonds. Drain away the liquid from the apples and place half of the mixture in the centre of the pastry. Brush the edges with the lightly beaten egg, and fold together, pressing firmly to seal.

3 Place the strudel on a prepared tray, seam-side down. Brush the top with egg and sprinkle with half of the combined brown sugar and cinnamon. Repeat the process with the other sheet and the remaining filling. Bake for 20–25 minutes or until the pastry is golden and crisp. Serve hot with cream or ice cream, or at room temperature as a teatime treat.

NOTE: Many types of fresh or canned fruit, such as pears, cherries or apricots, can be used to make strudel. Just make sure that the fruit is well drained before using, or the pastry will become soggy on the bottom.

BAKING HINTS
The secret to light, tender pastries, cakes and biscuits is all in the handling of the mixture. When a cake recipe says to 'fold' in the flour, use a large metal spoon or rubber spatula, and mix until the flour is just combined. Use a butter knife to 'cut' liquid into the dry ingredients in a pastry or biscuit recipe, then gather the dough together, using only your fingertips. It is the protein (gluten) in the flour which, if overhandled, causes the finished product to be tough and heavy.

ABOVE: Apple Strudel

7 cm (2¾ inch) fluted, round cutter, cut rounds from pastry. Gently press into patty tins. Lightly prick each round 3 times with a fork, bake for 10 minutes or until just starting to turn golden. Remove from oven and spoon 2 teaspoons of filling into each case. Return to oven for another 5 minutes or until filling has set. Cool slightly before removing from tins. Garnish with strips of candied lemon peel, if desired.

CHOCOLATE ECLAIRS

Preparation time: 20 minutes
Total cooking time: 40 minutes
Makes 18

1 cup (250 ml/8 fl oz) water
125 g (4 oz) butter
1 cup (125 g/4 oz) plain flour, sifted
4 eggs
315 ml (10 fl oz) cream, whipped
150 g (4¾ oz) dark chocolate, melted

1 Preheat oven to hot 210°C (415°F/Gas 6–7). Brush two baking trays with oil. Combine water and butter in pan. Stir over medium heat until butter melts. Bring to boil, remove from heat.
2 Add flour all at once. Return to heat and stir with a wooden spoon until mixture leaves side of pan and forms a ball around the spoon. Transfer to a large bowl; cool slightly. Add eggs one at a time, beating well after each addition until mixture is thick, smooth and shiny.

LITTLE LEMON TARTS

Preparation time: 40 minutes + refrigeration
Total cooking time: 15 minutes
Makes 24

2 cups (250 g/8 oz) plain flour
125 g (4 oz) butter, chopped
2 teaspoons caster sugar
1 teaspoon grated lemon rind
1 egg yolk

Filling

125 g (4 oz) cream cheese, softened
½ cup (125 g/4 oz) caster sugar
2 egg yolks
2 tablespoons lemon juice
½ cup (160 g/5¼ oz) sweetened
    condensed milk

1 Preheat oven to moderate 180°C (350°F/Gas 4). Brush two 12-cup shallow patty tins with oil. Sift flour and a pinch of salt into a bowl; rub in butter. Add sugar, rind, egg yolk and 2–3 tablespoons iced water; mix with a knife. Gently knead on lightly floured surface until smooth. Cover in plastic wrap and chill for 10 minutes.
2 **To make Filling:** Using electric beaters, beat combined cream cheese, sugar and egg yolks until smooth and thickened. Add lemon juice and condensed milk; beat until well combined.
3 Roll out the dough between sheets of baking paper to 3 mm (about ⅛ inch) thickness. Using a

CONDENSED MILK
Condensed milk is whole or skimmed milk that has been boiled down to about one third of its original volume and sweetened with sugar until it tastes more like a light caramel than milk. It is the sugar that ensures it keeps longer than evaporated milk once the can is opened. Condensed milk is wonderful for making fudge and ice cream.

ABOVE: Little Lemon Tarts RIGHT: Chocolate Eclairs

3 Spoon into a piping bag fitted with a 1.5 cm (⅝ inch) plain nozzle. Pipe 15 cm (6 inch) lengths onto trays, leaving room for expansion.
4 Bake for 10–15 minutes. Reduce heat to moderate 180°C (350°F/Gas 4). Bake another 15 minutes or until golden and firm. Split each éclair, removing uncooked dough. Fill with cream. Coat the tops with melted chocolate.

COFFEE KISSES

Preparation time: 40 minutes
Total cooking time: 10 minutes
Makes 30

3 cups (375 g/12 oz) self-raising flour
160 g (5¼ oz) butter, chopped
½ cup (125 g/4 oz) caster sugar
1 egg, lightly beaten
1 tablespoon instant coffee powder
1–2 tablespoons iced water

Coffee Butter Cream

80 g (2⅔ oz) butter
1 cup (125 g/4 oz) icing sugar, sifted
2 teaspoons water
2 teaspoons instant coffee powder
100 g (3⅓ oz) white chocolate, melted

1 Preheat oven to moderate 180°C (350°F/Gas 4). Brush two biscuit trays with oil. Line with baking paper. Sift flour into a bowl. Add butter and rub into flour, using your fingertips, until mixture resembles fine breadcrumbs. Add combined sugar, egg and coffee powder, dissolved in the water, all at once. Mix with a knife until the ingredients come together to form a soft dough. Lightly knead until smooth.
2 Roll out between two sheets of baking paper to 5 mm (¼ inch) thickness. Cut into 5 cm (2 inch) rounds, using a fluted biscuit cutter. Place on prepared trays. Bake 10 minutes or until lightly golden. Transfer to a wire rack.
3 To make Coffee Butter Cream: Using electric beaters, beat butter and icing sugar until light and creamy. Add combined water and coffee powder and beat until mixed. Place in a piping bag fitted with a fluted nozzle and pipe onto half of the biscuits. Top with another biscuit; sandwich together. Drizzle or pipe with melted chocolate. Top each with a chocolate-coated coffee bean, if desired.

CHOCOLATE WHEAT BISCUITS

Preparation time: 20 minutes
Total cooking time: 15–20 minutes
Makes 25

125 g (4 oz) butter
½ cup (95 g/3¼ oz) soft brown sugar
¼ cup (60 ml/2 fl oz) milk
1½ cups (225 g/7¼ oz) wholemeal plain flour
⅓ cup (40 g/1⅓ oz) self-raising flour
⅓ cup (30 g/1 oz) desiccated coconut
200 g (6½ oz) dark chocolate

1 Preheat the oven to moderate 180°C (350°F/Gas 4). Brush two oven trays with melted butter or oil and line with baking paper. Using electric beaters, beat the butter and sugar in a bowl until light and creamy. Add the milk and beat until combined.
2 Add the sifted flours and coconut. Using a knife, mix to a soft dough. Roll between two sheets of baking paper to 5 mm (¼ inch) thickness. Using a 5 cm (2 inch) round cutter, cut rounds from the dough and place on the tray. Bake for 15–20 minutes until golden; cool.
3 Melt the chocolate in a bowl over a pan of simmering water. Remove from heat, allow to cool slightly. Spread evenly over tops of biscuits and allow to set.

COFFEE ESSENCE
When cooking with coffee, dark roasted beans are best. To make a simple coffee essence, mix equal parts of finely ground instant coffee and boiling water and leave to steep for a day. For a stronger essence, boil freshly brewed coffee until reduced and thickened and then leave to cool. Both essences will last for up to two weeks if stored in the refrigerator. Commercial essences vary in strength and quality.

ABOVE: Coffee Kisses

283

3 Roll 1 level teaspoonful of mixture at a time into balls. Arrange about 5 cm (2 inches) apart on prepared trays. Flatten slightly with a fork. Bake 12 minutes or until golden. Stand biscuits on trays for 5 minutes before putting a wire rack to cool. Spread half the biscuits with ¼ teaspoon of jam on each. Spoon or pipe cream over jam, sandwich with remaining biscuits.

LEMON AND LIME BISCUITS

Preparation time: 40 minutes + 1 hour refrigeration
Total cooking time: 10–15 minutes
Makes 30

150 g (4¾ oz) butter, softened
¾ cup (185 g/6 oz) caster sugar
1 egg, lightly beaten
1 tablespoon lime juice
2 teaspoons grated lime rind
2 teaspoons grated lemon rind
1 cup (125 g/4 oz) plain flour
½ cup (60 g/2 oz) self-raising flour
60 g (2 oz) marzipan, grated

Lime Icing

1 cup (125 g/4 oz) icing sugar, sifted
1 teaspoon finely grated lime rind
1 tablespoon lime juice
2 teaspoons water

MELTING MOMENTS WITH JAM AND CREAM

Preparation time: 15 minutes
Total cooking time: 12 minutes
Makes 20

125 g (4 oz) unsalted butter
½ cup (125 g/4 oz) caster sugar
2 egg yolks
1 teaspoon vanilla essence
¼ cup (30 g/1 oz) custard powder
¾ cup (90 g/3 oz) plain flour
¾ cup (90 g/3 oz) self-raising flour
½ cup (160 g/5¼ oz) strawberry jam
¾ cup (185 ml/6 fl oz) thick cream, whipped

1 Preheat oven to moderate 180°C (350°F/Gas 4). Line two biscuit trays with baking paper. Using electric beaters, beat the butter and sugar until light and creamy. Add the egg yolks one at a time, beating thoroughly after each addition. Add the vanilla essence; beat until combined.
2 Transfer the mixture to a large bowl. Using a flat-bladed knife, incorporate the custard powder and sifted flours. Stir until ingredients are just combined. Gather the mixture together with fingertips to form a soft dough.

LIMES

Limes are the most perishable of the citrus fruits. They should be pale or dark green and have a tart, green pulp. If their skins are yellow they are usually overripe and will have lost much of their sour flavour. Lime juice is great instead of lemon juice in the avocado dip guacamole, and is also used in many desserts. The pale juice of fresh limes is also used in daiquiris and margheritas.

ABOVE: Melting Moments with Jam and Cream
RIGHT: Lemon and Lime Biscuits

1 Line two oven trays with baking paper. Using electric beaters, beat the butter and sugar in a bowl until light and creamy. Add the egg, juice and rinds, beating until well combined.

2 Transfer the mixture to a large bowl. Using a flat-bladed knife, mix the flours and marzipan until a soft dough forms. Divide the mixture in two. Turn one portion out onto a lightly floured surface and press together until smooth.

3 Form the biscuit dough into a log shape about 4 cm (1½ inches) in diameter. Wrap the log in plastic wrap and refrigerate for 1 hour. Repeat the process with the remaining dough. Preheat the oven to moderate 180°C (350°F/Gas 4). Cut the dough into 1 cm (½ inch) slices. Place the slices on the prepared trays and bake for 10–15 minutes or until the biscuits are lightly golden. Leave on the trays until cool. Dip the biscuits in the icing. Decorate if you like.

4 To make Lime Icing: Place the icing sugar, lime rind, lime juice and water in a small bowl. Stir to combine. Beat the mixture until smooth. If the mixture is too thick, add a little extra juice or water.

CONTINENTAL SLICE

Preparation time: 30 minutes + refrigeration
Total cooking time: 5 minutes
Makes 36

125 g (4 oz) butter

½ cup (125 g/4 oz) caster sugar

¼ cup (30 g/1 oz) cocoa

250 g (8 oz) shredded wheat
   biscuits, crushed

¾ cup (65 g/2¼ oz) desiccated coconut

¼ cup (30 g/1 oz) chopped hazelnuts

¼ cup (60 g/2 oz) chopped glacé cherries

1 egg, lightly beaten

1 teaspoon vanilla essence

Topping

60 g (2 oz) butter

1¾ cups (215 g/6¾ oz) icing sugar

2 tablespoons custard powder

1 tablespoon hot water

1 tablespoon Grand Marnier

125 g (4 oz) dark chocolate

60 g (2 oz) white vegetable shortening (copha)

1 Line the base and sides of an 18 x 28 cm (7 x 11 inch) shallow tin with foil. Combine the butter, sugar and cocoa in a small pan. Stir over low heat until the butter melts and mixture is well combined. Cook, stirring, for 1 minute. Remove from the heat and cool slightly.

2 Combine the biscuit crumbs, coconut, hazelnuts and cherries in a large bowl. Make a well in the centre; add the butter mixture, egg and vanilla all at once and stir well. Press the mixture firmly, with the back of a spoon, into the prepared tin. Refrigerate until firm.

3 To make Topping: Using electric beaters, beat the butter until creamy. Gradually add the combined icing sugar and custard powder, alternately with the combined water and Grand Marnier. Beat the mixture until light and fluffy. Spread evenly over the base and then refrigerate until set.

4 Combine the chocolate and shortening in a heatproof bowl; stand bowl over a pan of simmering water and stir over low heat until chocolate melts and mixture is smooth. Spread over the slice. Refrigerate for 4 hours or until firm. Cut the slice into squares to serve.

FRESH EGGS

When buying eggs, look for those that are less than two weeks old—they must be fresh if you want a good flavour. A fresh egg will lie horizontally on the bottom of a glass of water. If it stands upright it is old and if it actually rises it is stale. This test determines the amount of air in the rounded end of the egg. Although brown eggs are attractive, they have no more nutritional value than white ones. Eggs should be stored with the pointed end downwards and they will keep longer in the refrigerator. Eggs at room temperature will give more volume when beaten, while cold eggs are easier to separate as the yolk is less likely to break.

ABOVE: Continental Slice

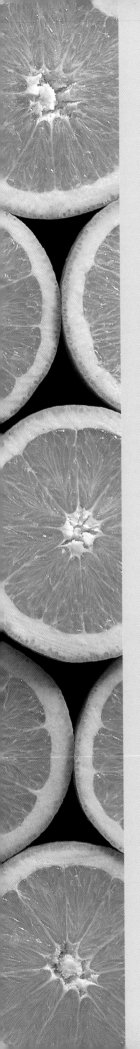

DRINKS

With brunch or after midnight (and at any time in between), the serving of a specially made drink always enhances the sense of occasion—and the cook's reputation as a host. Even healthy and delicious fruit drinks made for a family breakfast are a welcome change from everyday bottled juice, and coffee with that little something extra is the perfect finale for a hearty meal on a cold winter's night.

ABOVE, CLOCKWISE FROM BACK: Irish, Vienna and Spicy Coffee

VIENNA COFFEE

Preparation time: 10 minutes
Total cooking time: Nil
Serves 4

4 cups (1 litre) milky coffee
80 g (2²/3 oz) milk chocolate, grated
2 cups (500 ml/16 fl oz) cream, whipped

1 Stir 1 tablespoon of grated milk chocolate into each cup of milky coffee and top each with a generous dollop of whipped cream. Decorate with extra chocolate and serve immediately.

IRISH COFFEE

Preparation time: 10 minutes
Total cooking time: Nil
Serves 4

1 pot of strong black coffee (4 cups/1 litre)
sugar
Irish whiskey
thick cream

1 Pour the coffee into tall, preferably glass, mugs. Add sugar and Irish Whiskey, to taste.
2 Pour thick cream slowly over the back of a spoon onto the coffee to create a 6 mm (¹/4 inch) thick layer. Serve immediately. As a variation, substitute dark rum for the Irish Whiskey to make Jamaican Coffee.

SPICY COFFEE

Preparation time: 10 minutes
Total cooking time: Nil
Serves 4

¹/2–1 teaspoon ground cinnamon
1 pot of strong black coffee (4 cups/1 litre)
Kahlua
2 cups (500 ml/16 fl oz) cream, whipped
shredded orange rind, for decoration

1 Add the cinnamon to the coffee while it is still in the pot. Add 1–2 tablespoons of Kahlua to each cup or glass.
2 Top with the coffee, spoon or pipe the cream over the top and decorate with orange rind.

ICED TEA

Preparation time: 5 minutes
Total cooking time: Nil
Serves I

ice
¹/₂ cup (125 ml/4 fl oz) cold black tea
I teaspoon sugar

I Place ice, cold tea and sugar in a highball glass and stir with a swizzle stick. Garnish with lemon slices and mint leaves. Iced tea may also be made with cold herbal teas.

CLASSIC COCOA FOR TWO

Preparation time: 5 minutes
Total cooking time: 5 minutes
Serves 2

I tablespoon cocoa powder
I tablespoon sugar
¹/₄ cup (60 ml/2 fl oz) water
2 cups (500 ml/16 fl oz) hot milk
dash of rum or whisky (optional)

I Combine cocoa powder and sugar in a small pan. Add water and whisk until smooth. Bring to boil, reduce heat to low and add hot milk, whisking until frothy. Sprinkle with extra cocoa powder. Serve with a dash of rum or whisky.

ICED CHOCOLATE

Preparation time: 5 minutes
Total cooking time: Nil
Serves I

I–2 tablespoons drinking chocolate
I cup (250 ml/8 fl oz) ice-cold milk
whipped cream or vanilla ice cream

I In a long glass, mix drinking chocolate with a little milk until smooth. Top with ice-cold milk.
2 Float whipped cream or a scoop of vanilla ice cream (or both) on top.

CHOCOLATE THICK-SHAKE

Preparation time: 5 minutes
Total cooking time: Nil
Makes I shake

I cup (250 ml/8 fl oz) milk
I tablespoon chocolate syrup
2–3 scoops of chocolate ice cream

I Place milk and chocolate syrup in a blender; process briefly to combine. Add chocolate ice cream and blend until mixture is smooth but not runny. (The mixture should be very thick.) Pour into a large glass and serve with a wide straw.
NOTE: Chocolate syrup, often referred to as Chocolate Ice Cream Topping, is readily available from supermarkets.

*ABOVE: Classic
Cocoa for Two*

ENERGY SHAKE

Preparation time: 5 minutes
Total cooking time: Nil
Makes 2 shakes

1½ cups (375 ml/12 fl oz) skim or soy milk
1 tablespoon skim milk powder
½ cup (125 g/4 oz) yoghurt
1 tablespoon honey
1 banana, peeled
6 strawberries (optional)
ground cinnamon, for sprinkling

1 Blend all the ingredients except the cinnamon until smooth. Pour immediately into tall glasses and serve sprinkled with a little cinnamon.

FRUIT SALAD SMOOTHIE

Preparation time: 5 minutes
Total cooking time: Nil
Makes 2

2 scoops vanilla ice cream
1 cup (175 g/5⅔ oz) chopped fruit
    (passionfruit, strawberries, banana, etc)
3–4 ice cubes
2 tablespoons honey

1 Place all the ingredients in a blender and blend until smooth. Pour into tall glasses to serve.

BANANA EGG FLIP

Preparation time: 5 minutes
Total cooking time: Nil
Makes 2

1½ cups (375 ml/12 fl oz) milk
1 medium-sized banana
1 tablespoon honey
1 egg
2–3 tablespoons yoghurt
2 scoops vanilla ice cream
2 ice cubes

1 Pour the milk into a blender. Add the peeled and roughly chopped banana, honey, egg, yoghurt, ice cream and ice and blend well until the mixture is smooth. Pour into 2 glasses and serve.

PEACH DREAM

Preparation time: 5 minutes
Total cooking time: Nil
Serves 4

425 g (13½ oz) canned peach slices
3–4 scoops vanilla ice cream
¼ cup (60 ml/2 fl oz) orange juice
2–3 drops vanilla essence
2 cups (500 ml/16 fl oz) chilled milk
orange slices

1 Drain the peach slices and combine with ice cream, orange juice, vanilla and milk in a blender; blend until smooth. Serve at once in glasses, garnished with orange slices.

MANGO FRAPPE

Preparation time: 5 minutes
Total cooking time: Nil
Serves 2

20 ice cubes
3 large fresh mangoes, cut into pieces
sliced mango

1 Place the ice cubes in a blender or food processor. Process until the ice is roughly chopped. Add the mango pieces and process until thick and smooth.
2 Pour the mixture into glasses and serve immediately. Garnish with mango slices and a pineapple leaf, if you like.

COFFEE
The bewildering array of different coffee flavours and aromas depends on where the bean is grown, how it is roasted, how you brew it and the way it is served. But the only basic requirement for a good cup of coffee, no matter which method is used to make it, is that the bean is good quality. It's best to buy freshly ground beans, as grinding releases the flavour. True coffee lovers grind their own at home.

OPPOSITE PAGE:
Clockwise, from top left: Fruit Salad Smoothie; Energy Shake; Peach Dream; Banana Egg Flip; Mango Frappé

HOME-MADE LEMONADE

Preparation time: 10 minutes
+ overnight soaking
Total cooking time: 10–15 minutes
Makes about 5 cups (1.25 litres)

Lemon Syrup

6 large lemons
6 whole cloves
5 cups (1.25 litres) boiling water
2 cups (500 g/1 lb) sugar

ice
soda water

1 To make Lemon Syrup: Slice 6 lemons, place in a large bowl with cloves, cover with the boiling water. Leave to infuse overnight. Strain water into a large pan. Discard lemon slices and cloves. Add sugar and stir over low heat, without boiling, until dissolved. Bring to boil, simmer 10 minutes until reduced and slightly syrupy; cool.

2 To serve, place ice in a highball glass. Pour over 2 tablespoons lemon syrup, top with soda water. Garnish with lemon slices and mint leaves.

LEMON AND LIME BARLEY WATER

Preparation time: 5 minutes
Total cooking time: 30 minutes
Makes about 4 cups (1 litre)

1 cup (220 g/7 oz) pearl barley
8 cups (2 litres) water
1/4 cup (60 ml/2 fl oz) lemon juice
1/2 cup (125 ml/4 fl oz) lime juice
1/2 cup (125 g/4 oz) caster sugar

1 Boil barley and water in a large heavy-based pan for 30 minutes, or until liquid has reduced by half. Remove from heat and strain.
2 Add juices and sugar; mix well. Serve chilled with ice, and lemon and lime slices.

BARLEY WATER
Barley water is thought to provide relief for an upset stomach. Pearl barley has had the outer husk and bran removed. Barley was an essential part of life in Europe up until the 1500s and throughout history it has been used, not only as a food, but as a measuring standard, a medication and even a form of currency.

ABOVE: Home-made Lemonade

INDEX

Page numbers in *italics* refer to photographs.
Page numbers in **bold** type refer to margin notes.

ACKNOWLEDGEMENTS

HOME ECONOMISTS: Jody Vassallo, Jo Richardson, Michelle Earl, Michelle Lawton, Kerrie Mullins, Dimitra Stais, Tracey Port, Christine Sheppard, Jo Forrest, Melanie McDermott, Stephanie Souvilis
RECIPE DEVELOPMENT: Denise Munro, Voula Mantzouridis, Wendy Berecry, Wendy Goggin, Beverley Sutherland Smith, Kerrie Carr, Maria Sampsonis

PHOTOGRAPHY: Luis Martin, Jon Bader, Joe Filshie, Reg Morrison, Chris Jones, Ray Joyce, Tony Lyon, Andre Martin, Peter Scott, Andrew Payne, Andrew Furlong
STYLISTS: Rosemary De Santis, Mary Harris, Carolyn Fienberg, Amanda Cooper, Georgina Dolling, Donna Hay, Suzi Smith, Di Kirby, Elaine Rushbrooke